Language
and Living Things

Language and Living Things

Uniformities in Folk Classification and Naming

Cecil H. Brown

Rutgers University Press
New Brunswick, New Jersey

Library of Congress Cataloging in Publication Data

Brown, Cecil H., 1944–
  Language and living things.

  Bibliography: p.
  Includes index.
  1. Classification, Primitive.   2. Language and
culture.   3. Cognition and culture.   I. Title.
GN468.4.B76   1983   001'.01'2   83–3238
ISBN 0–8135–1008–2

TO PAMELA

CONTENTS

LIST OF FIGURES

LIST OF TABLES

PREFACE

Research on which this book is based began in 1975. Preliminary results were reported in two articles published in the *American Anthropologist* (Brown 1977, 1979a). In these, cross-language data are assembled showing uniformities in the manner in which humans name and classify plants and animals at the life-form level of abstraction. The present work presents an expanded and refined data base (Appendices A and B) which has led to some revisions in originally reported generalizations.[1] Also, a number of additional cross-language regularities in folk biological classification and nomenclature are described and the explanatory framework into which these uniformities plausibly fit is considerably broadened.

Several research strategies were employed in data collection for this book. Data from many languages were developed through library research. Bibliographic leads were frequently supplied by specialists (mostly ethnobiologists, anthropologists, and linguists) who were sent a circular letter requesting various kinds of information pertinent to the project, including actual data on folk biological classification in individual languages. In addition, requests for similar information were published in cooperation sections of scholarly journals and newsletters such as the *Anthropology Newsletter*, *Linguistic Reporter*, *Anthropos*, *The Eastern Anthropologist*, *Language Society of America Newsletter*, *Current Anthropology*, and others too numerous to mention here. The assistance of these publications is gratefully acknowledged.

A large amount of data compiled in this volume was supplied by missionary linguists (mainly members of the Summer Institute of Linguistics) who responded to a questionnaire-letter. Approximately 250 copies of the questionnaire-letter were mailed to missionary linguists located primarily in North, Middle, and South America, Southeast Asia, Australia, New Guinea, and Africa. I am grateful to the many individuals who responded with detailed information on plant and animal classification in their respective languages of study. In many cases, respondents had immediate access to native speakers. In almost all instances, follow-up letters were sent to respondents asking for various clarifications, many of which were made through direct informant contact.

The cooperation of many people made the present work possible. First, I would like to thank all of those individuals who provided data. These include Massimino Allam (Lotuho), Barbara J. Allen (Southern Tiwa), Haruo Aoki (Nez Perce), John Attinasi (Chol), Wilbur Aulie (Chol), Glenn Ayres (Ixil), Phillip Baer (Lacandon), Pierre L. Boiteau (Malagasy), S. K. Borthakur (Mikir), Al Boush, Jr. (Tifal), David Brambila (Tarahumara), Linda Kay Brown (Pocomchi), Michael F. Brown (Aguaruna Jivaro), Ralph Bulmer (Kyaka Enga), Don Burgess (Tarahumara), Inez Butler (Zoogocho Zapotec), Jim Butler (Tzutujil), Robert A. Bye, Jr. (Tarahumara), Eugene H. Casad (Cora), Shirley Chapman (Paumari), Chin See Chung (Kenyah), Ross Clark (Mele-Fila), Stephen Davis (Yolŋu), Christopher Day (Jacaltec), Mary De Boe (Popoloca), John M. Dedrick (Yaqui), Ronald K. Dennis (Jicaque), Robert K. Dentan (Semai), John R. Dorman (Akawaio), Susan Edgar (Tepehua), Roy F. Ellen (Nuaulu), Carol J. Erickson (Isirawa), Harry Feldman (Awtuw and Tok Pisin), William Fisher (Lacandon), Mark S. Fleisher (Clallam), Mark Flotow (Czech), Ray Freeze (Kekchi and Lacandon), Donna B. Gardiner (Southern Tiwa), Pierre Garnier (Bambara and Baoule), William C. Hall (Western Subanun), Thekla Hartmann (Bororo), Terence E. Hays (Ndumba), Jeffrey Heath (Mara, Ngandi, and Ritharngu), Kenneth Hilton (Tarahumara), P. B. Hollman (Lotuho), Ken Jacobs (Tzotzil, Chamula dialect), S. K. Jain (Mikir), Kathryn Keller (Chontal), Manfred and Barbara Kern (Pacaas Novos), John D. Kesby (Kilangi), Linda Amy Kimbal (Brunei Malay), Edward Lauber (Gouin), Linda Lauck (Patep), Robert M. Laughlin (Tzotzil, Zinacantan dialect), Inge Leenhouts (Teen), M. Denis Lemordant (Amharic), Dulcie Levitt (Anindilyakwa), John Lind (Sierra Popoluca), David Lithgow (Muyuw), Katharine Luomala (Gilbertese), Rundell Maree (Ibataan), Madeleine Mathiot (Papago), Kevin R. May (Nimboran), Roy and Georgia Lee Mayfield (Central Cagayan Agta), Robert H. McDaniel (Kayan), William L. Merrill (Tarahumara), Ronald G. Metzger (Carapana), Paul Milanowski (Upper Tanana), Bruce Moore (Colorado), Brian Morris (Chewa), John and Elizabeth Murane (Daga), Anthony Joshua Naden (Bisa and Sisaala), Neal Nellis (Atapec Zapotec), Velda C. Nicholson (Asurini), Muriel Parrott (Highland Tequistlatec and Lowland Tequistlatec), M. Catherine Peeke (Waodani), Anthony Peile (Gugadja), John C. Pfitzner (Western Aranda), Eunice V. Pike (Mazatec), Mrs. Mary Pitman (Araona), Arie Polderaart (Northern Paiute), Harold Popovich (Maxakali), Darrel A. Posey (Kayapo), André Prost (Bisa, Moore, and Songhay), Norren Pym (Iwaidja), Robert A. Randall (Samal), G. Reichel-Dolmatoff (Desana), Lawrence Reid (Bontoc), France-Marie Renard-Casevitz (Machiguenga), Peter Rivière (Tiriyo), Mary Black Rogers (Minnesota Ojibwa), the late Michelle Z. Rosaldo (Ilongot), Dean Saxton

(Papago), Hans-Jürgen Scholz (Igbira), N. C. Shah (Bengali, Hindi, Kumaoni, and Malyalam), William R. Sischo (Michoacan Nahuatl), Thom Smith-Stark (Pocomam), Dermot Smyth (Wik-Ngathana), Chuck Speck (Texmelucan Zapotec), Randall H. and Anna F. Speirs (Tewa), Sharon Stark (Popoloca), Andrew Strathern (Melpa), Morris Stubblefield (Mitla Zapotec), John R. von Sturmer (Kugu-Nganhchara), Horst Stute (Gaviao), Peter Sutton (Wik-Ngathana), Carole Swain (Ninam), John Taylor (Kaiwa), Kenneth Iain Taylor (Sanuma), Stephen A. Tyler (Koya), Rosemary Ulrich (Mopan), María Teresa Viñas Urquiza (Mataco), Paul W. Vollrath (Hewa), Julie Waddy (Anindilyakwa), Roy Wagner (Daribi), Dick Walker (Central Carrier), Jean Walker (Koiwai), James W. Walton (Muinane), Viola Warkentin (Chol), Viola Waterhouse (Highland Tequistlatec and Lowland Tequistlatec), Bruce E. Waters (Djinang), Michael R. Wilson (Kekchi), and Maurice L. Zigmond (Southern Paiute, Kawaiisu dialect).

I would also like to express my gratitude to many people who have supplied me with various kinds of help relevant to this project: Robert McC. Adams, Giovanni Aliotta, Bo Almqvist, Eugene N. Anderson, Mr. and Mrs. John Anderson, Myrdene Anderson, Frank G. Araujo, Angelika Auer, Joan Bamberger, S. A. Barnett, Jacques Barrau, the late Alfredo Barrera, Marie-Claire Bataille, Marcus A. M. Bell, Brent Berlin, Carmen Bernand, H. Russell Bernard, R. M. Berndt, Edmond Bernus, John H. Bodley, Barry A. Bogin, Serge Bouchard, Velma Bourque, Dominique Bourret, Juliette Brabant-Hamonic, David Brokensha, Stephen Brush, Vaughn M. Bryant, Jr., Pierre Cabalion, Ronald W. Casson, S. C. Chin, Miguel Civil, Kathleen Clark, Charles E. Cleland, Harold C. Conklin, Mr. and Mrs. Georges Cowan, I. M. Crawford, Frederick Dockstader, W. H. Douglas, Jacques Dournes, Simone Dreyfus, James A. Duke, Frederick L. Dunn, Mary Eubanks Dunn, Steven D. Emslie, Lawrence Feldman, Viola Frew, Claude Gadbin, Daniel W. Gade, Susan Gal, Wilson Galhego Garcia, Jean Goddard, Pierre B. Gravel, Pierre Grenund, Joseph E. Grimes, H. D. Gunn, Mireille Guyot, M. Jamil Hanifi, Michael J. Harner, John W. Harris, Carl H. Harrison, Mr. and Mrs. Roy Harrison, André Georges Haudricourt, Thomas N. Headland, Phyllis M. Healey, Albert Heinrich, Donald Hekman, Rosita Henry, James William Herrick, Barbara Hollenbach, Richard G. Holloway, Kenneth Honea, Robert Linville Hoover, Nicholas Hopkins, Claude Jardin, Allen W. Johnson, Joseph Jorgensen, Dorothy A. Kamen-Kaye, Rolf Kuschel, Aino Laagus, Weston LaBarre, Wayne Leman, René Letouzey, Stephen H. Levinsohn, Claude Lévi-Strauss, Jose A. Llaguno, Jacob A. Loewen, Michael H. Logan, Alfredo López Austin, Marguerite MacKenzie, J. K. Maheshwari, W. de Mahieu, José Mailhot, Evgeny Yu. Markov, Bonnie Jean McCay, Gerard McNulty, William R. Merrifield, Georges Metailie, V. Benno Meyer-Rochow, Wick R. Miller, Daniel E. Moerman, Elisabeth Motte, F. David Mulcahy, Guido

Munch, Timothy J. O'Leary, Michael L. Olson, Bernard Ortíz de Montellano, Gary B. Palmer, G. B. Panda, Campbell W. Pennington, Velma Pickett, Laurence Podselver, Leopold J. Pospisil, R. Pottier, Amadeo Rea, Paulette Roulon, John Rudder, Antonio Scarpa, Raymond A. Schlabach, Paul Schmidt, Richard Evans Schultes, Otto Schumann G., Anthony Seeger, J. J. Shah, Paul Sillitoe, Shirley Silver, R. L. Specht, Andrew F. Stimson, Benjamin Stone, Marilyn Strathern, Guy Stresser-Péan, Jorge A. Suárez, Paul Taylor, R. P. Marin Terrible, Nancy J. Turner, Paul Turner, J. E. Vidal, Carlos Viesca Treviño, Léontine E. Visser, Michael Walsh, N. Wander, Jerome Ward, S. Henry Wassen, L. J. Webb, Peter and Sue Westrum, Alva and Margaret Wheeler, James White, Clive Winmill, Kazimierz Wodzicki, Leland C. Wyman, and Douglas E. Yen.

The National Science Foundation supplied financial support for this work under Grant No. BNS-7906074. Northern Illinois University provided a paid sabbatical leave and physical resources for undertaking research. Aid from both institutions is greatly appreciated. I also wish to thank Anita Mozga and Paul K. Chase for assistance with the large amount of paper work involved and Kathy Voss who typed the manuscript. I am especially thankful to my wife, Pamela, who prepared the book's index. The late Donn V. Hart, Terence E. Hays, Eugene S. Hunn, and Stanley R. Witkowski read various sections of earlier drafts of this work and provided useful comments and suggestions for which I am grateful. The especially detailed response of Hays has led to several substantial changes. Finally, Witkowski is to be singled out for special thanks for providing me with many thought provoking discussions of the subject matter of this book and related issues. The extent of his intellectual stimulation and, thereby, his contribution to this book is very great indeed.

CHB

Language
and Living Things

» 1 «

INTRODUCTION

All human groups respond to the diversity of plants and animals in their habitats by grouping them into labeled or named categories of greater and lesser inclusiveness. For speakers of American English, white oaks, pin oaks, and post oaks are kinds of oak; oaks, walnuts, and maples are kinds of trees; and trees, vines, and bushes are kinds of plants. Such a system of inclusive relationships forms a *folk biological taxonomy*. "Folk" taxonomies are so named because they constitute classificatory knowledge shared by most mature speakers of a language rather than knowledge held by just a few specialists such as academic botanists and zoologists.

This book describes universal tendencies in ways in which folk biological taxonomies are constructed. It deals primarily with cross-language regularities in the development of named categories corresponding to large biological discontinuities in nature such as trees in general, birds in general, herbaceous plants in general, fish in general, and so on. Such categories are called "life-form" classes in this work.[1]

Cross-language data on which this study is based (assembled in Appendices A and B) indicate that certain large plant and animal discontinuities are pan-culturally encoded as labeled categories by languages. Another finding is that there is a strong tendency for this encoding process to involve relatively invariant sequences. In other words, life-form classes and the terms for them tend to be added to languages in more or less set orders. In addition to classificatory regularities, cross-language data attest to nomenclatural uniformities. Languages everywhere tend to use strikingly similar strategies in developing names for life-form categories.

Background

This book is rooted in two fields, ethnobiology and cognitive anthropology. Ethnobiology can be broadly defined as the study of humankind's relationship with the world of plants and animals. Cognitive anthropology is a more recent

1

development which focuses on the interrelationship of cognition, language, and culture.

The systematic investigation of human interaction with other living things has been closely linked to the development of modern cultural anthropology, especially so in the United States during the past 75 years or so. For example, in the early decades of this century the ethnobiology, particularly the ethnobotany, of North American Indian groups was the subject of numerous research projects arising from salvage ethnography efforts (e.g., Henderson and Harrington 1914; Stevenson 1915; Robbins, Harrington, and Freire-Marreco 1916). Monographs reporting findings of these early studies usually follow a similar format. This is a brief sketch of the peoples involved and their habitat and a list of the more important plants or animals. Native names for the latter are almost always given and there is typically a description of the ways in which organisms are used: e.g., as food, medicine, in ceremonies, and so on. Usually little or no attention is paid to native classification of plants and animals.

Hays (1974: 100–105) recognizes two phases of ethnobiological research which he labels the "old" and the "new." The old ethnobiology, typified by the above mentioned studies and still practiced by many today, focuses primarily on identifying plants and animals considered important in a material culture and the uses to which these are put by a people. The new ethnobiology, which began to emerge in the United States in the 1950's, emphasizes instead the linguistic and semantic aspects of folk biological knowledge and is particularly concerned with plant and animal classification and nomenclature.

If any one work can be singled out as ushering in the new ethnobiology, it is Harold Conklin's still unpublished doctoral dissertation, *The Relation of Hanunóo Culture to the Plant World* (1954). In this work and in subsequent papers, Conklin, an anthropologist, laid the groundwork for an ethnobiology which, while still concerned with the identification and utility of biological specimens in individual cultures, seeks to understand how knowledge of the world of plants and animals is systematically organized in the heads of people. Thus Conklin's work helped to direct anthropologists to a general concern with human cognition, one which mid-century linguistic and cultural anthropologists in the U.S. made a centerpiece of investigation under the various labels of ethnoscience, ethnographic semantics, the new ethnography, and the one preferred here—cognitive anthropology.

Cognitive anthropology developed as an attempt to understand human cultures as systems of concepts and rules that constitute cognitive maps (cf. Goodenough 1957; Frake 1964; Tyler 1969). Such systems are ordinarily approached through the vocabularies of languages. The words of a language are assumed to be a key to what is held to exist and what is thought important in human groups. Of particular significance to cognitive anthropologists are *lex-*

ical domains—groups of words that are closely connected in meaning, such as kinship terms, color terms, and botanical and zoological names. By attending to the interrelationship of words of a single lexical domain—for example, by fleshing out meaning similarities and differences—cognitive anthropologists have attempted to describe in copious detail how cultural knowledge is organized in the heads of people.

Cognitive anthropology, as worked out in ethnobiology by Conklin and other pioneers of the field, focused on folk biological taxonomies. In other words, the new ethnobiologists were chiefly concerned with ways in which different human groups partition the world of plants and animals into named classes (e.g., *maple* and *tree*) and how these classes are related to one another through hierarchic inclusion (e.g., *maple* is included in a class of things named *tree*). Early work also concerned itself, but to a somewhat lesser degree, with nomenclature (i.e., biological class name or label construction, an interest which was to develop fully in the important work of Brent Berlin beginning around 1970).

Insofar as cognitive anthropology initially sought to understand cultures in terms of interrelated conceptual units that *differ* from human group to human group, it was a continuation of the "relativistic" emphasis characterizing both linguistics and ethnology of the first half of this century. Berlin's work instigated a new direction of inquiry in cognitive anthropology by looking for similarities in addition to differences in cognitive structures underlying cultures. For example, by comparing folk biological taxonomies of seven different language groups, Berlin and his colleagues (Berlin, Breedlove, and Raven 1973) identified a set of general principles of classification and nomenclature that were described as throwing "considerable light on prescientific man's understanding of his biological universe" (1973: 214). Even more important, these generalizations indicate that humans everywhere use essentially the same strategies in organizing knowledge of biological phenomena.

Berlin's universalistic perspective also extended to his work with Paul Kay on color categorization. By comparing color vocabularies of 98 languages, Berlin and Kay (1969) discovered a lexical encoding sequence for basic color categories. In other words, their study attests to a universal tendency for languages to add basic color terms to their vocabularies in a more or less set order. For example, the first hue category encoded is always red. The encoding of red is invariably followed by adding terms for green and yellow; blue is encoded next, and so on.

While a universalistic orientation has not penetrated the research of all cognitive anthropologists (cf. Casson 1981), the number of works reporting generalizations involving the lexicons and categories of language published during the last decade or so is impressive, certainly if compared to the dearth of such work of earlier years. For example, in addition to the domains of folk biology and color terms, cross-language regularities have been reported for the domains of body-part terms, personality concepts, geometric-figure terms, and adjectives—to mention only a few (cf. Witkowski and Brown 1978a). The present work continues this orientation and owes much to the pioneering contributions of Berlin and his colleagues. It draws on Berlin's recognition that systems of folk biological classification are comparable, showing considerable cross-language uniformity, and on his emphasis—as most forcefully realized in his color-term study with Kay—on investigating lexical and classificatory regularities in a developmental framework.

Berlin's General Principles

At the core of Berlin's proposals of general principles of classification and nomenclature in folk biology is the concept of *ethnobiological rank*. According to Berlin and his colleagues (Berlin 1972, 1973, 1976; Berlin, Breedlove, and Raven 1973, 1974) each biological class within a folk taxonomy belongs to one of six ethnobiological ranks. Biological classes of the same rank "exhibit nomenclatural, biological, taxonomic, and psychological characteristics" that distinguish them from classes affiliated with other ranks (cf. Berlin 1976: 381). Some of the more important of these features are discussed here.

Berlin identifies fixed relationships between ethnobiological ranks and levels of taxonomic inclusion. These relationships are summarized in Figure 1. The most inclusive class of a folk taxonomy belongs to the "unique beginner" or "kingdom" rank. For example, the unique beginner class in American English folk botanical taxonomy is *plant*. The unique beginner is associated with the first level of taxonomic inclusion or Level 0, so designated by Berlin since unique beginners are very often unlabeled in languages. In other words, languages rarely have labeled botanical and zoological categories comparable to English's *plant* and *animal*.

Classes affiliated with the "life-form" rank occur only at Level 1 in folk taxonomies (see Figure 1). Examples of life-form classes from American English include *tree*, *vine*, and *bush*. Life-form classes are usually few in number, never exceeding 10 or so in any taxonomy. Categories of the "generic" rank also occur at Level 1, but the vast majority of these are found at Level 2 and are subordinate to life-form classes of Level 1.[2] Examples of the latter are American English *oak*, *maple*, and *walnut* which encompass organisms that are also kinds of *tree* (a life-form class). Generic classes are by far the most numerous in folk biological taxonomies; they constitute a level of abstraction that is psychologically basic or salient.

Categories of the "specific" rank are immediately included in generic classes at Levels 2 and 3. Examples are *white oak*, *pin oak*, and *post oak*, all of which are kinds of *oak* (a generic class). Specific categories are occasion-

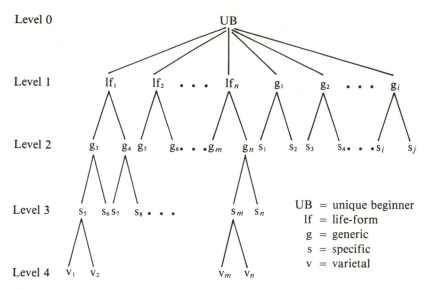

Level 0 — UB

Level 1 — lf_1 lf_2 • • • lf_n g_1 g_2 • • • g_i

Level 2 — g_3 $g_4\,g_5$ g_6• •g_m $g_n\,s_1$ $s_2\,s_3$ s_4• •s_i s_j

Level 3 — s_5 $s_6\,s_7$ s_8 • • • $s_m\,s_n$

UB = unique beginner
lf = life-form
g = generic
s = specific
v = varietal

Level 4 — v_1 v_2 v_m v_n

Figure 1. Ethnobiological ranks and taxonomic levels. Reproduced by permission of the American Anthropological Association, *American Anthropologist* 75(1):215 (1973).

ally partitioned into finer classes of a "varietal" rank, e.g., *swamp white oak*, a kind of *white oak*. There is a sixth enthnobiological rank not represented in Figure 1 since affiliated classes are very rarely found in biological taxonomies. Classes of an "intermediate" rank occur between life-forms of Level 1 and generics of Level 2. An English example is *evergreen tree*, a class immediately included in the life-form *tree*, which immediately includes generics such as *pine*, *fir*, *spruce*, etc.

There are other features in addition to taxonomic level by which rank affiliation is determined. For example, life-form classes are always *polytypic*, which is to say that they always include at least two members that are labeled—and typically very many more. Thus, the life-form *tree* in American English includes *oak*, *walnut*, and *maple* among many other labeled members. On the other hand, classes of generic and specific ranks, while sometimes polytypic, are very often *terminal* categories, that is, they do not include labeled members. For example, the generic class *bamboo* is typically a terminal category since most speakers of American English do not know names for different types of bamboo. In Berlin's framework, varietal classes are always terminal.

Other criteria are linguistic or nomenclatural in nature. For example, life-form classes are always labeled by *primary lexemes* (usually simple, unitary words such as *tree*) and immediately include generic categories that are also labeled by primary lexemes (e.g., *oak*, *walnut*, *maple*). Generic categories, if polytypic, include specific classes always labeled by *secondary lexemes*. A secondary lexeme is composed of the term for the class in which the item it labels is immediately included and a modifier, e.g., *white oak*, a kind of *oak*. If specific classes are polytypic, they include varietal classes which are also labeled by secondary lexemes, e.g., *swamp white oak*, a kind of *white oak*.

Secondary lexemes are not the only composite labels for biological classes found in folk taxonomies. For example, by Berlin's criteria English *tulip tree* is not a secondary lexeme but rather a type of primary lexeme (i.e., a productive primary lexeme), despite the fact that it consists of the term for the class in which tulip trees are immediately included, i.e., *tree*, and a modifier. A composite label is a secondary lexeme only if all items immediately included in the same biological class are labeled by equivalent composite terms.[3] Thus, for example, all members of the English class *oak* are labeled by secondary lexemes since *all* of their labels are composed of the word *oak* plus a modifier, e.g., *white oak*, *pin oak*, *post oak*, etc. On the other hand, *tulip tree* is not a secondary lexeme, since all members of the class *tree* are not labeled by equivalent composite terms. Unlike *tulip tree*, most labels for immediate kinds of *tree*, e.g., *oak*, *walnut*, *maple*, etc., are not composite.[4]

Nomenclatural considerations are the key to determination of ethnobiological rank in Berlin's framework. Polytypic categories of Level 1 are life-forms if they are labeled by primary lexemes and immediately include classes labeled by primary lexemes (i.e., generics). Biological categories are generics if they are labeled by primary lexemes and are either terminal or immediately include classes labeled by secondary lexemes (i.e., specifics). Categories are specific if they are labeled by secondary lexemes and are immediately included in classes labeled by primary lexemes (i.e., generics). And categories are varietal if they are labeled by secondary lexemes and are immediately included in classes labeled by secondary lexemes (i.e., specifics).

Several authors have raised questions concerning the applicability of some aspects of Berlin's framework. For example, Bulmer (1974) argues that his generalizations are premature, since they are based on only a small number of well-described native systems of plant and animal classification. This objection is not too disturbing since accumulating cross-language evidence for the most part has borne out the core of Berlin's proposals if not all details (Hays 1979: 268). A more serious reservation has been raised by Hunn (1977) who questions whether nomenclatural criteria for ranking classes necessarily correspond with certain psychological criteria for doing the same.

At the core of Berlin's framework is the observation that generic classes constitute a psychologically primary or basic level of naming. Generic categories, as mentioned above, tend to be the most numerous classes found in folk biological taxonomies. Berlin, Breedlove, and Raven (1973, 1974) report that generic classes in Tzeltal Mayan botanical classification are the most salient conceptual groupings of organisms and propose that this finding is a general condition. However, this may not hold for peoples of large-scale urban societies. Dougherty (1978) argues convincingly that in folk taxonomies of the latter human groups life-form classes (e.g., English *tree* and *fish*) are highly salient and thus are psychologically basic. This, according to Dougherty, is a function of the indifference towards plants and animals shown by most people who live in urban environments. (Chapter 5 investigates other ways in which classificatory systems of large-scale human groups differ from those of small-scale groups.)

Since generic classes constitute the most salient biological categories, at least for peoples of small-scale societies, terms for them exist as the "unmarked" core of folk biological vocabularies. In the framework of marking, developed over the years by Jakobson (1941), Greenberg (1966, 1969, 1975), and others, unmarked terms label highly salient referents and marked terms label somewhat less salient referents. Unmarked words differ in systematic ways from marked ones (marking features are discussed at length in Chapter 7). For instance, unmarked terms tend to be simpler (phonologically or morphologically) than marked ones. This is sometimes realized through overt marking. For example, in Spanish the term for "deep," *profundo*, is unmarked and its adjectival counterpart, *poco profundo* "shallow," is marked. The latter term is created by overtly marking the word for "deep" and translates literally "little depth" (*poco* "little" is an overt mark).

Many classification and nomenclature uniformities in folk biology probably trace to a universal core system based on marking relationships (Brown and Witkowski 1980). While systems of biological classification may altogether lack categories of the unique beginner, life-form, and varietal ranks (Brown 1977; Berlin 1972; Berlin et al. 1973), classes of the generic rank and possibly those of the specific rank are always encoded by languages. Thus in biological classification, use of generic and (possibly) specific categories may constitute a cross-language universal. Within this universal core, generic classes are unmarked and hence more salient and numerous than specific classes. Specific classes are always marked relative to unmarked generic classes in which they are immediately included. The marking relationship between generics and specifics in the core system is usually direct and overt. For example, *white oak* is a specific class immediately included in the generic category *oak*. The modifier *white* is an overt mark attached to the basic term *oak*.

Many of the cross-language uniformities outlined by Berlin and his colleagues (Berlin 1972, 1973, 1976; Berlin, Breedlove, and Raven 1973, 1974) are due at least in part to the probability that unmarked generic and marked specific classes make up a core system upon which folk taxonomies are usually built and expanded. We are only beginning to understand strategies for developing taxonomies beyond the universal core. Illumination of some of these strategies, especially those involving suprageneric classification, is a primary goal of the present work.

Language Universals

Works such as this one and investigations of Berlin, which focus on cross-language lexical uniformities, are also part of a larger study of language universals in general. Language universals constitute an important emphasis of contemporary linguistics since their description may shed considerable light on the nature of the human language faculty. Despite a growing interest in lexical universals among cognitive anthropologists and others, language regularities so far described pertain primarily to the phonological and syntactic components of languages. Most interpretations of the design properties of language have therefore been couched in terms of phonology and syntax. One goal of the present work is to show how lexical uniformities can contribute to a theory of the human language faculty.

The final chapter of this book (Chapter 9) attempts to evaluate principal competing models of the human language faculty. This is undertaken against the backdrop of an explanatory framework accounting for regularities in biological life-form encoding which also extends to uniformities in the encoding of basic color categories as delineated by Berlin and Kay (1969). Given that investigation of lexical universals has only barely begun, such an evaluation is clearly preliminary and tentative. Nonetheless, by relating this study and similar ones to such larger issues, I hope to make their usefulness and importance very apparent.

»2«

LIFE-FORM CLASSES AND DISCONTINUITIES IN NATURE

Interpretive Framework

Eugene Hunn (1977) has made an important contribution to the new ethnobiology pioneered by Conklin, Berlin, and others by directing attention to the relationship between folk classification and discontinuities in nature. A major proposal of his work is that folk taxonomic classes are built to a large extent on discontinuities occurring in the world of plants and animals. For the most part, biological organisms are not morphologically continuous, that is, in any given environment there is rarely a continuum of species grading from one to another with respect to their morphological features. Rather, there is typically much distinctiveness making for obvious breaks or gaps among species. While folk classification occasionally involves overlooking such breaks—resulting in the lumping together of morphologically distinct species—usually natural discontinuities are followed closely in folk categorization.

Discontinuities in nature are underlain by feature or attribute clustering. Bruner, Goodnow, and Austin (1956: 47) illustrate this by citing the example of birds in general, creatures possessing feathers, wings, a bill or beak, and characteristic legs. Any one of the latter features is highly predictive of the others. For example, if a creature possesses feathers, it will invariably also have wings, a bill or beak, and characteristic legs. Thus attributes of the discontinuity "birds in general" cluster together, or in other words, are highly correlated with one another.

Hunn (1977: 41–75) is especially interested in psychological processes through which discontinuities are translated into categories of folk taxonomies. Following Bruner et al. (1956: 47) he proposes that the mutual predictability of clustering features can lead to an expectancy in the minds of humans that attributes involved will always be found together. For example, through exposure to different kinds of birds, people build up in their minds an expec-

9

tation that feathers, wings, and so on, go together. Such an expectation underlies the conceptual development of the configurational or Gestalt property of
birdness. Thus, while many attributes may pertain to discontinuities in nature, such breaks tend to be recognized as single features, e.g., birdness,
rather than as a concatenation of several features (Hunn 1977: 46).

Some biological categories clearly are not so directly underlaid by discontinuities in nature. For example, the class *vegetable* is not directly linked to a
distinct biological discontinuity. In other words, there is no set of clustering
features that pertain to all things called vegetables. Rather, *vegetable* exists
by virtue of the fact that some botanical organisms are eaten while others are
not. Mere observation of a sample of plants called *vegetables* cannot lead to a
conception of "vegetableness" since these plants have little in common other
than their edibility.

Hunn (1977: 47) relates the distinction between biological classes directly
motivated by discontinuities in nature and those that are not to the distinction
between special purpose and general purpose folk categories (see also Berlin
et al. 1966; Bulmer 1970: 1084–1087; Hays 1982, 1983; Hunn 1982). A
special-purpose class is one whose membership is based primarily on some
single functional criterion rather than on a break in nature. For example, inclusion of plants in the category *vegetable* is determined primarily by their
edibility. Sometimes functional criteria are negative in nature; for instance,
the membership of *weed* extends to those plants totally lacking in use, which
interfere with the growth of other, more desirable plants. On the other hand,
inclusion in general-purpose categories is based on the complex gross morphology of biological organisms; for example, birds are included in the class
bird by virtue of the fact that they all share the clustering morphological features pertaining to the discontinuity "birds in general." Traditionally, studies
of folk biological taxonomy have focused almost exclusively on general purpose classification (e.g., Berlin et al. 1974; Hunn 1977; Hays 1974).

In the present work use of the expression *special purpose* is extended beyond those categories based on functional features to all biological classes
that are defined primarily in terms of a single, especially criterial attribute and
that are not directly underlain by discontinuities in nature. For example, the
English category *flower* (in the sense of type of plant) is a special-purpose
class since its membership is not based on several clustering morphological
features, but rather simply on the presence of prominent or ornamental blos-
soms. Other examples of special-purpose botanical categories in English based
on single, especially criterial attributes are *perennial* and *annual* (based on
seasonal habits), *desert shrub*, *tropical plant*, and *aquatic plant* (based on
environment or location), and *seedling* and *sprout* (based on life stage). Some
special-purpose zoological categories in English include *pet* (based on relationship to humans), *draft animal* (based on function), *mutt* (based on breed-
ing), and *puppy* (based on life stage).

Hunn (1977: 51) relates his proposals to Berlin's framework of ethnobiological ranks (see Chapter 1) by viewing specific, generic, life-form, and unique beginner classes (in that order) as usually reflecting a *continuum of discontinuities* that are increasingly heterogeneous. For example, the English specific class *white-breasted nuthatch* reflects a discontinuity associated with the abstracted attribute "white-breasted nuthatchness." The latter discontinuity encompasses organisms that are part of a larger and more diverse (heterogenous) discontinuity associated with the feature "nuthatchness." In turn, the "nuthatch" discontinuity extends to organisms that are part of an even larger discontinuity, "bird," reflected by the life-form category *bird*, and so on.

As noted in Chapter 1, classes of the generic rank constitute a psychologically primary or basic level of naming in folk biological taxonomies. Hunn (1977: 51–53) attempts to account for this by proposing that some discontinuities in nature are perceptually more salient than others (cf. Berlin, Boster, and O'Neill 1981). The perceptual salience of a discontinuity relates to both its heterogeneity (diversity of included organisms) and to its physical distinctiveness relative to other discontinuities. Essentially, the most perceptually salient discontinuities tend to be minimally heterogeneous and maximally physically distinct. In Berlin's words, these are "the smallest discontinuities in nature which are easily recognized on the basis of large numbers of gross morphological characteristics" (1973: 261).

Generic categories are the linguistic reflection of perceptually salient discontinuities in nature. When generic classes are lexically encoded, the perceptual salience of such breaks is translated or converted into linguistic salience. This is consistent with the fact that terms for generic categories generally are linguistically unmarked in languages—demonstrating, for example, phonological and morphological simplicity (see discussions of marking in Chapters 1 and 7). Thus, the fact that generic categories are usually labeled by primary lexemes is ultimately attributable to the considerable perceptual salience of the natural discontinuities on which these classes are based.

In Hunn's (1977: 53) framework specific classes encode discontinuities encompassing organisms that also participate in larger, more salient generic discontinuities. Since specific discontinuities are usually less salient than generic breaks in nature, terms for specific classes tend to be linguistically marked relative to terms for generic categories.

A specific discontinuity shows all the critical attributes of the larger, more salient generic discontinuity, which includes it plus attributes peculiar to itself alone and critical to its recognition as a distinct configuration. This special association is manifest in language by the fact that terms for specific classes are often formed through overt marking involving terms for generic classes (see Chapter 1). Thus, the greater lexical complexity of the label *white oak* relative to *oak* does not merely indicate that the former is linguistically marked vis-à-vis the latter, but also that the discontinuities reflected by these labels bear a special relationship to one another with respect to the sharing of attributes. The use of secondary lexemes as labels for specific classes, then, is due at least in part to relationships in nature.

Moving along the continuum of discontinuities from breaks in nature associated with specific classes to the single discontinuity associated with the unique beginner, not only is there an increase in diversity of included organisms, but there is also a decrease in the number of pertinent defining features. For example, while a generic discontinuity shares features with subordinate specific discontinuities, it lacks those particular attributes that make the latter distinctive. Similarly, a generic break compared to the life-form discontinuity which includes it has the attributes that define the life-form break plus those additional features which make it distinctive. There is, then, an inverse correlation between the heterogeneity of organisms pertaining to a discontinuity and the number of clustering attributes which characterize it. In any given environment, for any particular discontinuity, low heterogeneity usually indicates extensive criteria clustering and high heterogeneity indicates little criteria clustering.

Of course, this correlation is not perfect. Generic discontinuities, which are always underlain by extensive feature clustering, occasionally show considerable heterogeneity. This is especially true of cultivated plants. For instance, the Tzeltal generic category, čenek' "bean plant," is an exceptionally heterogeneous category that immediately includes 15 labeled specific classes (Berlin et al. 1974: 526). This is unusual, however, since generic categories rarely include more than two labeled specifics, and very often they are monotypic (terminal) (Berlin 1976: 389–390). For example, of the 471 generic plant classes established for Tzeltal, 398 or 85 percent are terminal (Berlin et al. 1974: 31), that is, they include no specific classes.

Discontinuities underlain by little criteria clustering occasionally show little heterogeneity. This is often the case when little species diversity is in evidence in an environment. For example, fish are sometimes totally lacking or very scarce in certain highland regions of New Guinea; and languages spoken in these areas sometimes encode a general "fish" class. The Siane language, for instance, has a "fish" term—which can, for example, be used to designate any canned fish—while only two types of native fish other than eels are known to speakers (Dywer 1978). The existence of such general labeled classes when exemplars are rare or even totally lacking may be explained by historical factors. For example, Siane speakers may have lived in an environment supporting a large and heterogeneous fish population before moving to their present habitat.

Such exceptions are relatively rare. For the most part, in any given environment, few clustering features predict heterogeneity, and many clustering features predict homogeneity. For convenience of reference, breaks in nature associated with the "few features/heterogeneous" end of the discontinuity continuum are called *large discontinuities* and those associated with the "many features/homogeneous" pole are called *small discontinuities*.

The world of plants and animals consists of large discontinuities that tend to be pan-environmental and small discontinuities that tend to be more limited in habitat. Thus as one moves along any particular discontinuity continuum from large to small breaks, ranges of habitat usually decrease significantly. For example, the large discontinuity "bird" has exemplars that occur in diversity and abundance in virtually all of the world's environments. "Bird" in turn encompasses the "nuthatch" discontinuity, which is considerably more restricted in range. Nuthatches are found in most parts of the Northern Hemisphere but do not occur south of the equator. Finally, exemplars of the small discontinuity "white-breasted nuthatch" are restricted to a relatively narrow range extending from southern Canada to southern Mexico (Peterson 1980: 212).

Large and small discontinuities also differ with respect to how many of each are supported by the world's environments. The total number of small, environment-specific plant and animal discontinuities is clearly massive. On the other hand, the number of large, pan-environmental discontinuities is probably very small in comparison. Thus, across languages large discontinuities that are lexically encoded tend to be highly similar while lexically encoded small discontinuities tend to be different. This presents the possibility that languages can be compared with respect to which of the large, pan-environmental breaks they do encode and which they do not. This possibility is pursued in the present work.

Large Biological Discontinuities

The largest pan-environmental biological discontinuities are only rarely lexically encoded by languages. In other words, languages commonly lack terms comparable to English *plant* and *animal* (or *creature*) (cf. Berlin et al. 1973).

After "plant" the largest and most diverse botanical discontinuities found in virtually all environments are as follows:

tree Large plant (relative to the plant inventory of a particular environment) whose parts are chiefly ligneous (woody).

grerb Small plant (relative to the plant inventory of a particular environment) whose parts are chiefly herbaceous (green, leafy, nonwoody).[1]

bush Plant of intermediate size (relative to the plant inventory of a particular environment) which is characteristically bushy (shows much branching and lacks a single, main support).

vine Elongated plant exhibiting a creeping or twining or climbing stem habit.

grass A flowerless, herbaceous plant with narrow, often bladelike or spear-shaped leaves.

In Chapter 8, clustering attributes pertaining to these large discontinuities, especially those underlying **tree** and **grerb**, are discussed in detail.

The five large botanical discontinuities listed here are not the only ones that are pan-environmental. For example, if not absolutely pan-environmental, fungi and lichens are clearly global in distribution. However, these five are singled out for special attention because among pan-environmental discontinuities they appear to be especially significant for humans. This special importance is mirrored cross-linguistically in folk botanical classification. For example, these five breaks in nature are consistently encoded by languages. In other words, they are realized as labeled botanical classes over and over again. In addition, categories reflecting them tend to be the most polytypic general-purpose plant classes of languages. For example, in five folk botanical taxonomies studied in exceptional detail by anthropologists, **tree**, **grerb**, **bush**, **vine**, and **grass**, when encoded, typically include more labeled categories than other general purpose plant classes. (See Tables 1, 2, 3, and 4, where the most polytypic general purpose plant classes in Ndumba [Hays 1974, 1979], Huastec [Brown 1972], Tzeltal [Berlin et al. 1974], and Aguaruna [Berlin 1976] respectively are listed [for further details see language cases 145a, 163a, 154a, and 46a in Appendix A]. Also Conklin [1954: 96] reports that **tree** [*kāyu*] encompasses 38 percent, **grerb** [*ʔilamnun*] 36 percent, and **vine** [*wākat*] 24 percent of the 1625 lowest-level, mutually exclusive named plant categories found in Hanunoo folk botanical taxonomy [see case 58a in Appendix A].)

The actual realization of large botanical discontinuities as classes in folk taxonomies can vary considerably with respect to range of inclusion. For example, while the category **tree** always encompasses trees, it often extends to woody plants in general including ligneous bushes and shrubs and occasionally even woody vines. In addition, **tree** sometimes includes large nonwoody plants such as coconut palms, banana trees, and large cactuses. In some instances, **tree** is restricted to large and/or woody plants that are not cultivated.

Grerb, when encoded, always includes nongrass herbaceous plants (denoted by *herb* in this work). However, it is frequently extended to grasses. It also often encompasses herbaceous plants in general including nonwoody bushes and shrubs and occasionally even herbaceous vines. In addition, the category sometimes extends to small woody plants such as saplings and stunted trees. In some instances, **grerb** is restricted to only those small and/or herbaceous plants that are not cultivated.

Table 1. Eight most polytypic general-purpose plant classes in Ndumba.

Class	Number of immediately included labeled classes
sa'tari (**tree**)	198
mauna (**grerb**)	68
sana (**vine**)	46
muso (**grass**)	37
kaa'mma ("sweet potato")	23
sara ("taro")	22
taana ("yam")	19
saaqaa ("sugar cane")	18

Source: Extracted from Hays 1974, 1979; cf. Brown n.d.

Table 2. Eight most polytypic general-purpose plant classes in Huastec.

Class	Number of immediately included labeled classes
te⁷ (**tree**)	97
č'oho·l (**grerb**)	51
č'ah (**vine**)	37
wayelte⁷ (**bush**)	11
tom (**grass**)	5
we·y ("maguey")	5
pakab ("sugar cane")	5
it'aθ ("banana plant")	5

Source: Extracted from Brown 1972; cf. Brown n.d.

After "animal" or "creature," the largest and most diverse zoological discontinuities found in nearly all environments are as follows:

bird Large creature (relative to creatures such as bugs) possessing wings and usually having feathers and a bill or beak. (Classes encoding this discontinuity always include birds. In their greatest extension they include birds and flying mammals such as bats.)

fish Creature possessing a streamlined body and fins, usually having gills. (Classes encoding this discontinuity always include true fish. In their greatest extension they include true fish and fish-shaped mammals such as dolphins and whales.)

snake Featherless, furless, elongated creature usually lacking appendages. (Classes encoding this discontinuity always include snakes and/or worms. In their greatest extension they include snakes, worms, lizards, eels, and, occasionally, other elongated creatures such as reptile-like insects.)

Table 3. Eight most polytypic general-purpose plant classes in Tzeltal.

Class	Number of immediately included labeled classes
te⁷ (**tree**)	178
wamal (**grerb**)	119
⁷ak (**grass**)	36
⁷ak' (**vine**)	24
čenek' ("bean plant")	15
lo⁷bal ("banana plant")	12
⁷eč' ("bromeliad")	10
čin ⁷ak' ("morning glory")[a]	9

Source: Extracted from Berlin, Breedlove, and Raven 1974; cf. Brown n.d.
[a] Čin ⁷ak' is immediately included in ⁷ak' (**vine**).

Table 4. Six most polytypic general-purpose plant classes in Aguaruna.

Class	Number of immediately included labeled classes
númi (**tree**)	275
daék (**vine**)	93
dúpa (**grerb**)	70
máma ("manioc")	±30(?)
šíŋki ("palm")[a]	30
páantam/pámpa ("banana plant")	21

Source: Extracted from Berlin 1976; cf. Brown n.d.
[a] Šíŋki is not included in númi (**tree**).

wug Small creature other than those pertaining to **bird**, **fish**, and **snake** discontinuities. (Classes encoding this discontinuity always encompass bugs, i.e., insects and other very small creatures such as spiders, and frequently are extended to worms. Occasionally they also include other creatures such as lizards, tortoises, and frogs if these are small.)[2]

mammal Large creature other than those pertaining to **bird**, **fish**, and **snake** discontinuities. (Classes encoding this discontinuity always include mammals. They are often extended to other large animals such as iguanas and crocodiles and, in addition, to creatures such as tortoises and frogs if these are large.)[3]

In Chapter 8 attributes pertaining to these large discontinuities are discussed in detail. However, it should be noted here that the status of **wug** and **mammal** as true discontinuities in nature is problematic. This issue is discussed in Chapter 8.

Clearly, other large zoological discontinuities in addition to these five are pan-environmental. These include ants, spiders, wasps, moths and butterflies, and toads and frogs to mention just a few. However, like the five plant discontinuities, these animal groupings are given special attention because among pan-environmental discontinuities they appear to be especially significant for humans. They are encoded as classes over and over again in the world's languages; and more significant, classes reflecting them tend to be the most polytypic animal categories of languages. Four folk zoological taxonomies studied in detail would appear to support this observation. Tables 5, 6, 7, and 8 list the most polytypic general purpose animal classes found in Chrau (Thomas 1966), Kyaka Enga (Ralph Bulmer, personal communication), Ndumba (Terence Hays, personal communication; Hays 1983), and Tzeltal (Hunn 1977) respectively. These show that **bird**, **fish**, **snake**, **wug**, and **mammal**, if encoded, are consistently among the most polytypic animal classes in a taxonomy.[4] Indeed, with the single exception of the Tzeltal **fish** category (Table 8), classes encoding the five zoological discontinuities are the most polytypic animal categories in all four languages. The Tzeltal exception is due to the fact that the language is spoken in a mountainous region of southern Mexico where fish are severely restricted in number and diversity. Similarly, Kyaka Enga and Ndumba are spoken in highland regions of New Guinea where fish are virtually lacking, accounting for the fact that these languages do not encode **fish**. For further details concerning animal classification in these four languages see language cases 32b, 69b, 119b, and 110b in Appendix B.

Occasionally terms for categories based on the above five animal discontinuities are extended to creatures that lack some or all of the associated clustering features. For example, **fish** terms sometimes encompass most, if not all, creatures that inhabit aquatic environments, including such organisms as turtles, frogs, crocodiles, and crustacea in addition to true fish (and fish-shaped mammals in some cases). Similarly, **bird** terms sometimes extend to winged creatures that are neither birds nor flying mammals, i.e., to flying insects. Such terms do not qualify as true **fish** and **bird** labels unless true fish (and fish-shaped mammals in some cases) and birds (and flying mammals in some cases) respectively constitute their referential foci. In other words, the latter creatures must be regarded by language speakers as the most typical or best representative of these classes.[5] In collecting data for this work, I have attempted to determine category focus whenever possible. When focus of biological classes is indeterminate, this is mentioned (see Appendices A and B for data).

A few languages surveyed for this work treat **wug** and **mammal** in a special manner. Instead of encoding **wug** and **mammal** in separate categories, they have lumped creatures of these groupings together in a single labeled class. These "combined **wug-mammal**" categories typically include bugs and mammals and frequently extend to other creatures that are neither birds, fish, or snakes—such as lizards, turtles, frogs, and so on.

Table 5. Seven most polytypic general-purpose animal classes in Chrau.

Class	Number of immediately included labeled classes
sŭm (**bird**)	17
ca (**fish**)	12
vih (**snake**)	7
kyôq ("frog"/"toad")	5
si ("louse")	5
khlang ("bird of prey")[a]	5
ong ("wasp")	5

Source: Extracted from Thomas 1966; cf. Brown 1982b.
[a]Khlang is not included in sŭm (**bird**).

Table 6. Eight most polytypic general-purpose animal classes in Kyaka Enga.

Class	Number of included terminal labeled classes
yaka (**bird**)	180
kau (**snake**)	71
sa (**mammal** ["large mammal"])	32
mugi ("frog"/"toad")	19
wi (**mammal** ["small mammal"])	13
mena ("pig")[a]	13
maemae ("butterfly"/"moth")	7
re ("ant")	7

Source: Ralph Bulmer, personal communication; cf. Brown 1982b.
[a]Mena is not included in either sa ("large mammal") or wi ("small mammal").

The Expression "Life-Form" as Used in this Work

As a rule, when languages encode classes reflecting one or more of the large discontinuities defined above, these categories fit the criteria of life-form rank as outlined by Berlin (1972, 1973, 1976; Berlin, Breedlove, and Raven 1973, 1974) (see Chapter 1). In other words, they occur at Berlin's Level 1; they are invariably polytypic; they are labeled by primary lexemes; and they immediately include classes labeled by primary lexemes (usually generics). There are, however, exceptions to this rule, described later. Nonetheless, in this work I use Berlin's expression "life-form" in reference to **tree**, **grerb**, **bush**, **vine**, **bird**, **fish**, **snake**, **wug**, **mammal**, and combined **wug-mammal** when these are lexically encoded, since these usually meet the strict criteria of life-form rank.

One way in which these categories occasionally do not meet Berlin's criteria is when dual life-form membership is in evidence. Consider, for example,

Table 7. Eight most polytypic general-purpose animal classes in Ndumba.

Class	Number of included labeled classes
kuri (**bird**)	143
to'vendi (**wug**)	80
fai (**mammal** ["large mammal"])	31
kaapa'raara (**snake**)[a]	29
feqana ("frog"/"toad")[b]	12
faahi (**mammal** ["small mammal"])	10
kaapura'rora ("butterfly"/"moth")[c]	8
kaa'puri ("ant")[c]	8

Source: Terence Hays, personal communication; Hays 1983.

[a] Kaapa'raara is immediately included in to'vendi (**wug**).

[b] Feqana is immediately included in to'vendi (**wug**).

[c] Kaapura'rora and kaa'puri are both immediately included in to'vendi (**wug**).

Table 8. Eight most polytypic general-purpose animal classes in Tzeltal.

Class	Number of immediately included labeled classes
mut (**bird**)	106
čanbalam (**mammal**)	36
čan (**snake**)	23
č'o ("small rodent")[a]	12
šuš ("wasp")	10
ʔam ("spider")	10
čay (**fish**)	8
čanul haʔ ("water bug")	8

Source: Extracted from Hunn 1977; cf. Brown 1982b.

[a] Č'o is immediately included in čanbalam (**mammal**).

Djinang (case 98a, Appendix A) which encodes both **grass** (*yurryarr*) and **grerb** (*murrur.rt*). Speakers of languages encoding both of these often consider their respective memberships to be mutually exclusive. However, for speakers of Djinang *yurryarr* are kinds of *murrur.rt*. In this example a large discontinuity (**grerb**) is reflected by a labeled class found at taxonomic Level 1 which immediately includes at Level 2 a labeled category mirroring another large discontinuity (**grass**). Because Djinang *yurryarr* (**grass**) does not occur at Level 1, it is not a proper life-form by Berlin's criteria, but rather a generic (or, possibly, an intermediate). Since labeled classes underlain by the 11 large discontinuities occasionally occur at Level 2, there is not always a perfect correlation between large, pan-environmental breaks and taxonomic level.

Encoded large discontinuities sometimes violate other criteria of life-form rank affiliation. For example, they may immediately include classes labeled by secondary lexemes, and thus they qualify as generics rather than as life-forms. For example, this is the case with respect to **snake** in the Chrau language (see case 32b, Appendix B). The class in question is labeled by *vih* and encompasses only creatures which are true snakes (Thomas 1966: 8). As it happens, all classes immediately included in *vih* are labeled by secondary (composite) lexemes: for example, *vih cungkring* "cobra," *vih chun* "a large, black poisonous snake," and *vih chhe aq* "a small snake, lives in grass roofs." In Berlin's framework, the latter are specific categories; and *vih* is therefore a generic rather than life-form class since only generic classes immediately include specific categories.

Grass, apparently more often than the other four plant "life-form" classes, is occasionally found to be affiliated with the generic rank with regard to Berlin's criteria. For instance, classes immediately included in Huastec *tom* (**grass**) are all labeled by secondary lexemes, e.g., *čataθ tom* "pangola grass" and *pakθa? tom* "Guinea grass" (Brown 1972). In some cases **grass** categories are just barely life-forms by nomenclatural criteria. For example, of the 36 classes immediately included in Tzeltal *?ak* (**grass**), 34 are denoted by composite labels consisting of the term *?ak* and a modifier (Berlin et al. 1974). Since two included classes are labeled by primary lexemes, Berlin and his colleagues (1974: 400) do not consider the 34 composite labels to be secondary lexemes but rather identify them as productive primary lexemes. Thus, by Berlin's formal criteria, *?ak* labels a life-form class. However, the predominant nomenclatural pattern indicates that Tzeltal *?ak* may be psychologically equivalent to a generic class (cf. Hunn 1977: 54).

There are, of course, instances where labeled **grass** classes are unambiguously life-forms by Berlin's criteria. For example, very few of the 37 classes immediately included at Level 2 in Ndumba *muso* (**grass**) are labeled by composite lexemes (Hays 1974). Nonetheless, **grass** is noteworthy among the five general botanical classes focused on in this work since there seems to be a cross-language tendency for it to demonstrate some or all characteristics of a generic category as described by Berlin.

A plausible explanation of this is that the **grass** discontinuity is underlain by more clustering attributes than the other four pan-environmental botanical discontinuities and, hence, is more like the perceptually salient small discontinuities typically reflected by generic classes in languages. Clearly, more clustering features pertain to the **grass** discontinuity than to the **grerb** break. **Grass** has all the clustering attributes of **grerb** (i.e., small herbaceous plants in general) plus others which pertain to it exclusively and make it distinct (e.g., bladed leaves and lack of a sturdy stem). However, the number of features underlying **grass** is still sufficiently small so that the discontinuity occurs pan-environmentally. **Grass**, in effect, seems to lie somewhere between the largest and smallest breaks on the continuum of plant discontinuities. As a result, labeled categories reflecting it in some languages fit the criteria of a generic class and in others, those of a life-form class as defined by Berlin.

As mentioned above, in this book, solely for convenience of reference, categories reflecting the discontinuities **tree**, **grerb**, **bush**, **vine**, **grass**, **bird**, **fish**, **snake**, **wug**, **mammal** and combined **wug-mammal** are called life-forms despite the fact that these on occasion do not formally qualify for affiliation with the life-form rank. There is, however, one important constraint on this adaptation of Berlin's term. Any category reflecting one of the five large discontinuities is *not* a life-form unless it is polytypic. In other words, a life-form, in my special use of the expression, is in evidence only if the pertinent class immediately includes at least two *labeled* categories.

One finding of the present investigation is that biological classes reflecting large discontinuities occasionally are *not* polytypic. For example, in the Iwaidja language (case 1a, Appendix A) the term *mirlag* is used to denote all small herbaceous plants including grasses (i.e., the **grerb** discontinuity). However, any particular small herbaceous plant identified by a more detailed term, such as a generic label, is not considered to be a *mirlag* by speakers. The latter term, then, labels a class of small herbaceous plants each of which cannot be identified by use of some other plant term. *Mirlag* in effect encompasses all unknown small herbaceous plants and no known ones. Since exemplars of *mirlag* are not labeled, the class is not judged to be a full-fledged **grerb** life-form. Such "empty" (cf. Turner 1974) general biological categories can be described as being "incipient" life-forms since they probably constitute a precursory stage in the development of full-fledged polytypic life-form classes (Brown and Chase 1981). This is discussed at length in Chapter 6.

Whereas large biological discontinuities are typically encoded through use of a single label, they are sometimes lexically realized in other ways. For example, languages may lack a term for **bird**, i.e., a class extended to birds in general, but lexically encode the life-form through the binary opposition "large bird"/"small bird." Languages doing so are judged (in Appendix B) as having a **bird** life-form. In some cases, languages may encode only one-half of a binary opposition, e.g., only "small bird." These languages are also judged as having **bird** life-forms. Binary opposition is particularly prevalent in the encoding of zoological life-forms. Among the latter, **snake**, which includes elongated animals in general, is most frequently recognized through binary contrast, i.e., "small elongated animal"/"large elongated animal." The "small elongated animal" category usually encompasses worms alone while the "large elongated animal" class is usually restricted to true snakes.

Binary opposition involving life-form classes is frequently based on the dimension size. However, other dimensions are sometimes used. For example, the **tree** discontinuity is occasionally realized by a "leafed tree"/"needled tree" contrast and the **vine** discontinuity by a "ligneous vine"/"herbaceous vine" contrast. There is even an example of **grass** encoded through a "clustering grass"/"nonclustering grass" opposition (see case 144a, Appendix A).

»3«

ANALYSIS OF CROSS-LANGUAGE DATA

A principal finding of this study is that the ubiquitously occurring life-form categories described in the preceding chapter are lexically encoded by languages in relatively invariant orders. Figures 2 and 3 summarize encoding sequences for plant and animal life-form classes respectively as determined through cross-language comparison.

The two encoding sequences are interpreted as series of stages in the growth of plant and animal life-form vocabularies, one life-form term being added at each stage. In the plant sequence, Stage 1 languages lack terms for all five botanical categories in question. Languages move to Stage 2 by lexically encoding **tree** and then to Stage 3 by adding a term for either **grerb** or **grass**. If **grerb** is encoded at Stage 3, **vine**, **grass**, and **bush** will be encoded from Stage 4 to 6. Addition of botanical life-forms from Stage 4 to 6 involves no strict order in either case.[1]

In the animal sequence (Figure 3), Stage 0 languages lack terms for the categories in question. Stage 1 languages encode one, Stage 2 languages encode two, and Stage 3 languages encode three of the life-forms **fish**, **bird**, and **snake**. At Stage 4, languages add a term for either **wug** or **mammal**. The remaining class is encoded at Stage 5.[2] (The addition of combined **wug-mammal** is discussed presently.)

The encoding uniformities summarized in Figures 2 and 3 have been determined by comparing plant life-form data from 188 languages and animal life-form data from 144 languages. These are presented in Appendices A and B respectively. The appendices are immediately preceded by a preamble on pages 129–132. This includes a description of methodology used in collecting data as well as an explanation of conventions adopted in data presentation.

The data base shows that while the categories in question are ubiquitous in languages, languages nonetheless differ with respect to the number of these classes they encode. Both plant and animal life-form vocabularies range in

23

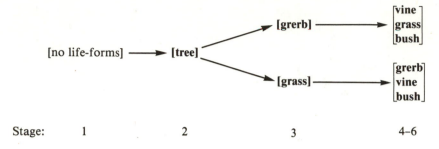

Stage: 1   2   3   4-6

Figure 2. Botanical life-form encoding sequence.

size from none to all five items of each encoding sequence. Another finding is
that all possible combinations of five life-forms of each sequence are not
found among languages surveyed. For example, the combination **fish** and
wug (minus **bird**, **snake**, and **mammal**) could occur in languages, but it does
not. In fact, only a rather limited number of possible combinations of both
plant and animal life-form terms actually occur. This indicates that constraints
of some nature on life-form classification limit the number and types of combinations to something less than what is logically possible.

The combinations that actually occur are to a certain extent patterned. For
example, if a language has only one animal life-form term, it will label **bird**
or **fish** or **snake**, but never **wug** or **mammal**. Such patterns attest to "implicational relationships" that are universal in scope. An implicational relationship
is evident when the occurrence of a certain term in languages implies or predicts the occurrence of another term, but not vice versa. For example, if a
language has a **wug** term, it will have terms for **bird**, **fish**, and **snake**. However, if a language has a term for any one of the latter three life-forms, it will
not necessarily have a label for **wug**. Thus **wug** implies **bird**, **fish**, and **snake**,
but none of these imply **wug**.

The existence of cross-language implicational relationships is often due to
regular ways in which languages change. For example, that **wug** implies
bird, **fish**, and **snake** but not vice versa is probably linked to the strong possibility that languages universally encode **bird**, **fish**, and **snake** before encod-

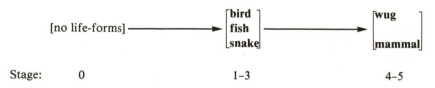

Stage: 0   1-3   4-5

Figure 3. Zoological life-form encoding sequence.

ing **wug**. The encoding sequences of Figures 2 and 3 are summations of regular change paths that would account for the implicational relationships evident in cross-language data (Appendices A and B). If languages encode life-forms only in the orders of Figures 2 and 3, then certain life-form combinations are possible and others are not. For example, the nonattested combination mentioned above, **fish** and **wug** (minus **bird**, **snake**, and **mammal**), does not occur because languages encode **bird** and **snake** in addition to **fish** before adding a **wug** term. The fact that plant and animal life-form vocabularies grow in a uniform manner, then, plausibly accounts for constraints on the occurrence of certain combinations of life-forms in languages and the nonoccurrence of others.

Botanical Life-Forms and Implicational Relationships

There are 32 (2^5) logically possible combinations of the five classes of the botanical life-form encoding sequence (Figure 2). Among the 188 languages surveyed for plant life-form classification (see Appendix A), only 14 of these combinations actually occur. These 14 combinations are as follows, with indication of their frequency of occurrence (in parentheses) among the 188 languages:

No life-forms   (2)
Tree   (7)
Tree + grerb   (21)
Tree + grass   (14)
Tree + vine   (1)
Tree + grerb + vine   (51)
Tree + grerb + grass   (13)
Tree + grerb + bush   (6)
Tree + grass + vine   (11)
Tree + grass + bush   (2)
Tree + grerb + grass + vine   (31)
Tree + grerb + vine + bush   (8)
Tree + grass + vine + bush   (7)
Tree + grerb + grass + vine + bush   (14)

Implicational relationships are apparent in these data. If a language has one or more of the life-forms **grerb**, **grass**, **vine**, and **bush**, it will also possess **tree**. However, languages having **tree** do not necessarily have any of the other life-forms. Thus, the presence of one or more of the life-forms **grerb**, **grass**, **vine**, and **bush** implies **tree**, but not vice versa. In addition, with only one language constituting an exception, if a language has **vine** and/or **bush**, it will also have **grerb** and/or **grass**. On the other hand, languages having **grerb** and/or **grass** do not necessarily have **vine** and/or **bush**. Thus, **vine** and/or

bush imply **grerb** and/or **grass**, but not the other way around. If these implicational relationships are interpreted as relating to a uniform manner in which life-form vocabularies grow, then languages first encode **tree**, then either **grerb** or **grass**, and then the remaining three plant life-forms (Figure 2).

Of the 14 life-form combinations found among the 188 languages, 13 are predicted by the botanical life-form encoding sequence. Thus, there is only one deviant combination, **tree + vine**; and this is possessed by only one language, Pacaas Novos (case 45a, Appendix A) or, in other words, by only 0.53 percent of surveyed languages. (In addition to **tree** and **vine**, Pacaas Novos also has incipient **grerb**.) As it happens, there are 14 combinations of botanical life-forms that are logically possible if languages follow the various encoding paths of Figure 2. Thus, the 188 languages surveyed nearly exhaust logical possibilities within the framework of the encoding sequence. (The expected combination **tree + grerb + grass + bush** is not attested.)

Zoological Life-Forms and Implicational Relationships

There are 64 (2^6) logically possible combinations of the five classes of the zoological life-form encoding sequence (Figure 3) plus combined **wug-mammal** that could occur in languages. Among the 144 languages surveyed only 17 of these combinations are found. Therefore, there are relatively severe constraints on the types of animal life-form classes that may occur together in the vocabularies of languages. The actually occurring combinations with their frequencies of occurrence (in parentheses) are given here (asterisks indicate combinations predicted by the encoding sequence):

* No life-forms   (1)
* **Fish**   (2)
* **Snake**   (1)
* **Bird + snake**   (9)
* **Fish + snake**   (6)
* **Bird + fish**   (1)
* **Bird + fish + snake**   (46)
  Fish + wug + mammal   (1)
  Bird + wug + mammal   (1)
  Bird + snake + mammal   (1)
* **Bird + fish + snake + wug**   (23)
* **Bird + fish + snake + mammal**   (21)
  Bird + fish + snake + combined **wug-mammal**   (3)
  Bird + snake + wug + mammal   (3)
* **Bird + fish + snake + wug + mammal**   (22)
  Bird + fish + snake + wug + combined **wug-mammal**   (2)
  Bird + fish + snake + wug + mammal + combined **wug-mammal**   (1)

Implicational relationships pertaining to these data are as follows. With only six languages constituting exceptions, if a language has **wug** or **mammal** or both, it will also possess **bird**, **fish**, and **snake** life-forms. However, languages having one, two, or all of the latter three classes do not necessarily have **wug** or **mammal** or both. Thus, the presence of **wug** or **mammal** or both of these implies the presence of **bird**, **fish**, and **snake**, but not vice versa. If these implicational relationships are interpreted as relating to a uniform manner in which life-form vocabularies grow, then **bird**, **fish**, and **snake** are added to languages before **wug** and **mammal** (Figure 3).

*   *   *

Another implicational relationship is also apparent. Languages having combined **wug-mammal** also have **bird**, **fish**, and **snake**. On the other hand, languages encoding one, two, or all of the latter three categories do not necessarily have combined **wug-mammal**. Consequently, combined **wug-mammal** implies **bird**, **fish**, and **snake**, but not vice versa. The latter three life-forms, then, precede combined **wug-mammal** in encoding order as well as preceding **wug** and **mammal**. This additional regularity is not incorporated into the formal representation of the encoding sequence (Figure 3) since combined **wug-mammal** apparently is a relatively rare life-form class (occurring in only six languages of the 144 surveyed).

Of the 17 life-form combinations found among the 144 languages, 10 are predicted by the life-form encoding sequence (these are marked with asterisks in the list given earlier).[3] In other words, these 10 combinations are expected to occur if life-form vocabularies are built up in the order of Figure 3. In addition, 3 combinations accord with the additional encoding uniformity involving combined **wug-mammal** (see preceding paragraph). Thus there are only 4 combinations that do not accord with cross-language regularities in animal life-form encoding. The 13 expected combinations are possessed by 138 languages of the 144 surveyed or, in other words, by 95.83 percent. On the other hand, the 4 unexpected combinations are possessed by only 6 languages or 4.17 percent. While animal life-form encoding regularities are not strictly "universal," since all languages do not participate in them, there is, nonetheless an obviously strong universal tendency for languages to encode zoological life-forms in the order of Figure 3.

Languages and Stage Affiliations: Plant Life-Forms

Only two languages, Iwaidja (1a) and Southern Paiute (Kawaiisu dialect) (2a) totally lack terms for botanical life-forms of the encoding sequence (Figure 2) and, thus, are affiliated with Stage 1 of plant life-form growth. As it happens,

Iwaidja does have incipient **tree** and **grerb** classes. In other words, it has terms for botanical organisms typically fitting into these two categories but not designated by any other Iwaidja plant name. Named exemplars are not included. Incipient life-forms by convention are not considered in life-form counts determining stage affiliation. The source for Southern Paiute (Kawaiiau dialect) reports that he recorded "no words referring to general types of plant growth: trees, grass, etc., and nothing that clearly distinguished between 'that which is edible' and that which is not." However, a term for weed is mentioned by the source.

Of the sample of 188 languages, 7 are affiliated with Stage 2 of plant life-form growth having only one life-form class, **tree**. These are Bella Coola (3a), Bontoc (4a), Dalabon (5a), Northern Paiute (Oregon dialect) (6a), Sahaptin (7a), Shuswap (8a), and Wasco (9a). Two of these languages, Bella Coola and Sahaptin, have incipient **grass** classes in addition to **tree**. According to the source for Dalabon, it is possible that the language has botanical life-forms beyond **tree**. The source for Wasco reports that with the exception of "a rarely-used extension from 'wood,' there is not even a word for tree." If extension of "wood" to "tree" in fact has little currency in the language, then Wasco should perhaps be judged as lacking **tree** and affiliated with Stage 1.

Thirty-six languages are affiliated with Stage 3, having two botanical life-forms. Of these, 21 have **tree + grerb**, 14 have **tree + grass**, and 1 has the deviant combination **tree + vine** (Pacaas Novos [45a]). Two languages, Lillooet (36a) and Tarahumara (43a) having **tree + grass** also have incipient **grerb**. In addition, 3 other **tree + grass** languages, Dugum Dani (31a), Minnesota Ojibwa (37a), and Shoshoni (39a) may eventually be shown to have **grerb** life-forms as well (see discussions associated with these cases in Appendix A). It should also be noted that a dialect of Shoshoni has a term for **grass** while it possibly lacks one for **tree** (see discussion of this case). It therefore may constitute a second language case that is not in accord with the encoding sequence.

Unusual general plant classes pertain to two Stage 3 languages having **tree + grerb**. Khmer (18a) encodes a botanical category which encompasses bushes and vines. This class seems to be a "residual" category whose membership consists of all plants not included in **tree** and **grerb**.[4] Gouin (15a) lumps vines and reeds together in a labeled grouping. Since this class is apparently focused on reeds (its best exemplars), it is not codified as being **vine**.

Stage 4 languages are by far most common among those surveyed; 83 of the 188 have some combination of three plant life-forms of the botanical encoding sequence. Among these, those having **grerb** combined with two other life-forms other than **grass** are 57 in number; while only 13 languages have **grass** combined with two life-forms other than **grerb**. This indicates that languages are somewhat more inclined to add **grerb** at Stage 3 than to add **grass**.

In addition, since **vine** constitutes a third life-form in 62 of the 83 Stage 4 languages, there appears to be a strong tendency to encode **vine** before **bush** and before **grass** as well if **grerb** is encoded at Stage 3.

Three languages judged affiliated with Stage 4, Mende (80a), Ngbaka Ma'bo (83a), and Mitla Zapotec (103a), may actually have more than three botanical life-forms (see discussion associated with these cases). Two languages, Awtuw (49a) and Southern Paiute (Cedar City dialect) (106a), may have fewer than three. Awtuw may lack **grerb** and/or **vine** (see discussion associated with this case). The Cedar City dialect of Southern Paiute may lack **tree** and thus may constitute another deviant Stage 3 language having **grerb + grass**. The source for the latter case reports that the term elicited for **tree** "was recorded only in the context of taxonomic discussion [and] may be somewhat artificial."

Forty-six languages are judged affiliated with Stage 5, having four plant life-forms. The vast majority of these (31) have the combination **tree + grerb + grass + vine**. One of these, Yucatec (158a), may have an additional life-form, **bush**, and thus in fact may be a Stage 6 language (see associated discussion). Three languages, Muinane (144a), Sierra Popoluca (147a), and Yaqui (157a), may have fewer than four plant life-forms (see associated discussions). It is possible that one of these, Yaqui, is a deviant case, lacking **tree** but having other plant life-forms of the encoding sequence. In addition, the Yaqui **grass** term may label an incipient rather than a full-fledged life-form class.

Only 14 languages have all five classes of the botanical life-form encoding sequence and are thus affiliated with Stage 6. Two of these may actually have fewer than five life-forms. **Grass** in Clallam (181a) may turn out to be an incipient rather than a full-fledged life-form category. Choctaw (178a) possibly lacks a **tree** term and therefore may not be in accord with the encoding sequence.

Languages and Stage Affiliations: Animal Life-Forms

Only 1 language of the 144 surveyed, Iwaidja (1b), totally lacks classes of the zoological life-form encoding sequence. Iwaidja, then, is the only language affiliated with Stage 0 of life-form growth. However, the language does have incipient **bird**, **fish**, and **snake** life-form classes.

Three languages of the 144 are affiliated with Stage 1 of animal life-form growth, having only one life-form term. Two of these, Desana (2b) and Ngandi (3b) have only **fish**. It is possible that Ngandi has another life-form in addition to **fish**. The source for Ngandi mentions that absence of a "snake" label may be an elicitation gap. The third Stage 1 language, Muyuw (4b), has only **snake**.

Sixteen languages have only two animal life-forms and thus are affiliated with Stage 2. Amahuaca (5b), Ilongot (6b), Jicaque (7b), Karok (8b), Nimboran (9b), Northern Paiute (Nevada) (10b), Papago (11b), Smith River (12b), and Wik-Ngathana (13b) have a **bird + snake** combination. Ilongot and Northern Paiute (Nevada) also have incipient **fish** life-forms. Highland Tequistlatec (14b), Juchitan Zapotec (15b), Mitla Zapotec (16b), Paumari (17b), Ritharngu (18b), and Sanuma (19b) have **fish + snake**. Juchitan Zapotec also has incipient **wug** and **mammal** life-forms. Only 1 language, Sahaptin (20b), has a **bird + fish** combination. Sahaptin also has incipient "snake" and "worm" classes. Four languages of the 15 Stage 2 languages having **snake** lack terms restricted to true snakes. Papago and Northern Paiute (Nevada) encode only one half of the binary opposition "large elongated creature" (snake)/"small elongated creature" (worm) having a term for "worm" but none for "snake." Nimboran has a term covering lizards and snakes and another term for "worm." Mitla Zapotec lumps snakes and worms together in a single labeled class and also has a separate term for "worm." Some of the languages judged affiliated with Stage 2 possibly have more than two animal life-forms (see discussions associated with cases 5b, 13b, 17b, and 19b in Appendix B).

Stage 3 and 4 languages are most numerous among the 144 sampled. Forty-nine languages are affiliated with Stage 3, having three zoological life-forms. Forty-six of these have the expected combination **bird + fish + snake**. Three have unexpected combinations: Dalabon (67b) with **fish + wug + mammal**, Dugum Dani (68b) with **bird + wug + mammal**, and Kyaka Enga (69b) with **bird + snake + mammal**. Deviant cases are discussed presently. Some of the 49 languages judged affiliated with Stage 3 may have fewer than three life-forms (see discussions associated with cases 27b, 29b, 30b, 54b, and 68b) and some may have more (see discussions associated with cases 21b, 24b, 35b, 37b, 50b, 53b, 61b, 63b, and 67b).

There are 50 languages affiliated with Stage 4, having four animal life-forms each. Twenty-three of these have the combination **bird + fish + snake + wug** and 21 have **bird + fish + snake + mammal**. This breakdown indicates that **wug** and **mammal** have roughly equal chances of being encoded by languages at Stage 4. Three languages have combinations of four life-form terms not in accord with the encoding sequence: Gimi (117b), Maring (118b), and Ndumba (119b), each with **bird + snake + wug + mammal**. Three languages, Koiwai (114b), Mokilese (115b), and Tzotzil (Zinacantan) (116b), have **bird**, **fish**, **snake**, and combined **wug-mammal**. Some of the 50 languages judged affiliated with Stage 4 may have fewer than four life-forms (see discussions associated with cases 78b, 79b, 100b, 103b, 106b, 110b, and 116b) and some may have more (see discussions associated with cases 71b, 72b, 77b, 82b, 84b, 89b, 98b, 101b, and 109b).

Twenty-five languages of the 144 are affiliated with Stage 5. Of these, 22 have all five zoological life-forms of the encoding sequence. Two languages, Daga (142b) and Southern Paiute (Chemehuevi dialect) (143b) have **bird**, **fish**, **snake**, **wug**, and combined **wug-mammal**. Tahitian (144b), as noted in the preamble to Appendices A and B, is treated here as a Stage 5 language, even though it actually has six life-forms. These are the five of the encoding sequence plus combined **wug-mammal**. Three of the languages judged affiliated with Stage 5 possibly have fewer than five animal life-forms (see discussions associated with cases 126b, 131b, and 134b).

Problematic Cases Involving Animal Life-Forms

As noted earlier, six languages or 4.17 percent of 144 surveyed have combinations of animal life-form terms not in accord with cross-language encoding regularities. These six are Dalabon (67b) with **fish + wug + mammal**, Dugum Dani (68b) with **bird + wug + mammal**, Kyaka Enga (69b) with **bird + snake + mammal**, and Gimi (117b), Maring (118b) and Ndumba (119b) all with **bird + snake + wug + mammal**.

Five of these six languages, Dugum Dani, Kyaka Enga, Gimi, Maring, and Ndumba, are spoken in highland regions of New Guinea. Deviant life-form combinations of the latter are traced to ecological deficiencies of highland environments. For example, all of these languages lack **fish** but have **wug** and/or **mammal**. Fish are either totally lacking, rare, or extremely limited in variety in environments in which they are spoken (see discussions associated with the cases in Appendix B). Dugum Dani lacks a **snake** life-form in addition to **fish**. The source for this case reports that snakes are rare in the Dugum Dani habitat, there being only two sorts of nonpoisonous ones.

To my knowledge, there are no ecological factors that would similarly account for the unexpected combination of Dalabon (67b). There is, then, only one language among the 144 sampled that inexplicably violates the animal life-form encoding sequence. This case constitutes only 0.69 percent of the languages surveyed.

Environmental factors are also associated with several unusual groupings of creatures encountered among the 144 languages. Three languages, Papago (11b), Kayaka Enga (69b), and Siane (40b), include fish in **snake** life-forms. A fourth language, Kilangi (133b) apparently did so in the not so distant past. Papago lacks a term for fish but lumps these creatures with small elongated animals in a "worm" life-form. Kyaka Enga, also lacking a **fish** term, includes fish in a highly heterogeneous **snake** life-form encompassing snakes, worms, lizards, caterpillars, reptile-like insects, and other elongated creatures. While Siane has a **fish** label, *laiva*, some speakers nonetheless insist that fish are also *hoiafa*, a term for another highly heterogenous **snake** category. All three languages are spoken in environments in which fish are rare and/or extremely limited in diversity. Papago is spoken in desert areas of the United States Southwest and Northern Mexico and Kyaka Enga and Siane in highland regions of New Guinea. The source for Kilangi notes that in the past there were no fish in Kilangi territory. Apparently, when Kilangi speakers encountered fish, they were forbidden to eat them because they considered fish to be snakes (*njoka*) (see associated discussion, Appendix B). The inclusion of fish in **snake** is understandable since these animals typically share the feature "elongation" with other included creatures.

Another language, Patep (107b), also treats fish in an unusual manner. While true fish have their own label, *beac*, they are also lumped with mammals and water creatures such as frogs and turtles in a **mammal** life-form class. Environmental deficiency is also associated with this classificatory strategy. Patep speakers (Papua New Guinea) are mountain people acquainted with only a few varieties of fish (see associated discussion, Appendix B). Patep (107b) and Siane (140b) are similar cases in that they both have **fish** terms but nonetheless recognize fish as affiliated with other, more inclusive life-form classes, **mammal** and **snake** respectively. Apparently, since native exemplars of fish are so few in number and/or variety, speakers of these languages do not feel justified in maintaining labeled **fish** categories as unaffiliated groupings equivalent to or coordinate with **bird**, **snake**, **mammal**, and so on.

Ecological factors may also occasionally relate to unusual treatment of snakes. Several languages surveyed here have terms for "large elongated creatures" (snakes) but also include these animals in either **wug** or **mammal** or combined **wug-mammal** life-forms (see cases 83b, 112b, 116b, 119b, 124b, 133b, 135b, 136b, 138b, and 139b). Three of these, which lump snakes with bugs in **wug**, Minnesota Ojibwa (136b), Northern Ojibwa (138b), and North Saami (139b), are spoken in northern latitudes where snakes are scarce, of few varieties, and inconspicuous because of small size. Environmental deficiencies do not seem to be correlated with other cases treating snakes in similar ways. Some of these cases are discussed in following chapters.

»4«

LANGUAGE RELATEDNESS AND GROWTH STAGES

"Galton's Problem" could be raised in response to the findings reported here. In other words, it is possible that implicational relationships discovered in the data are merely artifacts of the "relatedness" of languages. If so, the validity of the proposals that plant and animal life-form terms are added to languages in fixed orders is questionable. If geographically and/or genetically related languages tend to be affiliated with the same stage of life-form growth, then many of the logically possible combinations of life-forms do not occur in languages because of areal diffusion of only a limited number of patterns and/or because only a few combinations were originally represented in the vocabularies of parent languages.

Galton's Problem and Botanical Life-Forms

Table 9 organizes the 188 languages surveyed for plant classification according to genetic relationship, and roughly by geography, and indicates botanical life-form stage affiliation. Genetically related languages of the sample are not regularly associated with the same life-form stage. For example, the three Dravidian languages are affiliated with Stages 4, 5, and 6 respectively, and the four Mon-Khmer languages with Stages 3, 4, and 5. In some cases, even dialects of the same language are associated with different stages: e.g., the three dialects of Southern Paiute (Kawaiisu, Chemehuevi, and Cedar City) are affiliated with Stages 1, 3, and 4 respectively and the two dialects of Tzotzil (Zinacantan and Chamula) with Stages 5 and 6 respectively.

Geographically contiguous languages also tend not to share the same stage of plant life-form growth. For example, the 20 Western United States languages (Clallam, Hopi, Kiowa Apache, Kootenai, Montana Salish, Navaho, Nez Perce, Northern Paiute [Nevada], Northern Paiute [Oregon], Papago, Sahaptin, Smith River, Southern Paiute [Cedar City], Southern Paiute [Cheme-

Table 9. Classification of languages with botanical stage affiliations.

Eskimo Aleut: Eskimo (Stage 3).
Salish:
   Interior Salish: Shuswap (Stage 2), Lillooet (Stage 3), Montana Salish (Stage 5).
   Coast Salish: Halkomelem Salish (Stage 3), Clallam (Stage 6).
   Bella Coola: Bella Coola (Stage 2).
Wakashan: Southern Kwakiutl (Stage 3).
Unclassified language: Kootenai (Stage 5).
Athapascan-Eyak:
   Athapascan:
      Apachean: Kiowa Apache (Stage 3), Navaho (Stage 5).
      Northern Athapascan: Upper Tanana (Stage 4), Central Carrier (Stage 6).
      Pacific Coast Athapascan: Smith River (Stage 3).
   Other: Haida (Stage 4).
Algonquian: Delaware, Minnesota Ojibwa (Stage 3).
Muskogean: Choctaw (Stage 6).
Penutian:
   Sahaptin–Nez Perce: Sahaptin (Stage 2), Nez Perce (Stage 4).
   Chinookan: Wasco (Stage 2).
Unclassified language: Zuni (Stage 4).
Hokan:
   Tequistlatecan: Highland Tequistlatec, Lowland Tequistlatec (Stage 5).
   Other: Karok (Stage 4).
Aztec-Tanoan:
   Tanoan: Southern Tiwa (Stage 3), Tewa (Stage 5).
   Uto-Aztecan:
      Numic: Southern Paiute (Kawaiisu) (Stage 1), Northern Paiute (Oregon) (Stage 2),
         Northern Paiute (Nevada), Shoshoni, Southern Paiute (Chemehuevi) (Stage 3),
         Southern Paiute (Cedar City) (Stage 4).
      Sonoran: Tarahumara (Stage 3), Papago (Stage 4), Huichol, Yaqui (Stage 5), Cora
         (Stage 6).
      Aztecan: Classical Nahuatl (Stage 4), Michoacan Nahuatl (Stage 5).
      Other: Hopi (Stage 3).
Mesoamerican:[a]
   Mayan: Chontal, Chuj, Ixil, Jacaltec, Pocomchi (Stage 4), Kekchi, Mopan, Tzeltal,
      Tzotzil (Zinacantan), Tzutujil, Yucatec (Stage 5), Chol, Chorti, Huastec, Lacandon,
      Pocomam, Tzotzil (Chamula) (Stage 6).
   Oto-Manguean:
      Zapotecan: Atapec Zapotec, Juchitan Zapotec, Mitla Zapotec (Stage 4), Texmelucan
         Zapotec, Zoogocho Zapotec (Stage 5).
      Popolocan: Popoloca (Stage 3), Mazatec (Stage 5).
      Other: Amuzgo (Stage 5).
   Totonacan: Tepehua (Stage 5).
   Zoquean: Sierra Popoluca (Stage 5).
Unclassified language: Jicaque (Stage 4).
Macro-Chibchan: Ninam (Stage 4), Colorado (Stage 5).
Ge-Pano-Carib:
   Macro-Carib: Tiriyo (Stage 4), Akawaio, Makiritare, Muinane (Stage 5).
   Macro-Panoan: Amahuaca, Araona, Mataco (Stage 4).

Table 9. *continued*

Macro-Ge-Bororo: Bororo (Stage 5).
Unclassified language: Waodani (Stage 4).
Andean-Equatorial:
  Equatorial:
    Tupi: Asurini (Stage 3), Gaviao (Stage 4), Kaiwa, Kayova (Stage 5).
    Arawakan: Pacaas Novos (Stage 3), Machiguenga, Paumari (Stage 4).
    Macro-Tucanoan: Carapana, Desana (Stage 5).
    Jivaroan: Aguaruna Jivaro (Stage 4).
  Andean: Quechua (Stage 5).
Austronesian:
  Oceanic:
    Papua Austronesian: Kiriwinian, Muyuw, Patep (Stage 4).
    Micronesian: Gilbertese (Stage 3), Mokilese (Stage 5).
    Polynesian: Mele-Fila (Stage 4).
  Northwest Austronesian:
    Philippine:
      Sulic: Hanunoo, Manobo Blit, Taubuid, Western Subanun (Stage 4), Tasaday
        (Stage 5).
      Cordilleran: Bontoc (Stage 2), Central Cagayan Agta, Ibataan, Iloko, Itawis,
        Pagan Gaddang (Stage 4).
      Others: Casiguran Damagat, Samal, Sambal (Stage 4).
    Other: Ilongot (Stage 4).
  West Indonesian: Jarai, Kenyah, Roglai (Stage 4), Brunei Malay (Stage 5), Malagasy
    (Stage 6).
  East Indonesian: Nuaulu (Stage 4).
  Moluccan Austronesian: Koiwai (Stage 4).
Indo-Pacific:
  Central New Guinea:
    East New Guinea Highlands: Gimi (Stage 3), Melpa (Stage 4), Kalam, Ndumba
      (Stage 5).
    Sepik: Awtuw, Hewa (Stage 4).
    Central and South New Guinea: Tifal (Stage 5).
    South-East New Guinea: Daga (Stage 5).
    West New Guinea Highlands: Dugum Dani (Stage 3).
    North Papuan: Nimboran (Stage 4).
  North New Guinea?: Isirawa (Stage 4).
  West Papuan: Tobelo (Stage 5), Bunaq (Stage 5).
Australian:
  Pama-Nyungan:
    Pama-Maric: Wik Moŋkan (Stage 3), Kugu-Nganhchara, Wik-Ngathana (Stage 4).
    Murngic: Ritharngu, Yolŋu (Stage 3), Djinang (Stage 4).
    Southwest Pama-Nyungan: Gugadja (Stage 4).
    Arandic: Western Aranda (Stage 3).
  Gunwingguan: Dalabon (Stage 2), Ngandi (Stage 3).
  Maran: Mara (Stage 3).
  Iwaidjan: Iwaidja (Stage 1).
  Others: Nunggubuyu, Anindilyakwa (Stage 3).
Mon-Khmer: Khmer (Stage 3), Brou, Nya Hon (Stage 4), Sre (Stage 5).

Table 9. *continued*

Miao-Yao: Hmong (Stage 4).
Kam-Tai: Lao (Stage 4).
Tibeto-Burman (Naga-Kuki-Chin): Mikir (Stage 4).
Altaic?: Japanese (Stage 4).
Dravidian: Hill Pandaram (Stage 4), Malyalam (Stage 5), Koya (Stage 6).
Afro-Asiatic: Amharic (Stage 4).
Nilo-Saharan: Songhay (Stage 3), Lotuho (Stage 5).
Niger-Congo:
    West Atlantic: Sherbro (Stage 3), Basari, Bedik, Kisi, Temne (Stage 4).
    Gur: Gouin, Sisaala (Stage 3), Dogon, Moore (Stage 4), Teen (Stage 5).
    Kwa: Igbira (Stage 3), Baoule (Stage 4), Ando (Stage 5).
    Mande: Bisa (Stage 3), Bambara, Mende (Stage 4).
    Adamawa: Banda, Manja, Ngbaka Ma'bo (Stage 4).
    Bantu-Proper: Kilangi (Stage 3), Chewa, Kaguru (Stage 4).
Uralic (Lappic): North Saami (Stage 4).
Indo-European:
    Indic: Hindi, Kumaoni (Stage 5), Bengali (Stage 6).
    Latin: Puerto Rican Spanish (Stage 4).
    Germanic: American English (Stage 6).

---

[a]Witkowski and Brown 1978b.

huevi], Southern Paiute [Kawaiisu], Southern Tiwa, Tewa, Wasco, Yaqui, and Zuni) range from Stage 1 to Stage 6 in affiliation. Moreover, these 20 cases are fairly evenly distributed across stages:

Stage 1: 1 case
Stage 2: 3 cases
Stage 3: 6 cases
Stage 4: 4 cases
Stage 5: 5 cases
Stage 6: 1 case

Neither diffusion nor genetic relationship appears to have figured significantly in the observed distribution of plant life-form inventories. It therefore appears that discovered implicational relationships are the product of a uniform way in which plant life-forms are added to vocabularies rather than an artifact of language relatedness.

This is not to propose that diffusion and genetic relationship never influence plant life-form growth. For example, Chapter 5 cites evidence showing that genetically related languages usually possess more biological life-form terms than their parent language did. Thus, the number of life-form terms pertaining to a parent language apparently affects daughter language-stage affiliation by imposing a "lower limit" on the number of life-form terms that daughter languages can possess.

In addition, there are instances in which plant life-form classes (but not necessarily terms for them) have probably diffused. For example, of the 15 Northwest Austronesian languages, all spoken in the Philippines, all but two are associated with Stage 4 in plant life-form growth. This appears to be a greater number than that expected by chance. Of the 188 languages surveyed, 83 or 44.1 percent are affiliated with Stage 4. On the other hand, 85.7 percent of Philippine languages sampled are Stage 4 cases. This is roughly two times the size of anticipated findings if the 44.1 percent figure is roughly indicative of chance expectations. In addition, of the 13 Stage 4 Philippine languages, all but one has the combination **tree + grerb + vine**. Extrapolation from all languages surveyed indicates that approximately 63 percent or only 8 of these 13 languages should have this combination if chance alone is pertinent. Consequently, it seems that either genetic relationship or diffusion, or conceivably both, underlie Philippine language-stage homogeneity. Diffusion is the more likely factor since terms for **grerb** and **vine**—but not terms for **tree**—vary significantly from language to language, suggesting that these two life-forms were not present in a common ancestral language. However, detailed comparative work using the methods of historical linguistics must be undertaken before relative influences of diffusion and genetic relationship can be accurately assessed in this case.

Galton's Problem and Zoological Life-Forms

Table 10 organizes the 144 languages surveyed for animal classification according to genetic relationship, and roughly by geography, and indicates zoological life-form stage affiliation. Languages that are genetically related are not found to be regularly associated with the same animal life-form stage. For example, all but one of the well-represented major language groupings (Andean-Equatorial, Australian, Austronesian, Aztec-Tanoan, Ge-Pano-Carib, Indo-Pacific, Mesoamerican, and Niger-Congo) are affiliated with at least four of the six growth stages. Niger-Congo is affiliated with three. Australian is especially noteworthy since it is associated with all six stages. In addition, subgroupings within major groups tend to show stage heterogeneity: for example, Numic (of Aztec-Tanoan) with four stages, Philippine (of Austronesian) with three stages, Pama-Nyungan (of Australian) with three stages, and Arawakan (of Andean-Equatorial) with three.

Geographically contiguous languages also tend not to share the same stage of zoological life-form growth. For example, 16 Western United States languages (Clallam, Smith River, Navaho, Yurok, Sahaptin, Nez Perce, Keres, Karok, Southern Tiwa, Tewa, Northern Paiute, Shoshoni, Southern Paiute [Cedar City], Southern Paiute [Chemehuevi], Papago, and Hopi) range from Stage 2 to Stage 5 in affiliation. Thus, as in the plant case, neither diffusion

Table 10. Classification of languages with zoological stage affiliations.

Eskimo Aleut: Eskimo (Stage 5).
Salish: Clallam (Stage 4).
Athapascan:
   Northern Athapascan: Upper Tanana (Stage 3), Central Carrier (Stage 4).
   Pacific Coast Athapascan: Smith River (Stage 2).
   Apachen: Navaho (Stage 4).
Macro-Algonquian:
   Algonquian: Delaware, Minnesota Ojibwa, Montagnais, Northern Ojibwa (Stage 5).
   Other: Yurok (Stage 4).
Macro-Siouan:
   Siouan: Omaha (Stage 4).
   Other: Catawba (Stage 4).
Penutian:
   Sahaptin–Nez Perce: Sahaptin (Stage 2), Nez Perce (Stage 3).
Unclassified language: Keres (Stage 3).
Hokan:
   Tequistlatecan: Highland Tequistlatec (Stage 2), Lowland Tequistlatec (Stage 3).
   Other: Karok (Stage 2).
Aztec-Tanoan:
   Tanoan: Southern Tiwa (Stage 3), Tewa (Stage 4).
   Uto-Aztecan:
     Numic: Northern Paiute (Stage 2), Shoshoni (Stage 3), Southern Paiute (Cedar City)
       (Stage 4), Southern Paiute (Chemehuevi) (Stage 5).
     Sonoran: Papago (Stage 2), Huichol, Tarahumara (Stage 3), Cora, Yaqui (Stage 4).
     Aztecan: Michoacan Nahuatl (Stage 3), Classical Nahuatl (Stage 5).
   Other: Hopi (Stage 3).
Mesoamerican:[a]
   Oto-Manguean:
     Zapotecan: Juchitan Zapotec, Mitla Zapotec (Stage 2), Atapec Zapotec, Texmelucan
       Zapotec, Zoogocho Zapotec (Stage 3).
     Popolocan: Mazatec (Stage 3).
   Mayan: Chuj, Huastec (Stage 3), Tzeltal, Tzotzil (Stage 4), Chorti (Stage 5).
   Zoquean: Sierra Popoluca (Stage 4).
   Totonacan: Tepehua (Stage 4).
Unclassified language: Jicaque (Stage 2).
Macro-Chibchan:
   Waican: Sanuma (Stage 2).
   Barbacoan: Colorado (Stage 3).
Ge-Pano-Carib:
   Macro-Panoan:
     Pano-Tacana: Amahuaca (Stage 2), Araona (Stage 3).
     Mataco: Mataco (Stage 5).
   Macro-Carib:
     Carib: Akawaio (Stage 3), Makiritare (Stage 4).
     Witotoan: Nuinane (Stage 4).
   Macro-Ge: Kaingan (Stage 3), Kayapo, Maxakali (Stage 4).
   Unclassified language: Waodoni (Stage 4).

Table 10. *continued*

Andean-Equatorial:
  Equatorial:
    Arawakan: Paumari (Stage 2), Machiguenga (Stage 3), Pacaas Novos (Stage 4).
    Tupi:
      Tupi-Guarani: Asurini, Kaiwa (Stage 3).
      Monde: Gaviao (Stage 3).
  Macro-Tucanoan:
    Tucanoan: Desana (Stage 1), Carapana (Stage 3).
  Jivaroan: Aguaruna Jivaro (Stage 3).
Austronesian:
  Oceanic:
    Polynesian: Mele-Fila (Stage 3), Tahitian (Stage 5).
    Micronesian: Mokilese (Stage 4).
    Papua Austronesian: Muyuw (Stage 1), Patep (Stage 4).
  Northwest Austronesian:
    Philippine:
      Sulic: Western Subanun (Stage 4).
      Cordilleran: Bontoc, Central Cagayan Agta (Stage 3), Ibataan (Stage 4).
    Other: Ilongot (Stage 2).
  West Indonesian: Brunei Malay, Kenyah (Stage 3), Indonesian, Kayan, Malagasy (Stage 4).
  East Indonesian:
    Ambon-Timor: Nuaulu (Stage 3).
  Moluccan Austronesian: Koiwai (Stage 4).
Indo-Pacific:
  Central New Guinea:
    East New Guinea Highlands:
      Gende-Siane-Gahuku-Kamano-Fore:
        Fore: Gimi (Stage 4), Fore (Stage 5).
        Siane: Siane (Stage 5).
      Hagen-Wahgi-Jimi-Chimbu: Maring, Melpa (Stage 4).
      Enga-Hule-Wiru: Kyaka Enga (Stage 3).
      Karam: Kalam (Stage 4).
      Mikaru: Daribi (Stage 4).
      Gadsup-Anyana-Awa-Tairora: Ndumba (Tairora) (Stage 4).
    Central and South New Guinea:
      Ok: Faiwol (Stage 4), Tifal (Stage 5).
    North Papuan: Nimboran (Stage 2).
    West New Guinea Highlands: Dugum Dani (Stage 3).
    Sepik: Awtuw, Hewa (Stage 4).
    South-East New Guinea: Daga (Stage 5).
  North New Guinea?:
    Upper Tor: Isirawa (Stage 4).
Australian:
  Pama-Nyungan:
    Pama-Maric:
      Middle Pama: Wik Moŋkan (Stage 3), Kugu-Nganhchara (Stage 4).

Other: Wik-Ngathana (Stage 2).
  Murngic: Ritharngu (Stage 2), Djinang (Stage 3), Yolŋu (Stage 4).
  Arandic: Western Aranda (Stage 3).
Gunwingguan: Ngandi (Stage 1), Dalabon (Stage 3).
Iwaidjan: Iwaidja (Stage 0).
Maran: Mara (Stage 3).
Others: Nunggubuyu (Stage 3), Anindilyakwa (Stage 5).
Austro-Asiatic:
  Mon-Khmer: Chrau (Stage 3).
  Malacca: Semai (Stage 3).
Kam-Tai: Northeastern Thai (Stage 4).
Chinese: Cantonese, Penang Hokkien (Stage 3), Mandarin (Stage 4).
Altaic?: Japanese (Stage 5).
Dravidian: Hill Pandaram (Stage 5).
Nilo-Saharan: Songhay (Stage 3), Lotuho (Stage 4).
Niger-Congo:
  Bantu Proper:
    North Eastern Bantu: Kikamba (Stage 4), Kilangi, Komo (Stage 5).
    Central Eastern Bantu: Ila (Stage 4), Fipa (Stage 5).
  Adamawa-Eastern: Azande, Gbaya Kara (Stage 5).
  Mande: Bisa (Stage 3), Mende (Stage 4).
  Gur: Gouin, Moore, Sisaala (Stage 3), Teen (Stage 4).
  Kwa: Igbira (Stage 4).
Lappic: North Saami (Stage 5).
Indo-European:
  Indo-Iranian: Pashto (Stage 4).
  Balto-Slavic: Czech (Stage 5).
  Germanic: American English (Stage 5).
Pidgin (English based): Tok Pisin (Stage 4).

---

[a] Witkowski and Brown 1978b.

nor genetic relationship appears to have figured significantly in the observed distribution of animal life-form inventories. From this it can be concluded that implicational relationships involving animal life-forms are also the product of a uniform way in which life-forms are added to vocabularies rather than an artifact of language relatedness.

As in the plant case, diffusion and genetic relationship may occasionally influence animal life-form growth. There are instances in which animal life-form classes (but not necessarily terms for them) have probably diffused. For example, in two widely separated areas of the world, the distinction "large mammal"/"small mammal" may have spread by borrowing. Seven of nine East New Guinea Highland languages lexically encode **mammal** through binary contrast by use of dissimilar sets of two terms. These are Gimi (117b), Fore (129b), Siane (140b), Maring (118b), Kyaka Enga (69b), Kalam (101b), and Ndumba (119b). In addition, one other New Guinea language, Isirawa (100b), encodes one-half of the binary contrast, i.e., "small mammal."

While these languages are genetically related, it is unlikely that the classificatory strategy they share is traced to common ancestry since **mammal** tends to emerge very late in animal life-form growth. Independent development of the large/small contrast for **mammal** by each of these languages also seems unlikely since this distinction is rare, having a significant occurrence in only one other region of the world, northern North America.[1] Of the six languages of the latter region found in the sample (cases 63b, 94b, 127b, 136b, 137b, and 138b) four encode **mammal** through binary opposition or by labeling one-half of the contrast. These are Northern Ojibwa (138b), Minnesota Ojibwa (136b), Eskimo (127b), and Central Carrier (94b). Since only the former two languages are clearly genetically related, it is possible that the "small mammal"/"large mammal" distinction is an areal feature of northern North America. Of course, many more languages of the area must be investigated before this can be proposed with confidence.

»5«

LEXICAL RECONSTRUCTION AND LIFE-FORM GROWTH

The plant and animal life-form encoding sequences (Figures 2 and 3) are supported by studies employing the comparative method of historical linguistics. This approach provides a means for reconstructing vocabularies of languages of the remote past (proto-languages) ancestral to groups of genetically related modern languages. This chapter describes reconstructed plant and animal life-form vocabularies of parent languages of three unrelated genetic groupings of languages. These groupings are the Mayan languages of Mesoamerica (Brown 1979b; Brown and Witkowski 1982), the Polynesian languages of Oceania (Brown 1981b, 1982a), and the Numic languages of the Western U.S. (Fowler 1972). In all three cases, lexical reconstruction of biological life-form growth accords with encoding sequences.

Mayan Life-Form Growth

Contemporary Mayan languages for the most part are located in a relatively continuous zone encompassing parts of Guatemala, Belize, Honduras, and Mexico. These are descended from a parent language spoken at the latest roughly four thousand years ago. By comparing vocabularies of 26 of the 31 reported contemporary Mayan languages, the plant life-form term inventory of Proto-Mayan has been reconstructed and details of plant life-form growth in the language family from Proto-Mayan times to the present have been recovered (Brown 1979b).

All contemporary Mayan languages have combinations of life-form terms predicted by the plant encoding sequence. All but one of the 26 languages have at least three of the five life-forms of the encoding sequence, and about two-thirds have four or more life-forms. Thus nearly all Mayan languages are associated with higher stages of botanical life-form growth (Stages 4–6).

43

Mayan languages are well represented among the 188 languages surveyed for plant classification (Appendix A, see cases 56a, 57a, 66a, 67a, 87a, 139a, 143a, 154a, 155a, 156a, 158a, 179a, 180a, 183a, 185a, 187a, and 188a).

Lexical reconstruction of Mayan botanical life-form growth is as follows. Proto-Mayan of four thousand years ago had only one plant life-form, **tree**, and, thus, was associated with Stage 2 of life-form growth (see Figure 2). Daughter languages maintained the life-form system of Proto-Mayan for approximately three thousand years. About one thousand years ago, botanical life-form lexicons began to increase in size, so that today all Mayan languages possess at least **tree** and **grerb**, and most possess life-forms beyond these. This reconstruction of course is consistent with the plant life-form encoding sequence. If a language has only one life-form of the encoding sequence, it should be **tree**. Mayan languages, then, have precisely the kind of reconstructed plant life-form inventory expected if life-form vocabularies are in fact built up in accordance with the encoding sequence.

Reconstruction of Mayan zoological life-form growth is based on all 31 reported languages (Brown and Witkowski 1982). Animal life-form combinations found in all of these languages match those predicted by the zoological life-form encoding sequence (Figure 3). In addition, all have at least three of the five life-forms. Approximately one-half of the 31 languages are affiliated with Stage 3 of animal life-form growth having the expected combination **bird + fish + snake**.[1] Other languages are affiliated with stages beyond 3, having **wug** or **mammal** or **wug** and **mammal** in addition to the latter three. At least two languages possess a combined **wug-mammal** life-form. Five Mayan languages are included among the 144 surveyed for animal classification: Chuj (33b), Huastec (39b), Tzeltal (110b), Tzotzil (116b), and Chorti (123b).

Reconstruction of the growth of folk zoological life-forms in Mayan is as follows. Proto-Mayan of four thousand years ago had one animal life-form, **snake**, and it thus was associated with Stage 1 of animal life-form growth (see Figure 3). Subsequently, terms for **bird** developed independently in most Mayan subgroups, occasionally diffusing from languages of one subgroup to neighboring languages of another. All Mayan terms for **fish** were innovated in post Proto-Mayan times. One **fish** term diffused to most Mayan languages except the geographically peripheral ones. By a thousand years ago, most Mayan languages were at Stage 3 with three life-form forms: **snake**, **bird**, and **fish**. Since then, a few languages have developed terms for **wug** and/or **mammal** or combined **wug-mammal**.

This reconstruction provides evidence consistent with the animal life-form encoding sequence. Only one animal life-form, **snake**, reconstructs for Proto-Mayan. On the other hand, if, for example, **wug** reconstructed but not **snake**, this would contravene the predicted order in which languages acquire animal life-forms. To **snake**, daughter languages subsequently added **bird** and **fish** before any one of them encoded the remaining life-forms of the sequence, also in accordance with the animal encoding order.

Polynesian Life-Form Growth

Polynesian languages are dispersed over a vast area of the Pacific Ocean. They are descended from Proto-Polynesian which broke up approximately twenty-five hundred years ago. The Polynesian grouping belongs to the Oceanic division of the large and widespread Austronesian language family. Reconstruction of Polynesian plant life-form growth is based on data from 24 languages (Brown 1982a).[2] These include representatives from all major and minor subgroups of Polynesian. Only one Polynesian language, Mele-Fila (122a), is included among those surveyed for plant classification.

With one exception, combinations of plant life-form terms found in Polynesian languages all conform with the plant life-form encoding sequence. The exception is Nukuoro, a Polynesian Outlier language, which encodes only **vine**, an unexpected singleton life-form.[3] Polynesian languages range in stage affiliation from Stage 2 to Stage 6 with most languages associated with Stages 3 and 4, having two and three life-forms respectively. In addition to Nukuoro, another Polynesian Outlier, Kampingamarangi, has only one plant life-form term. In this case, the singleton life-form is the expected **tree**. Only two languages of the twenty-four surveyed have all five plant life-forms of the encoding sequence.

Like Proto-Mayan, Proto-Polynesian of twenty-five hundred years ago possessed only one botanical life-form, **tree**, and it thus was at Stage 2 in life-form growth. Shortly after the parent language's breakup, a daughter language innovated **grass**, and this life-form diffused widely to other daughter languages. No other botanical life-forms were encoded by Polynesian languages for about fifteen hundred years. During the last thousand years, many Polynesian languages have encoded life-forms beyond **tree** and **grass**. This reconstruction, of course, is in accord with the encoding proposal (Figure 2), with **tree** coming first followed by **grass** and subsequently by the remaining life-forms of the encoding order.

*　*　*

Reconstruction of Polynesian zoological life-form growth is also based on data from 24 languages (Brown 1981b), including 2 found among the 144 surveyed here for animal classification: Mele-Fila (49b) and Tahitian (144b).

Combinations of animal life-form terms found in Polynesian languages all conform with the zoological encoding sequence. All but 3 of the 24 languages' have at least three animal life-forms of the encoding sequence. Those encoding fewer than three have terms for **bird** and **fish**, but these also encode combined **wug-mammal**. This is unexpected since these languages lack **snake** and thus have failed to encode all three life-forms of the initial triad before adding combined **wug-mammal**. However, as discussed presently, lack of **snake** terms in Polynesian languages is attributable to ecological factors.

Thirteen Polynesian languages have **wug** as well as **bird**, **fish**, and **snake**. In addition, the combined **wug-mammal** life-form class is a relatively common feature of Polynesian languages. Fourteen languages of those surveyed apparently encode it. Only one of the twenty-four languages, Tahitian (144b), encodes **mammal**. The rarity of **mammal** is attributable in part to the fact that Polynesian islands support few native terrestrial mammals.

Proto-Polynesian of some twenty-five hundred years ago was somewhat further along than Proto-Mayan with respect to zoological life-form growth. Proto-Polynesian was associated with growth Stage 3, having the initial three life-forms of the encoding sequence, **bird**, **fish**, and **snake**. In addition, Polynesian language history differs from Mayan language history since some Polynesian languages actually lost an animal life-form, **snake**, which was present in their parent language.

The reconstructed Proto-Polynesian term for **snake** is *ŋata*. This term apparently extended to all true snakes. The proto-language, like several of its modern daughter languages, lacked a term for "worm." Many daughter languages have reflexes (i.e. descendant forms) of *ŋata* which designate "snake." These include languages of all the major subgroups of Polynesian except those of the Eastern Polynesian subgroup (i.e. Easter Island, Hawaiian, Marquesan, Tahitian, Mangaian, Rarotongan, Mangarevan, Maori, Tuamotuan, and others).

There is abundant evidence, both archaeological and linguistic, that the islands of Fiji are the point from which pre-Polynesians moved into Polynesia (Pawley and Green 1971: 14–15). Pawley and Green (1971: 22) note that Fiji is the only region close to the Triangle area of Polynesia that has snakes. (Easter Island, Hawaii, and New Zealand constitute the three defining points of Triangle Polynesia.) In addition, with the exception of Samoa, all of the islands of the latter area lack snakes. It is noteworthy that Samoan (a Polynesian language) has a reflex of Proto-Polynesian *ŋata* which means "snake" and that most of its genetic cousins in the Samoic-Outlier subgroup of Polynesian spoken to the west of the Triangle area have the same. Some languages of the Eastern Polynesian subgroup have reflexes of *ŋata*, but none of these designates "snake." These languages are all spoken in the Triangle area of Polynesia where snakes are lacking.

When Polynesian speakers moved into the Triangle area, they diversified linguistically and at the same time tended to lose **snake** life-forms in response to the absence of snakes. In some cases, this meant that reflexes of *ŋata* were entirely lost and in others that their meanings were shifted to referents other than snakes. At least two Eastern Polynesian languages, Easter Island and Marquesan, have completely lost *ŋata reflexes. The acquisition of new referents took different paths in different languages. Several languages shifted *ŋata reflexes to other elongated creatures which are not snakes: Hawaiian *naka* "a land shell (snail?)/a sea shell," Mangaian *ŋata* "sea slug," Rarotongan *ŋata* "a species of shellfish," Maori *ŋata* "slug, snail." In another language, Tuamotuan, the reflex shifted to nonzoological living objects characterized by elongation: *ŋata* "a stem, stalk, vine." And, finally, in two other languages reflexes totally lost a substantive application: Tahitian *ʔataʔata* (reduplication) "shocking, disgusting," and Mangarevan *ŋatatata* (partial reduplication) "to crawl."

Today, most Eastern Polynesian languages have reacquired "snake" terms, in most cases in response to contact with Europeans. The fact that very few of these languages share terms for "snake" is strong evidence that they all lacked such words in the recent past despite the fact that their ancestors of twenty-five hundred years ago had a "snake" term.

After breakup of all subgroup parent languages, completed roughly one thousand years ago, most Polynesian animal life-form inventories began to expand (from either a **bird + fish + snake** or a **bird + fish** base). This involved addition of terms for "worm" and **wug** and also terms for "snake" in most languages which had lost the life-form. In addition, many languages developed combined **wug-mammal** life-forms, in most cases by extending referential application of **bird** terms to bugs and mammals (this is described in detail in Chapter 6).

It is probable that much of this late growth took place in response to cultural changes brought about through contact with Europeans during the last several hundred years. This is clearly the case with respect to reacquisition of "snake" by some Eastern Polynesian languages. Both Hawaiian and Maori borrowed their "snake" terms from English. Maori also acquired a second "snake" term by adopting the Hebrew label for "snake," a result of missionary influence. In order to translate the Bible into Polynesian languages, missionaries created a large number of animal names from Hebrew, Greek, and Latin. Missionary influence also accounts for "snake" terms of Tahitian and Rarotongan which are native corruptions of the Greek label for "serpent" (see discussion, case 144b). The Easter Island "snake" term is probably an adaptation of the Spanish word for large elongated creatures.

Like the Mayan case, reconstructed Polynesian life-form growth conforms with the animal life-form encoding sequence. **Bird, fish,** and **snake** reconstruct for Proto-Polynesian rather than deviant combinations of three life-forms such as **bird + wug + snake** or **snake + mammal + fish**. The Polynesian case differs from Mayan since some daughter languages in the past lost an originally encoded life-form because of environmental conditions. However, subsequent life-form growth has nonetheless followed the predicted sequence.

Numic Life-Form Growth

The Numic language group studied by Fowler (1972) consists of several languages located in the Great Basin region of the Western United States. The group parent language, Proto-Numic, was spoken approximately two thousand years ago. Numic is a branch of the Uto-Aztecan family of languages whose members are widely distributed from the United States Great Basin through Mexico to parts of Central America.

* * *

Six Numic language cases are found among the 188 surveyed for plant classification. Four of these, Southern Paiute (Chemehuevi) (28a), Northern Paiute (Nevada) (38a), Shoshoni (39a), and Southern Paiute (Cedar City) (106a), are either entirely or in part extracted from Fowler's (1972) work: Two others, Southern Paiute (Kawaiisu) (2a) and Northern Paiute (Oregon) (6a), come from other sources. A remaining Numic language, Mono, is not represented.

The six Numic cases range in stage affiliation from 1 to 4. Southern Paiute (Kawaiisu) totally lacks plant life-form terms. Northern Paiute (Oregon) has one life-form, the expected **tree**. Three cases have two life-forms: Northern Paiute (Nevada) and Shoshoni with **tree** and **grass** and Southern Paiute (Chemehuevi) with **tree** and **grerb**. Finally, Southern Paiute (Cedar City) has **tree**, **grerb**, and **grass**.

Evidence assembled by Fowler (1972) indicates that plant life-forms are very weakly developed in Numic languages. Indeed, no life-form terms are widely shared among these languages, strongly suggesting that Proto-Numic totally lacked them. After careful analysis of the data, Fowler (1972) is reluctant to propose certain antiquity for any botanical life-form class. For example, in a discussion of a term that may have denoted **grass** in Proto-Numic she is willing to acknowledge only the possibility that "it had achieved . . . *partial* [?] status as a life-form prior to Numic internal divergence" (italics added). Similarly, in discussing contemporary **tree** terms, she (1972: 247–248) writes, "they seem to reflect the life-form concept only covertly" and adds "that there was no Proto-Numic life-form meaning specifically and only 'tree'." After reviewing the detailed evidence compiled by Fowler, I have ascertained no grounds whatsoever for proposing that any of the five life-forms of the botanical encoding sequence pertained to the Numic parent language.

If Proto-Numic altogether lacked plant life-forms (as does the modern Kawaiisu dialect of Southern Paiute), then it is clear that botanical life-form terms have been encoded independently by most daughter languages since Proto-Numic times and that this addition has followed the encoding sequence. This is so since none of the language cases having plant life-form terms demonstrate combinations of these other than those predicted by the encoding sequence.

$$* \quad * \quad *$$

Four Numic language cases are found among the 144 languages surveyed for animal classification: Northern Paiute (Nevada) (10b), Shoshoni (57b), Southern Paiute (Cedar City) (88b), and Southern Paiute (Chemehuevi) (143b). These cases, for the most part, have been extracted from Fowler's study. Two of these, Northern Paiute (Nevada) and Shoshoni, have been supplemented here with data from other sources (see cases in Appendix B).

The four Numic cases range in animal life-form stage affiliation from 2 to 5. Northern Paiute (Nevada) has **bird** and **snake** plus an incipient **fish** life-form and is thus at Stage 2. Shoshoni is at Stage 3 with an expected **bird + fish + snake** combination. In addition to the latter three life-forms, Southern Paiute (Cedar City) has **wug** and Southern Paiute (Chemehuevi) has both **wug** and combined **wug-mammal**. Thus the latter two cases are affiliated with Stages 4 and 5 respectively. Life-form combinations pertaining to all four cases, of course, accord with cross-language encoding regularities.

Of the five life-forms of the animal encoding sequence, three possibly reconstruct for Proto-Numic according to Fowler (1972). These are the expected **bird**, **fish**, and **snake**. Of these three, Fowler (1972) reconstructs only one, **snake** (restricted to true snakes), with confidence. There are certain technical problems underlying reconstructions for **bird** and **fish** which make these somewhat tentative. In any case, it appears that Proto-Numic had as few as one and as many as three of the initial triad of life-forms of the animal encoding sequence.

If **fish** were encoded by Proto-Numic, then one daughter language, Northern Paiute (Nevada), has lost a life-form, **fish**, at some point during its development from the parent language. Nevertheless, Northern Paiute has a label for an incipient **fish** life-form, that is, a word that is used to designate unknown, unnamed fish. In addition, it is probable that the Northern Paiute term is a reflex of the **fish** label tentatively reconstructed for Proto-Numic by Fowler. Perhaps this indicates that the form, if it actually pertained to the parent language, labeled an incipient rather than a full-fledged **fish** class in Proto-Numic times.

If Proto-Numic was at Stage 3, having a **bird + fish + snake** combination, then Shoshoni (57b) has maintained the life-form system of its parent language, and the two dialects of Southern Paiute (cases 88b and 143b) have acquired additional animal life-form classes, **wug** and combined **wug-mammal** respectively. Numic animal life-form growth apparently has not deviated from that predicted by the encoding sequence.[4]

Societal Scale and Life-Form Growth

Lexical reconstructions for Mayan, Polynesian, and Numic indicate that plant and animal life-form vocabularies generally grow rather than shrink over time. There is other evidence suggesting that the two life-form encoding sequences are basically additive or cumulative in nature.

Size of both botanical and zoological life-form vocabularies is positively correlated with societal scale (Brown 1977, 1979a). Languages having few biological life-form terms are usually spoken by people living in small-scale societies with little of the political integration, social stratification, and technological elaboration found in large urban societies where people speak languages usually having many life-form terms.[5] This indicates that life-form classes are particularly useful in the latter societies.

The special aptness of biological life-forms in large-scale societies may relate to the increasing separation of humans from direct reliance and dependence on the natural environment in these societies. The typical individual in a small-scale society can usually name and identify hundreds of separate plant species (Berlin et al. 1974; Conklin 1954; Hays 1976), while typical nonspecialist members of modern urban society might do well to name and identify even one hundred (Dougherty 1978). When people lose detailed knowledge of plants and animals, including names for them, less specific terms, such as life-form labels, become increasingly salient and tend to grow in number. The addition of biological life-form classes to languages, then, indexes a general decrease of interest in and concern with the world of plants and animals.

Salience of biological classes can be measured through frequency of use of terms for them in ordinary language. More frequently used words of a language tend to label more salient classes and less frequently used words to label less salient categories. Thus, in languages of modern nation-state societies, terms for plant and animal life-form classes generally should be more frequent in use than terms for less general biological classes. Tables 11, 12, 13, 14, and 15 organize information relating to the salience of plant and animal concepts (classes) as measured by frequency of use of terms for them in nation-state languages. As expected, these tables show that biological life-form classes are ranked among the most salient plant categories in these languages.

Salience rankings of plant and animal concepts (classes) presented in Ta-

Table 11. Ranking of the sixty most salient plant concepts in American English based on frequency of occurrence of terms for them in written language.

Frequency	Plant concept(s)
1254	**tree** (tree)
1050	plant
354	wheat
319	"corn" (294 corn, 25 maize)
313	**grass** (grass)
218	**bush** (175 bush, 43 shrub)
205	pine
105	oak
89	mint
74	willow
61	**vine** (52 vine, 9 creeper)
58	flax
52	cedar
46	moss, barley
45	reed
44	oat
43	lilly
41	chestnut
40	maple
37	peach
35	evergreen
32	pear, birch, lichen
31	clover
30	rye
29	parsnip
28	bamboo, onion, poplar, walnut
26	cabbage, fern, fir, plum
24	lilac
23	elm
22	tulip
20	lettuce
19	heather, turnip
18	daisy, mahogany, papyrus, spinach
17	myrtle
16	algae
15	hemlock, redwood, sycamore
14	hickory, huckleberry
13	sassafras, honeysuckle
12	blackberry, daffodil, linseed, magnolia, mushroom

Source: Extracted from the "Lorge-Thorndike Semantic Count" found in Thorndike and Lorge 1944; cf. Brown n.d.

Note: Tokens (running words counted) = 4,500,000.

Table 12. Ranking of the nineteen most salient plant concepts in Arabic based on frequency of occurrence of terms for them in written language.

Frequency	Plant concept(s)
36	**tree**
32	"wheat"
15	"plant," "rose"
8	**grerb**
7	"barley"
4	"pine tree"
3	"aromatic plant," "lotus," "reed"
2	"palm tree"
1	"parsley/clover," "mulberry," "a weak plant" (?), "hashish," "corn," "pomegranates," "flax"

Source: Extracted from Landau 1959; cf. Brown n.d.
Note: Tokens (running words counted) = 272,178.

Table 13. Ranking of the sixty-six most salient animal concepts in American English based on frequency of occurrence of terms for them in written language.

Frequency	Animal concept(s)
2874	horse
1375	"animal/creature/beast" (849 animal, 324 creature, 202 beast)
582	dog
482	**fish** (fish)
348	**bird** (bird)
266	robbin
247	**wug** (216 insect, 31 bug)
246	**snake** (127 snake, 54 serpent, 65 worm)
234	cattle
205	lion
202	cat
195	sheep
175	goose
162	rabbit
160	deer
155	cow
148	toad
145	wolf
143	pig
131	bee, crow, monkey, seal
114	rat
112	eagle
111	duck
108	cardinal
103	chicken

Table 13. *continued*

Frequency	Animal concept(s)
98	bull
90	lamb, mule
89	spider
87	ant
84	elephant
81	hound
75	goat, mouse, possum
72	beaver
69	ox
68	cock
62	shark
61	trout
58	muskrat
56	mole
54	cricket
52	owl
50	calf, dragon, dragonfly, hen, kitten, pony
48	fowl
47	buffalo
44	badger
43	donkey, hare, hog
42	fox
41	squirrel, gorilla, hawk
40	turtle, lark, tiger

Source: Extracted from the "Lorge-Thorndike Semantic Count" found in Thorndike and Lorge 1944; cf. Brown 1982b.

Note: Tokens (running words counted) = 4,500,000.

bles 11–15 are based on frequency of occurrence of terms for them in written language rather than spoken.[6] Biological concepts ranked in each table constitute a group of the most salient plant and animal classes in a language. For example, those of Table 11 are the sixty most salient plant categories in American English by frequency of use criteria. In each table plant or animal concepts are ranked from the most salient one in a language to the least salient of the pertinent group. In a number of cases different terms of a language label the same plant or animal class. Frequency counts for these are added together to yield an overall count for the class. For example, American English "corn" has a frequency score of 319 which is the sum of the occurrences of *corn* (294) and *maize* (25) in a token of approximately 4,500,000 running words (Table 11). The frequency score for the concept **snake** (Tables 13, 14, and 15) is the sum of counts for "snake" and "worm" classes. Individual scores for the latter two animal concepts are also given.

Tables 11 and 12 show that botanical life-forms are among the most salient

Table 14. Ranking of the forty-four most salient animal concepts in Arabic based on frequency of occurrence of terms for them in written language.

Frequency	Animal concept(s)
59	"animal/creature"
31	**bird**
30	"dog"
27	"lion"
26	"camel"
16	**fish**
12	"horse"
10	**snake** (9 "snake," 1 "worm"), "locust"
9	**wug**
8	"cow"
6	"deer," "mule," "elephant," "bee"
5	"monkey/ape"
4	"reptile/burden animal," "goat," "spider," "cat"
3	"mosquito," "sheep," "wolf," "ostrich," "cock"
2	"swine," "hen," "fly," "leech," "vulture/eagle," "ant"
1	"duck," "fox," "ox," "buffalo," "dove," "donkey," "giraffe," "hawk," "hyena," "scorpion," "lynx/leopard," "cobra," "tiger"

Source: Extracted from Landau 1959; cf. Brown 1982b.
Note: Tokens (running words counted) = 272,178.

Table 15. Ranking of the sixty-five most salient animal concepts in Peninsular Spanish based on frequency of occurrence of terms for them in written language.

Frequency	Animal concept(s)
214	"animal/creature"
207	**bird**
188	"horse"
160	"dog"
117	"bull"
115	**fish**
82	"lion"
73	"cat"
71	"cow"
58	"cock," "ox"
53	**snake** (35 "snake," 18 "worm")
45	"goat," "chicken"
41	"mouse"
40	"fly (insect)"
39	"pig"
38	"eagle"
37	"sardine"
34	"cattle," "pigeon," "donkey"
33	"mule"

Table 15. *continued*

Frequency	Animal concept(s)
32	"wolf"
31	"fox"
29	"butterfly"
27	"hare," "turkey"
26	"parrot"
25	"spider," "snail," "frog," "tiger," "sheep"
23	"mosquito"
22	"bee"
21	"ant," "toad"
20	"partridge," "rabbit," "raven"
19	"duck"
18	"grub," "monkey," "crab," "blackbird"
15	**wug**
14	"elephant"
13	"thrush," "cricket"
12	"locust"
11	"mole"
10	"hog," "cardinal," "bear"
9	"flea," "falcon"
8	"turtledove," "reptile," "lizard," "woodpecker"
7	"deer," "swallow"
6	"whale," "clam"

Source: Extracted from Buchanan 1941; cf. Brown 1982b.
Note: Tokens (running words counted) = approximately 1,200,000.

plant concepts in both American English and Arabic. In American English **tree** is first in frequency of use and **grass, bush**, and **vine** are found among the eleven most salient plant concepts. In Arabic, **tree** and **grerb** are respectively first and fourth in frequency of use. It should also be noted that the American English **grerb** term, *plant*, ranks second after **tree** in frequency of use. However, it is impossible to calculate what percentage of this frequency is linked to the word's use as a unique beginner or kingdom label as opposed to its more restricted referential application to small herbaceous plants.

Tables 13–15 show that two zoological life-forms, **bird** and **fish** are among the six most salient animal concepts in American English, Arabic, and Spanish. In addition, **snake** is found among the eleven most salient animal concepts in all three. In two languages, American English (Table 13) and Arabic (Table 14), **snake** and **wug** have virtually the same high degree of salience (see frequency scores for these). Only Spanish (Table 15) has a life-form concept, **wug**, which shows a relatively low salience ranking. It should also be noted that the most general faunal concept of all, "creatures, beasts, or animals in general," is ranked first in salience in Arabic and Spanish, and second in American English.[7]

Since people living in small-scale societies have less need for general plant and animal concepts than people of nation-state societies, it is probably the case that life-form classes, if encoded, are not especially salient for them. Word frequency data from small-scale society languages should show that many, if not most, generic plant and animal classes are ranked higher in salience than respective plant and animal life-form classes, in sharp contrast to the relative rankings of generics vis-à-vis life-forms presented in Tables 11–15 for nation-state languages. Unfortunately, adequate word frequency counts for small-scale society languages are not now available to test this proposition.

In addition to the association with societal scale, size of plant life-form vocabulary is positively correlated with botanical species diversity.[8] Languages of desert and arctic peoples usually have few plant life-form terms, while languages of peoples living in areas favoring botanical variety, such as temperate woodlands or tropical rain forests, have a greater number. Species diversity and societal scale are themselves positively correlated.[9] This might suggest that either species diversity or societal scale, but not both, is the crucial factor influencing size of plant life-form inventory. In other words, one of these two associations may simply be an artifact of the other.

While languages spoken in environments severely lacking botanical species diversity regularly have few plant life-form terms, languages spoken in environments supporting much species diversity do *not* regularly have large plant life-form vocabularies. Consequently, most of the strength of the correlation between size of plant life-form lexicon and botanical species diversity derives from the fact that severe lack of species variety, such as that found in desert or arctic regions, strongly tends to constrain growth of plant life-form vocabularies. There is no evidence that extreme botanical variety, such as that found in tropical rain forests, encourages botanical life-form growth.

On the other hand, there is evidence that increases in societal scale promote life-form addition. Large urban societies are primarily associated with temperate woodlands and grasslands rather than with lush tropical rain forests. As a consequence, large plant life-form inventories are by and large characteristic of languages spoken in areas of only moderate species diversity. This is unexpected if degree of species diversity is the primary factor influencing the size of plant life-form vocabularies. Thus increases in societal scale promote life-form growth even in areas where species diversity is not particularly great.

It appears that neither of the two positive correlations is entirely an artifact of the other. Very low botanical species diversity constrains the expansion of plant life-form lexicons whereas increasing societal scale encourages plant life-form growth.

The association between size of biological life-form inventories and societal scale indicates a tendency for the number of life-form terms to grow with increases in societal scale. The reverse is also indicated: decrease in number of life-form terms with decreases in societal scale. However, since societal scale has generally increased during the course of human history, especially during the last several thousand years, it follows that plant and animal life-form vocabularies in the vast majority of cases have grown rather than shrunk in size. Thus the two life-form encoding sequences are basically additive or cumulative in nature.

The cumulative nature of the encoding sequences implies that earlier language states do not usually have more plant and animal life-form terms than later language states. Thus, languages of several thousands of years ago should not have had more life-form terms than their daughter languages of today. In addition, considering that major increases in societal scale and widespread urbanization have occurred during recent millennia of human history, we should expect that such parent languages only rarely had even the same number of terms as their modern offspring.

Lexical reconstructions described in the preceding sections indicate that such expectations are justified. Contemporary Mayan languages have more plant and animal life-form terms than Proto-Mayan, for which only **tree** and **bird** respectively reconstruct. Among modern Polynesian languages surveyed, all but two have more plant life-forms than Proto-Polynesian, which possessed only **tree**. In addition, it is doubtful that any Polynesian languages have fewer than three animal life-forms (counting combined **wug-mammal**), the number of life-forms reconstructing for their parent language. Also, only a handful of contemporary Polynesian languages have the same number of animal life-form labels as that of Proto-Polynesian. This is the case despite the fact that many Polynesian languages in the past actually lost a life-form class, **snake**, which pertained to the parent language.

Finally, five of the six Numic language cases surveyed for botanical classification have more plant life-form terms than Proto-Numic, which apparently totally lacked them. In addition, of the four Numic language cases investigated for zoological classification by Fowler (1972), only one, Northern Paiute, may have a smaller animal life-form inventory than Proto-Numic, which according to Fowler, possibly had **bird**, **fish**, and **snake**. It is also possible that Proto-Numic had only one animal life-form term, in which case all four daughter languages have bigger zoological life-form vocabularies than their common precursor did.

In summary, several lines of evidence indicate that the two life-form encoding sequences are basically additive in nature, that as societal scale has increased over time languages have tended to acquire life-form classes rather than lose them. In addition, lexical reconstruction shows that as languages accumulate life-form terms they do so in the order of the encoding sequences.

In addition to the lexical encoding sequences for plant and animal life-forms, others have been described in the literature, including a sequence for basic color categories (Berlin and Kay 1969), one for geometric figures (Burris 1979), and one for dimensions of size (Brown and Witkowski n.d.). These encoding sequences, like the ones dealt with here, are all positively correlated with societal scale and are therefore basically additive in nature. This indicates that languages spoken several thousands of years ago had few, if any, general terms for colors, geometric figures, and size dimensions just as they had few plant and animal life-form labels (Witkowski and Brown 1978a, 1981).

Lexical encoding sequences discovered so far are almost certainly only a few of those that remain to be found. Since the lexicon is that part of language which most closely reflects human cultural concerns and relationships with the natural environment, such sequences can shed much light on the conceptual inventory and life-ways of human groups of the remote past. This new area of investigation amounts to a kind of human conceptual prehistory that has the potential of contributing much richness and detail to more conventional methods, such as archaeology and traditional historical linguistics, of recovering the human past.

»6«

NOMENCLATURAL DEVELOPMENT

This chapter describes uniform ways individual languages have acquired plant and animal life-forms, continuing investigation of biological nomenclatural development begun by Brent Berlin (1972). Languages acquire life-forms either by borrowing them from other languages or by innovating them. Life-form diffusion is usually of interest insofar as its recognition contributes to reconstructing histories of life-form growth pertaining to language families (cf. Brown 1979b, 1981b, 1982a; Brown and Witkowski 1982). The present chapter focuses on life-form acquisition through independent innovation.

Languages utilize four strategies in innovating plant and animal life-forms: (1) expansion of reference, (2) restriction of reference, (3) use of metaphor, and (4) description.

Expansion of reference involves extending the referential range of a term for a particular kind of organism to a grouping of organisms of which the latter is a member, for example, using a term for swordgrass to refer to grasses in general or a term for salmon to refer to fish in general. Restriction of reference is the reverse strategy, for example, using a word for plants in general to designate a less comprehensive grouping of plants, say, small herbaceous ones (i.e., **grerb**).

Innovation of plant and animal life-forms through metaphor entails drawing parallels between organisms and other objects that they may somewhat resemble, whereby terms for the latter are used to denote the former. For example, a language might use a word for tongue (flexible, elongated body part) to refer to vines in general, or a term for root to label small elongated creatures in general (i.e., worms).

Innovation through description merely involves production of descriptive labels for life-form classes, for example, "creeping plant" for **vine** or "little creature" for **wug**. Descriptive labels for plant and animal life-form classes found among languages surveyed here are noted in discussions associated with language cases presented in Appendices A and B.

BOTANICAL LIFE-FORM INNOVATION

Innovation of **Tree**

Berlin (1972) proposes that **tree** life-forms often develop through expansion of reference. This entails extending the range of a word for an especially important kind of tree in an environment to trees in general. This proposal is based on the observation that **tree** terms in several langauges are polysemous, referring to a specific type of tree in addition to trees in general. For example, in Indian languages of the Southwestern United States a single term often designates both cottonwood tree and **tree** (Trager 1939). Discussions associated with language cases presented in Appendices A and B frequently note such polysemous uses of life-form terms. In most cases, application of a life-form term to a more restricted referent is probably indicative of innovation of the life-form class through expansion of reference.

Expansion of reference often takes place along a "kind of" path: sword-grass is a kind of **grass**, and a cottonwood tree is a kind of **tree**. Another form of expansion involves a "part of" path whereby a word for a principal component or part of an object is used in reference to the whole object (cf. "tube" to designate television set). Witkowski, Brown, and Chase (1981) have assembled extensive cross-language evidence indicating that languages have often developed **tree** life-forms by extending application of a word for wood (a major component or part of trees) to trees in general.[1]

As in cases of expansion of reference along "kind of" paths, expansion involving "part of" channels is often indicated by polysemy. Witkowski, Brown, and Chase's (1981) investigation shows that approximately two-thirds of the world's languages have terms that denote both wood and **tree**. Among the 188 language cases surveyed for plant classification, at least 93 have wood/**tree** polysemy (see Appendix A). Since many sources do not provide information on term polysemy, considerably more languages of the sample than these 93 probably use a single term to designate both wood and **tree**.

Documentation of extensive wood/**tree** polysemy alone is not, of course, certain indication that **tree** usually develops through referential expansion from "wood." It is just as indicative of the reverse possibility, that "wood" develops from **tree**. However, several lines of evidence supporting the former interpretation rather than the latter can be cited.

In the preceding chapter, it is noted that as societal scale increases biological life-form terms tend to increase in number and salience. In small-scale societies, then, those few plant life-forms that are encoded, including **tree**, are not particularly salient. On the other hand, there are no reasons for presuming that "wood" terms are also of low salience in these societies. Indeed, a word for wood would have high utility for peoples accustomed to using the material for construction purposes, as fuel, tools, and so on.

Plausibly, small-scale society languages of the past usually had a term for wood but either lacked a term for **tree** or encoded it only as a low salience category. If this is correct, then wood/**tree** polysemy has developed in most languages having it through extension of a salient term for wood to **tree** rather than vice versa. This would have occurred when increases in societal scale enhanced the aptness and usefulness of life-form categories such as **tree**.

Just this sort of development seems to have taken place in Wasco (9a). In a description of Wasco plant categories, French writes "there are almost no terms which refer to broad classes or categories of plants. For example, there are no words corresponding to these in English: bush, herb, or berry. Except for a rarely-used extension from 'wood,' there is not even a word for 'tree'" (1957: 225–226). Wasco, of course, has wood/**tree** polysemy. However, the concept "wood" is clearly more salient that **tree** and thus almost certainly developmentally prior to **tree**.

Other evidence indicating the priority of "wood" is linguistic in nature. Languages sometimes construct **tree** labels by modifying a word for wood. For example, the Chamorro (Austronesian family) label for **tree** is *tronkon hayu*, which consists of the "wood" term, *hayu*, and the modifier, *tronkon* "trunk" (probably borrowed from Spanish as are many other Chamorro words). Invariably when one of the pair wood/**tree** exists as a modified version of the other, it is **tree** rather than "wood" which is so constructed. This pattern accords with the overall greater salience and developmental priority of wood versus **tree**.

There is a strong positive correlation between societal scale and wood/**tree** polysemy.[2] Speakers of languages uniting wood and **tree** under a single term usually live in small-scale societies while speakers of languages separating them usually live in large, urban, or state societies. This indicates that as societies increase in size and complexity, wood/**tree** polysemy tends to be lost.

If **tree** life-forms usually develop from "wood," it follows that many languages spoken in large-scale societies having separate words for **tree** and wood had both referents united under one or the other of the terms at some point in the past. For instance, the contemporary English word *tree* designated both **tree** and wood in Old English (*trēow*) and in Middle English (*tre*). The modern word has lost the latter meaning, which is now carried solely by *wood*. *Wood* in turn can be traced to Old English *wudu* and Middle English *wode*, both of which denoted "woods, forest, wood" (cf. Buck 1949). Loss of wood/**tree** polysemy in English, then, involved deletion of the "wood" referent in response to a competing word for wood and retention of the old term as a label for **tree** alone.

Loss of wood/**tree** polysemy may be attributed to two specific changes associated with increases in societal scale. First, as outlined in Chapter 5, there is an increase in the aptness and usefulness of **tree** and other life-form classes. When **tree** becomes just as salient as wood, the two referents tend to become separately labeled. Second, elaboration of woodworking technology tends to accompany societal expansion. This creates a perceptual distance between the concepts **tree** and "wood" resulting in their lexical separation.

In small-scale societies, woodworking seldom involves radical alteration of tree products. Branches, logs, sticks, and the like rarely require extensive modification for the construction of shelters, use as firewood, and as tools. On the other hand, in large-scale societies, manipulation by woodworking specialists occurs to such an extent that the appearance of wood is often only remotely suggestive of its affinity with trees in the wild. Of course, wood in small-scale societies can at times be greatly altered such as in mask carving. It seems likely, however, that many more instances of radical alteration occur in large societies. Thus the wide perceptual distance between living trees and many of the wooden products of modern urban peoples may also contribute to wood/**tree** separation.

Innovation of **Grerb**

In this section and in those immediately following, many examples of plant and animal life-form innovation are from Mayan and Polynesian languages. These were uncovered through use of the comparative method of historical linguistics (Brown 1979b, 1981b, 1982a; Brown and Witkowski 1982).

Grerb innovation in Mayan and Polynesian languages for the most part has entailed expansion of reference. In some instances, this has involved striking parallels with respect to the detailed manner in which languages of both groups have drawn on existing vocabulary to create life-form classes. For example, terms for **grerb** in both Polynesian and Mayan languages have developed from words for rubbish, garbage, trash, litter, rotten stuff, and the like. In most cases such words were first extended to weeds, i.e., useless and bothersome small herbaceous plants, and then through expansion of reference to small herbaceous plants in general.

An example of the latter development is Maori (Polynesian) *otaota* **grerb**. Comparison of related words (cognates) in other Polynesian languages suggests a reconstructed Proto-Polynesian term *ʔotaʔota* which meant "residue, refuse, rubbish." Some descendant forms (reflexes) in addition to the Maori term are Hawaiian *okaoka* "dust, fine particles," Nukuoro *odaoda* "driftwood (any sort)," Tikopian *otaota* "rubbish," Samoan *otaota* "rubbish, refuse, excrement," Tongan *ʔotaʔota* "sweepings, rubbish," and Niuean *otaota* "rubbish, refuse, excreta." The Maori **grerb** term originally had a similar meaning and subsequently was extended to small herbaceous plants in general. This almost certainly involved weed as an intervening referent. In fact, the term's derivational history is suggested by its contemporary alternate applications, i.e., to both litter and weed, in addition to **grerb**.

Unrelated **grerb** terms in a number of Polynesian languages have referential histories closely paralleling that described for Maori *otaota*. Perhaps surprising is the fact that a number of **grerb** terms in languages of the Mayan family (which are both genetically and geographically removed from Polynesian languages) have also developed in a very similar manner. For example, two Mayan languages of the Quichean branch of the family, Cakchiquel and Quiche, have related terms for **grerb**, *q'ayis* and *q'ayes* respectively. Related forms in other Quichean languages focus referentially on useless objects, especially useless plants: Tzutujil *q'ayis* "weeds, garbage" and Pocomam *q'ahes* "bush, bushes, scrub, rubbish, junk." Proto-Quichean **q'ahis*, from which the Cakchiquel, Quiche, Tzutujil, and Pocomam forms are descended, is derived from Proto-Mayan **q'ah* "rotten." Thus, the original botanical referent of Proto-Quichean **q'ahis* appears to have been rotten plant or weed. Cakchiquel and Quiche **grerb** classes then are traced developmentally to expansion of a "weed" term, which is itself traced to a form meaning "rotten."

Derivation of **grerb** from words such as "rotten," "litter," "garbage," "filth," and so on is almost certainly a global phenomenon. This is indicated by the fact that in addition to the Mayan and Polynesian examples several languages of those surveyed in Appendix A have **grerb** terms with alternative meanings that are similarly negative in nature. These include Igbira (17a) with *avị* **grerb**/"backwardness," Papago (105a) with *ṣá'i* **grerb**/"brush, trash, waste," Carapana (133a) with three terms, *moetīē* **grerb**/"useless stuff," *capunirījē* **grerb**/"hurtful stuff," and *carorije* **grerb**/"bad stuff," Mokilese (142a) with *tuptup* **grerb**/"weed," Muinane (144a) with *beeva* **grerb**/"plant filth," and Tewa (152a) with *ɸéʔñ̨évi* **grerb**/"rubbish, litter, weed." In addition, the source for Kekchi (139a) notes that its **grerb** term, *pim*, implies contempt.

Both Polynesian and Mayan languages have also innovated **grerb** by use of terms originally meaning "forest." The link between forest and **grerb** is fairly clear. Forests are often places of thickly growing vegetation, including both trees and small herbaceous plants. Through restriction of reference a term for forest may come to refer to the bush or areas that are extensively overgrown and not so much to a collection of trees. A further development is application of the term to thickly growing useless herbaceous plants or more simply, to underbrush. Expansion of reference of a word for underbrush to small herbaceous plants in general, whether thickly growing and useless or not, would account for development of a **grerb** referent. Such a change sequence underlies innovation of **grerb** in at least two Polynesian languages and in at least one Mayan language.

Mayan and Polynesian languages do not share all strategies used in innovating **grerb** through expansion of reference. For example, several Mayan languages have extended application of terms for medicine to **grerb**. Underlying this development is the fact that most Mayan medicines are herbal in nature. Thus these languages have expanded terms restricted to medicinal herbaceous plants to small herbaceous plants in general. Comparable derivational histories are not known for Polynesian languages. In addition, at least one Mayan language has expanded a term for greens (i.e., edible small herbaceous plants) to **grerb**, another development not attested in Polynesian languages.

Such unshared developments do not detract from the fact that innovation of **grerb** terms in Polynesian and Mayan languages for the most part has involved substantially the same developmental details. Presently I argue that these striking parallels are largely attributable to similar ways in which Polynesian and Mayan societies have changed over time.

Restriction of reference apparently only rarely figures into innovation of **grerb**. For instance, there are no examples in Polynesian and Mayan languages of **grerb** life-forms created through restriction of reference. As it happens, American English (175a) represents a rare case in which the latter development has occurred.

The American English **grerb** term, *plant*, originally designated botanical organisms in general. *Plant*, which is Latin in origin, probably entered English with its original modern sense from French.[3] In Latin, *planta* referred to a sprout, slip, or cutting. In French, the word took on the verbal sense of "planting," and eventually the nominative sense of botanical organisms in general. *The Oxford English Dictionary* does not identify use of the term in English with the latter meaning before the sixteenth century. Apparently even at that early date the term was occasionally restricted in reference to small herbaceous plants.

During the course of its history, English has had at least three different **grerb** terms. In Old English (Anglo-Saxon), the term *wort* designated small herbaceous plants in general. This usage is now mirrored only in compounds such as *colewort*, *mugwort*, etc. *Wort* was eventually replaced by *herb*, originally Latin for **grerb**, which entered English from French. In most modern dialects of English, *herb* is now restricted in meaning to herbaceous plants used as medicines and seasonings. This restriction may have taken place partly in response to competitition with *plant* for the referential space "small herbaceous plants in general."

In modern dialects of English, *plant* is almost always polysemous—designating botanical organisms in general and, more restrictively, only the herbaceous ones. Within dialects, it is probably the case that some speakers know only the more comprehensive use, some only the less comprehensive use, and some both. For example, Groves (1978), by interviewing fifty native speakers of American English, has determined that roughly 35 percent of speakers apply the term only to botanical organisms in general, 24 percent only to small herbaceous plants in general, and 41 percent to both ranges. These figures suggest that the derived referent of *plant*, i.e., **grerb**, is now well established, at least in American English.

There is at least one other way in which languages innovate **grerb**. Since **grerb** usually includes most plants that are not trees, languages sometimes descriptively identify **grerb** as constrasting with **tree** through use of compound labels translating literally something like "small-tree," "tree-opposite," "non-tree," and so on. This strategy is probably not as common as my earlier articles (Brown 1977, 1979b) suggest since it pertains to only 3 of the 188 languages surveyed for plant classification: Jacaltec (67a), Gugadja (99a), and Dogon (112a). In 2 of these languages, Jacaltec and Dogon, **grerb** terms are compound labels consisting of **tree** terms and modifiers whose meanings are not clear. However, the Gugadja example is unambiguous with *wada lambanba* **grerb** translating literally "small tree."

Innovation of **Vine**

Terms for **vine** are frequently polysemous, referring to various materials used for binding and tying such as rope, string, and cord in addition to plants having creeping, twining, or climbing stem habits. For example, among the 188 language cases, at least 15 have **vine** terms that also designate binding or tying material. Moreover, these languages are global in distribution such that similar polysemous applications are probably not due to diffusion or genetic relationship (see cases 45a, 49a, 52a, 75a, 78a, 92a, 93a, 121a, 122a, 123a, 135a, 139a, 141a, 162a, and 180a).

Vine term polysemy indicates that the life-form is more than occasionally independently innovated by extending a term for binding or tying material to elongated plants in general. Of course, the reverse is also a possibility, that is, extending a **vine** term to binding or tying material. However, there is evidence supporting the proposal that the former development usually, if not always, has underlain **vine** term polysemy.

For example, several Mayan languages have related (cognate) **vine** terms that also denote rope and/or string. Cognate forms that apply only to tying material are found in many other Mayan languages. This indicates that the ancestral word (proto-stem) from which all of these forms are descended designated only rope/string. Consequently, the **vine** referent of some reflexes is a secondary development.

A tying-material-to-**vine** extension is also documented for a Polynesian language through the comparative approach. Pileni, a Polynesian outlier, uses the term *fau* in reference to both **vine** and string. This form is a reflex of Proto-Polynesian **fau*, which designated a certain kind of tree, *Hibiscus tiliaceus*, whose fibrous bark is widely used by modern Polynesians for making binding material. In a number of languages, **fau* reflexes are used in reference to the binding material itself in addition to the tree of which it is made. Thus it is virtually certain that the "string" referent of Pileni *fau* was developmentally prior to **vine**.

Other Oceanic languages (Austronesian family) provide additional evidence of the priority of "tying material" vis-à-vis **vine**. Many have related terms which designate tying material or **vine** or both referents. These are all reflexes of a Proto-Oceanic stem reconstructing as **waRos*. Oceanic languages commonly develop new meanings for terms by reduplicating them. Two Oceanic languages have both unitary and reduplicated reflexes of **waRos*: Moto *waro* "fishing line"/*warowaro* "vines of all kinds" (Lister-Turner 1931) and Arosi *waro* "piece of string, twine"/*warowaro* "vines" (Fox 1970). In both languages, the "vine" referent is associated only with the reduplicated form, thus indicating that it is a secondary, derived meaning.[4] On the other hand, I have encountered no cases in which Oceanic languages associate tying material with reduplicated reflexes. In other words, there is no similar evidence suggesting that tying material is ever a secondary, derived meaning. This indicates that Proto-Oceanic **waRos* designated tying material alone. In post Proto-Oceanic times, some reflexes of course took on the meaning **vine**.

Extension of a term for tying material to **vine** may be accomplished through either expansion of reference or use of metaphor. Expansion of reference may be the underlying strategy in cases in which vines are or were extensively used for binding and tying. For example, it is possibly the case that vines constituted the primary material out of which rope, string, and the like were constructed in Proto-Oceanic times and in subsequent periods. Modern use of vines as tying materials by speakers of Oceanic languages suggests this possibility. Indeed, glosses of reflexes of Proto-Oceanic **waRos* sometimes indicate that vines are the principal type of tying material designated: e.g., Eddystone *aroso* "creeper or similar plant used as string" (Lanyon-Orgill 1969) and Kove *waho* "vine binding" (Ann Chowning, personal communication). The fact that many contemporary reflexes of **waRos* "tying material" denote **vine**, then, may be attributed to referential expansion from a category of tying materials consisting mostly of vines to a class of vines in general, including both those used for binding or tying and those *not* so used.

If expansion of reference is not the underlying factor, then tying-material/ **vine** polysemy is probably linked to metaphor. For example, a term for rope may be extended to **vine** simply because vines somewhat resemble ropes. Such extensions on occasion involve linguistic modification of the "tying-material" term. This produces metaphorical expressions for **vine** with literal translations such as "green rope," "bush rope," and "wood rope." Examples of the latter are found in 3 of the 188 language cases in Appendix A (see discussions associated with cases 73a, 156a, and 165a).

Vine is also occasionally innovated by expanding a term for a specific kind of vine to vines in general. For example, the Proto-Polynesian word for morning glory has developed contemporary reflexes that designated **vine**. Innovation of **vine** can also involve expansions that take place along "part of" paths. For example, at least two Polynesian languages have acquired **vine** as a referent for terms originally designating the stems of plants. In these cases, expansive change has entailed using a word for a principal part of a vine, i.e., its stem, to refer to the whole plant.

Several interesting metaphors underlie **vine** innovation in Mayan and Polynesian languages. A number of Mayan **vine** terms are derived from the Proto-Mayan word for tongue. This is perhaps a surprising equation since the human tongue and tongues of other mammals are usually short and thick, hardly reminiscent of vines. On the other hand, tongues of various reptiles and amphibians are long and thin, having more in common with long flexible vines than, say, the human tongue. The former, then, probably constitute the analogical basis of the metaphor.

Several Mayan languages have metaphorically equated the body part neck with **vine** by applying a term for the former to the latter. One of these (Ixil [case 68a]) in fact also uses a reflex of the Proto-Mayan "tongue" term in reference to **vine**. In this case, the "tongue" word designates nonwoody vines with flexible stems that can be used as tying material and the "neck" term denotes thick ligneous vines that do not easily bend. This distinction reflects differences between the anatomical parts to which these terms originally applied: long, thin, and flexible tongues and long, thick, and somewhat rigid necks.

Both Mayan and Polynesian languages have developed **vine** life-forms by metaphorically equating elongated plants with elongated animals. At least one Mayan language has extended a term that originally meant "worm" to **vine**, and at least one Polynesian language has extended a "snake" term to the life-form class.

Finally, languages occasionally innovate descriptive labels for **vine**. For example, 4 of the 24 Polynesian languages treated in my comparative study have expressions for **vine** translating literally "creeping plant" or "climbing grerb" (Brown 1982a). Among the 188 language cases surveyed for plant classification, at least 4 have similar descriptive **vine** labels (see cases 142a, 145a, 172a, and 174a).

Innovation of **Grass**

Comparison of Polynesian and Mayan developments does not indicate cross-language trends in the innovation of **grass**. As mentioned in the preceding chapter, **grass** was innovated by a Polynesian language shortly after the parent language's breakup, and this life-form diffused widely to other daughter languages. There is some evidence that this innovation involved extending a term for a particular kind of grass to grasses in general. Other Polynesian **grass** terms may have emerged in a similar fashion, although evidence bearing on such developments is not extensive.

Grass life-forms in most Mayan languages have clearly developed through expansion of reference. However, unlike Polynesian **grass** labels, **grass** terms in Mayan languages were initially restricted to a special purpose plant category, "roofing grass" or "thatch," rather than to a particular kind of grass. This is indicated by the fact that **grass** terms are invariably polysemous, referring to thatch in addition to having a life-form application. Also, distributions of forms and meanings indicate that "thatch" referents were developmentally prior to **grass** referents.

Innovation of **Bush**

Almost all examples of **bush** labels found in Mayan and Polynesian languages are descriptive in nature. These include expressions translating literally "small tree," "low tree," "young tree," "sleeping tree," and "tree in round clumps." At least 9 languages among the 188 surveyed in Appendix A have similar descriptive labels for **bush** (see cases 164a, 165a, 170a, 179a, 183a, 185a, 186a, 187a, and 188a).

Cross-Language Tendencies in Plant Life-Form Innovation

Cross-language tendencies are evident in the innovation of four out of five plant life-forms of the botanical encoding sequence (the odd man out is **grass**). For example, languages strongly tend to innovate **bush** through production of descriptive labels. Even more striking is the tendency of languages to draw on substantially the same vocabulary items in innovating **tree**, **grerb**, and **vine** life-forms. This tendency is especially strong with respect to development of **tree**. As noted earlier, roughly two-thirds of the world's languages appear to have innovated **tree** by referentially expanding a term for wood.

In addition, relatively large percentages of languages, but clearly far less than two-thirds, have developed **grerb** and **vine** life-forms by extending terms for useless plants and tying material respectively.

In general, there is a tendency for languages to develop plant life-form classes based on gross morphology from utilitarian or special-purpose botanical categories. For example, **tree** often develops from "wood," a botanical category usually identified for utilitarian purposes (fuel, construction, etc.). Similarly, **grerb** and **vine** are frequently developed from "useless plants" (underbrush or weeds) and "tying material" respectively, categories whose identification is mainly in terms of function or, at least, lack of function, rather than gross morphology. In light of this general tendency, it is noteworthy that most Mayan **grass** life-forms have developed through expansion of reference of terms for "thatch," another utilitarian special-purpose botanical class.

Languages, of course, do not always develop plant life-forms from special-purpose classes. In the preceding pages, several examples of other developments are described—for example, innovation of life-form classes through expansion of reference of terms for particular botanical species. Given that other innovative strategies are possible, why is there a relatively strong preference for deriving plant life-forms from utilitarian or special purpose categories?

This preference is possibly explained by the fact that terms for special-purpose classes are usually words of currency that already relate to broad classes of plants. Such terms are in effect highly apt lexical materials for constructing botanical life-forms. For example, words for wood are general in reference since they refer to the ligneous parts of all large plants typically included in **tree** rather than to woody components of only one or two species. Similarly, "weed" terms encompass a broad category of small herbaceous plants, all of which are typically included in **grerb**. Such categories are about as close as you can get to plant life-form classes without actually being plant life-form classes. Thus it would be natural to draw on terms for these in innovating botanical life-forms. In addition, such innovations have good chances of being understood and, thus, of gaining currency in languages since life-form referential ranges are not radically different from ranges originally associated with "wood" terms, "weed" terms, and so on.

Clearly, derivation of **tree** from "wood" is the most common development of a plant life-form class from a utilitarian category. As noted earlier, terms for wood have high utility. Thus they are usually added to languages long before life-form classes such as **tree** are encoded. Consequently, "wood" terms have been readily available in most languages to be pressed into service as **tree** life-form labels. There are also reasons for believing that similarly apt lexical materials for constructing other life-form classes, especially **grerb**, have not always been so available or so convenient. This may in part explain why other plant life-form classes rarely, if ever, precede **tree** in lexical encoding (see Chapter 8).

While pressures for adding plant life-forms to vocabularies are linked to increases in societal scale, presumably such additions will tend not to be made unless languages are able to provide apt raw lexical materials for innovating life-forms with relative ease. For example, if a language lacks terms for useless plants in general ("weed," "underbrush," "scrub," and the like), chances that **grerb** will be innovated are possibly less than otherwise.

As it happens, the encoding of "weed" and related categories is influenced by societal scale. People of small-scale, nonagricultural societies obviously have little need for lexically distinguishing weeds, i.e., bothersome plants that interfere with the growth of cultivated ones. Indeed, it may be the case that languages usually do not innovate "weed" until their speakers are committed to highly intensive forms of agriculture supporting reasonably large economies. Thus development of "weed" and similar terms, a usual raw lexical material for constructing **grerb** life-forms, generally has taken place late in the histories of most languages. Such factors, for example, may explain why **grerb** life-forms are relatively late additions to both Mayan and Polynesian languages.

As outlined in Chapter 5, neither Mayan nor Polynesian languages began any major phase of life-form term expansion beyond **tree** until roughly one thousand years ago. Indeed, distributions of forms and meanings indicate that all modern Mayan and Polynesian **grerb** life-forms have emerged quite recently. It is also apparent that Mayan and Polynesian terms for weed, underbrush, and similar botanical classes are late additions (Brown 1979b, 1982a). Although terms for some domesticated plants reconstruct for both parent languages, terms for weed, underbrush, etc., apparently do not.[5] The lateness of "weed" terms in both groups is of course also attested by the fact that their derivations—and ultimately those of **grerb** terms as well—are easily traced to terms for rubbish, litter, filth, garbage, and so on. **Grerb** life-forms, then, may have emerged late in Mayan and Polynesian language histories in part because apt raw lexical materials for constructing them have themselves been developmentally late.

Because changes in societal scale and complexity underlying several parallel developments in Mayan and Polynesian have in fact been worldwide, such features of botanical life-form growth and development almost certainly extend to other genetic groupings of languages as well. It is therefore likely that similar developments in Mayan and Polynesian languages reported here will prove global, if not near universal, in future investigations.

ZOOLOGICAL LIFE-FORM INNOVATION

Expansion of Reference and Animal Life-Forms

In two studies (Brown and Witkowski 1982 and Brown 1981b), use of the comparative approach has revealed numerous examples of expansion of reference in Mayan and Polynesian languages underlying innovation of animal life-forms. For example, comparison of related words (cognates) meaning "maggot" found in many Polynesian languages indicates that *iLo* "maggot" pertained to Proto-Polynesian's lexicon. Two Polynesian languages, Nukuoro and Tahitian (144b) have descendant forms (reflexes) of this proto-word (*ilo* and *iro* respectively) that refer to worms in general. These two languages, then, have created "worm" life-forms by extending referential application of a term originally designating maggot to small elongated creatures in general.

Reconstructed referential histories of words that develop as animal life-form terms through expansion of reference are occasionally somewhat more complex than the latter Polynesian example. Consider, for instance, the "snake" term, *k'anti*, found in Kekchi, a Mayan language. This term is traced to not just one but two ancestral stems, Proto-Mayan *q'an* "yellow, ripe" and *ti·* "mouth." Several Mayan languages have combined reflexes of these two proto-words to produce descriptive labels for a much feared species of snake, *Agkistrodon bilineatus*, which has a very obvious yellow line around its mouth. For example, *k'anti*, translating literally "yellow mouth," designates *Agkistrodon bilineatus* in two Cholan Mayan languages, Cholti and Chorti (123b), which geographically neighbor Kekchi. Phonological considerations clearly indicate that Kekchi borrowed *k'anti* from one of these two languages. When it did, the term almost certainly referred to *Agkistrodon bilineatus*. Subsequently, Kekchi extended the meaning of the term to snakes in general.

Because **wug, mammal**, and combined **wug-mammal** are always the last animal life-forms to be encoded by languages, referential histories of terms for these are usually more transparent and therefore more easily recovered than those of labels for **bird, fish**, and **snake**. In other words, referential histories of terms for the former classes have usually not yet been obscured by language changes that tend to accumulate over extended periods of time. Consequently, most of the following examples of animal life-form innovation involve **wug, mammal**, and combined **wug-mammal** rather than the initial triad of life-forms of the zoological encoding sequence.

Polynesian languages show considerable variety in the ways in which they have innovated **wug** through expansion of reference. Different languages have done so by extending referential application of terms for several different creatures typically included in **wug** life-forms. For example, the Marquesan term for **wug**, *i?o*, is a reflex of the Proto-Polynesian word for maggot (**iLo*) referred to above. It is possible that Marquesan first expanded its "maggot" term to worms in general (such as Nukuoro and Tahitian have done) and then subsequently expanded it to **wug** (encompassing bugs and worms). Two other Polynesian languages, Mangaia and Niuean, have created **wug** classes that encompass bugs, lizards, and certain small elongated creatures by expanding application of their reflexes of the Proto-Polynesian term for lizard (**moko*). A common Polynesian strategy for developing **wug** has involved referential expansion of terms originally denoting specific bugs such as lice (Rennellese), sandflies or midges (Tikopian), fleas (Easter Island), and moths (Maori).

Several languages of those surveyed for animal classification may have developed **mammal** life-forms through expansion of reference of words originally designating meat. Eight languages have **mammal** terms that also mean "meat" or refer more restrictively to the special-purpose category "game animals" or, in other words, to mammals sought for their flesh. These include Awtuw (93b), Hewa (97b), Igbiro (99b), Muinane (105b), Pacaas Novos (106b), Patep (107b), Waodani (111b), and Gbaya Kara (130b). In addition, the Daga (142b) label for combined **wug-mammal** has "meat" as a second sense. There are also several languages having "meat"/"game animal"/"edible animal" terms that may be in the process of expanding to **mammal**. See discussions associated with Aguaruna Jivaro (21b), Asurini (24b), Carapana (30b), Djinang (35b), Gaviao (36b), Nuaulu (53b), and Teen (89b).

Among the 144 languages surveyed in Appendix B, only 6 lump bugs and mammals together in a combined **wug-mammal** life-form class. Given the apparent rarity of combined **wug-mammal** in this sample, it is perhaps surprising to find that it occurs quite frequently in languages of the two genetic groupings, Mayan and Polynesian, studied in depth for animal life-form development. Perhaps even more surprising is that combined **wug-mammal** in languages of both groups has developed through expansion of reference of terms for life-forms of the initial triad of the animal encoding sequence.

Zinacantan Tzotzil, a Mayan language included among those surveyed in Appendix B (case 116b), can be used to illustrate this feature of reference expansion. This language uses the term *čon* (or *chon*) to label a zoological grouping that includes mammals, reptiles, frogs, turtles, bugs, and worms. As is usual for combined **wug-mammal** classes, creatures associated with the initial triad of the encoding sequence, such as fish and birds, are excluded from this grouping; but snakes are not. This fairly unusual treatment of snakes traces to the fact that *čon* originally served as a "snake" label before expanding in reference to combined **wug-mammal**. This is known since the term is a phonologically regular reflex of Proto-Mayan **ka·n* "snake" (Brown and Witkowski 1979, 1982).

When *čon* "snake" expanded to combined **wug-mammal**, it almost certainly retained its original sense (i.e., "snake") while adding the additional broader meaning. In fact, *čon* apparently is still used on occasion by Tzotzil speakers to designate "snake" (cf. Laughlin 1975). However, a new term, *kiletel čon*, has developed—referring specifically to snakes and more generally to all reptiles. It translates literally "dragging **wug-mammal** creature."

Several Mayan languages geographically neighboring Tzotzil (Tzeltal, Tojolobal, and Chol) participated in similar developments, most likely the result of areal diffusion. The Bachajon dialect of Tzeltal uses its reflex of Proto-Mayan *ka·n* "snake," i.e., *čan*, as a label for both "snake" and **wug**. Tojolobal's reflex of the same, *čan*, specifically designates snakes and apparently is used more broadly to refer to **mammal**, perhaps even extending to creatures in general. The Chol **wug** term, *činil*, is also a reflex of Proto-Mayan "snake," and its **wug** application also developed through expansion of meaning. Chol **wug** encompasses little frogs, little turtles, and even little fish in addition to bugs. Snakes, however, are excluded. These elongated creatures are now designated by another term, *lukum*, which originally denoted earthworms.

Several languages of the Quichean subgroup of the Mayan family also seem to have combined **wug-mammal** life-forms. These include Quiche, Tzutujil, Cakchiquel, and Pocomchi. Similar to Tzotzil, these languages apparently developed combined **wug-mammal** by expanding referential application of a label for one of the three initial life-forms of the encoding sequence. However, in the Quichean case **bird** rather than **snake** expanded.

All four Quichean Mayan languages use the same term, *čikop*, in reference to combined **wug-mammal**, probably an areal effect. Use of the term in Quiche is typical. Quiche *čikop* restrictively denotes **bird** and expansively designates combined **wug-mammal**, which includes birds in addition to bugs and mammals. While it is not entirely certain that **bird** was the original referent of the term, the fact that birds are included in **wug-mammal** and are the category's focus is some evidence that it was. Paralleling the Tzotzil case, expansion of reference would explain the unusual inclusion of birds in combined **wug-mammal**. At least one of the four languages, Cakchiquel, has developed a new **bird** label through modification of *čikop*. Cakchiquel *šik' čikop* **bird** translates literally "feathered **wug-mammal** creature."

A development very similar to that described for Quichean languages has occurred in a number of languages of the Polynesian grouping. At least thirteen Polynesian languages use their reflex of Proto-Polynesian *manu* **bird** to designate a combined **wug-mammal** class encompassing birds in addition to bugs and mammals. Most of these languages have retained **bird** as a specific referent of the term. Tahitian (144b) is a typical example. Its reflex of the Proto-Polynesian term, *manu*, specifically denotes **bird** and expansively designates combined **wug-mammal**, which includes birds. In some Polynesian languages, **bird** was lost as a specific referent of *manu* after it expanded to combined **wug-mammal**. Most of these languages have developed new **bird** terms by modifying old ones. For example, Rennellese uses *manu gege* for **bird**, which translates literally "flying **wug-mammal** creature." This closely parallels two Mayan naming strategies resorted to in similar contexts: Tzotzil "dragging **wug-mammal** creature" for "snake" and Cakchiquel "feathered **wug-mammal** creature" for **bird**.

In addition to Tzotzil (116b) and Tahitian (144b), several other languages of the 144 surveyed for animal classification apparently have created categories by expanding terms for **bird** or **snake**. Mokilese (115b), a Micronesian language, has a combined **wug-mammal** class labeled by *maan*. The fact that birds are constituents of this grouping is evidence of innovation of the category through referential expansion of a **bird** term. In Mokilese birds are designated by *maan səng*, which translates literally "flying **wug-mammal** creature."

Two Australian languages, Yolŋu (112b) and Anindilyakwa (121b), apparently have created **mammal** and **wug** classes respectively by expanding terms for **bird**. The Yolŋu term *warrakan* designates **mammal**, a category encompassing land mammals, reptiles, and birds. The inclusion of birds and the fact that the most typical *warrakan* are judged to be birds by speakers indicate that the term originally denoted **bird**. Similarly, Anindilyakwa speakers have a **wug** life-form, *wurrajija*, which extends to birds and has these creatures as its focus. This, of course, suggests that its label originally designated only birds.

Komo (134b), an African Benue-Congo language, also includes birds in a **mammal** category. This language encodes **mammal** through binary opposition. Birds are lumped with rodents and other small mammals in a "small mammal" class, *mbaú*, contrasting with a "large mammal" grouping, *nyama*. The expression *mbau aoyala* denotes **bird** and translates literally "flying small mammal." **Bird** almost certainly constituted the original referent of *mbaú*. Probable cognates of the latter term are found in other Benue-Congo languages with meanings associated with birdness: e.g., Swahili *mbawa* "feathers of the wing" and Efik *mba* "wing." Thus, Komo "small mammal" probably developed through expansion of reference of a term for **bird**.

Western Subanun (91b), a Philippine language, has developed **wug** through referential expansion of a term for "snake." This has involved reduplication, a grammatical feature of the language which produces the diminutive. The term *mamak* denotes "snake" and its reduplicated form, *mamakmamak*, labels a **wug** class encompassing bugs, worms, snakes, and small lizards. While *mamakmamak* is literally "little snake," the source for the language reports that its literal sense is not conceptually significant. In other words, *mamakmamak* are thought of as being **wug**s rather than little snakes. Possibly *mamakmamak* originally designated only worms ("little snake"?) and later expanded referentially to bugs and other small residual creatures. However, such a proposal does not explain the inclusion of snakes in **wug**. Western Subanun **bird** had a similar derivational history. The **bird** term, *manukmanuk*, is the reduplicated word for "chicken" (*manuk*). *Manukmanuk*, according to the source for Western Subanun, are conceptually birds rather than little chickens.

Why languages, more often than might be expected, use terms for **bird** and **snake** to create **wug**, **mammal**, and combined **wug-mammal** categories is far from clear at present. I can suggest only one plausible contributing factor. Since **bird** and **snake** classes are very broad in membership compared to generic groupings (for example, English *robin* and *cobra*), perhaps it is sometimes easier for people to envision these as having even greater referential breadth than to think of less comprehensive generic classes as so extended.

Some factors contributing to the specific case of Polynesian referential expansion of **bird** to combined **wug-mammal** are relatively clear. Most of the islands settled by Polynesian speakers have limited faunal inventories today, and these were even more restricted in the past. Native mammals, other than those adapted to aquatic environments, are rarely found in Polynesia or in other parts of the Pacific. Most of the land mammals that are now common were imported by man either on purpose (domesticated beasts) or accidently (rats). Other creatures, such as snakes and even bugs on some islands, are also noteworthy for their scarcity. On the other hand, birds, while also somewhat restricted in number and variety in some parts of Oceania, nevertheless must have been relatively prominent creatures in the past compared to exemplars of other animal life-form classes.

Assuming this prominence of birds, for Proto-Polynesian speakers and speakers of early daughter languages, animals that were not fish or sea creatures (labeled *ika*) were, for the most part, *manu* (the Proto-Polynesian word for **bird**). This may mean that things called *manu* conceptually were not just "birds," but also "creatures that do not live in the sea." If so, it would have been natural to extend referential application of *manu* reflexes to other nonsea creatures when these were introduced into Polynesian habitats. Fuentes (1960: 782) mentions just this sort of extension for the Easter Island language: "the original meaning of *manu* was bird, but once animals were brought into the island they became *manu* since Pascuense [Easter Island] was lacking a word to describe them."

Environmental and historical factors, then, may partly account for referential extension of Polynesian **bird** terms. Possibly similar developments in other languages are also due to ecology-and/or culture-specific influences.

Languages occasionally develop animal life-form classes through restriction of reference of terms for broader zoological categories. For example, the English term *animal* originally referred only to living creatures in general. In modern usage, it retains this meaning, but it has also absorbed the more restricted referent **mammal**. Since most languages tend to lack general biological categories such as English *plant* and *animal* (Berlin 1972; Berlin et al. 1973), few have actually developed animal life-forms through restriction of reference. Most of the few examples of reference restriction known to me have involved reductions in the ranges of terms for combined **wug-mammal**.

Several examples of restriction of reference are mentioned above in connection with development of combined **wug-mammal** classes. For instance, Tzotzil (116b) reacquired a "snake" class through reference restriction after its original "snake" term, *čon*, became applied primarily to combined **wug-mammal**. It did so by linguistically modifying the combined **wug-mammal** label creating *kiletel čon* "snake," literally, "dragging **wug-mammal** creature." There are, of course, similar examples from Cakchiquel, Mokilese, Komo, and numerous Polynesian languages described in the preceding section.

Tahitian's (144b) **wug** life-form developed through restriction of reference of a term for combined **wug-mammal**. This also entailed linguistic modification, specifically reduplication, which is the common Tahitian method of giving the idea of smallness and great numbers (Lemaitre 1977: 174). The Tahitian word for combined **wug-mammal**, *manu*, has become restricted in reference to a subset of the membership of that category, bugs, through reduplication (*manumanu*). A similar development occurred in Southern Paiute (Chemehuevi dialect) (143b), which uses the plural form (*paʔávivim*) of its term for combined **wug-mammal** (*paʔabi*) to denote insects and other small creatures.

Metaphor and Animal Life-Forms

Metaphor, like restriction of reference, is far less commonly involved in developing animal life-form classes than is expansion of reference. Only a few examples are attested for Mayan and Polynesian languages. Most of these involve elongated-creature categories. For instance, two Mayan languages, Pocomam and Pocomchi, use reflexes of the Proto-Mayan word for tongue to refer to snakes. Tongues, like snakes, are characteristically long and flexible, especially those of creatures such as lizards, frogs, and so on. Other Mayan languages, Kanjobal and Jacaltec, have derived "snake" terms from a Proto-Mayan word which denoted malicious supernatural entities (e.g., animal spirits, ghosts, etc.). "Worm" life-forms apparently have been innovated in at least two Mayan languages, Chol and Kekchi, by applying a term for root to those small elongated creatures. Finally, Marquesan, a Polynesian language, reacquired "snake" after losing it (see Chapter 5) by metaphorically equating such creatures with eels. The language has two compound terms for "snake" both of which translate literally "land eel."

Only one example of the use of figurative language in the derivation of life-forms for creatures other than elongated animals has come to my attention. The Chontal (Mayan) **wug** term, *ahčuk'aʔtak*, is derived from *ahčuk'aʔ* which means "so and so" or "an unnamed person." Chontal **wug**, then, translates literally something like "the unnamed ones." This suggests that **wug** in Chontal is now or was in the past an "incipient" life-form category.

Incipient Life-Form Classes

Life-form innovation may occasionally involve a developmental phase in which life-form categories are only embryonic in nature, showing most, but not all characteristics of full-fledged life-form classes. These are the so-called "incipient" life-forms mentioned here and in several preceding chapters. Terms for incipient life-forms label general biological groupings, but these include only organisms that do not have individual plant or animal names. The emergence of incipient life-form classes may often have preceded innovation of full-fledged biological life-forms in languages. The latter is accomplished when named varieties are included along with unnamed ones in previously incipient plant and animal classes.

Incipient plant life-form classes are known to occur for certain in 7 languages of the 188 surveyed in Appendix A: Iwaidja (1a), Bella Coola (3a), Sahaptin (7a), Lillooet (36a), Tarahumara (43a), Pacaas Novos (45a), and Itawis (65a). In addition, 6 other languages probably have incipient plant life-form categories (see discussions in Appendix A associated with Awtuw [49a], Paumari [86a], Zuni [109a], Ninam [125a], Yaqui [157a], and Clallam [181a]). Incipient animal life-forms are known for certain to occur in 8 languages of the 144 surveyed in Appendix B: Iwaidja (1b), Ilongot (6b), Northern Paiute (10b), Juchitan Zapotec (15b), Sahaptin (20b), Brunei Malay (28b), Central Cagayan Agta (31b), and Waodani (111b, see discussion of this case). In addition, 3 other languages probably have incipient animal life-forms (see discussions in Appendix B associated with Paumari [17b], Tarahumara [61b], and Navaho [83b]). Other languages of those sampled in Appendices A and B probably have incipient life-forms, but for one reason or another these were not recognized and reported as such by sources. Because I personally investigated Juchitan Zapotec (with Paul K. Chase), I have chosen this language to illustrate some of the salient features of a classificatory system having incipient life-forms.[6]

Juchitan Zapotec (15b), spoken in the Mexican state of Oaxaca, is affiliated with Stage 2 of animal life-form growth, having only **fish** and **snake** of the five life-forms of the zoological encoding sequence. However, **mammal** and **wug** exist as incipient life-form classes. The term *mani'* designates incipient **mammal**, and in a modified version, *mani huiini'*, it denotes incipient **wug** as well. *Mani'* is used to refer to all larger creatures that cannot be identified by any other Zapotec animal term, and *mani huiini'* refers to all smaller unidentifiable creatures. (The modifier *huiini'* translates "little.") Usage of these terms as described here is overtly recognized by adult speakers of Juchitan Zapotec.

Since any fish can be identified by use of the **fish** life-form term and any snake by the "snake" life-form term, fish and snakes are always excluded from the categories *mani'* and *mani huiini'*. Worms are also excluded since there is a term for any small, legless, elongated creature. In addition, all other animals, with some exceptions to be mentioned presently, that can be identified through use of a generic term are excluded. Examples of the latter are turtles, ants, mice, spiders, eagles, buzzards, rabbits, dogs, crickets, and so on. Since Juchitan Zapotec lacks terms for full-fledged **bird**, **wug**, and **mammal** life-form classes, unidentifiable creatures characteristically fitting into these three categories constitute the bulk of animals designated by use of *mani'* and *mani huiini'*. In addition, since birds are generally considered to be small creatures, unknown birds are typically lumped with other unknown small creatures (mostly bugs) in the class *mani huiini'*. Unknown mammals, of which there are very few, are designated *mani'* since mammals are generally considered to be large.

Mani' and *mani huiini'* resemble full-fleded **mammal** and **wug** life-forms since they encompass mammals and bugs respectively. They differ from full-fledged **mammal** and **wug** categories in two respects. First, inclusion of birds is atypical of a **wug** class (cf. *mani huiini'*). Second and most important, *mani'* and *mani huiini'* differ from **mammal** and **wug** since their membership is limited to unidentifiable creatures. Full-fledged **mammal** and **wug** typically include most, if not all, creatures not included in **bird**, **fish**, and **snake** whether they are identifiable or not. In addition, full-fledged life-form classes are always polytypic, having at least two members, and usually many more than two, which have their own labels (see Chapter 2). Since *mani'* and *mani huiini'* are not polytypic, they do not qualify as true life-form classes.

The term *mani'* apparently was borrowed into Zapotec from Nahuatl (Aztec) four hundred or more years ago (for details, see Brown and Chase 1981). Its original meaning was "creatures in general." Through restriction of reference, *mani'* and its derived counterpart, *mani huiini'* acquired their present referential ranges.

Restriction of the referential range of *mani'* (and by implication of *mani huiini'*) to unidentifiable creatures seems a reasonable development from its original wider meaning. When *mani'* first entered the language, it probably was principally applied to animals that could not be readily identified by use of well-established Zapotec names, and only occasionally used for known creatures. This tendency could have set the stage for the eventual restriction of the term to unknown animals, the current Juchitan Zapotec application.

Mani' was subjected to even further restriction of meaning in Juchitan Zapotec. In addition to its use as a label for "large unknown creature," *mani'* now serves as the generic term for horse. This is attributable in part to the fact that horses were introduced by the Spanish and were therefore originally "unknown" to Zapotec speakers and other indigenous peoples. The horse is in effect the archetypal large unknown animal for speakers of Juchitan Zapotec.

In Chapter 5, evidence is assembled showing that although languages may occasionally lose biological life-forms, the general tendency has been for life-form growth, i.e., category addition, rather than loss. As societies move increasingly towards urbanization and large-scale organization, people are more and more removed from direct contact and intimate interaction with the world of plants and animals. As a consequence, they lose detailed knowledge of biological organisms, including generic and specific names for them, and more general terms, such as life-form labels, become increasingly useful and salient and tend to grow in number.

Since addition of life-form classes has been the tendency over time, Juchitan Zapotec may eventually add zoological life-form categories beyond **fish** and **snake**. If so, the incipient categories, *mani'* and *mani huiini'*, would be natural candidates for consolidation into full-fledged **mammal** and **wug** life-forms. With decreases in detailed knowledge of animals, the number of creatures designated by *mani'* and *mani huiini'* would tend to increase. Fish, snakes, and worms, however, would continue to be excluded from these categories since these creatures are maintained in labeled life-form classes of their own. As membership of *mani'* and *mani huiini'* categories grows, these would begin to resemble in size full-fledged life-form classes. As a result, a tendency may develop to generalize them to known creatures as well as unknown.

Such generalization in fact appears to have already begun. Adult speakers consistently identify certain creatures by use of *mani'* and *mani huiini'* despite the fact that they have well-known Zapotec generic names. This is, for example, the case for frogs, toads, iguanas, and Mexican opossums or tlacuaches, all of which are classified as either *mani'* or *mani huiini'* depending on size. When informants were reminded that this classification is not in accordance with the stated rule governing use of *mani'* and its counterpart, most were bewildered. In some instances, however, ad hoc responses of a substantive nature were evoked. One informant, for example, claimed that the tlacuache is *mani'* because it comes out only at night and hence is not a well-known creature.

Since Juchitan Zapotec does not encode **bird** and since unknown birds are included in *mani huiini'*, consolidation of *mani'* and *mani huiini'* as full life-form classes might result in an atypical **wug** category, one encompassing birds in addition to other small creatures such as bugs. However, factors underlying such a development presumably would lead to the lexical encoding of **bird** before consolidation of **mammal** and **wug**. **Bird**, of course, strongly tends to emerge before full-fledged **wug** and **mammal** classes are encoded by languages.

As described in detail in Chapter 7, Chase (1980a, b) in an investigation of folk zoological life-form acquisition by American children finds that younger child informants (three to five and one-half years in age) assign the word *bird* only to those birds they are unable to identify by some generic label such as *duck, parrot, owl*, and so on. Thus for these children, *bird* labels an incipient life-form class. Child acquisition of incipient **bird** always precedes learning the full **bird** life-form of adult speakers of American English. It constitutes a transitional stage between having no **bird** category and acquiring the adult range of the class.

Parallels to the acquisition sequence described by Chase (1980a, b) may pertain to the development of folk biological life-forms in languages in general. In other words, incipient life-form classes may have often served as transitional stages in the innovation of full plant and animal life-form categories. Presumably the need for general terms for plants and animals grows and the pool of unknown, unnamed organisms enlarges with increases in societal scale and removal of people from intimate contact with nature. The development of incipient life-form classes would constitute an appropriate, if not natural, response to an ever increasing number of *unknown* biological entities. As incipient life-forms expand in membership, these would begin to resemble in size full-fledged life-form classes. As a result, a tendency may develop to generalize them to named creatures as well, thus completing the process of life-form innovation.

The fact that incipient life-form classes are found only occasionally in languages does not necessarily detract from the proposal outlined here. Two related factors are probable contributors to the contemporaneous scarcity of incipient life-forms. First, many of the world's languages, especially those with large numbers of speakers, already have fully developed life-form systems since many are spoken by peoples living in urban environments or in other ways removed from nature. In other words, from a worldwide perspective, biological life-form development has mostly run full course, or nearly full course, in response to removal of people from direct and continuous contact with the world of plants and animals. Second, the predominant way in which languages have acquired life-forms in recent history probably has involved borrowing from external sources rather than independent innovation. This is related to the fact that worldwide increases in societal scale and complexity have led to the mobility of people and consequent high frequency of contact of speakers of diverse languages. In short, most languages in recent times probably have acquired full life-forms (concepts, not necessarily labels) through language contact and thus bypassed the incipient life-form stage that more than occasionally may be associated with biological life-form innovation.

»7«

LIFE-FORMS AND LINGUISTIC MARKING

This chapter relates cross-language regularities in life-form classification to linguistic marking.[1] The framework of marking has been developed
over the years by Jakobson (1941), Greenberg (1966, 1969, 1975), and others. Marking involves all components of language: phonology, grammar, and
the lexicon. Marking in the lexicon entails a distinction between marked and
unmarked words. Unmarked words differ in systematic ways from marked
ones. For example, unmarked terms tend to occur more frequently in ordinary
language use than do marked terms; unmarked items tend to be simpler (phonologically or morphologically) than marked ones; and unmarked labels tend
to be acquired before marked labels by children learning language.

The plant and animal life-form encoding sequences (Figures 2 and 3, Chapter 3) reflect universal marking sequences or marking hierarchies. These are
manifested as chains of marking relationships. In the plant life-form hierarchy, **tree** is unmarked vis-à-vis **grerb** and **grass**, which are marked. **Grerb**
and **grass** in turn are unmarked relative to **vine** and **bush** which are marked.
In the animal life-form hierarchy, **bird**, **fish**, and **snake** are unmarked vis-à-
vis **wug** and **mammal**, which are marked. This chapter explores several interrelated ways in which marking hierarchies for botanical and zoological life-
forms are linguistically realized.

Marking Features

Several diagnostic features of marking tend to cooccur in typical marking relationships. Some of these are as follows:

Unmarked Item	*Marked Item*
1. The implied in an implicational relationship	1. The implier in an implicational relationship
2. Earlier acquisition by languages	2. Later acquisition by languages

3. Greater frequency of use (in text or spoken language)	3. Lesser frequency of use
4. Less complex (phonologically or morphologically)	4. More complex
5. Earlier child acquisition	5. Later child acquisition

Marking features 1 and 2, which are closely interrelated, entail a cross-language perspective. Implicational relationships (feature 1) have been discussed in detail (Chapter 3). **Tree** is unmarked cross-linguistically since it is implied in such relationships and **grerb** and **grass** are themselves implied by **vine** and **bush**, meaning that the former pair is unmarked vis-à-vis the latter pair, which is marked. Similarly, **bird**, **fish**, and **snake** are unmarked cross-linguistically since they are implied by **wug** and **mammal**, which are of course marked since they are impliers.

Implicational associations involving lexical items are often the synchronic result of cross-language regularities in the order in which these items are acquired by languages (feature 2). Such relationships, of course, form the basis for proposals of both botanical and zoological life-form encoding sequences. However, there is evidence independent of cross-language implicational relationships that corroborates the two acquisition hypotheses. This is evidence developed through the comparative approach of historical linguistics described in Chapter 5, showing that languages historically have added plant and animal life-form terms to their vocabularies in the orders of the two encoding sequences.

Marking features 3, 4, and 5 are also closely interrelated, but these associations are realized in individual languages rather than across languages. For example, Zipf (1935, 1949) has shown that frequency of use (feature 3) correlates strongly with phonological (or orthographic) length of words (feature 4). High frequency is associated with short word length and thus with less complexity; low frequency with long length and more complexity. Because unmarked items are less complex than marked items and because they occur more frequently, it is not surprising that they tend to be acquired by children learning language before they acquire marked items (feature 5).

Inasmuch as the two life-form encoding sequences are also marking hierarchies, they should reflect other criteria of marking in addition to features 1 and 2. For example, in individual languages we should expect that terms for **tree** occur more frequently in ordinary use than terms for the four other botanical life-forms or that labels for **bird**, **fish**, and **snake** are used more often than words for **wug** and **mammal**. The following sections of this chapter assemble evidence showing how the plant and animal life-form marking hierarchies are realized in individual languages through frequency of use, complexity of form, and child acquisition criteria.

In Chapter 5 (Tables 11–15), data are presented showing that plant and animal life-form names are among the most frequently used biological terms in languages affiliated with nation-state societies. Tables 16 and 17 compile similar data showing that frequency of use of terms for plant and animal life-forms correlates strongly with orders in which these are added to languages. In other words, an additional feature of marking, frequency of use, attests to the universal marking hierarchies for plant and animal life-forms which are also evidenced by other marking features such as implicational relationships and language acquisition order.

Frequency data presented in Tables 16 and 17 are extracted from word frequency counts based on written rather than spoken language. Frequency figures (given in parentheses) are based on counts for more than one lexical item when more than one word denotes the same life-form in a language. For example, in Rumanian two terms, *pom* and *copac*, designate **tree**. The individual frequencies of these items are 35 and 25 occurrences respectively yielding a total frequency for Rumanian **tree** of 60. Similarly, the American English **wug** figure, 372, is an aggregation of counts for the terms *bug* (65 occurrences) and *insect* (307 occurrences). In addition, frequency counts for **snake** (Table 17) in several languages (American English, Arabic, Brazilian Portuguese, French, German, and Peninsular Spanish) are aggregations of counts for "snake" and "worm" terms. In some cases frequencies of "worm" terms are so low that they are not given in sources, meaning that for some languages counts for "snake" terms alone yield figures for **snake**. Chinese and Japanese are exceptional among the eleven languages since they both lump worms and bugs in **wug** and lack "worm" labels (see cases 81b and 132b, Appendix B).[2]

Some of the plant life-form terms pertaining to Table 16 have additional referents, and thus they are polysemous. For example, the English **grerb** term, *plant*, also refers to botanical organisms in general. Consequently, only part of its frequency score (1050 occurrences) relates to its use as a **grerb** label. This is probably something less than 500 occurrences, although this is only a guess based on observed frequencies of occurrence of nonpolysemous **grerb** terms in other languages. Several other plant life-form terms are similarly polysemous, and this is indicated in Table 16. As in the case of English *plant*, frequencies actually pertaining to life-form applications of these terms are undoubtedly less than the scores given in Table 16.

The data of Table 16 show a very close correspondence between the encoding sequence for plant life-forms and the frequency of use of terms for them. For example, in most, if not all, of the eleven languages, **tree** occurs most frequently.[3] In addition, in all but one language the second most frequent life-form is either **grerb** or **grass**. (The exception is German.) Also, in nearly all

Table 16. Frequency ranking of folk botanical life-forms in eleven nation-state languages.

Languages	Frequency ranking				
	High				Low
American English	tree (1254)	grerb[a] (1050)	grass (313)	bush (218)	vine (61)
Arabic	tree (36)	grerb (8)	———	———	———
Brazilian Portuguese	tree (365)	grerb (44)	grass (17)	bush (16)	vine[b] (14)
Chinese	tree (19)	grass (9)	———	———	———
French	tree (211)	grerb (85)	vine[b] (42)	bush (24)[c]	———
German	tree (2325)[c]	bush (405)[c]	grass (315)[c]	grerb (265)[c]	vine (<100)[c]
Italian	tree (43)	grerb (31)	vine (<4)[c]	bush (<4)[c]	———
Japanese	tree (20)	grerb (12)	grass (<4)[c]	vine (<4)[c]	bush (<4)[c]
Peninsular Spanish	tree (136)	grerb (49)	bush (15)[c]	vine (<5)[c]	———
Rumanian	tree (60)	grerb (35)	vine (27)	bush (<4)[c]	———
Russian	tree[d] (166)	grerb (146)	bush (85)	vine (<13)	———

Note: Cf. Brown n.d.

[a] Term also denotes plants in general.

[b] Term also means "vineyard."

[c] Close estimate.

[d] Term also means "wood."

cases **bush** and **vine** are lower in frequency than other life-forms of the encoding sequence. Thus, by frequency of use criteria, **tree** is generally unmarked vis-à-vis **grerb** and **grass**, and **grerb** and **grass** are generally unmarked vis-à-vis **bush** and **vine**. This, of course, is the same marking hierarchy implied in the botanical life-form encoding sequence.

Without exception, in each of the eleven languages (Table 17) **bird**, **fish**, and **snake** occur more frequently in written usage than **wug**. Table 17 also shows that these three are more frequent than **mammal** in all languages. However, frequency counts for **mammal** are almost certainly deflated for some languages, and hence they are not entirely reliable. Terms for creatures in general are sometimes used secondarily to designate **mammal**, as occurs in American English with *animal* (see case 120b). The same is probably true of "animal" terms in the several Romance languages represented. Terms for creatures in general occur in these languages at very high frequencies. For example, American English *animal* has a frequency of 1226 compared to 1079 for **fish**, the most frequently occurring English animal life-form (see Table 17). It is impossible to calculate with any degree of reliability what proportion of *animal*'s occurrences involve **mammal** as the intended referent, as opposed to "creatures in general." Since counts for **mammal** in Table 17 do

Table 17. Frequency ranking of folk zoological life-forms in eleven nation-state languages.

Languages	Frequency ranking				
	High				Low
American English	fish (1079)	bird (770)	snake (380)	wug (372)	mammal (27)
Arabic	bird (29)	fish (16)	snake (10)	wug (9)	mammal ([a])
Brazilian Portuguese	bird (291)	snake (142)	fish (133)	wug (43)	mammal (<5)
Chinese	fish (12)	bird (9)	snake (<9)	wug (<9)	mammal (<9)
French	bird (108)	snake (62)	fish (54)	wug (45)	mammal (<5)
German	fish (1025)[b]	bird (612)[b]	snake (598)[b]	wug (<100)	mammal (<100)
Italian	fish (17)	bird (10)	snake (8)	wug (4)	mammal (<4)
Japanese	bird (16)	snake (11)	fish (8)	wug (6)	mammal (6)
Peninsular Spanish	bird (207)	fish (115)	snake (53)	wug (15)	mammal (<5)
Rumanian	bird (53)	snake (28)	fish (19)	wug (<4)	mammal (<4)
Russian	bird (114)	fish (84)	snake (32)	wug (<13)	mammal (<13)

Note: Cf. Brown 1982b.

[a] Not found among tokens surveyed.

[b] Close estimate.

not include these unknown values, they undoubtedly underrepresent **mammal**'s true frequency of use in some languages.[4]

Snake is the only life-form of the initial encoding triad that is not found as the most frequently occurring animal life-form in a language (see Table 17). Thus on the average, **snake** is somewhat less unmarked than **bird** and **fish** in languages affiliated with nation-state societies. This becomes even more evident when frequency counts for "snake" and "worm" terms are considered separately. These figures are as follows (counts are given in parentheses):

> American English: "snake" (254)
> "worm" (126)
> Arabic: "snake" (9)
> "worm" (1)
> Brazilian Portuguese: "snake" (124)
> "worm" (18)
> Chinese: "snake" (<9)
> "worm" (no term)
> French: "snake" (23)
> "worm" (39)
> German: "snake" (395-close estimate)
> "worm" (203-close estimate)

Italian: "snake" (8)
"worm" (<4)
Japanese: "snake" (11)
"worm" (no term)
Rumanian: "snake" (28)
"worm" (<4)
Russian: "snake" (32)
"worm" (<13)
Spanish: "snake" (35)
"worm" (18)

In all but two of the eleven languages, Japanese and Rumanian, "snake" (large elongated creature) occurs at frequencies lower than those of both **bird** and **fish** (compare the above counts with those of Table 17). In addition, in two languages (French and American English) "snake" actually occurs less frequently than does **wug** and in Arabic "snake" and **wug** have identical frequency scores.

The marked status of "snake" relative to the marking values of **bird** and **fish** in languages affiliated with nation-state societies is perhaps attributable to a general lack of salience for snakes for people residing in such societies. Snakes, for example, are usually rare in areas where the human population is dense such as cities and surrounding suburban and agricultural regions. In addition, those that are present are usually inconspicuous because of small size. On the other hand, birds and fish are usually somewhat more prominent in these habitats either as naturally occurring creatures or as market produce. Apparently the relative lack of salience of snakes among people of nation-state societies is reflected by the relatively low frequency of use of "snake" terms vis-à-vis that of **bird** and **fish** terms. Presumably "snake" terms in languages spoken in small-scale societies where snakes are often more prominent would tend to rival, if not occasionally to surpass, terms for **bird** and **fish** in frequency of use. Unfortunately, to my knowledge such counts are not at present available.

Another cross-language marking relationship is evident in the above frequency data for "snake" and "worm." Excluding from consideration Chinese and Japanese, which lack "worm" terms, among the remaining nine languages with only one exception "snake" terms occur more frequently than "worm" labels. Thus words for "worm" tend to be marked in nation-state languages relative to terms for "snake."[5]

A final observation is that among the nine languages having "worm" terms, six have "worm" labels used less frequently than **wug** terms, and three have "worm" labels surpassing **wug** words in frequency of use only narrowly (compare the above counts for "worm" with those for **wug** in Table 17). This indicates that at least among nation-state languages "worm" is rarely, if ever, unmarked (at least strongly) vis-à-vis **wug**.

Complexity of Form

Unmarked words tend to be less complex (morphologically or phonologically) than marked words. For example, in Kilangi (19a) **tree**, *miti*, is disyllabic while **grerb**, *masambi*, is trisyllabic. Similarly, in American English *bird*, *fish*, and *snake* are all monosyllabic while *insect*, *mammal*, and *animal* (secondarily **mammal**) are disyllabic and trisyllabic. However, complexity of form is a somewhat less certain measure of markedness than frequency of use since exceptions are relatively often encountered. For example, in Southern Paiute (Chemehuevi) (28a) **tree**, *mahábi*, is trisyllabic while **grerb**, *tisi*, is disyllabic. The criterion of complexity of form, then, reflects a strong tendency rather than an absolutely determinate phenomenon.

When lexical items maintain the same relative marking values across languages, as do biological life-form terms, then on the average unmarked terms should be less complex than marked terms. With this expectation in mind, I have calculated the average orthographic length of plant life-form terms associated with language cases of Appendix A and the average orthographic length of animal life-form terms associated with language cases of Appendix B. This was accomplished by simply counting the number of orthographic segments of words for a life-form class, summing them, and then dividing that sum by the number of terms counted.[6]

Average orthographic lengths of plant life-form labels are as follows (from shortest and least complex to longest and most complex):

> **Tree:** 4.56 segments
> **Grass:** 5.25 segments
> **Grerb:** 5.35 segments
> **Vine:** 5.38 segments
> **Bush:** 6.22 segments

These figures, of course, are another reflection of the universal marking hierarchy for folk botanical life-forms. On the average, terms for **tree**, the most unmarked plant life-form by other marking criteria, are orthographically least complex. Most complex in terms of average orthographic length are terms for **vine** and **bush**, the most marked botanical life-form classes. In between these extremes of average length are terms for **grass** and **grerb** which are universally marked vis-à-vis **tree** and unmarked vis-à-vis **vine** and **bush**.

Average orthographic length of animal life-form labels are as follows (from shortest to longest):

Fish: 4.87 segments
Snake: 5.53 segments
Bird: 5.66 segments
Mammal: 5.75 segments
Wug: 6.70 segments

These figures, of course, accord with the marking hierarchy for folk zoological life-forms. On the average, terms for **bird**, **fish**, and **snake**, which are unmarked, are shorter in orthographic length than terms for **wug** and **mammal**, which are marked. This marking relationship can also be expressed in a slightly different manner using averages. The average length of terms for **bird**, **fish**, and **snake** considered together is 5.38 segments compared to an average length of 6.14 segments for terms for **wug**, **mammal**, and combined **wug-mammal** considered together.

In Chapter 5, several lines of evidence are described which indicate that life-form terms tend to be more numerous and salient in languages spoken in large-scale societies than in those spoken in small-scale ones. For example, frequency data are presented showing that animal life-form words tend to be among the most frequently used names for creatures in three languages affiliated with nation-state societies. Since frequency of use is inversely correlated with complexity of form, it follows that average orthographic length of animal life-form terms in nation-state languages should be less than that of corresponding terms in small-scale society languages.

Of the 144 languages surveyed for animal classification, 7 are regularly spoken by peoples living in large-scale, nation-state societies: Cantonese (29b), Indonesian (74b), Mandarin (80b), Northeastern Thai (84b), American English (120b), Czech (125b), and Japanese (132b). Table 18 presents the average orthographic length of life-forms in these languages compared to the average lengths calculated for life-forms in all 144 languages surveyed (the overwhelming majority of which are affiliated with small-scale societies). With the exception of calculations for **mammal**, these figures accord with the hypothesis that animal life-form classes are more salient for people of large-scale societies than for those of small-scale ones. Another way of putting this is that animal life-form terms of nation-state languages are unmarked vis-à-vis corresponding terms of small-scale-society languages (cf. Dougherty 1978).

It is noted above that **snake** is somewhat less unmarked by frequency of use measures than **bird** and **fish** in languages affiliated with nation-state societies. However, this is not entirely borne out by complexity of form measures. On the average, terms for **snake** in the 144 languages surveyed are shorter than terms for **bird** (see Table 18). This may indicate that **snake** is somewhat more unmarked (or less marked) relative to **bird** and **fish** in small-scale societies

Table 18. Average orthographic length of animal life-form terms of nation-state languages compared to average length of life-form terms of all 144 languages surveyed.

| | Average orthographic length | |
Life-forms	Nation-state languages	All languages
fish	3.14 segments	4.87 segments
snake	4.10 segments	5.53 segments
bird	4.14 segments	5.66 segments
wug	5.00 segments	6.70 segments
mammal	6.00 segments	5.75 segments

Note: Cf. Brown 1982b.

than in large-scale ones. This accords with my proposal that snakes are often relatively prominent creatures in environments where small-scale societies are located and thus tend to rival, if not occasionally to surpass, birds and fish in salience.

Table 18 also shows that **snake** terms on the average are shorter than **bird** terms in nation-state languages. Terms for true snakes ("snake") are even shorter in these languages, averaging 3.57 segments. This is unexpected since labels for true snakes occur in nation-state languages at considerably lower frequencies than terms for either **bird** or **fish** (see preceding section). This anomaly may be linked to the possibility that there is often a time lag between changes in frequency of use and corresponding adjustments in complexity of form. Thus, for instance, the fact that "snake" terms are on the average shorter than **bird** terms in nation-state languages may indicate that such terms were shorter than **bird** terms in these languages in the past when speakers still lived in small-scale societies. Nation-state languages, then, may have simply maintained past forms of "snake" and **bird** labels while changing their frequencies of occurrence to match the altered relative prominence of these respective creatures in increasingly urbanized environments.

Complexity of form and frequency of use criteria are in accord with respect to the relative marking values of "snake" and "worm" terms in nation-state languages. In the latter, "worm" labels are marked relative to "snake" labels by frequency of use measures. The same marking relationship for these items is evidenced in these languages by complexity of form criteria: "worm" terms on the average are longer (5.33 segments) than "snake" terms (3.57 segments). In addition, when all 144 languages are considered, the same relative marking values are attested: "worm" terms averaging 6.10 orthographic segments and "snake" labels averaging 5.28 segments. This indicates that across languages, regardless of degree of associated societal scale, "worm" terms are marked vis-à-vis terms for "snake."

Finally, complexity of form and frequency of use measures are also in agreement with regard to marking relationships between "worm" and **wug** labels. It is noted earlier that "worm" in nation-state languages is rarely, if ever, unmarked (at least strongly) relative to **wug** by frequency of use criteria. In nation-state languages the average length of "worm" terms (5.33 segments) is greater than that for **wug** labels (5.00 segments), indicating that "worm" is in fact marked vis-à-vis **wug**. On the other hand, when all sampled languages are considered, "worm" terms appear to be unmarked relative to **wug** terms, averaging 6.10 and 6.70 segments respectively. However, this average for "worm" is greater than the average for **mammal** terms (5.75 segments) indicating that cross-linguistically "worm" is marked vis-à-vis at least one class not belonging to the initial triad of the zoological encoding sequence. In addition, the average length of "worm" labels across languages is not significantly smaller than the average length of terms for **wug**, **mammal**, and combined **wug-mammal** considered together (6.14 segments). When several different relationships are considered, cross-linguistically "worm" labels appear to have marking values roughly comparable to those of terms for **wug**, **mammal**, and combined **wug-mammal**. Thus, "worm" terms, like labels for the latter three classes, are not particularly salient in languages. As dicussed presently, this finding may relate to the fact that worms are often included in **wug** life-forms.

Child Acquisition

Dougherty (1979) has investigated acquisition of botanical terminology by American children. Her study indicates that American children first learn **tree** and **grerb** and later acquire **grass**, **vine**, and **bush**. This acquisition order, of course, parallels the plant life-form encoding sequence and thus is additional evidence of a universal marking pattern.

Dougherty's (1979) study was cross-sectional rather than longitudinal in nature. It involved twelve children, six ranging from three to eight years in age and six between the ages of two and three years. All children lived in an older homogeneous section of the city of Berkeley, California. Dougherty elicited information from children through use of standard ethnoscientific questioning techniques (cf. Black 1969). This was usually done with actual plants in full view of informants.

The earliest classification of plants by children involving discontinuities in nature occurs with the recognition of two life-forms, **tree** and **grerb**, encoded by use of the words *tree* and *plant* respectively (Dougherty 1979: 299). However, these categories are considerably broader in membership than categories labeled by these terms in the system of adults. *Tree* is used to designate most large woody plants, including bushes, and *plant* to denote most small herbaceous plants. The next life-forms to be encoded encompass plants which are most distinctive morphologically according to Dougherty (1979: 299). These include **grass** (labeled *grass*) and **bush** (labeled *bush*). Apparently when **vine** (labeled *vine*) is first encoded, it is subsumed under **grerb** (*plant*) along with some other general classes, for example, *flowers* and *leaves*. Eventually **vine** and other general categories are extracted from the referential range of **grerb** and achieve a coordinate status with **tree**, **grerb**, **grass**, and **bush**. At this point, ranges of **tree** and **grerb** more closely match those of the adult system.

The developmental sequence described by Dougherty (1979) very closely parallels details of plant life-form growth in languages. When languages first encode **tree** and **grerb**, these categories extend to most large woody plants and to most small herbaceous plants respectively (see Stage 2 and 3 languages, Appendix A). As other life-form classes are added, the ranges of **tree** and **grerb** tend to shrink (see Stage 4–6 languages, Appendix A). For example, the lexical encoding of **bush** usually involves pulling bushes and shrubs from the range of **tree** or **grerb**, or from the ranges of both, as the case may be.

Acquisition of botanical terminology by Tzeltal (Mayan) children has been investigated by Stross (1973). While Stross does not address himself specifically to the order in which plant life-forms are acquired, he provides some information suggesting that Tzeltal children also recognize **tree** and **grerb** before other life-form classes.

Tzeltal (case 154a) is a Stage 5 language with four coordinate plant life-forms: *te?* (**tree**), *wamal* (**grerb** [herb]), *?ak* (**grass**), and *?ak'* (**vine**). Stross (1973: 135–136) notes that by the age of 2½ years children probably know the four life-form terms but imperfectly associate them with their referents. Such associations usually rest on a foundation of functions. Stross writes: "Thus *te?* 'tree' may be identified when the child associates a specimen with its capacity to yield *te?* 'stick', 'twig', 'pole'. Grasses will often be called *wamal* when encountered outdoors, although a tuft of thatch grass on the roof might be immediately recognized as *?ak*" (1973: 136).

By the age of four, according to Stross (1973: 136), the Tzeltal child can generally use all four life-form terms appropriately. However, on occasion mistakes are made. For example, he may sometimes use *wamal* **grerb** in reference to an *?ak* (**grass**) or *?ak'* (**vine**) or he may use *te?* (**tree**) to denote an *?ak'* (**vine**). The reverse mistakes apparently do not occur: i.e., use of *?ak* or *?ak'* to designate a *te?* or *wamal*. This suggests that prior to four years of age **tree** and **grerb** may have been encoded by Tzeltal children with broader referential ranges than those associated with adult usage. For example, **tree** may have been extended to ligneous vines and **grerb** to grasses and herbaceous vines. If so, as in the American English case, Tzeltal children probably encode broad **tree** and **grerb** life-forms before other general plant categories.

Chase (1980a, b) has investigated child acquisition of folk zoological life-forms in two languages, Juchitan Zapotec (Oaxaca, Mexico) and American English. His general conclusions are that child speakers of both languages learn animal life-form terms and associated concepts in the order of the animal life-form encoding sequence (Figure 3). Thus, by child acquisition criteria, **bird**, **fish**, and **snake** are unmarked relative to **wug** and **mammal** which are marked.

Of Chase's two investigations, the American English study provides more insights into life-form acquisition by children than the Juchitan Zapotec study. Juchitan Zapotec (15b) has only two animal life-forms of the encoding sequence, **fish** and **snake**. Since all children interviewed by Chase controlled terms for these life-forms, the Juchitan Zapotec study sheds little light on order of life-form acquisition. However, as outlined in the preceding chapter, the language also has incipient **wug** and **mammal** life-form classes. Thus, in Juchitan Zapotec only unknown and unnamed bugs are included in incipient **wug** and only unnamed and unknown mammals are included in incipient **mammal**. This is overtly recognized by adult speakers of the language (Brown and Chase 1981). On the other hand, child speakers of Juchitan Zapotec often extend terms for incipient **wug** and **mammal** to named creatures as well as to unnamed ones. This parallels lexical overextensions by children frequently cited in the psycholinguistic literature (cf. Lindfors 1980: 170–171). Of course, children later acquire the adult usage of these terms.

Chase's (1980a, b) American English study has both stratificational and longitudinal aspects. Initially, Chase interviewed ten white middle-class children living in northeastern Illinois and ranging in age from approximately three to nine years. Seventeen months later, seven of these ten were reinterviewed, and six additional children were incorporated into the study at that time. Chase found that the number of animal life-forms possessed by children correlates perfectly with age, the youngest having fewest and the oldest having most. In addition, the composition of life-form inventories possessed by these children indicates that they acquired them in the order of the animal encoding sequence. For example, no child was discovered to have a combination of life-forms such as **bird**, **fish**, and **wug** (lacking **snake** and **mammal**). In the follow-up study of some children, most had acquired additional animal life-forms, again in accordance with the order of the encoding sequence.

Chase (1980a, b) used two strategies for determining possession of knowledge of folk zoological life-forms. All children were first presented with a stack of cards with realistic animal pictures (mostly in color) pasted on them. Among these, all major animal groupings (mammals, insects, amphibians, reptiles, etc.) were well represented. Children were asked to sort these into piles of creatures that "go together." They were then asked to supply names for both piles and individual cards. In addition to stimulus materials, Chase used traditional ethnoscientific techniques (cf. Black 1969) to elicit inclusive relationships.

In addition to paralleling the zoological encoding sequence, order of acquisition of animal life-forms by American children shows some interesting language-specific details. This order is outlined in Figure 4. Children ranging in age from roughly 3 to 5½ years have knowledge of only two life-forms, **fish** and **snake** (labeled *fish* and *snake* respectively). Before reaching 6 years in age, they learn a third life-form, **bird** (labeled *bird*). At around the age of 7 years, **wug** is acquired (labeled variously *bug* or *insect*). Finally, **mammal** (labeled variously *animal* or *mammal*) is learned after the age of 8 years or thereabout.

Figure 4. Order in which American children acquire folk zoological life-forms (Chase 1980a, b).

This acquisitional order seems to be related in part to American children's knowledge of generic terms for creatures. The younger children interviewed by Chase were unable to identify individual fish pictures by generic names (e.g., *trout*, *bass*, *catfish*, etc.) with the exception of the shark (called *jaws* by some); and names for individual snakes were not known. On the other hand, they were able to assign generic terms to numerous bird pictures (e.g., *penguin*, *seagull*, *parrot*, *duck*, *owl*, and so on). Perhaps as a consequence, when sorting pictures, the children usually put all fish into a single pile and all snakes in another (sometimes also including worm pictures). Birds were often left ungrouped; that is, each bird picture constituted its own pile of one. Children sorting pictures thus appear to possess knowledge of **fish** and **snake** life-form classes but not **bird**.

Children lacking a **bird** life-form are not unfamiliar with the word *bird*. However, they simply do not use the term in a way corresponding to adult usage; in other words, they do not use it as if it were a label for a full-fledged life-form class. Rather, they apply *bird* only to those creatures with feathers, wings, and a bill or beak which are unknown to them and cannot be identified by use of a generic term. Consequently, for these children, known creatures such as ducks, parrots, owls, and so on are definitely not *birds* in their system. Younger American children thus use *bird* as a label for a zoological class having all the characteristics of incipient life-form categories described earlier.[7]

Chase's (1980) study also shows that worms are not particularly salient for

American children as a class. All of the very youngest children (under four years of age) identified pictures of worms as *snakes*. While some of the other younger children clearly had a "worm" class independent of "snake," others lumped worms with snakes in piles variously called *snakes*, *snakeworms*, or *snakes and worms*. The acquisitional and syntactic priority of the label *snake* relative to *worm* is another indication of the marked status of the latter relative to the former in American English. Finally, it is interesting to note that some of the older children even include worm in **wug** life-forms.

Marking and the Encoding of "Snake" and "Worm"

By frequency of use, complexity of form, and child acquisition criteria cross-linguistically "snake" is unmarked vis-à-vis "worm," which is marked. Universal marking values of these items should also be reflected by the two other features of marking outlined earlier, implicational relationships and language acquisition.

Among the 144 languages surveyed for animal classification 117 have "snake" terms, 59 have "worm" terms, and 17 have terms for categories combining snakes and worms.[8] Among those languages having two or more of these, 52 have both "snake" and "worm" labels, 2 have both "snake and worm" and "worm" terms, and 1 has labels for all three categories of elongated creatures (see case 71b). Languages having a label for only one of these classes breakdown as follows: 65 with "snake" only, 14 with "snake and worm" only, and 4 with "worm" only. Thus, if a language has a term for "worm," chances are extremely high that it will also have a term for "snake." On the other hand, accurately predicting the presence of a "worm" term by the occurrence of a "snake" term in a language is considerably more difficult. Thus, generally, "worm" implies "snake" but not vice versa.[9] This implicational relationship accords with other features of marking showing that "worm" is marked vis-à-vis "snake."

The implicational relationship holding between "snake" and "worm" indicates that "snake" is regularly encoded by languages before "worm." There is independent evidence supporting this from comparative investigations of Mayan and Polynesian languages. While "snake" reconstructs for Proto-Mayan, no such evidence exists supporting a reconstruction of Proto-Mayan "worm." Indeed, "worm" terms are very late developments in contemporary daughter languages, some of which have yet to acquire them. Similarly, the zoological life-form inventory of Proto-Polynesian included a term for "snake" but not one for "worm." The several contemporary Polynesian languages that have "worm" terms acquired them quite recently. Thus in both Mayan and Polynesian languages encoding of "snake" has preceded encoding of "worm." This too, of course, is indicative of the marked status of "worm" vis-à-vis "snake."

The universally marked status of "worm" vis-à-vis "snake" is plausibly linked to relative size. Because of their small size, worms are inconspicuous elongated creatures compared to snakes. In addition, worms are habitually found living in things or under something, factors contributing to a general lack of visibility. Although worms constitute a clear break in nature, their distinctiveness as a natural discontinuity is somewhat minimized by their smallness and their living habits. In other words, compared to snakes, worms are not perceptually salient.

Evidence assembled in preceding sections also indicates that terms for "worm," if not marked relative to terms for **wug**, **mammal**, and combined **wug-mammal**, have roughly the same marking values as the latter labels. The occurrence of "worm" terms among the 144 surveyed languages in relation to the occurrence of labels for **wug**, **mammal**, and combined **wug-mammal** supports this observation. For example, terms for "worms" are found in 28 languages which altogether lack **wug**, **mammal**, and combined **wug-mammal**. On the other hand, there are 47 languages having one or more of the latter classes which lack "worm." Therefore, the occurrence of a "worm" term in a language does not necessarily imply **wug** or **mammal** or **wug-mammal**, or vice versa. Since implicational relationships do not hold between "worm" and the latter categories, there is no reason to presume that "worm" regularly precedes or follows them in encoding.

As mentioned in preceding chapters, snakes and worms are relatively often included in **wug** or **mammal** or **wug-mammal** in languages actually having labeled "snake" and "worm" categories. This tendency is somewhat stronger for worms than for snakes. In addition, when labels for "snake" and/or "worm" are lacking in a language, there is a tendency to include these creatures in **wug** or **mammal** or **wug-mammal** if these exist. This is somewhat more the case for worms than for snakes since general terms for the former are more often missing in languages than terms for the latter. When worms are so classified, they are lumped with bugs in **wug** (or with bugs and mammals in combined **wug-mammal**), and they are never grouped with large creatures in **mammal**. This tendency is another reflection of the fact that worms as a grouping are roughly equivalent in salience to **wug/mammal/wug-mammal** as measured by marking criteria. Thus, lack of perceptual salience of worms due primarily to small size leads more than occasionally to their grouping with other small creatures which are also relatively lacking in salience.

EXPLANATORY
FRAMEWORK

What factors determine linguistic marking? Specifically, in the present context, what generates marking hierarchies for folk botanical and zoological life-forms? Since relative marking values of **tree**, **grerb**, **grass**, **vine**, and **bush** and of **bird**, **fish**, **snake**, **wug**, and **mammal** are uniform across languages, conditions affecting these values must themselves, for the most part, be regular across languages.

In this chapter, possible influences are considered in detail. An explanatory framework is proposed to account for plant and animal life-form encoding sequences and related features of marking. Incorporated into this framework are several factors that seem to influence naming behavior to a significant extent, including (1) conjunctivity (underlying binary opposition), (2) dimension salience, and (3) criteria clustering (relating to discontinuities in nature).[1]

BOTANICAL LIFE-FORMS

The special encoding priority of **tree** and **grerb** (cf. Figure 2, Chapter 3) is probably attributable in part to the general human tendency to classify by means of binary opposition. When **grerb** is encoded at Stage 3 as a second plant life-form class, it and **tree** completely or nearly completely partition the botanical world into two large contrasting groups of plants. By so doing, **tree** and **grerb** categories constitute a binary opposition.

Classification through binary opposition is a common feature of language. Physical and conceptual dimensions are universally encoded initially through binary contrast, e.g., deep/shallow, long/short, sharp/blunt, rough/smooth, good/bad. Only later are such dimensions recognized by single terms, e.g., depth, length, sharpness, texture, and value respectively. The priority of binary contrast in dimension encoding is often apparent in the development of terms for whole dimensions. These are frequently derived from one of the two labels for associated oppositions: for example, depth from deep and sharpness from sharp.

Sometimes classification of natural objects involves their "dimensionalization." In other words, they are treated as if they are distributed along a dimension and accordingly encoded through binary contrast. Encoding of both plant and animal life-form classes through binary opposition is relatively common. This often involves the dimension size, especially in the zoological realm. For example, among languages surveyed for animal classification a relatively large number encode **bird** through a "large bird"/"small bird" contrast. In addition, **snake** is typically encoded through binary contrast based on size: "snake" (large elongated creature)/"worm" (small elongated creature). Other animal life-form classes are also encoded through binary opposition (e.g., "large fish"/"small fish") but usually somewhat less frequently across languages than **bird** and **snake**.

Examples of individual botanical life-forms realized as binary oppositions based on size are not as pervasive as those found for the animal domain. One example is Ngbaka Ma'bo (83a) which encodes **grerb** by lexically distinguishing a "big herbaceous plant"/"small herbaceous plant" contrast. Another example is Amahuaca (116a) which lexically encodes both a "large grass" category and a "small grass" one. Life-form categories can be distinguished through binary contrast in terms of other dimensions as well. In the plant domain a common one is "ligneousness" versus "herbaceousness." For example, some languages encode **vine** through a "woody vine"/"nonwoody vine" contrast, e.g., Ixil (66a), Ngbaka Ma'bo (83a), and Malagasy (186a).

Binary opposition exists as the only way of encoding a dimension through use of two terms while not violating the principle of conjunctivity (Witkowski and Brown 1978a; Brown and Witkowski 1980). Recognition of dimensional concepts such as depth, sharpness, texture, and value through binary contrast is conjunctive naming behavior. A logically possible alternate way of encoding a dimension would be to name its midsection with a single term and its two extremes with another. However, this never occurs in dimensional naming because it would contravene conjunctivity. The category combining dimensional extremes would be disjunctive, and such categories are rare in human naming systems. Binary opposition represents the only conjunctive way of encoding a dimension through use of two terms. Thus use of binary contrast in dimension encoding is the surface result of conjunctivity considerations.

For the same reason, classifying by dimensionalizing natural objects always entails binary opposition. Languages could, for instance, categorize birds through attention to size by assigning a name to all midsized birds and another to all very large and very small birds. Because treating birds in such a way would violate conjunctivity, this does not occur. Combining very large and very small birds (minus midsized ones) would be disjunctive. Consequently, oppositional categorization of objects in terms of underlying dimensions is also a surface result of conjunctivity.

When botanical objects are dimensionalized and encoded through binary contrast, this most frequently involves either the dimension size or the dimension "ligneousness" (versus "herbaceousness"). The importance of these two dimensions in botanical classification illustrates the principle of dimension salience. Highly salient dimensions pertain to large and varied sets of objects. Dimensions are not particularly salient if they apply only to a small number of different objects. Since all botanical organisms vary by size and ligneousness, there is a tendency for these dimensions to underlie encoding of plant classes through binary contrast.

This tendency is highlighted by the fact that the common **tree/grerb** opposition involves both size and ligneousness. **Tree** encompasses plants that are both large and ligneous and contrasts with **grerb**, which includes plants that are both small and herbaceous.

The priority of the **tree/grerb** contrast in plant life-form encoding is in part attributable to criteria clustering. As discussed at length in Chapter 2, feature or attribute clustering underlies discontinuities in nature. A discontinuity is in evidence when certain features of natural objects correlate or cluster so that the presence of any one feature is highly predictive of the presence of other features. The example referred to in Chapter 2 is that of birds in general, i.e., creatures possessing feathers, wings, a bill or beak, and characteristic legs. Any one of the latter features is anticipatory of the others. For example, if a creature has feathers, it will inevitably also have wings, a bill or beak, and characteristic legs. Thus, attributes of the discontinuity "birds in general" cluster together, that is, they are highly correlated with one another.

The possibility that classes of botanical objects will be encoded through binary opposition is greatly enhanced if a discontinuity in nature is also pertinent. This is especially true if the discontinuity is underlain by feature clustering involving variables of two or more highly salient dimensions. For example, in the plant world large size is naturally correlated with ligneousness (woodiness) and small size is correlated with herbaceousness (nonwoodiness or leafiness). These physical associations create natural breaks that reinforce the tendency to make an initial **tree/grerb** distinction in plant life-form encoding. Figure 5 graphically illustrates this binary contrast and associated criteria clustering. It shows that by encoding **tree** and **grerb** languages simultaneously make two sets of dimensional oppositions, i.e., large/small and woody/nonwoody, through use of only two terms.

Languages tend to vary with respect to the definitional weight their speak-

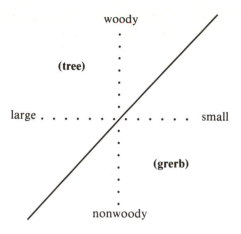

Figure 5. Binary distinctions pertaining to the encoding of **tree** and **grerb**.

ers assign to each of the two dimensions underlying the **tree/grerb** contrast. Some tend to emphasize ligneousness, some size, and some treat both dimensions as equal components in distinguishing **tree/grerb**. An example of the latter is Daga (135a). The source for this language writes that Daga **tree** "includes any vegetation that is large [and] has a wood texture to the trunk (thus bananas are excluded)," while plants identified by Daga **grerb** "basically . . . are any types of vegetation that are smaller than a tree [and] have no wood texture."

When both dimensions are not weighted equally, there is a tendency to include plants in **tree** that are not woody or are not large, and to include plants in **grerb** that are not herbaceous or are not small. For example, "woodiness" versus "nonwoodiness" apparently is emphasized by speakers of Cora (182a). Since herbaceousness rather than size is significant in its definition, Cora **grerb** encompasses some very large herbaceous plants indeed. These include, among others, the elephant-ear plant, the sunflower, sugar cane, and the maguey plant. The situation is reversed for speakers of Koiwai (74a), who clearly focus on size. As a result, any large plant—i.e., any plant roughly more than one-foot off the ground—regardless of stem texture is denoted by Koiwai **tree**: e.g., banana plants, palms, rotans, and all vines. When size is emphasized, **grerb** terms are often used to designate small trees (e.g., young or stunted ones) in addition to small herbaceous plants. Similarly, **tree** terms are often extended to herbaceous plants that are typically small but for one reason or another have grown with exceptional vigor. Such varying emphases and applications relating to **tree** and **grerb**, when pertinent, are described in discussions accompanying language cases presented in Appendix A.

When languages encode only one-half of the **tree**/**grerb** opposition, **tree** rather than **grerb** is regularly encoded. **Tree**, of course, precedes **grass**, **vine**, and **bush**, as well as **grerb**, in botanical life-form growth (cf. Figure 2). The priority of **tree** probably relates in part to the fact that trees are the largest plants in environments and thus "stand out" vis-à-vis other plants. In other words, in addition to constituting a clear discontinuity in nature trees are especially distinct or salient because of their large size. As a consequence, the **tree** discontinuity is more compelling in botanical life-form classification than the **grerb** discontinuity. Since **tree** precedes all other life-forms of the encoding sequence, this indicates that it is the most distinctive large botanical discontinuity of all.

In addition to its developmental priority, **tree** is of course unmarked vis-à-vis **grerb** and other botanical life-forms. The unmarked status of **tree** conforms with a zero-to-infinity principle associated with the linguistic marking of adjectival oppositions. Greenberg (1975: 90) cites several adjectival pairs—deep/shallow, wide/narrow, long/short, and large/small—which enter into universal marking patterns. In all cases, the marked item of the adjectival pair is associated with the "zero" point of the relevant dimension, while the unmarked item is associated with deviation from the zero point, the "infinite" end. For example, "deep" is universally unmarked while "shallow" is marked, "wide" is unmarked while "narrow" is marked and so forth. For all dimensions with a clear physical interpretation and a zero point, there is a tendency to treat the "infinite" pole preferentially, resulting in its unmarked status. This tendency also occurs in botanical life-form classification where **tree** or "large plant" universally emerges as unmarked vis-à-vis **grerb** or "small plant." The dimension involved is, of course, size.[2]

According to Clark (1973) the zero-to-infinity principle is attributable in part to the canonical posture and movement of human beings (i.e., upright and forward). Consequently, humans universally perceive physical space from the same perspective and in much the same manner, for example, recognizing the same "zero" and "infinite" ends of physical dimensions. However, this does not account for why "infinite" poles are always treated preferentially. A plausible explanation is that humans are in some way internally predisposed or constrained to do so. In other words, our species may be innately wired in some general way to process dimensional information by focusing primarily on "infinite" poles and only secondarily on "zero" poles.

There is another factor which possibly contributes to the priority of **tree**. It is argued in Chapter 6 that lack of apt lexical materials for constructing life-forms possibly inhibits life-form encoding. For example, the recency of **grerb** terms in Polynesian and Mayan languages may be due in part to the probability that "weed," "underbrush," and similar categories were encoded late in these languages. Terms for such special purpose classes are commonly extended to **grerb** since they are about as close in referential extension to that life-form as one can get without actually labeling **grerb**. If such categories are lacking in languages, as they often are in those spoken by nonagricultural groups, chances that **grerb** will be innovated are possibly less than otherwise.

While apt lexical materials for innovating **grerb** have not always been available in languages, this is clearly not the case for **tree**. As noted in Chapter 6, most of the world's languages (roughly two-thirds) probably have innovated **tree** by extending a term for wood to the life-form class. Terms for wood, of course, are of high utility and usually have been added to languages long before plant life-form classes such as **tree** and **grerb** (which tend to develop rather late in languages in response to increases in societal scale [see Chapter 5]). As a result, "wood" terms have been readily available in most languages to be pressed into service as **tree** life-form labels. In brief, the common availability of a highly apt lexical item for innovating **tree**, i.e., "wood," probably partly explains the developmental priority of this life-form class.

Grerb and Grass

When languages encode only one-half of the **tree**/**grerb** opposition, i.e., **tree**, they sometimes subsequently add one or more other botanical life-forms before encoding the other half, i.e., **grerb**. When such is the case, **grass** is virtually always added before **vine** and **bush** at Stage 3 (cf. Figure 2).

The encoding priority of **grass** at Stage 3, relative to **vine** and **bush**, possibly relates in part to the fact that like **grerb**, **grass** contrasts with **tree** along more than one physically continuous dimension. In fact, grasses are more unlike trees than any other plants typically included in botanical life-form classes: (1) grasses are usually small, while trees are large, (2) grasses are herbaceous, while trees are ligneous, (3) grasses typically lack substantial central supports, while trees have trunks (on the other hand, nongrass herbaceous plants included in **grerb** often have sturdy stems), and (4) grasses have narrow leaf morphology, while trees usually have broadleaf morphology or needles (on the other hand, nongrass herbaceous plants included in **grerb** usually have broadleaf morphology).

If the initial encoding of plant life-forms always entails binary opposition, then the usual encoding of either **grerb** or **grass**, but not **vine** or **bush**, at Stage 3 is understandable. Both **grerb** and **grass** are obvious physical opposites of **tree**. **Grerb** opposes **tree** since it encompasses most, if not all, plants other than trees (at least at Stage 3). **Grass** opposes **tree** since it includes those herbaceous plants which are most unlike trees. Thus the encoding of both **grerb** and **grass** at Stage 3 involves binary opposition: **grerb** as the *general* opposite of **tree**, and **grass** as the *specific* opposite of **tree**.[3]

As noted in Chapter 3, languages are somewhat more likely to encode **grerb** at Stage 3 than **grass**. Thus there is a tendency for languages to encode the general opposite of **tree** rather than its specific opposite. In fact, a **tree/grerb** partitioning of the plant world may have a certain utilitarian edge over a **tree/grass** partitioning. As outlined in Chapter 6, languages add botanical life-forms in response to a general decrease of interest in and concern with nature. Life-form categories become important when people need only to refer to plants in a general manner. In this context a **tree/grerb** contrast is highly apt and useful since it permits people to refer to virtually *all* plants in their environments through use of general terms. On the other hand, since a **tree/grass** distinction does not extend to all plants—it does not encompass nongrass herbaceous plants—it may be somewhat less apt and useful.

However, it is also the case that **grass** has a certain encoding advantage not pertaining to **grerb**. This is that grasses constitute a more salient discontinuity in nature than small herbaceous plants in general. **Grass** is clearly a less heterogeneous category than **grerb** and, therefore, more distinctive. In addition to both bladed and nonbladed small herbaceous plants, **grerb** life-forms frequently encompass vines and bushes, and, occasionally, even small trees. On the other hand, **grass** life-forms are restricted to only those small herbaceous plants with bladed leaves. Since highly distinctive breaks in nature are usually closely followed in the folk classification of biological organisms (cf. Hunn 1976, 1977), it is perhaps surprising that morphologically less distinct **grerb** tends to precede **grass** in encoding. This suggests that gross utilitarian considerations may sometimes override morphological ones in life-form encoding. Thus **grerb** is more often encoded at Stage 3 than **grass**, a more distinctive break in nature than **grerb**, possibly because **grerb** is a better utilitarian category, that is, it extends to a larger range of plants than does **grass**.[4]

The fact that **grass** is sometimes encoded at Stage 3 is difficult to explain if **grerb** indeed has a utilitarian advantage. One plausible explanation is that life-form encoding at Stage 3 is also environmentally sensitive. This would be the case if languages having **grass** but lacking **grerb** are usually associated (a) with environments such as savannahs, prairies, and high altitude areas in which grasses are the most conspicuous and ubiquitous small herbaceous plants or (b) with environments such as deserts and tundra in which diversity of small herbaceous plants is minimal. While I have not collected detailed information on environmental associations of language cases, clearly many languages of the sample having **grass** but not **grerb** are spoken in world regions in which environments such as those described in (a) and (b) above are common (e.g., Dugum Dani [31a], Eskimo [32a], Gilbertese [33a], Kiowa Apache [35a], Northern Paiute [38a], Shoshoni [39a], Southern Tiwa [42a],

Tarahumara [43a], Wik Moŋkan [44a], Atapec Zapotec [117a], Bororo [168a], and Lotuho [172a]). It is also clear that the vast majority of these languages are not spoken in areas characterized by extensive botanical species diversity such as found in tropical rain forests.

The addition of **grass** rather than **grerb** at Stage 3 may also relate to another factor. If apt lexical materials for constructing **grerb** (e.g., terms for weed, scrub, etc.) are not readily available in a language when pressures initially develop for adding a life-form beyond **tree**, then encoding of **grerb** may be inhibited or, at least, delayed. As a result, a language may seize upon the less functional, specific opposite of **tree**, i.e., **grass**, in completing life-form classification through binary opposition. This, of course, assumes that apt lexical materials of some sort for constructing **grass** are available in the language.

Vine and Bush

Only one Stage 3 language, Paacas Novos (40a), combines **tree** with a life-form, i.e., **vine**, other than **grerb** or **grass**. The possible Stage 3 combinations **tree + vine** and **tree + bush** are extremely rare (the latter may not occur at all in languages) for several possible reasons. First, assuming that binary opposition is always the initial strategy in plant life-form encoding, **vine** and **bush** are not added at Stage 3 since neither is obviously an opposite of **tree** along any physical dimension. For example, vines do not contrast with trees along the dimension size since both very large vines and very small ones are often present in environments; nor do vines oppose trees along the dimension "ligneousness" since both woody and nonwoody varieties occur. Similarly, bushes are both ligneous and herbaceous. In addition, while bushes are smaller than trees, they are not proper opposites of trees since they do not include all plants which are smaller than trees. Bushes are, in fact, intermediate in size between trees and small herbaceous plants such as grasses.

Another factor possibly relating to the rarity of **tree + vine** and **tree + bush** in Stage 3 languages is that these, like the **tree + grass** combination, would not seem to be as useful or as utilitarian as the usual **tree + grerb** combination. In other words, these distinctions do not facilitate reference to virtually all plants in an environment through use of general terms. Of course, **tree + grass** does occur at Stage 3 with some regularity even though not especially utilitarian (at least relative to the **tree + grerb** combination), but this relates to the fact that this combination at least makes sense in a framework of binary contrast. The Stage 3 combinations **tree + vine** and **tree + bush**, then, are neither particularly functional nor involve binary oppositions. Possibly these two factors partly explain why neither **vine** nor **bush** is commonly encoded after **tree** at Stage 3 in life-form growth.

The late encoding of **vine** is perhaps surprising since, like grasses, vines constitute a relatively distinct discontinuity in nature. Plants included in **vine** are relatively homogenous all having elongated stems with varying degrees of flexibility. Of course, despite its distinctiveness as a natural break, **vine** is only very rarely encoded before **grass** and **grerb** at Stage 3. Considerations outlined in the preceding two paragraphs presumably mean that the significance of morphological distinctiveness as a factor leading to the lexical encoding of **vine** is lessened. However, the lateness of **vine** possibly also involves another factor. Even though vines constitute a clear discontinuity in nature, they are not usually very conspicuous in the wild compared to plants pertaining to other life-form classes. This is primarily due to the fact that most vines require other plants to support their growth. As a consequence, vines typically do not grow in open, clear areas on their own and, thus, lack the visibility of plants such as trees, bushes, and grasses. This lack of conspicuousness (relative to that of other plants) may function to minimize somewhat their salience as a discontinuity in nature.

Of the five life-forms of the encoding sequence, **bush** perhaps constitutes the least distinctive discontinuity and this undoubtedly contributes to its late addition to languages. Basically **bush** encompasses those plants with extensive branching which are intermediate in size relative to the plant inventory of an environment. No clearcut dimensions other than bushiness and size seem to pertain to the life-form and, therefore, criteria clustering is only weakly in evidence.

Within the marking hierarchy for folk botanical life-forms, **tree**, **grerb**, and **bush** form a special marking sequence based on a shared physical dimension. The lexical encoding of **bush** involves further attention to the size dimension underlying the **tree/grerb** opposition. **Bush** is of intermediate size relative to the latter two life-forms. Usually only after the **tree/grerb** distinction is made and biggest plants are distinguished from smallest ones, will a **bush** class be recognized which consists of those botanical organisms that are smaller than the largest plants and larger than the smallest plants in any given environment. Thus **tree**, **grerb**, and **bush** form a marking sequence based on size in which **tree** is least marked, **bush** is most marked, and **grerb** is in between in marking value.[5]

ZOOLOGICAL LIFE-FORMS

The unmarked status and encoding priority of **bird**, **fish**, and **snake** vis-à-vis **wug** and **mammal** (Figure 3, Chapter 3) is due in part to the fact that these constitute highly distinctive discontinuities in nature and thus are especially salient. The nature of clustering attributes pertaining to the **bird** discontinuity was discussed earlier. Similarly, **fish** and **snake** have respective sets of defining features showing high levels of mutual predictability. The occurrence of fins predicts a streamlined body and gills, and greatly elongated creatures usually lack appendages as well as feathers and fur.

The marked status and late encoding of **wug** and **mammal** is in part attributable to their relative indistinctiveness as natural discontinuities vis-à-vis the distinctiveness of **bird**, **fish**, and **snake**. In fact, these may not constitute true discontinuities in nature. Both **wug** and **mammal** are exceptionally heterogeneous, demonstrating little criteria clustering. For example, while most mammals have four appendages used for locomotion and/or object manipulation, so do many other animals including such common creatures as lizards, salamanders, frogs, and turtles. Consequently, possession of four appendages is not particularly predictive of other faunal characteristics such as fur or hair. Exemplars of **wug** have even less in common than creatures included in **mammal**. **Wug**, for example, encompasses animals having legs and lacking them, having wings and lacking them, having segments and lacking them, and so on.

* * *

After the three major zoological discontinuities are encoded as life-form classes, there remains a large and varied group of creatures none of which unambiguously fit into any life-form classes based on discontinuities in nature. These left over or "residual" creatures often include mammals, lizards, frogs, turtles, snails, worms, and bugs to mention just the more obvious ones. Life-form encoding beyond **bird**, **fish**, and **snake** regularly involves lexical recognition of subgroupings of these animals. However, among residual creatures distinct large discontinuities are not easily discerned since criteria clustering is not much, if at all, in evidence. As a consequence, languages usually resort to a common classificatory strategy that need not necessarily involve distinct discontinuities, that is, binary opposition based on the salient dimension size. Thus the addition of **wug** and **mammal** encodes the contrast "small residual creature"/"large residual creature."[6]

That the residual life-form classes **wug** and **mammal** are encoded late by languages, that is, after **bird**, **fish**, and **snake**, is due in part to the fact that the possibility of lexically distinguishing creatures by size is not enhanced by criteria clustering. There are, of course, several languages among those surveyed in Appendix B that have encoded one or both residual life-form classes before encoding all of the triad **bird**, **fish**, and **snake**. However, the rarity of such cases attests to lack of empirical motivation (i.e., true discontinuities) for making a "big creature"/"little creature" distinction. Such a contrast will usually be made only after all other more obvious possibilities have been exhausted, that is, only after the distinct large discontinuities **bird**, **fish**, and **snake** have been lexically encoded.

Of course, some habitats may support fewer of these obvious possibilities (distinct large discontinuities) than others. In other words, exemplars of nonresidual life-form classes may be lacking or scarce in some environments. In this event languages may exhaust all obvious possibilities in animal life-form classification without encoding all three of the triad **bird**, **fish**, and **snake**. If such languages then go on to encode residual creatures through binary opposition, this, of course, would create combinations of life-form terms not in accord with the encoding sequence (for examples, see language cases 68b, 69b, 117b, 118b, and 119b, Appendix B).

There is another way of dealing with residual creatures which is occasionally resorted to by languages. Instead of lexically recognizing them through binary opposition based on size, some languages simply regard residual creatures, both large and small, as forming a unified grouping which is encoded by use of a single term. This, of course, creates combined **wug-mammal** life-form classes (see language cases 114b, 115b, 116b, 142b, 143b, and 144b).

The relative rarity of combined **wug-mammal** among the 144 languages surveyed suggests that humans are usually disinclined to use classificatory strategies that do not incorporate substantive defining features. Membership in a combined **wug-mammal** category does not involve actual morphological characteristics of creatures but rather their lack of membership in other life-form classes. On the other hand, the binary contrast **wug/mammal** does entail a morphological feature, that is, animal size. The relatively high frequency of occurrence of the latter contrast indicates that humans are somehow more comfortable with life-form classes which are anchored in objective reality, even if only minimally so.

A classic example of the **wug/mammal** contrast is described by Evans-Pritchard (1963) for the Azande (122b). He reports the following extensions for Azande **mammal** (*anya*) and **wug** (*agbiro*), respectively: "Reptiles, except the snakes, tend to be described as *anya* . . . if they are large and as *agbiro* . . . if they are small" (1963: 139). Thus Azande *anya* encompasses such creatures as iguanas in addition to mammals. Evans-Pritchard also notes that Azande *agbiro* encompasses toads and tortoises in addition to bugs and small nonsnake reptiles.

Mammal and **wug** in Hill Pandaram (131b) parallel Azande life-forms. Morris describes Hill Pandaram **mammal** as follows:

The category *mrgam* includes not only all known species of mammals . . . but several of the large species of reptiles. It excludes however snakes . . . and smaller reptiles and amphibia which are normally referred to, if categorized at all, as *puchi* (1976: 349–350).

Morris (1976: 348) describes *puchi* (**wug**) as "a residual category . . . which includes insects, crustaceans and several other creatures."

The lumping of large creatures that are not mammals with mammals in **mammal** and small creatures that are not bugs with bugs in **wug** is evidence that these categories are based on animal residualness and size rather than on discontinuities in nature. In addition to Azande and Hill Pandaram, many languages of those surveyed (Appendix B) incorporate creatures such as lizards, salamanders, toads, frogs, tortoises, and turtles into **wug** and **mammal** life-form classes. Worms, of course, are also frequently included in **wug**. Apparently in many cases the fact that worms are elongated creatures is not as important with respect to their life-form class affiliation as is the fact that they are small.

Other creatures are found in residual life-form classes but somewhat less frequently. For example, Siane (140b) speakers include fresh water eels and cassowaries in their "large mammal" category. The inclusion of eels may relate to the fact that they are not found in the Siane environment and are known only through trade. Cassowaries, probably because they are large and flightless, are excluded from **bird** life-forms in Siane and in several other related New Guinea languages such as Fore (129b) and Kalam (101b). Siane differs from the latter languages since instead of treating aberrant cassowaries as unaffiliated with all major life-form classes, its speakers have incorporated these creatures into their named grouping of the largest residual animals. Daga (142b) speakers have responded in a similar manner to the unusualness of cassowaries by including them in their combined **wug-mammal** class. Some speakers of Awtuw (93b) recognize cassowaries as belonging to both **bird** and **mammal** life-form classes.

While bugs are regularly included in **wug** and mammals in **mammal**, certain other residual creatures, such as frogs and toads, are just as likely to be found in one of these classes as the other. For example, frogs and/or toads are lumped with mammals in **mammal** in at least nine languages of those sampled: Kalam (101b), Muinane (105b), Patep (107b), Tepehua (108b), American English (120b), Czech (125b), Gbaya Kara (130b), Mataco (135b), and North Saami (139b). On the other hand, at least nine other languages include frogs and/or toads in **wug**: Dugum Dani (68b), Ndumba (119b), Anindilyakwa (121b), Azande (122b), Hill Pandaram (131b), Kilangi (133b), Minnesota Ojibwa (136b), Northern Ojibwa (138b) (see associated discussion), and Siane (140b). In addition, according to the *Oxford English Dictionary* the British English **wug** term, *insect*, in the past extended to frogs and other small creatures which are not true insects or true bugs: an entry for *insect* reads, "formerly (and still by the uneducated) applied still more widely, e.g., to earthworms, snails, and even some small vertebrates, as frogs and tortoises."

Variability across languages with respect to inclusion of frogs and toads in **wug** or **mammal** probably relates to the fact that in typical habitats these residual animals are smaller than most mammals and larger than most bugs; in other words, they are midsized. As a consequence, their assignment to either **wug** or **mammal** is highly sensitive to fine distinctions concerning animal size. Thus, those languages including frogs and toads in **wug** have drawn the line separating big residual creatures from little residual creatures at a place along a continuum of animals ranked by size which is different from the point at which it is drawn by languages placing frogs and toads in **mammal**.

On occasion variability with respect to drawing such a line is found even within a single language community. Such is the case for Minnesota Ojibwa (136b) which has both a **wug** category and a **mammal** life-form encoded through binary opposition, i.e., "small mammal"/"large mammal." Certain residual creatures tend to shift between these three categories apparently depending on context and speaker. Creatures involved are turtles, crabs, frogs, toads, mice, woodchucks, squirrels, foxes, gophers, and the dog. The latter six mammals, with the possible exception of mice, presumably shift between "small mammal" and "large mammal." Crabs, frogs, and toads (and possibly mice) presumably shift between **wug** and "small mammal." One creature, the turtle, in fact can be placed in any one of the three residual classes apparently depending on actual size.

Nomenclature is sometimes indicative of the roles of size and residualness in the derivation of residual life-form classes. For instance, languages having zoological unique beginners, such as English *creature*, will occasionally encode **wug** through use of descriptive labels translating "little creature": for examples, see Kikamba (77b), Malagasy (79b), and Sierra Popoluca (87b). The residualness of creatures such as bugs is sometimes indicated by their designation through use of modified general terms that are even broader in referential scope than "creature." For example, Mende's (82b) **wug** term is a compound label translating literally "living thing" (also see discussions associated with cases 72b and 89b).

Though the tendency to add **bird, fish,** and **snake** before **wug** and **mammal** is obviously strong, a few languages have encoded one or both of the latter two life-forms before all three of the initial triad have been encoded. In most instances the premature addition of **wug** and/or **mammal** is traced to environmental factors as described in Chapter 3 (see cases 68b, 69b, 117b, 118b, and 119b). When the latter is not the case, the residual nature of **wug** and **mammal** should be evidenced by the inclusion in these categories of creatures normally affiliated with life-forms encoded before **wug** and **mammal**, but which have not in fact been encoded. This is so since the latter creatures would in fact be "residual," that is left over after a language has lexically recognized all of the distinct discontinuities it desires to at a particular point in time. For example, if a language has **wug** and/or **mammal** but not **bird**, then we should expect birds to be treated as additional residual creatures categorized by size.

This in fact has occurred in the one deviant language case not explained by ecological factors. Dalabon (67b) having **fish** but lacking both **bird** and **snake** lumps residual birds and residual snakes with insects, small marsupials, and other residual creatures in **wug**. Similarly, Ibataan (98b), a nondeviant language which has encoded "worm" but not "snake," includes residual snakes in **mammal** along with mammals, lizards, and sea turtles.

Lack of residualness is sometimes overlooked in assigning creatures to **wug**, **mammal**, or combined **wug-mammal**. In other words, occasionally creatures affiliated with a labeled nonresidual life-form category, such as **snake**, are considered to belong to a labeled residual class as well. Dual life-form classification of this type involves only the elongated creatures, worms and snakes. For example, seven languages surveyed, Navaho (83b), Western Subanun (91b), Ndumba (119b), Classical Nahuatl (124b), Kilangi (133b), Minnesota Ojibwa (136b), and North Saami (139b) have labeled "snake" classes but also include snakes in **wug**. Two of the latter, Kilangi and North Saami, also include worms in **wug** even though these creatures are recognized by their own unique labels. Other languages having similar systems of dual life-form classification involving elongated creatures are Pashto (86b), Tepehua (108b), Yolŋu (112b), Mokilese (115b), Tzotzil (116b), Czech (125b), Eskimo (127b), Mataco (135b), Daga (142b), and Southern Paiute (Chemehuevi dialect) (143b).

Nonresidual worms included in a residual category are always placed in **wug** (or combined **wug-mammal**) and never in **mammal**. Of course, when worms are in fact residual creatures—that is, when they are not included in a labeled "worm" class or in a heterogeneous **snake** life-form encompassing snakes and worms—these small elongated creatures are frequently lumped with bugs in **wug**. The inclusion of worms in **wug**, whether residual or not, obviously relates to their small size.

On the other hand, nonresidual snakes are found included in both **wug** and **mammal** classes. However, in the majority of cases they are affiliated with **wug** rather than **mammal**. In Chapter 3 it is suggested that in some instances the inclusion of snakes in **wug** is traced to ecological factors. This explanation handles three languages spoken in northern latitudes where snakes are scarce, of few varieties, and inconspicuous because of small size (Minnesota Ojibwa [136b], Northern Ojibwa [138b], and North Saami [139b]). In other cases such inclusions may be based on perceived similarities between focal small residual creatures, i.e., bugs, and snakes which have nothing to do with residualness and size. People may conceptualize snakes as being like bugs because they are unattractive creatures, annoying creatures, feared creatures, biting creatures, dangerous creatures, mysterious creatures, and so on. For example, such criteria apparently underlie the inclusion of snakes in **wug** by speakers of Ndumba (119b) (Hays 1983).

COMPARATIVE OVERVIEW

Addition of animal life-form terms to languages departs noticeably from the pattern found for plant life-form encoding. The latter pattern, of course, involves an initial partitioning of an entire domain into two opposing halves: **tree** vs. **grerb**. On the other hand, in the case of animals an initial binary distinction, i.e., "small creature" vs. "large creature," is not made. Rather, if a binary contrast is to be encoded at all, it is made only after a large part of the domain is already referentially covered by general animal terms, that is, by terms for **bird**, **fish**, and **snake**. In other words, the animal life-form encoding sequence differs from the plant sequence in that binary opposition (i.e., **wug/mammal**) occurs at the end of the sequence and does not extend to the entire domain (i.e., to all creatures).

There is no evidence that languages regularly, or even occasionally follow the plant life-form pattern when *initially* encoding animal life-forms by partitioning the universe of creatures into large and small ones. For example, of the sample of 144 languages surveyed for animal classification, only three Highland Tequistlatec (14b), Kayapo (76b), and Gbaya Kara (130b), have two terms which completely segregate the animal kingdom into large and small creatures. However, there are no reasons for assuming that these binary oppositions were lexically encoded *before* other general animal categories of the languages, i.e., before **bird**, **fish**, and **snake** (see discussions associated with cases 14b, 76b, 130b). In addition, one other language, Kikamba (77b), lexically encloses a "large creature"/"small creature" contrast, but this distinction does not extend completely to the universe of animals since it does not encompass birds (see discussion associated with case 77b).

Differences in the ways in which the worlds of plants and animals are physically structured apparently results in different approaches to life-form classification involving each domain. That binary contrast based on the salient dimension size regularly figures into the initial encoding of plant, but not animal, life-form classes is probably due to the fact that criteria clustering underlies a botanical size distinction but not a zoological one. Big plants are usually also woody and little plants are usually also herbaceous. On the other hand, big creatures do not show any prominent characteristics which regularly go along with being large and little creatures do not show any prominent features which go along with being small. Thus a possible initial encoding of a "big creature"/"little creature" contrast does not occur since it lacks reinforcement through criteria clustering. However, criteria clustering does produce certain discontinuities in the faunal realm which are associated with initial phases of animal life-form encoding. These are, of course, **bird**, **fish**, and **snake**.

Above it is argued that binary opposition is the preferred classificatory strategy in the initial encoding of broad plant categories since it has a utilitarian advantage over other strategies; that is, it facilitates total referential coverage of a domain through use of general terms. The initial encoding of animal life-form classes, of course, involves only partial referential coverage of the domain of creatures. This indicates that the utilitarian advantage of initial encoding through binary contrast is not a sufficient condition for this distinction to be made. Apparently, such a strategy will be resorted to in initial encoding only if reinforced by other factors. In the case of plants initial binary opposition is reinforced by criteria clustering. In the case of animals it is not, and, hence, initial binary contrast does not occur despite its utilitarian edge over other classificatory strategies.

MARKING AND THE EXPLANATORY FRAMEWORK

This chapter began by asking what generates the universal marking hierarchies for botanical and zoological life-forms. Fundamentally it appears that these hierarchies are products of the manner in which the variables of binary opposition, criteria clustering, and dimension salience, coupled with utilitarian concerns influence naming behavior.

Criteria clustering appears to be an especially important variable in the generation of life-form marking values. For example, the animal life-form marking sequence reflects the indistinctiveness of **wug** and **mammal** as large groupings in nature relative to the distinctiveness of **bird**, **fish**, and **snake**. In other words, terms, for **bird**, **fish**, and **snake** are regularly unmarked vis-à-vis terms for **wug** and **mammal** because the physical objects labeled by the former three words figure into salient large discontinuities in nature while those labeled by the latter two do not. Similarly, of the several large plant discontinuities, **tree** is clearly the most distinctive primarily because it encompasses the largest and, hence, the most conspicuous plants in an environment. As a consequence of its exceptional natural salience, **tree** is unmarked vis-à-vis all other plant life-form classes.

Other details of marking reflect the often complex interaction of criteria clustering and other factors. For example, since **grerb** is a relatively heterogeneous category, it constitutes a somewhat less distinctive break in nature than, say, **grass** or **vine**. However, its very heterogeneity means that **grerb** is a more useful life-form since, in conjunction with **tree**, it facilitates reference to virtually all plants in an environment through use of general terms. Thus a utilitarian consideration tends to magnify **grerb**'s salience as a natural discontinuity resulting in its usual unmarked status relative to other plant life-form classes (excepting, of course, **tree**).

Criteria clustering obviously would not figure prominently into lexical marking if humans were not innately inclined to follow discontinuities in nature when classifying and naming objects. The marking hierarchies, then, are in large part attributable to internal constraints on humans in the processing of external stimuli.

The close agreement of physical-perceptual constraints and linguistic marking values of plant and animal life-forms indicates that the former are converted or translated into the latter. For example, the category **tree** is naturally most salient and is always encoded first in the development of botanical life-form lexicons. Of course, the same is true of **bird, fish,** and **snake** which are encoded first in the zoological sequence. The physical salience of these classes is converted through lexical encoding into linguistic salience which is manifested through typical marking effects such as high frequency of use, simplicity of form, and early acquisition by children learning language.

»9«

CONCLUSION

Preceding chapters describe cross-language regularities in the classification and naming of biological organisms. General purpose categories in folk biological taxonomies are invariably built on discontinuities found in the world of plants and animals. These range from "small" discontinuities which are homogeneous groupings of organisms sharing many morphological features, such as oaks, bluejays, begonias, and trout, to "large" discontinuities which are highly heterogeneous groupings of organisms sharing few morphological features, such as trees in general, birds in general, herbaceous plants in general, and fish in general.

Large and small discontinuities differ in other respects. The number of small discontinuities supported by the world's environments is clearly massive while the number of large discontinuities is very small in comparison. In addition, small discontinuities tend to be environment-specific while large ones are pan-environmental in occurrence. This means that across languages categories based on small discontinuities tend to be very different while those based on large discontinuities tend to be very similar.

In this book languages are compared with regard to which of the large, pan-environmental discontinuities they do and do not encode. Ten large discontinuities, which are encoded by languages over and over again, are singled out for special attention because the classes which reflect them tend to be the most polytypic general purpose categories of folk biological taxonomies. In other words, they regularly include more labeled members than other biological classes of languages. These categories, referred to as "life-form" classes, are **tree**, **grerb** (small herbaceous plant), **bush**, **vine**, and **grass**, and **bird**, **fish**, **snake**, **wug** (e.g., American English *bug*), and **mammal**.[1] There are other large biological discontinuities which are encoded by languages, but categories reflecting them are not regularly found among the most polytypic plant and animal classes of taxonomies. Examples of the latter are lichens and fungi, ants, spiders, wasps, and moths and butterflies, to mention just a few.

Cross-language comparison reveals implicational relationships holding among botanical and zoological subsets of the ten life-form classes identified above. From these relationships are inferred lexical encoding sequences for both plant and animal life-form categories (Figures 2 and 3, Chapter 3). The two encoding sequences are interpreted as a series of stages in the growth of plant and animal life-form vocabularies.

Stage 1 languages in the plant sequence (Figure 2) do not encode any of the five botanical life-forms. At Stage 2 **tree** is lexically encoded. A **tree** term in early stage languages usually extends to a wider range of plants than **tree** terms in later stage languages. It frequently includes woody bushes and shrubs in addition to trees and, occasionally even woody vines. At Stage 3 either a **grerb** or **grass** term is added, the former being somewhat more likely to emerge at this stage than the latter. If **grerb** is encoded at Stage 3, **vine**, **grass**, and **bush** will be added from Stage 4 to Stage 6. While the latter addition involves no strict order, there is a tendency for **vine** to precede **grass** and **bush** in encoding. If **grass** is added at Stage 3, **grerb**, **vine**, and **bush** will be encoded from Stage 4 to 6, although in no particular order.

When a **grerb** term is added at Stage 3, it typically encompasses most, if not all, small herbaceous plants including grasses, i.e., those plants not included in the **tree** class. When languages have encoded both **grerb** and **grass**, **grerb** tends to include only nongrass herbaceous plants. **Grass**, **vine**, and **bush** categories are often composed of plants previously included in **grerb** and **tree**. Thus, the lexical encoding of **bush**, for example, involves pulling bushes and shrubs from the range of **grerb** or **tree**, or from the ranges of both, as the case may be.

Stage 0 languages in the animal sequence (Figure 3) encode none of the five zoological life-forms. **Fish**, **bird**, and **snake** are added from Stage 1 to 3, although in no particular order. At Stage 4 languages encode either **wug** or **mammal** and the remaining animal life-form is encoded at Stage 5. **Wug** and **mammal** are "residual" life-form classes, encompassing small and large creatures respectively that are not included in earlier encoded **fish**, **bird**, and **snake** categories. Occasionally residual creatures, both small and large, are lumped together in a single labeled class creating a combined **wug-mammal** life-form. Implicational relationships apparent in cross-language data indicate that combined **wug-mammal** is typically encoded by languages after **fish**, **bird**, and **snake**.

In addition to implicational relationships, other types of evidence attest to the life-form encoding orders. For example, reconstruction of plant and animal life-form growth through use of the comparative method of historical linguistics shows that languages have historically added life-form terms to their vocabularies in the orders of Figures 2 and 3. Most significantly, the encoding sequences are shown to be merely one index of universal marking hierarchies for plant and animal life-form classes. These marking hierarchies are also evidenced in individual languages by frequency of use of life-form terms, by term complexity (morphological and phonological), and by order in which these are acquired by children learning language.

Other regularities pertain to life-form classification. For instance, there are relatively strong positive correlations between size of life-form vocabularies of languages and the societal scale associated with their speakers. Languages spoken by people of large urban societies tend to encode more plant and animal life-form classes than languages spoken by individuals of small scale, nonurbanized societies. Since societal scale has generally increased during the last several millennia of human history, these associations indicate that languages have tended to acquire life-form categories over time rather than lose them. This proposal is supported by language reconstruction showing that proto-languages (ancestral languages) spoken in the remote past usually had fewer life-form terms than their modern descendent languages.

In addition to classificatory uniformities, nomenclatural regularities are in evidence. In other words, across languages similar strategies for developing names for life-form classes tend to be employed. In many cases these strategies involve strikingly detailed similarities. For example, terms for **grerb** in many genetically and geographically unrelated languages have developed from words for rubbish, garbage, trash, litter, rotten stuff, and the like. Such parallels plausibly arise due to similar constraints on life-form growth stemming from similar ways in which societies in different parts of the world have changed over time with increases in size and complexity.

Larger Issues

While documentation of uniformities in biological classification and nomenclature is of interest itself, of equal importance are frameworks of understanding that can be developed to account for them. Such frameworks can help delineate shared processes underlying human language and cognition. An explanatory framework is proposed in Chapter 8. Whether this particular proposal is definitive or not, it is important to recognize that cross-language research will advance our understanding of the nature of language and cognition only if such interpretations are forthcoming. In concluding this book, an attempt is made to relate regularities uncovered and their provisional explanations to larger issues by focusing on their possible implications for a theory of the human language faculty.

In discussing the nature of the human language faculty, a distinction must be drawn between knowledge of an individual language such as Chinese, English, or Hopi—knowledge which is entirely learned—and knowledge of the design principles of "language" itself. Since the rise of transformational-generative grammar and more recent derivative grammatical theories, it has been argued that the underlying template of human "language" is innate. For example, Chomsky (1975: 219) proposes that humans start life with innate knowledge of "the form and character of grammars and the principles by which grammars operate."

At issue is the degree of specificity of these design principles. Chomsky's discussions of universals of syntax stress the detailed specificity of these uniformities. He rejects attempts to account for language universals by appealing to very general, non-specific mechanisms. Cognitive psychologists and others tend to appeal to "information processing" models of the human language faculty. Language learning is explained in terms of innate but very general mechanisms for processing primary linguistic data of individual languages. A position combining detailed specificity and information processing, a "rich cognition" model, has been proposed by Witkowski and me (Witkowski and Brown 1978a; Brown and Witkowski 1980). This model supposes that some aspects of the human language faculty involve detailed design principles; however, the remainder and much the larger part is attributed to innate information processing devices, some of which may be quite specific, but most of which are probably very general.

The question of specificity can be directly approached by comparing plausible explanations of lexical uniformities to ascertain their range of applicability across lexical domains. Explanations that are domain-specific would be indicative of specific design features of language, and those that extend across domains would suggest general information processing mechanisms. Of course, the explanatory framework proposed in the preceding chapter extends to regularities in the lexical encoding of *both* plant and animal classes and, hence, might not be considered domain-specific. If the framework also extends to uniformities involving lexical domains in addition to the biological ones, then a reasonable case can be made for an information processing model of the human language faculty.

The remainder of this chapter details encoding regularities involving a non-biological lexical domain, color, and considers explanations of these uniformities. Comparison of the latter with those proposed for biological life-form encoding reveals several parallels, a result which is in accord with a generalized model of the human language faculty. However, the explanatory framework pertaining to color encoding regularities also involves some explanations which are domain-specific. Thus lexical regularities and their explanations suggest that the most appropriate model of the language faculty is one involving both detailed specifications and general information processing mechanisms, that is, a "rich cognition" model.

In 1969 Berlin and Kay compiled a large body of cross-language data showing strong constraints on the co-occurrence of "basic color terms" in languages. From these data they drew conclusions concerning the order in which color terms are added to vocabularies, proposing a lexical encoding sequence for basic color categories. Since 1969 numerous field studies of native color vocabularies have been published which are in overall accord with the encoding sequence. This new evidence, however, has led to minor changes in the initially described encoding order (Witkowski and Brown 1977; Kay and McDaniel 1978). The revised encoding sequence for color is presented in Figure 6.[2]

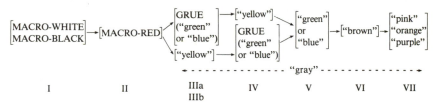

Figure 6. Revised Berlin and Kay color encoding sequence (Witkowski and Brown 1977).

Like biological life-form encoding orders, the encoding of basic color categories is depicted as involving growth stages. Stage I languages encode two categories, "macro-white" and "macro-black." "Macro-white" includes whites and most warm hues (reds, yellows, oranges, browns, pinks, and purples) and "macro-black" includes blacks and most cool hues (blues and greens). At Stage II "macro-red," which includes most warm hues, is encoded. With the addition of "macro-red," "macro-white" is reduced to white and very light hues. Either "grue" or "yellow" may be added at Stage III as a fourth category. "Grue" is a category including most cool hues. The encoding of "grue" restricts "macro-black" to black and very dark hues. If "grue" is added at Stage III, "yellow" is added at Stage IV and vice versa. The lexical encoding of the remaining color classes involves subdividing "macro-red" and "grue." (For further details see Witkowski and Brown 1977; Kay and McDaniel 1978.)

In Figure 6 a term in quotation marks refers to the focus of a color class. Color foci are the most representative members of color classes in the judgment of informants. Berlin and Kay (1969) have shown that the foci of all basic color categories fall into eleven small areas of color space. Expressions in uppercase type, of course, designate categories composed of various combinations of black and white and the hues red, yellow, green, and blue. These "composite" categories also have focal members. "Macro-white" is variously focused in white or red (usually red), "macro-black" is focused in black, "macro-red" in red, and "grue" variously in either green or blue.

* * *

There are a few languages among those surveyed by Berlin and Kay (1969) which have combinations of basic color terms not in accord with the sequence of Figure 6. Figure 7 is a reformulation of the color encoding sequence which agrees with all existing color nomenclature data. This reformulation, which treats only focal hues, shows that "red" is always encoded first (Stage A), followed by "yellow," "green," and/or "blue," but in no particular order (Stage B). These in turn are followed by "brown," "pink," "purple," and "orange," again in no particular order (Stage C). Since Figure 7 is a weaker sequence than Figure 6, it is less likely to be compromised by accumulating color data. More important, it provides a clear picture of color universals and suggests an explanation of these regularities.

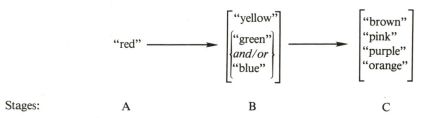

Stages: A   B   C

Figure 7. Encoding sequence for hue (Witkowski and Brown 1977).

Most observers now agree that a set of sublinguistic perceptual regularities linked to a neurophysiological substrate profoundly affect human color categorization (see reviews of Bornstein 1975, Kay and McDaniel 1978, and von Wattenwyl and Zollinger 1979). These unformities are such that the physically continuous hue spectrum is divided perceptually into four natural categories: "red," "yellow," "green," and "blue." In other words, these four classes are in some way wired into the neural circuitry of humans. For example, Bornstein, Kessen, and Weiskopf (1976) have experimentally shown that prelinguistic human infants react to color stimuli in a manner according with innate recognition of the categories "red," "yellow," "green," and "blue." In addition, their investigation reveals that of the four wired hues "red" is especially salient for infants.

Evidence of detailed neural specifications and linguistic evidence gathered by Berlin and Kay (1969) fit together well. Consider, for example, ways in which the reformulated sequence dealing with hue (Figure 7) and neural wiring findings are in accord. The four wired hue categories ("red," "yellow," "green," and "blue") are encoded first at Stages A and B. Non-wired categories ("brown," "pink," "purple," and "orange") emerge only secondarily at Stage C. In addition, "red," which is shown to be especially salient in Bornstein et al.'s (1976) infant study, is always the first of the four wired hues to be encoded (Stage A). Thus specific neural design for the categories "red," "yellow," "green," and "blue" underlies some of the encoding regularities described by Berlin and Kay (1969).

The color encoding sequence, like the two life-form encoding sequences, is also a marking hierarchy (see Chapter 7). As such it is manifested in languages through several other features of marking in addition to implicational relationships and language acquisition order (cf. Hays, Margolis, Naroll, and Perkins 1972). For example, Durbin (1972) has shown a correlation between the color encoding sequence and average orthographic length of color terms. Hays et al. (1972) have shown that intralanguage frequency of use of color terms correlates with the encoding sequence. And several studies (e.g., Cruse 1977; Johnson 1977) show that children learn basic color terms largely in the encoding order.

Underlying the marking hierarchy for basic color categories are neurophysiologically wired color classes. When lexically encoded, the neurophysiological priority of these categories is converted into high linguistic salience manifested through typical marking effects such as high frequency of use, brevity of name, early child acquisition, and so on. These wired classes are similar to discontinuities which underlie the plant and animal life-form marking hierarchies. For example, "red," like **tree**, constitutes an exceptionally salient natural break. However, discontinuities pertaining to color and those pertaining to plants and animals have quite different realizations. In the latter case **tree**, **bird**, **grass**, **fish**, **vine**, etc., are discontinuities in the external physical world underlain by criteria clustering. In the case of colors, "red," "yellow," "green," and "blue" are internal breaks, existing only in the neurophysiological mechanisms of humans.

Despite their naturalness, the wired hue categories are never the first color classes to be lexically encoded by languages. The composite color categories, "macro-black," "macro-white," "macro-red," and "grue," precede "red," "yellow," "green," and "blue" in the development of color lexicons (Figure 6).

Six combinations of the four primary hue classes are possible in composite categories: 1. red-yellow ("macro-red"), 2. yellow-green (a rare but attested category, Bornstein 1973), 3. green-blue ("grue"), 4. blue-yellow, 5. red-blue, and 6. red-green. However, only the first three of these actually occur.

The nonattested macro-colors provide evidence that a dimension based on wavelength order, i.e. red-yellow-green-blue, is important in human color categorization. Only conjunctive primary colors, i.e. those adjacent to each other in wavelength order, can be combined in composite classes. Nonadjacent combinations, 4-6, would be disjunctive, and, hence, do not occur. Conjunctivity considerations, then, provide important constraints limiting the variety of composite color classes.

As outlined in the preceding chapter, binary opposition is another way in which the principle of conjunctivity is realized in natural language categorization. Similar to plant life-form classification, the initial distinction in basic color encoding is a binary opposition, that is, "macro-black"/"macro-white." This distinction, like the **tree**/**grerb** contrast (cf. Figure 5, Chapter 8), involves two physical dimensions. "Macro-black" (black-green-blue) and "macro-white" (white-red-yellow) oppose light and dark along a brightness dimension and warm and cool along a hue dimension, always associating dark shades with cool hues and light shades with warm hues (see Figure 8).

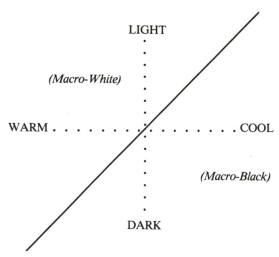

Figure 8. Binary distinctions pertaining to the encoding of "macro-black" and "macro-white" (Witkowski and Brown 1977).

In the case of the **tree**/**grerb** opposition, the invariable welding of large size with ligneousness and small size with herbaceousness (cf. Figure 5) is due to the natural structure of the physical world. On the other hand, neurophysical wiring underlies the invariable pairing of warm hues with white and cool hues with black in the categories "macro-white" and "macro-black" respectively (Figure 8). The focus of "yellow" in all languages which have this category is always displaced very strongly toward light hues and white, while the cross-language foci of the three other wired hue classes, "red," "blue," and "green," are in the medium to dark brightness range. Thus "yellow" is naturally associated with the light part of the color space. Red goes along with yellow in a "macro-white" class because of conjunctivity considerations. As a result, warm colors are universally associated with white in a "macro-white" category and cool colors with black in a "macro-black" category.

*   *   *

The association of warm hues with white and cool hues with black is another example of criteria clustering. Processes yielding the opposition "macro-black"/"macro-white," therefore, are similar to those resulting in the contrast **tree**/**grerb** in botanical classification. In both cases two dimensions are pertinent, size and woodiness for plants and brightness and hue for colors. Both contrasts partition two dimensions simultaneously by using only two terms (compare Figure 5 for plants and Figure 8 for color). One is based on criteria clustering in the external physical world and the other on criteria clustering produced through neurophysiological wiring.

The fact that warm hues cluster with white and cool hues with dark contributes to the likelihood that languages will make a "macro-white"/"macro-black" distinction in the initial encoding of basic color categories. A utilitarian factor may also contribute to this development. Basic color categories become important when people develop a need to refer to colors in a general manner.[3] An initial "macro-white"/"macro-black" contrast is highly apt and useful since it permits people to refer to virtually all colors through use of general terms. On the other hand, initial encoding of, say, one or more of the four wired hue categories would be less functional than a "macro-white"/"macro-black" distinction since some major parts of the color space would be excluded from ranges of general color terms.[4]

At Stage II, a third composite color, "macro-red," emerges, probably the result of another binary opposition (light versus warm). When "macro-red" is lexically encoded this in effect represents the separation of brightness from hue in the light-warm range of the color space (see Figure 9). Similarly, the emergence of "grue" represents separation of brightness and hue in the dark-cool range of the color space. Thus "macro-red" is distinguished from an essentially nonhue-associated white and "grue" is distinguished from an essentially nonhue-associated black as languages add terms beyond "macro-white" and "macro-black."

The encoding of hue categories beyond "grue" basically involves subdividing composite categories. However, the emergence of "gray" relates to special treatment of the brightness dimension. "Gray" is a wild-card category

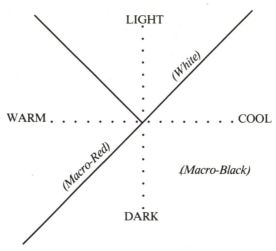

Figure 9. Binary distinctions pertaining to the encoding of "macro-red" and "white" (Witkowski and Brown 1977).

which can be encoded at any point after the early stages (see Figure 6). When nonhue-associated black and nonhue-associated white emerge with the encoding of "macro-red" and "grue," the brightness dimension in effect becomes separated from the hue dimension. When this occurs, "gray" can develop as a category intermediate to "black" and "white" along the separate dimension of brightness. Thus the brightness dimension is treated similarly to the size dimension underlying **tree**, **grerb**, and **bush**; namely an opposition (**tree/ grerb**) is recognized and only later is a middle segment (**bush**) distinguished.

Of the two biological life-form encoding sequences, the color encoding order more closely resembles the sequence for plant life-forms since in both cases (color and plants) an initial binary opposition is pertinent (respectively "macro-white"/"macro-black" and **tree/grerb**). Of course, initial encoding of general categories for the domain of animals does not involve a binary contrast. In other words, creatures are not at first partitioned into two groupings of large and small animals. This is due to the fact that such a division lacks reinforcement through criteria clustering. Animals do not demonstrate continuous variation along any dimension other than size, and, consequently, creature size is not especially predictive of other animal features (see Chapter 8). Of course, criteria clustering figures prominently into the encoding priority of **bird**, **fish**, and **snake** which are highly distinct large discontinuities in nature. In addition, after encoding of the latter three classes, languages may distinguish remaining residual creatures by creating a **wug/mammal** binary op-

126 / Language and Living Things

position. However, unlike binary oppositions of color and plant classification, that pertaining to animal categorization involves only one dimension, size, and, therefore, is not reinforced by criteria clustering. This helps to explain why binary contrast in animal life-form classification occurs only late in zoological life-form growth, if at all (see Chapter 8).

Rich Cognition

Explanatory frameworks proposed in this work suggest that both specific design principles and more general mechanisms constitute aspects of the human language faculty. Some variables influencing biological life-form encoding and basic color encoding are not domain-specific. This suggests that they are associated with information processing mechanisms. Conjunctivity (including binary opposition), criteria clustering, and dimension salience (Chapter 8) are variables affecting naming behavior which relate to very general cognitive faculties. On the other hand, color encoding is in part explained through reference to four natural categories of hue which apparently are directly wired into the neural circuitry of humans. These particular design features of languages are very specific, indeed.

Lexical regularities studied in this book suggest that general design principles play a considerably more important role in shaping actual language than do detailed design principles. The character of lexicons almost certainly would be quite different without conjunctivity, criteria clustering, and so on. On the other hand, language would be much the same if humans were not programmed for "red," "yellow," "green," and "blue." Lack of specific wiring for biological categorization, for example, has not prevented lexical encoding of general plant and animal classes. If detailed wiring for color did not exist, there is no reason to believe that languages would not encode basic color classes, although probably somewhat different ones.

Since some aspects of innate language are based on specific design features, it is not inconceivable that further examples will emerge as investigation of language universals proceeds. It seems unlikely, however, that they will figure prominently into explanations of language uniformities. In any case, neither an information processing model nor a detailed design model alone sufficiently captures the variety and complexity of the human language faculty. Rather, a "rich cognition" model, combining both possibilities, appears warranted by this study and related investigations of cross-language uniformities involving the lexicon.

PREAMBLE TO
APPENDICES A AND B

Appendices A and B assemble plant and animal life-form data from 188 and 144 languages respectively. These materials have been gathered from published and unpublished articles and monographs treating plant and animal classification in various languages and from personal communications with linguists and others who have specialized knowledge of the languages in question. In many cases persons in the field directly investigated folk biological classification for me by interviewing native speakers. In addition, life-form data from several languages were collected by me personally, either in the field (Veracruz and Oaxaca, Mexico) or from native speakers of languages other than English residing in this country.

No sampling procedure per se was used in selecting language cases to be included in this study. Rather, the procedure followed was to incorporate *all* life-form data encountered, the only constraint being that data extracted solely from dictionaries were excluded. Published investigations of plant and animal life-form encoding based primarily on dictionary data (Brown 1977, 1979a) precede this study. One goal of the present work is to anchor the plant and animal life-form encoding regularities in a corpus of data which is generally unafflicted by the lack of thoroughness and accuracy of biological reference usually found in typical dictionaries. However, some dictionary data are used, but only to supplement nondictionary information collected in the manner described above.

The exhaustive data collection approach employed means that some language cases are more thorough than others with respect to accuracy of biological reference. However, it needs to be emphasized that these cases, although very important in the aggregate with respect to conclusions reached in this book, are not critically important on a one by one basis. Thus if a few cases fall short of reasonable accuracy, this does not negate the aggregate weight of the majority of cases. This, of course, is the advantage of using such large

129

numbers of cases. Since abundant evidence is brought to bear, removal of a few cases on grounds of inaccuracy is not particularly serious.

The order of presentation of data is in terms of plant and animal growth stages (see Figures 2 and 3, Chapter 3), moving from initial stages (Stage 1 for plants, Stage 0 for animals) sequentially through final stages (Stage 6 for plants, Stage 5 for animals). Language cases are organized within growth stages according to the specific combinations of plant or animal life-form classes which they happen to share. Within each such organizational unit ordering of language cases is alphabetical by language name. Language cases are also assigned case numbers which are utilized in the text of this work for easy referral back to the data. Each case number is followed by a lowercase letter, a or b, which indicates appendix affiliation, respectively A or B.

The following information is provided for each language case:

1. *Language name and stage affiliation.* Language name is as provided by sources. Stage affiliation is determined by number of full-fledged plant or animal life-forms judged present in a language: for plants, Stage 1 = no life-forms, Stage 2 = one life-form, Stage 3 = two life-forms, and so on; for animals, Stage 0 = no life-forms, Stage 1 = one life-form, etc. In Appendix B this count includes combined **wug-mammal** classes. However, there is one exception. Tahitian (case 144b) has all five life-forms of the animal encoding sequence plus combined **wug-mammal**. Tahitian is treated as affiliated with Stage 5 despite the fact that it actually has six life-forms. Since only Tahitian among the 144 languages of Appendix B has more than five life-forms, a growth stage beyond Stage 5 is not proposed.

   In some instances languages have two or more words which denominate the same life-form class. For example, Carapana (133a) has three terms for **grerb**, *moetĩē*, *capunirĩjē*, and *carorije*. In such cases the life-form is counted only once in determining life-form stage affiliation. Incipient life-forms (abbreviated *I.L.-F.*, see Chapter 6) do not figure into stage affiliation calculations.

2. *Language classification.* Affiliation with major and minor genetic groupings has been determined for each language. The smallest subgrouping with which a language is affiliated is listed first followed by superordinate groupings of increasing inclusiveness. Assigned classifications for the most part are based on Voegelin and Voegelin's *Classification and Index of the World's Languages* (1977). Classifications of Mesoamerican languages are based on Witkowski and Brown (1978b). A few classifications have been determined from other sources.

3. *Geographic area.* An attempt has been made to be as detailed as possible in locating geographic areas in which languages are spoken. How-

ever, because of limitations of some sources, in some cases only very rough locations are supplied.

4. *Source*. Names of individuals who have supplied data through personal communications are indicated. When data have been extracted from published or unpublished articles or monographs, bibliographic reference is given. A few cases have been collected firsthand by me and this is indicated. In some cases more than one source may be pertinent.

5. *Life-form terms and glosses*. In all cases the orthography of sources is utilized. While it would have been preferable to employ a standard orthography throughout, to do so would have required a major research undertaking for which resources and time were lacking. Glosses following terms attempt to match as closely as possible in an encapsulated format those given in sources. These consist of a major life-form gloss in boldface type (e.g., **tree**, **bird**, etc.) followed by parenthetical information outlining more specifically the referential ranges of terms, for example, **grerb** (grass+herb), which indicates that the class in question encompasses both grasses and small herbaceous plants lacking bladed leaves. (The word *herb* in this work denotes small herbaceous plants other than grasses.) In some cases the referential range of one life-form term may encompass that of another. For example, in Koiwai (case 74a) **vine**, labeled by *waras*, includes botanical organisms which are also members of a more comprehensive **tree** class, labeled by *ai*. The parenthetical information for **tree** captures this fact: (large plant+vine). The degree of specificity of parenthetical information varies from case to case since some sources are more thorough than others. When a gloss given in a source adds information beyond that which can be parsimoniously presented in parentheses, this is mentioned in a following discussion section (see below). The symbol *I.L.-F.* following a term's gloss indicates that the term labels an incipient life-form class. Many **tree** terms are polysemous, also denoting wood. If it is known that a **tree** term designates wood, this is indicated in the associated gloss by use of the symbol **wood**. The latter is occasionally followed by parenthetical information specifying details of application, e.g., **wood** (lumber/firewood).

6. *Discussion*. In many cases commentary follows presentation of life-form terms and glosses. This usually provides information beyond that which is supplied by glosses. For example, it may identify focal members of biological classes. (Focal members are the "best" or most typical exemplars of a class in the judgment of informants.) Discussion may note variable applications of life-form terms across speakers, dialects, and so on or mention other terms which are possibly life-form labels. It may also call readers' attention to plausible alternative interpretations of

the data when they are in some way ambiguous or unclear. In some cases commentary consists of speculative observations concerning a life-form system's past or future development. Parallels between the case in question and other cases are also occasionally noted.

Finally, if a language found in Appendix B also occurs in Appendix A, then the reader is referred to Appendix A for that language's classification and geographic area. In addition, if a source is not listed for a language in Appendix B, then the source given for the same language in Appendix A is pertinent.

» A «

BOTANICAL LIFE-FORM DATA

STAGE 1 LANGUAGES.

No Life-Forms.
1a. Iwaidja (Australia) (has incipient **tree** and **grerb**)
2a. Southern Paiute (Kawaiisu dialect) (California, U.S.A.)

Case 1a.

Language Iwaidja (Stage 1)
Classification Iwaidjan, Australian
Area Coburg Peninsula, Australia
Source Noreen Pym (personal communication)
Life-Form Terms arlirr **tree** (tree) *I.L.-F.*
  mirlag **grerb** (grass+herb) *I.L.-F.*
Discussion Pym notes that useful trees, grasses, herbaceous plants, etc., are known by their own names and not identified as being either *arlirr* or *mirlag*. Incipient life-forms, such as these, by convention are not considered in life-form counts determining stage affiliation. Since all Iwaidja life-form classes are incipient, it ranks as a Stage 1 language entirely lacking full-fledged botanical life-forms.

Case 2a.

Language Southern Paiute (Kawaiisu dialect) (Stage 1)
Classification Numic, Uto-Aztecan, Aztec-Tanoan
Area California, U.S.A.
Source Maurice L. Zigmond (personal communication)
Life-Form Terms (there are none)

133

Discussion Zigmond writes that he recorded "no words referring to general types of plant growth: trees, grass, etc., and nothing that clearly distinguished between 'that which is edible' and that which is not." He found only one word, *mahavt*, having a general meaning, i.e., "weed." For dialectal differences see Southern Paiute (Chemehuevi dialect) (28a) and Southern Paiute (Cedar City dialect) (106a).

STAGE 2 LANGUAGES.

One Life-Form: **tree**.
3a. Bella Coola (British Columbia, Canada) (has incipient **grass**)
4a. Bontoc (Guinaang Dialect) (The Philippines)
5a. Dalabon (Australia)
6a. Northern Paiute (Oregon dialect) (Oregon, U.S.A.)
7a. Sahaptin (Washington State, U.S.A.) (has incipient **grass**)
8a. Shuswap (British Columbia, Canada)
9a. Wasco (Oregon and Washington, U.S.A.)

Case 3a.

Language Bella Coola (Stage 2)
Classification Bella Coola, Salish
Area British Columbia, Canada
Source Nancy Jean Turner (1974)
Life-Form Terms stn **tree** (tree)
　　　　　　　　　slaws **grass** (grass) *I.L.-F.*
Discussion The word *slaws* refers to "grasses and grass-like plants." Turner (p. 35) describes *slaws* as an "empty" category containing "many recognizably different members but few or none of these possess generic names." The term, then, labels an incipient life-form class.

Case 4a.

Language Bontoc (Guinaang dialect) (Stage 2)
Classification Cordilleran, Philippine, Northwest Austronesian, Austronesian
Area Mountain Province, Luzon, the Philippines
Source Lawrence Reid and Domingo Madulid (1972)
Life-Form Term pagpag **tree** (tree+bush)
Discussion The **tree** life-form excludes cultivated trees (coffee, guava, mango, avocado) and pine trees. There is a general term which is possibly a

grerb label, *lógam*, glossed "weed, useless herbaceous plant." As identified, however, it appears to be a special purpose class rather than a life-form category. Another general term, *taaw*, refers to "any of several species of grass used for thatching," and *wakal* is a "general name for any vine used for tying." These two classes as well are special purpose categories.

Case 5a.

Language Dalabon (Stage 2)
Classification Gunwingguan, Australian
Area Southern Arnhem Land, Australia
Source Kenneth Maddock (1975)
Life-Form Term dul **tree** (tree)
Discussion Maddock (p. 102) writes, "I did not discover that plants, excepting trees, are grouped into genera, but whether none exist is doubtful, for my taxonomic inquiries were conducted incidentally to what seemed then to be more pressing concerns and were not at all systematic."

Case 6a.

Language Northern Paiute (Oregon dialect) (Stage 2)
Classification Numic, Uto-Aztecan, Aztec-Tanoan
Area Oregon, U.S.A.
Source James Michael Mahar (1953)
Life-Form Term wünüdi **tree** (tree)
Discussion For dialectal variation see Northern Paiute (Nevada dialect) (38a).

Case 7a.

Language Sahaptin (Stage 2)
Classification Sahaptin-Nez Perce, Penutian
Area Columbia River Basin, Washington State, U.S.A.
Source Eugene Hunn (1980a)
Life-Form Terms pátat **tree** (tree)
 c'íc'k **grass** (grass) *I.L.-F.*
Discussion The **tree** term is a verbal noun derived from *páta-* "to stand up, to be placed upright." Hunn notes that a minority of his informants used *pátat* to refer to inanimate objects such as poles and snags. There is also a term for coniferous tree, *pátatuwi*, which apparently has expanded in meaning from an original referent, subalpine fir. The **grass** term and a term for flower, *latít*, are used by speakers to refer to residual collections of nameless plants. The

grass term, then, is an incipient life-form label. Hunn also mentions two special purpose categories, *x̣nít* "edible root" and *tmaanít* "edible fruit," which are highly salient suprageneric classes for Sahaptin speakers.

Case 8a.
_____

Language Shuswap (Stage 2)
Classification Interior Salish, Salish
Area British Columbia, Canada
Source Gary Palmer (1975)
Life-Form Term tsegáp **tree** (tree)
Discussion The language does have a term for weed, *swupúlexw*, which refers to "plants which are not good for anything." The term translates literally "hair or growth on the ground" and is probably cognate with the incipient **grerb** label described for Lillooet (36a), another Interior Salish language.

Case 9a.
_____

Language Wasco (Stage 2)
Classification Chinookan, Penutian
Area Oregon and Washington, U.S.A.
Source David French (1957)
Life-Form Term (term?) **tree** (tree)/**wood**
Discussion French writes:

> These Indians lack not only a commonly used term for plant (or for animal), but there are almost no terms which refer to broad classes or categories of plants. For example, there are no words corresponding to these in English: bush, herb, or berry. Except for a rarely-used extension from 'wood,' there is not even a word for tree."

STAGE 3 LANGUAGES.

Two Life-Forms: **tree+grerb**.
10a. Anindilyakwa (Australia)
11a. Asurini (Brazil)
12a. Bisa (Upper Volta, Ghana)
13a. Delaware (Oklahoma, U.S.A.)
14a. Gimi (Papua New Guinea)
15a. Gouin (Upper Volta)

16a. Hopi (Arizona, U.S.A.)
17a. Igbira (Nigeria)
18a. Khmer (Cambodia)
19a. Kilangi (Tanzania)
20a. Mara (Australia)
21a. Ngandi (Australia)
22a. Nunggubuyu (Australia)
23a. Popoloca (Mexico)
24a. Ritharngu (Australia)
25a. Sherbro (Sierra Leone)
26a. Sisaala (Ghana)
27a. Songhay (Nigeria, Niger, Mali, Upper Volta, Dahomey)
28a. Southern Paiute (Chemehuevi dialect) (Nevada, U.S.A.)
29a. Western Aranda (Australia)
30a. Yolŋu (Australia)

Case 10a.

Language Anindilyakwa (Stage 3)
Classification Australian
Area Groote Eylandt, Australia
Source (1) Julie Waddy (personal communication); (2) Dulcie Levitt (personal communication); (3) Julie Waddy (1980, 1982); (4) John W. Harris (1979).
Life-Form Terms eka **tree** (tree + woody bush)/**wood**
　　　　　　　　amarda **grerb** (grass + herb + fern)
Discussion The **grerb** term is also used more expansively to refer to botanical organisms in general. Levitt writes that *amarda* "refers to all green plants, but in the case of trees the reference is more to the foliage of the trees than to the trees themselves." Waddy (1982: 70) notes that the two life-form classes "are based on binary opposition of woody vs. nonwoody."

Case 11a.

Language Asurini (Stage 3)
Classification Tupi-Guarani, Tupi, Equatorial, Andean-Equatorial
Area Brazil
Source Velda C. Nicholson (personal communication)
Life-Form Terms ywa **tree** (tree)/**wood**
　　　　　　　　soowia **grerb** (grass + herb)

Case 12a.

Language Bisa (Stage 3)

Classification Eastern Mande, Southern-Eastern Branch, Mande, Niger-Congo, Niger-Kordofanian

Area Upper Volta, Ghana

Source (1) André Prost (personal communication); (2) Anthony Joshua Naden (personal communication).

Life-Form Terms gɔ **tree** (tree)/**wood**

              bur **grerb** (grass+herb)

Discussion Prost writes that *bur* includes all plants that are not ligneous (woody). The category apparently excludes fungi.

Case 13a.

Language Delaware (Stage 3)

Classification Algonquian, Macro-Algonquian

Area Oklahoma (formerly in the Delaware Basin in Pennsylvania, New York, New Jersey, and Delaware)

Source Jay Miller (1975)

Life-Form Terms hʊtukw **tree** (tree)

              skikw **grerb** (grass+herb)

Discussion Miller's informant used the "tree" term to denote "any plant over human height." The attributes of plants designated by the **grerb** term "are ubiquity and being shorter than a human adult."

Case 14a.

Language Gimi (Stage 3)

Classification Fore, Gende-Siane-Gahuku-Kamano-Fore, East New Guinea Highlands, Central New Guinea, Indo-Pacific

Area Eastern Highlands of Papua New Guinea

Source Leonard B. Glick (1964)

Life-Form Terms da **tree** (tree)

              doni **grerb** (grass+herb)

Discussion Glick describes *doni* as follows: "roughly equivalent to 'grass,' but it also covers most weeds, a few vines, and so on. . . ."

Case 15a.

Language Gouin (Stage 3)

Classification Kirma-Tyurama, Gur, Niger-Congo, Niger-Kordofanian

Area Upper Volta

Source Edward Lauber (personal communication)
Life-Form Terms tíbìŋgu- **tree** (tree+bush)
               hĩḛ̂ŋgù- **grerb** (grass+herb)
Discussion The **grerb** term encompasses all nonwoody plants except vines and reeds. Vines and reeds form their own general grouping designated *kɛ̃ĩŋo-*. This category apparently is focused on reeds.

Case 16a.

Language Hopi (Stage 3)
Classification Uto-Aztecan, Aztec-Tanoan
Area Arizona, U.S.A.
Source (1) Alfred F. Whiting (1939); (2) Charles F. Voegelin and Florence M. Voegelin (1957).
Life-Form Terms ho´hu **tree** (tree)/**wood**
               tu: ´saka **grerb** (grass+herb)
Discussion The above terms and referential extensions are from Whiting. Whiting writes that the range of *tu: ´saka* extends to "grasses and many other herbs." The Voegelins, on the other hand, identify the term (*tí:saga*) as restricted to "1. wild grass, 2. alfalfa." This may indicate that grass constitutes the focal type of the Hopi **grerb** life-form.

Case 17a.

Language Igbira (Stage 3)
Classification Nupe-Gbari, Kwa, Niger-Congo, Niger-Kordofanian
Area Nigeria
Source Hans-Jürgen Scholz (personal communication)
Life-Form Terms ọchí **tree** (woody plant+banana plant+bamboo+date
                     palm+coconut tree)/**wood**
               aví **grerb** (grass+herb+bush)
Discussion The **tree** term encompasses all ligneous plants and large plants with strong trunks or stems. Greenness and soft stems are common characteristics of plants designated *aví*. The **grerb** term also denotes "any bushland, i.e. large areas with either green or dried grass, shrubs and trees." Used figuratively the word refers to "backwardness."

Case 18a.

Language Khmer (Stage 3)
Classification Mon-Khmer, Austro-Asiatic
Area Cambodia

Source Marie A. Martin (1971)
Life-Form Terms daəm **tree** (tree)
smav **grerb** (grass+herb)
Discussion Martin assigns the French gloss *arbre* ("tree") to *daəm* and describes the class as consisting of plants with thick, sturdy stems. *Smav* is glossed *herbes* ("herbaceous plant") and described as encompassing slender plants that do not stand erect. There is a third general plant term *vɔ:r*, glossed by *lianes* ("vines") which is in fact a label for a residual botanical category. The latter includes plants not identified as *daəm* or *smav*, i.e. bushes and vines, which are left over after encoding the initial dyad **tree** and **grerb**.

Case 19a.

Language Kilangi (Stage 3)
Classification North Eastern, Bantu Proper, Bantoid, Benue-Congo, Niger-Congo, Niger-Kordofanian
Area Tanzania
Source (1) John D. Kesby (1979); (2) John D. Kesby (personal communication)
Life-Form Terms miti **tree** (tree+bush+large herb)
masambi **grerb** (grass+small herb)
Discussion Kesby (1979: 46) writes that the above two categories are distinguished along the dimensions size and woodiness: "*miti* being large and/or woody and *masambi* being small and non-woody." He (personal communication) also writes that Kilangi speakers "may have a word for vine, but I have never heard it . . . even if there is a term, few people know it. Vines are certainly not an important category in daily . . . experience."

Case 20a.

Language Mara (Stage 3)
Classification Maran, Australian
Area North Central Australia
Source Jeffrey Heath (personal communication)
Life-Form Terms ḍabaliya **tree** (tree)/**wood**
wiji **grerb** (grass+herb)
naṛanji **grerb** (grass+herb)

Case 21a.

Language Ngandi (Stage 3)
Classification Gunwingguan, Australian

Area Northern Territory, Australia
Source Jeffrey Heath (personal communication)
Life-Form Terms gu-ḍandaʔ **tree** (tree+any woody plant)/**wood**
gu-mulmu **grerb** (grass+herb)

Case 22a.

Language Nunggubuyu (Stage 3)
Classification Australian
Area Eastern Coast of Arnhem Land, Australia
Source Jeffrey Heath (1978)
Life-Form Terms ṛaŋag- **tree** (tree+woody bush)
maḍa- **grerb** (grass+herb)
Discussion According to the source the **tree** term refers to "woody" plants and the **grerb** term to "non-woody" plants. Aquatic plants such as water lilies, seaweeds, seagrasses, and algae are excluded from both categories.

Case 23a.

Language Popoloca (Stage 3)
Classification Popolocan, Oto-Manguean, Mesoamerican
Area Puebla, Mexico
Source (1) Mary De Boe and Sharon Stark (personal communication); (2) Andrés Peña (1980).
Life-Form Terms nttá **tree** (tree+large cactus)/**wood**
ca **grerb** (grass+herb)

Case 24a.

Language Ritharngu (Stage 3)
Classification Murngic, Pama-Nyungan, Australian
Area Arnhem Land, Northern Territory, Australia
Source Jeffrey Heath (personal communication)
Life-Form Terms ḍaṛpa **tree** (tree)/**wood**
mulmu **grerb** (grass+herb)

Case 25a.

Language Sherbro (Stage 3)
Classification Southern Branch, West Atlantic, Niger-Congo, Niger-Kordo-fanian
Area Sierra Leone

Source F. C. Deighton (1957).
Life-Form Terms thɔk-lɛ **tree** (tree)
puluk-lɛ **grerb** (grass+herb)

Case 26a.

Language Sisaala (Tumu dialect) (Stage 3)
Classification Grusi, Central Gur, Gur, Niger-Congo, Niger-Kordofanian
Area Ghana
Source Anthony Joshua Naden (personal communication)
Life-Form Terms tia **tree** (tree)
yaŋ **grerb** (grass+herb)

Case 27a.

Language Songhay (Stage 3)
Classification Nilo-Saharan
Area Nigeria, Niger, Mali, Upper Volta, Dahomey
Source André Prost (personal communication)
Life-Form Terms turi **tree** (tree)/**wood**
subu **grerb** (grass+herb)
Discussion The **grerb** term is described as encompassing all plants that are
not ligneous.

Case 28a.

Language Southern Paiute (Chemehuevi dialect) (Stage 3)
Classification Numic, Uto-Aztecan, Aztec-Tanoan
Area Las Vegas, Nevada, U.S.A.
Source Catherine Louise Sweeney Fowler (1972)
Life-Form Terms mahábɨ **tree**(tree+large brush-tree)
tɨsɨ **grerb** (grass+herb)
Discussion The term *mahábɨ* apparently is also used to refer to plants in
general in some contexts. However, Fowler notes that it is most commonly
applied to trees and large brush-trees. For dialectal differences see Southern
Paiute (Cedar City dialect) (106a) and Southern Paiute (Kawaiisu dialect) (2a).

Case 29a.

Language Western Aranda (Stage 3)
Classification Arandic, Pama-Nyungan, Australian
Area Central Australia

Source John C. Pfitzner (personal communication)
Life-Form Terms irna **tree** (tree+bush)
                thirrka **grerb** (grass+herb)
Discussion The **tree** term can also be used to refer to plants in general. Any plant which is woody and has a rigid stem and branches is *irna* (**tree**). Any herbaceous plant without a rigid stem and branches is *thirrka* (**grerb**). The source writes that "the distinction between *irna* and *thirrka* appears to lie in the distinction between 'hard' plants and 'soft' plants."

Case 30a.

Language Yolŋu (Stage 3)
Classification Murngic, Pama-Nyungan, Australian
Area Arnhem Land, Northern Territory, Australia
Source (1) Stephen L. Davis (1981); (2) John Rudder (1979).
Life-Form Terms dharpa **tree** (tree)/**wood**
                mulmu **grerb** (grass+herb)
Discussion According to Davis, a tree is tree by right of its "woodiness" for speakers of the language. Davis also identifies grasses as the focus of **grerb**. Vines are excluded from both life-form classes.

      Two Life-Forms: **tree+grass**.
31a. Dugum Dani (West Irian)
32a. Eskimo (Canada)
33a. Gilbertese (Gilbert Islands)
34a. Halkomelem Salish (Cowichan dialect) (British Columbia, Canada)
35a. Kiowa Apache (Oklahoma, U.S.A.)
36a. Lillooet (British Columbia, Canada) (has incipient **grerb**)
37a. Minnesota Ojibwa (Minnesota, U.S.A.)
38a. Northern Paiute (Nevada dialect) (Nevada, U.S.A.)
39a. Shoshoni (Utah, Nevada, U.S.A.)
40a. Smith River (California, U.S.A.)
41a. Southern Kwakiutl (British Columbia, Canada)
42a. Southern Tiwa (New Mexico, U.S.A.)
43a. Tarahumara (Mexico) (has incipient **grerb**)
44a. Wik Moŋkan (Australia)

Case 31a.

Language Dugum Dani (Stage 3)

Classification West New Guinea Highlands, Central New Guinea, Indo-Pacific

Area West Irian

Source Karl G. Heider (1970)

Life-Form Terms o **tree** (tree+woody bush)

etesiga **grass** (grass)

Discussion There is a third general botanical label, *oga*, described by Heider as "a generic term . . . sometimes used for all wild flora." Since the inclusion of trees in the latter range is not entirely clear, it is possible that *oga* encompasses only uncultivated herbaceous plants and, thus, is a **grerb** label.

Case 32a.

Language Eskimo (Stage 3)

Classification Eskimo-Aleut

Area Baker Lake, Northwest Territory, Canada

Source Jean Pierre R. Paillet (1973)

Life-Form Terms qiyuk **tree** (woody plant)

ivit **grass** (grass)

Discussion Paillet compares his data with that of L. Schneider collected from the Ungava region and the west coast of Hudson's Bay and finds that they, including life-form terms, correspond fairly extensively. However, he reports that Schneider gives a lexical form, *nunaaraq* (with variants *nunaaruq, nunayaq*), not found at Baker Lake which refers to "little plants in general" or, in other words, labels **grerb**.

Case 33a.

Language Gilbertese (Stage 3)

Classification Micronesian, Oceanic, Austronesian

Area Gilbert Islands, Micronesia

Source (1) Katharine Luomala (personal communication); (2) Katharine Luomala (1953).

Life-Form Terms kai **tree** (tree)/**wood**

uteute **grass** (grass+sedge)

Case 34a.

Language Halkomelem Salish (Cowichan dialect) (Stage 3)
Classification Coast Salish, Salish
Area British Columbia, Canada
Source Nancy Chapman Turner and Marcus A. M. Bell (1971).
Life-Form Terms θqɛ́t **tree** (tree)
                  sáx̣ʷəl **grass** (grass)

Case 35a.

Language Kiowa Apache (Stage 3)
Classification Apachean, Athapascan, Athapascan-Eyak, Na-Dene
Area Oklahoma, U.S.A.
Source Julia Anne Jordan (1965)
Life-Form Terms -kǫ́'é **tree** (tree)/**wood**
                  -čìš **tree** (tree)/**wood**
                  ɫòh **grass** (grass)

Case 36a.

Language Lillooet (Stage 3)
Classification Interior Salish, Salish
Area British Columbia, Canada
Source Nancy Jean Turner (1974)
Life-Form Terms segáp **tree** (tree)
                 slék̲em **grass** (grass)
                 swa7púlmexw **grerb** (herb) *I.L.-F.*
Discussion The "tree" term also refers specifically to *Pseudotsuga. Agropyron spicatun* or "bunchgrass" is the specific referent of the "grass" term. The label for incipient **grerb** translates literally "ground hair." Turner describes the latter category as including "various introduced and native herbs not recognized with generic names." A probable cognate of incipient **grerb** designating weed is found in Shuswap (8a), an Interior Salish language.

Case 37a.

Language Minnesota Ojibwa (Stage 3)
Classification Algonquian, Macro-Algonquian
Area Northern Minnesota, U.S.A.
Source (1) Mary Black Rogers (personal communication); (2) Mary Rose Bartholomew Black (1967).

Life-Form Terms mitig **tree** (tree)/**wood**

maškosį.nsan **grass** (grass)

Discussion A **grerb** life-form appears to be emerging in the language through referential extension of the word for leaves, i.e. *ani.bi.šan*. Rogers (personal communication) notes that two of six informants initially glossed the latter term as "leaves, flowers, weeds, vegetables, berries—all things growing except grass." She adds, "I see now that *ani.bi.šan* in its larger range could be or have been a term excluding woody plants."

Case 38a.

Language Northern Paiute (Nevada dialect) (Stage 3)

Classification Numic, Uto-Aztecan, Aztec-Tanoan

Area West-Central Nevada, U.S.A.

Source Catherine Louise Sweeney Fowler (1972)

Life-Form Terms sagapi **tree** (deciduous tree)

wahábɨ **grass** (grass+rush)

Discussion Fowler (p. 63) writes that *sagapi* also specifically designates "cottonwood tree." The term can be expanded at one level to include the willow tree and also "used in popular speech today for any deciduous tree." The **grass** category includes species having slender parallel-sided leaves which grow in clumps. Small rushes (*Juncaceae*) and other slender-stemmed plants are also included. For dialectal variation see Northern Paiute (Oregon dialect) (6a).

Case 39a.

Language Shoshoni (Stage 3)

Classification Numic, Uto-Aztecan, Aztec-Tanoan

Area Utah, Nevada, U.S.A.

Source (1) Ralph V. Chamberlin (1964); (2) Catherine Louise Sweeney Fowler (1972).

Life-Form Terms ó-pi or wú-pi **tree** (tree+woody bush)/**wood**

só-nɨp **grass** (grass)

Discussion The above terms and referential extensions are from Chamberlin. Chamberlin's data are from the Gosiute dialect of Shoshoni spoken in Utah and Fowler's data are from a dialect spoken in Owyhee, Nevada. Fowler reports an identical "grass" term, but failed to uncover in her investigation a label for "tree." The concept "tree" is clearly of low salience for speakers of the language having it. Chamberlin, for example, indicates that the primary meaning of *ó-pi* or *wú-pi* is "wood" which is extended to woody plants, and, at times, even to plants in general. Chamberlin also describes a term which may label **grerb**. The word *pú-i-si-a-ka* is a "general name for green or growing plants" (literally, "green plant"). However, Chamberlin does not state whether or not trees are excluded from the latter group.

Case 40a.

Language Smith River (Stage 3)
Classification Pacific Coast Athapascan, Athapascan, Athapascan-Eyak, Na-
 Dene
Area Northwestern California, U.S.A.
Source Jane O. Bright and William Bright (1965)
Life-Form Terms tš'aamé⁷ **tree** (coniferous tree)
　　　　　　　　　tšéeneh **tree** (non-coniferous tree+bush)
　　　　　　　　　xəmšən **grass** (grass)

Case 41a.

Language Southern Kwakiutl (Stage 3)
Classification Wakashan
Area British Columbia, Canada
Source Nancy Chapman Turner and Marcus A. M. Bell (1973)
Life-Form Terms dlo7s **tree** (tree)
　　　　　　　　　k'ítem **grass** (grass)
Discussion The "grass" term also refers specifically to *Elymus mollis*.

Case 42a.

Language Southern Tiwa (Stage 3)
Classification Tanoan, Aztec-Tanoan
Area New Mexico, U.S.A.
Source Barbara J. Allen and Donna B. Gardiner (personal communication)
Life-Form Terms tuła **tree** (tree)
　　　　　　　　　łi **grass** (grass)
Discussion The **tree** term is a compound form based on the word for wood, *ła*, and another element.

Case 43a.

Language Tarahumara (Stage 3)
Classification Sonoran, Uto-Aztecan, Aztec-Tanoan
Area Northern Mexico
Source (1) Robert A. Bye, Jr. (personal communication); (2) David Brambila

(personal communication); (3) Don Burgess (personal communication); (4) Kenneth Hilton (personal communication); (5) Andrés Lionnet (1972); (6) I. Thord-Gray (1955)

Life-Form Terms gusí or gusiki **tree** (tree)
                    rojá **tree** (tree)
                    okó **tree** (tree)
                    kasará **grass** (grass)
                    sawaré **grerb** (herb) *I.L.-F.*
                    urike **grerb** (herb) *I.L.-F.*

Discussion The above terms and referential extensions are from Bye who alone of the above sources has systematically investigated Tarahumara folk classification of plants. There appears to be considerable dialectal and/or idiolectal variation with respect to the encoding of **tree** indicating its probable low salience in the language. The term *gusí* (or *gusiki*) seems to be the most widely recognized "tree" label since it is the only one of the above three which is reported by more than two sources (Thord-Gray and Lionnet in addition to Bye). *Gusí* (or *gusiki*) appears to have been derived from the "wood" term *gu*. Burgess as well as Bye identifies *rojá* as a "tree" label. The primary meaning of the term is "oak." Bye reports that he has most often heard *rojá* used in reference to trees in general in the mountainous countryside. Among the sources, Bye alone mentions use of *okó* as a "tree" label. Similar to *rojá*, *okó* refers primarily to a type of tree, the "ocote" pine, and is expanded to "tree" mainly by folk of mountainous areas. Two of the sources, Brambila and Hilton, have failed to find a "tree" term at all in their lexical investigations. The incipient **grerb** terms *sawaré* and *urike*, are reported only by Bye. He describes these as designating "unidentified herbaceous plants" which are generally "weedy" in appearance. *Sawaré* appears to be linguistically derived from the word for leaf, *sawa*. The "grass" term is the only life-form label and class which is reported by all six sources. Finally, one source, Burgess, gives a term for "vine," *banaká*. It is likely that the latter term in fact refers more precisely to the "shoot of a plant or vine," a meaning which is assigned to it in Lionnet's dictionary (cf. *ban-e-wá*).

Case 44a.

Language Wik Moŋkan (Stage 3)
Classification Middle Pama, Pama-Maric, Pama-Nyungan, Australian
Area Southern Cape York Peninsula, Australia
Source D. F. Thomson (1946)
Life-Form Terms yukk **tree** (tree)/**wood**
                    wäkk **grass** (grass)
Discussion The "tree" term also means "thing."

Two Life-Forms: **tree+vine**.
45a. Pacaas Novos (Brazil) (has incipient **grerb**)

Case 45a.
_____

Language Pacaas Novos (Stage 3)
Classification Madeira Group, Chapacura-Wanhaman, Arawakan, Equatorial, Andean-Equatorial
Area Rondonia Territory, Brazil
Source Manfred and Barbara Kern (personal communication)
Life-Form Terms pana **tree** (tree+bush+palm)/**wood**
        macon **vine** (vine)
        nahwarac **grerb** (grass+herb) *I.L.-F.*
Discussion The Kerns describe *nahwarac* as follows: "any weed, jungle growth, grass . . . 'noncultivated small herbaceous plants' and you could say it is a general category on par with *pana*. There are, however, *no* specific classes of *nahwarac*" (emphasis supplied by C.H.B.). The term also means "jungle." The "vine" term also denotes string, rope, fishing line, and back strap for carrying children.

STAGE 4 LANGUAGES

Three Life-Forms: **tree+grerb+vine**
46a. Aguaruna Jivaro (Peru)
47a. Amharic (Ethiopia)
48a. Araona (Bolivia)
49a. Awtuw (Papua New Guinea)
50a. Bambara (Senegal, Mali, Upper Volta)
51a. Banda (Central African Republic)
52a. Baoule (Ivory Coast)
53a. Brou (Cambodia)
54a. Casiguran Dumagat (The Philippines)
55a. Central Cagayan Agta (The Philippines)
56a. Chontal (Mexico)
57a. Chuj (Guatemala and Mexico)
58a. Hanunoo (The Philippines)
59a. Hewa (Papua New Guinea)
60a. Hill Pandaram (India)
61a. Hmong (Laos)
62a. Ibataan (The Philippines)
63a. Iloko (The Philippines)

64a. Ilongot (The Philippines)
65a. Itawis (The Philippines) (has incipient **grass**)
66a. Ixil (Guatemala)
67a. Jacaltec (Guatemala)
68a. Jarai (Vietnam)
69a. Juchitan Zapotec (Mexico)
70a. Karok (California, U.S.A.)
71a. Kenyah (Malaysia)
72a. Kiriwinian (Trobriand Islands)
73a. Kisi (Sierra Leone)
74a. Koiwai (West Irian)
75a. Kugu-Nganhchara (Australia)
76a. Lao (Laos)
77a. Machiguenga (Peru)
78a. Manja (Central African Republic)
79a. Manobo Blit (The Philippines)
80a. Mende (Sierra Leone, Liberia)
81a. Mikir (India)
82a. Muyuw (Papua New Guinea)
83a. Ngbaka Ma'bo (Central African Republic)
84a. Nuaulu (Indonesia)
85a. Patep (Papua New Guinea)
86a. Paumari (Brazil)
87a. Pocomchi (Guatemala)
88a. Roglai (Vietnam)
89a. Samal (The Philippines)
90a. Sambal (The Philippines)
91a. Taubuid (Batangan dialect) (The Philippines)
92a. Temne (Sierra Leone)
93a. Tobelo (Indonesia)
94a. Waodani (Ecuador)
95a. Western Subanun (The Philippines)
96a. Wik-Ngathana (Australia)

Case 46a.
_____

Language Aguaruna Jivaro (Stage 4)
Classification Jivaroan, Andean-Equatorial
Area Department of Amazonas, Peru
Source Brent Berlin and Elois Ann Berlin (1977)
Life-Form Terms númi **tree** (tree)

dúpa **grerb** (grass + herb)

daék **vine** (woody vine)

Discussion The **tree** life-form excludes palms which have their own general label.

Case 47a.

Language Amharic (Stage 4)

Classification Ethiopic, South Semitic, Semitic, Afro-Asiatic

Area Ethiopia

Source M. Denis Lemordant (personal communication)

Life-Form Terms zaf **tree** (tree)

aräq **vine** (vine)

Case 48a.

Language Araona (Stage 4)

Classification Tacana, Pano-Tacana, Macro-Panoan, Ge-Pano-Carib

Area Bolivia

Source Mrs. Mary Pitman (personal communication)

Life-Form Terms ákwi **tree** (tree + bush)/**wood**

nóȼa **grerb** (grass + herb)

hóno **vine** (vine)

Case 49a.

Language Awtuw (Stage 4)

Classification Ram, Upper Sepik, Sepik, Central New Guinea, Indo-Pacific

Area West Sepik Province, Papua New Guinea

Source Harry Feldman (personal communication)

Life-Form Terms taw **tree** (tree)/**wood**

yawnow **grerb** (grass + herb + bush)

mæt **vine** (vine + cane)

Discussion The **tree** life-form includes ligneous plants that have branches. It excludes such large plants as palm trees, coconut trees, and banana trees. The **tree** term extends to at least one nonwoody plant, i.e. tobacco, and probably to several others. The source describes *yawnow* as encompassing "all grasses, many herbs, and many bushes . . . mostly wild plants, but many cultivated plants as well." However, he notes that the single feature that applies most broadly to plants designated by *yawnow* is uselessness. Consequently, the term may in fact label weed rather than **grerb**. On the other hand, that some *yawnow* are cultivated and clearly have uses, e.g., cultivated ginger, indicates a **grerb** range. It may be the case that the term is polysemous denoting both weed and **grerb**. The fact that *mæt* encompasses various types of cane in addition to all vines may indicate that a **vine** codification is not appropriate. The term also designates rope. The lumping of canes with vines possibly is due to the use of strips of cane fiber as lashing material. The source also adds that more "naive" (unacculturated?) speakers apply the above three terms only to unnamed, unknown plants having the characteristics associated with the classes they denote. These, then, may be incipient life-form labels for some individuals.

Case 50a.

Language Bambara (Stage 4)
Classification Northern, Northern-Western, Mande, Niger-Congo, Niger-Kordofanian
Area Senegal, Mali, Upper Volta
Source (1) Pierre Garnier (personal communication); (2) Pierre Garnier (n.d.).
Life-Form Terms yíri **tree** (tree)/**wood**
bí **grerb** (grass+herb)
nőfő **vine** (woody vine)
Discussion The primary meaning of *yíri* is "wood."

Case 51a.

Language Banda (Stage 4)
Classification Eastern (of Adamawa-Eastern), Niger-Congo, Niger-Kordofanian
Area Central African Republic
Source A.-M. Vergiat (1969)
Life-Form Terms oyo **tree** (tree)/**wood**
gusu **grerb** (grass+herb)
nduku **vine** (vine)

Case 52a.

Language Baoule (Stage 4)
Classification Volta-Comoe, Kwa, Niger-Congo, Niger-Kordofanian
Area Ivory Coast
Source (1) Pierre Garnier (personal communication); (2) Pierre Garnier (n.d.).

Life-Form Terms uaka **tree** (tree)/**wood**

nya-nya **grerb** (grass+herb)

nyama **vine** (vine)

Discussion The primary meaning of *uaka* is "wood." The **grerb** term is re-duplicated *nya* "leaf." The "vine" term also denotes rope.

Case 53a.

Language Brou (Stage 4)

Classification Katuic, Mon-Khmer, Austro-Asiatic

Area Cambodia

Source Jacqueline Matras and Marie A. Martin (1972)

Life-Form Terms loong **tree** (tree)

bat **grerb** (grass+herb)

jömüü **vine** (vine)

Discussion Plants classified as *loong* are usually taller than an adult human, while those classified as *bat* are usually less than 1.5 meters in height.

Case 54a.

Language Casiguran Dumagat (Stage 4)

Classification Philippine, Northwest Austronesian, Austronesian

Area Luzon, the Philippines

Source Thomas N. Headland (1981)

Life-Form Terms kayo **tree** (tree+woody plant)/**wood**

lamon **grerb** (grass+herb)

lanot **vine** (vine)

Case 55a.

Language Central Cagayan Agta (Stage 4)

Classification Cordilleran, Philippine, Northwest Austronesian, Austronesian

Area Cagayan Province, Luzon, the Philippines

Source Roy and Georgia Lee Mayfield (personal communication)

Life-Form Terms kayu **tree** (tree)/**wood**

kadat **grerb** (grass+herb)

lanut **vine** (vine)

Discussion The **tree** term designates all and only solid wood trees and thus does not extend to items such as palm trees and banana plants. The source describes *kadat* as encompassing grasses, weeds, and small herb types. Some herbaceous plants excluded from *kadat* are various root crops (sweet potato, taro, cassava, etc.), legumes, aerial plants, and cactuses. Grasses seem to constitute the focus of **grerb**. The source also mentions that in most situations any plant life may be described as either *mula* "planted" or *nagtuhu* "sprouted" (self propagated). The latter terms, of course, label special purpose classes whose memberships are based on manner of propagation. Specific plants on one occasion may be *mula*, but on another, *nagtuhu*.

Case 56a.

Language Chontal (Stage 4)
Classification Mayan, Mesoamerican
Area Tabasco, Mexico
Source Kathryn Keller (personal communication)
Life-Form Terms te⁷ **tree** (tree)/**wood**
             binila or bilina **grerb** (grass+herb)
             ac' **vine** (vine)

Case 57a.

Language Chuj (Stage 4)
Classification Mayan, Mesoamerican
Area Huehuetenango, Guatemala
Source Dennis E. Breedlove and Nicholas A. Hopkins (1970)
Life-Form Terms te⁷ **tree** (tree)/**wood**
             ⁷aN **grerb** (grass+herb)
             č'aN **vine** (vine)
Discussion. The following glosses are assigned to the above terms by the source: *te⁷* "woody-stemmed plants and their products," *č'aN* "vines and their products," *⁷aN* "plants [other than grains] not covered by . . . *č'aN*, or *te⁷*, mostly herbs."

Case 58a.

Language Hanunoo (Stage 4)
Classification Hanunoic, Mesophilippine, Sulic, Philippine, Northwest Austronesian, Austronesian
Area Mindoro, the Philippines
Source Harold C. Conklin (1954)
Life-Form Terms kāyu **tree** (woody plant)/**wood**
             ⁷ilamnun **grerb** (grass+herb+fern+moss+lichen+fungus+alga)
             wākat **vine** (vine)

Discussion The **tree** life-form encompasses all plants whose stems are woody, but not vinelike. **Grerb** includes all herbaceous plants or very small plants that lack a vinelike stem. Conklin (1954: 92) writes that in certain contexts *ʔilamnun* refers primarily to gramineous herbs but adds that where contrast is desired at a higher level "there is no ambiguity and most ferns and fern allies, mosses, lichen, fungi, and algae are thus classed together with all non-vinelike herbaceous plants." The **vine** life-form includes both ligneous and herbaceous vines.

Case 59a.

Language Hewa (Stage 4)
Classification Sepik Hill, Sepik, Central New Guinea, Indo-Pacific
Area Sepik District, Papua New Guinea
Source Paul W. Vollrath (personal communication)
Life-Form Terms me **tree** (tree+woody bush)/**wood**
  pokole **grerb** (grass+herb)
  le **vine** (vine)

Discussion The **tree** category encompasses only trees and other woody plants that are found in the wild and, thus, excludes planted specimens. The **grerb** term is also specifically the name of a short grass that takes hold in bare spots. While **grerb** primarily encompasses grasses and is almost certainly focused in "grass," the source notes that the category includes everything called weeds.

Case 60a.

Language Hill Pandaram (Stage 4)
Classification Dravidian
Area South India
Source Brian Morris (1976)
Life-Form Terms maram **tree** (woody plant (tree+shrub))
  chedi **grerb** (grass+herb)
  valli **vine** (vine)
  kodi **vine** (vine)

Discussion Morris describes the **tree** term as follows: "is often used to refer to the forest generally . . . but more specifically it refers to woody plants, and includes trees and shrubs." The **grerb** life-form consists of "epiphytes, ferns and herbaceous plants" and is glossed by Morris as "small plant." It is assumed here that grasses are included in **grerb** since they are kinds of herbaceous plants.

Case 61a.

Language Hmong (Stage 4)
Classification Miao-Yao
Area Laos
Source J. E. Vidal and J. Lemoine (1970)
Life-Form Terms ntoo **tree** (tree)
                 nroj **grerb** (grass+herb)
                 hmab **vine** (vine)

Case 62a.

Language Ibataan (Stage 4)
Classification (Ivatan dialect), Cordilleran, Philippine, Northwest Austronesian, Austronesian
Area The Philippines
Source Rundell Maree (personal communication)
Life-Form Terms kayokayo **tree** (tree)
                 tamek **grerb** (grass+herb+bush)
                 oloten **vine** (vine)
Discussion The "tree" term is reduplicated *kayo* "wood." Plants included in **grerb** are basically those which are not usable or otherwise not classified.

Case 63a.

Language Iloko (Stage 4)
Classification Cordilleran, Philippine, Northwest Austronesian, Austronesian
Area The Philippines
Source Morice Vanoverbergh (1927)
Life-Form Terms káyo **tree** (tree)/**wood**
                 róot **grerb** (grass+herb)
                 lánot **vine** (vine)

Case 64a.

Language Ilongot (Stage 4)
Classification Northwest Austronesian, Austronesian
Area Luzon, the Philippines
Source Michelle Z. Rosaldo (personal communication)

Life-Form Terms keyu **tree** (tree)/**wood**

　　　　　　　　ra'ek **grerb** (grass+herb)

　　　　　　　　wakar **vine** (vine)

Discussion In some contexts the **grerb** term is used as if it were a label for plants in general.

Case 65a.

Language Itawis (Stage 4)

Classification Banagic, Cordilleran, Philippine, Northwest Austronesian, Austronesian

Area The Philippines

Source Investigated by the author

Life-Form Terms ka'yu **tree** (tree)/**wood**

　　　　　　　　mulla **grerb** (herb+bush)

　　　　　　　　lanut **vine** (vine)

　　　　　　　　kadat **grass** (grass) *I.L.-F.*

Discussion My Itawis informant stated that there are no individually named species of grass included in *kadat*. Thus the term labels an incipient life-form.

Case 66a.

Language Ixil (Stage 4)

Classification Mayan, Mesoamerican

Area Guatemala

Source Glenn Ayres (personal communication)

Life-Form Terms ¢e⁹ **tree** (tree)/**wood**

　　　　　　　　k'oač **grerb** (grass+herb)

　　　　　　　　aq' **vine** (herbaceous vine)

　　　　　　　　qul **vine** (ligneous vine)

Discussion Ayres mentions that women often use a different term for **grerb**, *k'opač*, which is probably a variant of *k'oač*.

Case 67a.

Language Jacaltec (Stage 4)

Classification Mayan, Mesoamerican

Area Guatemala

Source Christopher Day (personal communication)

Life-Form Terms te⁹ **tree** (tree+cactus)/**wood**

　　　　　　　　telax **grerb** (grass+herb+bush)

　　　　　　　　aq' **vine** (vine)

Discussion The **grerb** label is apparently derived from the **tree** term and the "locative of abundance" suffix *-lax*. The term is now a frozen form with no analyzable meaning. According to Day, *telax* is a double-sensed word designating (1) land with certain types of plant cover, or under cultivation, and (2) plants other than trees that are not cultivated. In addition, the term refers to trees and shrubs *if they are small*.

Case 68a.

Language Jarai (Stage 4)
Classification Chamic, West Indonesian, Hesperonesian, Austronesian
Area Central South Vietnam
Source Jacques Dournes (1968)
Life-Form Terms köyau **tree** (tree)/**wood**
           phun köyau **tree** (tree)
           rok **grerb** (grass+herb)
           hre' **vine** (woody vine)

Case 69a.

Language Juchitan Zapotec (Stage 4)
Classification Zapotecan, Mesoamerican
Area Oaxaca, Mexico
Source Investigated by the author with Paul K. Chase
Life-Form Terms yaga **tree** (tree+erect cactus)/**wood**
           guixi **grerb** (grass+herb+fungus+corn plant)
           lubá' **vine** (vine)
Discussion The **tree** category encompasses all large plants that are erect and have a main support (trunk, stem) and, consequently, includes palm and coconut plants in addition to ordinary trees. It also extends to some fairly small erect plants, but these are almost always ligneous. Most informants agree that erect cacti such as the nopal belong in the **tree** category, but some deny this. The term *yaga* also refers to botanical organisms in general including both trees and herbaceous plants. The **grerb** category encompasses all small herbaceous plants usually lacking rigid stems. The corn plant is included in **grerb** perhaps because of its resemblance to grasses. Most, but not all, speakers consider fungi to be kinds of *guixi*.

Case 70a.

Language Karok (Stage 4)
Classification Hokan
Area Northwestern California, U.S.A.
Source John P. Harrington (1932)
Life-Form Terms 'íppa' **tree** (tree)
pírⁱc **grerb** (grass+herb+bush)
'atatúrá·n'nar **vine** (vine)
Discussion The "tree" term also has the expanded sense of "plants in general." The **grerb** term also denotes leaf and foliage.

Case 71a.

Language Kenyah (Stage 4)
Classification West Indonesian, Hesperonesian, Austronesian
Area Sarawak, Malaysia
Source Chin See Chung (personal communication)
Life-Form Terms kayu **tree** (tree+bush+woody plant)/**wood**
u'du **grerb** (grass+herb+sedge)
akar **vine** (vine)
Discussion The **grerb** term designates all low vegetation up to two meters in height. In addition to grasses and small herbaceous plants **grerb** encompasses low woody plants such as sub-shrubs and seedlings. The source notes that there are very few strictly herbaceous plants in the Kenyan environment. The **grerb** term is often used to mean "weeds" in cultivated fields.

Case 72a.

Language Kiriwinian (Stage 4)
Classification Papua Austronesian, Oceanic, Austronesian
Area Trobriand Islands
Source Bronislaw Malinowski (1965)
Life-Form Terms ka'i **tree** (tree+bush)/**wood**
munumunu **grerb** (grass+herb)
wotunu **vine** (vine)
Discussion In a broader sense the word *ka'i* means "plants in general." Malinowski writes that *munumunu* "is any plant which is neither a tree or a creeper; a plant, that is, which has no woody stem and which does not wind round a support or creep along the soil . . . always signifies a plant which is not cultivated in the gardens, nor grown in the village, nor round the houses. . . ."

Case 73a.

Language Kisi (Stage 4)

Classification Southern Branch, West Atlantic, Niger-Congo, Niger-Kordofanian

Area Sierra Leone

Source F. C. Deighton (1957)

Life-Form Terms yɔmdo **tree** (tree)

bilõ **grerb** (grass+herb)

pundule **vine** (woody vine)

Discussion The "vine" term translates literally "bush-rope."

Case 74a.

Language Koiwai (Stage 4)

Classification Moluccan Austronesian, Austronesian

Area Bomberai Peninsula, West Irian

Source Jean Walker (personal communication)

Life-Form Terms ai **tree** (large plant+vine)/**wood**

mariut **grerb** (small plant)

waras **vine** (vine)

Discussion The source describes *ai* as "any plant larger than very low shrubs
and grass, examples: coconut palm, sago palm, iron wood, frangiapani, rotan
and all vines, banana tree, any bush higher than 1 ft. off the ground." The
grerb term extends to grasses, shrubs and any ground-cover less than approximately one foot off the ground.

Case 75a.

Language Kugu-Nganhchara (Stage 4)

Classification Middle Pama, Pama-Maric, Pama-Nyungan, Australian

Area Cape York Peninsula, Australia

Source John R. von Sturmer (personal communication)

Life-Form Terms yuku **tree** (tree)

waka **grerb** (grass+reed+herb)

nhaye **vine** (vine)

Discussion The "vine" term also denotes fabricated strings made from plants
other than vines.

Case 76a.

Language Lao (Stage 4)
Classification Southwestern Tai, Kam-Tai
Area Laos
Source Jules Vidal (1963)
Life-Form Terms tōn **tree** (tree+bush)
              'nha **grerb** (grass+herb)
              khua **vine** (vine)
Discussion The **grerb** term does not apply to plants greater than approximately two meters in height.

Case 77a.

Language Machiguenga (Stage 4)
Classification Maipuran, Arawakan, Equatorial, Andean-Equatorial
Area Peru
Source France-Marie Renard-Casevitz (personal communication)
Life-Form Terms intšato **tree** (tree)
              tobaširi **grerb** (grass+herb)
              šibitsa **vine** (vine)
Discussion The **grerb** term translates literally "many vegetation shoots."

Case 78a.

Language Manja (Stage 4)
Classification Eastern (of Adamawa-Eastern), Niger-Congo, Niger-Kordo-
   fanian
Area Central African Republic
Source A.-M. Vergiat (1969)
Life-Form Terms te **tree** (tree)/**wood**
              zo **grerb** (grass+herb)
              nya **vine** (vine)
Discussion The "vine" term also denotes rope. The same life-form terms and referential extensions occur in Gbaya, a closely related language.

Case 79a.

Language Manobo Blit (Stage 4)
Classification Sulic, Philippine, Northwest Austronesian, Austronesian
Area Mindanao, the Philippines
Source D. E. Yen (1976)

Life-Form Terms kayu **tree** (tree)
　　　　　　　klu'on **grerb** (grass+herb+bush)
　　　　　　　kagbul **vine** (vine)

Case 80a.

Language Mende (Stage 4)
Classification Southwestern Mande, Mande, Niger-Congo, Niger-Kordofanian
Area Sierra Leone, Liberia
Source (1) F. C. Deighton (1957); (2) Frederick William Hugh Migeod
(1913).
Life-Form Terms ngulu **tree** (tree)
　　　　　　　gbiti **grerb** (grass+herb)
　　　　　　　ngeya-kɔ **vine** (woody vine)
Discussion The above terms and referential extensions are from Deighton.
Migeod gives what is probably an alternate **grerb** label, *tifa/lifa*, glossed
"plant," this used in the sense of "plants versus trees." (Migeod does not list
gbiti.) Deighton also gives a number of different terms for grasses some of
which have fairly broad referential ranges, e.g., *ngala* "more or less general
name for tall grasses." None of the latter can be determined with certainty to
be true **grass** life-form labels.

Case 81a.

Language Mikir (Stage 4)
Classification Naga, Naga-Kuki-Chin, Tibeto-Burman
Area Northeastern India
Source S. K. Jain and S. K. Borthakur (personal communication)
Life-Form Terms araung **tree** (tree)
　　　　　　　tipli **grerb** (grass+herb)
　　　　　　　rikang **vine** (vine+straggling shrub)

Case 82a.

Language Muyuw (Stage 4)
Classification Papua Austronesian, Oceanic, Austronesian
Area Woodlark Island, Papua New Guinea
Source David Lithgow (personal communication)
Life-Form Terms kay **tree** (tree+bush)
　　　　　　　awuyow **grerb** (grass+herb)
　　　　　　　vatul **vine** (vine)

Discussion The source describes the **tree** class as including "trees, and bush-plants with straight stems, or bushes with hard stems." **Grerb** encompasses "grass and weeds with soft stems."

Case 83a.

Language Ngbaka Ma'bo (Stage 4)
Classification Eastern (of Adamawa-Eastern), Niger-Congo, Niger-Kordo-fanian
Area Central African Republic
Source Jacqueline Thomas (1977)
Life-Form Terms náā **tree** (tree+woody bush)
　　　　　　　　ndí **grerb** (large herb (+large grass?))
　　　　　　　　nzákánì **grerb** (small herb (+small grass?))
　　　　　　　　kpó **vine** (large woody vine)
　　　　　　　　kú **vine** (herbaceous vine)
Discussion This is the only language surveyed that encodes **grerb** through binary opposition, i.e. "large herb"/"small herb." Both **grerb** terms are described as encompassing "herbaceous plants." It is not clear whether grasses are included among the latter. The source gives another general term, *kpìkìsi.kpáā*, which might be appropriately codified as **grass**. This term is described in French as referring to " 'plantes grasses' à tiges ou feuilles charnues," indicating that it may not encompass all grasses. The source adds that this category is of less importance than the others listed above.

Case 84a.

Language Nuaulu (Stage 4)
Classification West Ceram, Ambon-Timor, East Indonesian, Austronesian
Area Ceram Island, Indonesia
Source Roy F. Ellen (1973, 1975a)
Life-Form Terms ai **tree** (tree+woody bush)
　　　　　　　　rahue **grerb** (herb+bush (+grass?))
　　　　　　　　wane **vine** (vine)
Discussion The gloss for **grerb**, "herbs and shrubby plants," does not clearly indicate the inclusion or exclusion of grasses.

Case 85a.

Language Patep (Stage 4)
Classification Buang, Papuan Austronesian, Oceanic, Austronesian
Area Morobe Province, Papua New Guinea

Source Linda Lauck (personal communication)
Life-Form Terms xax **tree** (tree+bamboo+banana+sugar cane)/**wood**
nita **grerb** (grass+herb+corn)
yihi **vine** (vine)
Discussion The **tree** class includes trees and other tall, sturdy plants which stand upright. The **grerb** category encompasses grasses and other herbaceous plants which stand up but are not sturdy. According to the source most exemplars of **grerb** are grasses. This perhaps indicates a "grass" focus.

Case 86a.

Language Paumari (Stage 4)
Classification Arauan, Arawakan, Equatorial, Andean-Equatorial
Area Amazonas State, Brazil
Source Shirley Chapman (personal communication)
Life-Form Terms ava **tree** (tree+palmeira)/**wood**
hogoi **grerb** (grass+herb)
ahoi **vine** (vine)
Discussion The **grerb** term encompasses all uncultivated small herbaceous plants. Chapman notes that the Paumari tend not to use a generic form when the specific plant is known. This indicates that the above classes may be incipient rather than full life-forms.

Case 87a.

Language Pocomchi (Stage 4)
Classification Mayan, Mesoamerican
Area Guatemala
Source (1) Linda Kay Brown (personal communication); (2) Marvin K. Mayers (1958).
Life-Form Terms če·ʔ **tree** (tree)/**wood**
k'iče·ʔ **grerb** (grass+herb+vine)
k'aham **vine** (vine)
Discussion The above terms, except that for "vine," and referential extension are from Brown. The "vine" term, from Mayers and not reported by Brown, is transliterated into standard linguistic symbols to accord with the orthography of Brown.

Case 88a.

Language Roglai (Stage 4)
Classification West Indonesian, Hesperonesian, Austronesian

Area Vietnam
Source Jacque Dournes (1973)
Life-Form Terms köyöu **tree** (tree)/**wood**
köyöu phun köyöu **tree** (tree)
harö **grerb** (grass+herb)
tölöi **vine** (vine)

Case 89a.

Language Samal (Stage 4)
Classification Philippine, Northwest Austronesian, Austronesian
Area Linuŋan Island, Basilan Strait, Southwestern Mindanao, the Philippines
Source (1) Robert A. Randall (personal communication); (2) Robert A. Randall (1976).
Life-Form Terms kayu **tree** (tree+woody plant)
sagbot **grerb** (grass+herb+vine+mushroom+nonwoody plant)
bahan **vine** (vine)

Case 90a.

Language Sambal (Stage 4)
Classification Philippine, Northwest Austronesian, Austronesian
Area Luzon, the Philippines
Source Robert B. Fox (1952)
Life-Form Terms káyu **tree** (tree)/**wood**
dikót **grerb** (grass+herb)
lamón **grerb** (grass+herb)
kíniw **vine** (vine)
Discussion Both of the **grerb** terms are glossed "grass." However, both clearly extend to herbaceous plants having a broad leaf morphology in addition to plants with bladed, narrow leaves. Whether the two terms cover distinct referential ranges, the same referential range, or partially overlapping ranges is not clear. It is possible that one is focused in grasses and the other in nongrasses, but this is only speculation.

Case 91a.

Language Taubuid (Batangan) (Stage 4)
Classification Hanunoic, Mesophilippine, Sulic, Philippine, Northwest Austronesian, Austronesian
Area Mindoro, the Philippines

Source Fredrick Douglas Pennoyer III (1975)
Life-Form Terms kayu **tree** (tree+woody bush)
makmak **grerb** (grass+herb+herbaceous bush)
uat **vine** (vine)

Case 92a.

Language Temne (Stage 4)
Classification Southern Branch, West Atlantic, Niger-Congo, Niger-Kordofanian
Area Sierra Leone
Source F. C. Deighton (1957)
Life-Form Terms a-kənt **tree** (tree)
a-kereŋ or a-kirin **grerb** (grass+herb)
an-ruŋanɛ **vine** (vine)
ra-beŋa **vine** (woody vine)
an-gbam **vine** (vine)
ra-lel **vine** (vine)
Discussion The last three **vine** terms listed above also designate rope.

Case 93a.

Language Tobelo (Stage 4)
Classification North Halmahera, West Papuan, Indo-Pacific
Area North Moluccas, Indonesia
Source Paul Michael Taylor (1979)
Life-Form Terms o gota **tree** (tree)/**wood** (lumber/firewood)
o rurubu **grerb** (grass+herb)
o gumini **vine** (vine)
Discussion Taylor describes dialectal variation with respect to inclusion of plants in the **tree** life-form class:

> The defining features of *o gota* 'tree' minimally include woodiness of the stem (thus herbaceous plants are not included), ascendant or erect stems (thus woody vines are not included), and that woody tissue is found throughout a cross-section of the stem (thus palms, manioc, etc. also are distinct). For Tobelo-Boeng speakers at Loleba these features will adequately distinguish 'trees' from 'vines', 'herbaceous weeds' and other plants. For "Dodinga"-dialect speakers at Pasir Putih (Kec, Jailolo), however, the small woody plants like *o digo* (. . . *Sida sp.* . . . .) or *o kokereehe* (*Crotalaria retusa L.*) are classed with *o rurubu* 'herbaceous weeds' rather than with *o gota* 'tree'; these and other cases lead us

to posit another distinctive feature of the 'tree' class in the Dodinga dialect: fairly large size (approximate minimal full-grown diameter of about 3–4 cm and height over 2 m).

Taylor also notes that any young uncultivated "tree" may be called *o rurubu* in the word's sense of "weed." On this point he writes:

One often hears of a particular small sapling, *o rurubu nenanga o gota* 'this weed (*o rurubu*) is a tree (*o gota*)' (non-contrastive sense of *o rurubu*); or, of the same sapling, *nenanga o rurubuua, o gota ho* 'this is not a (member of the) herbaceous weed (class), it is a tree' (*o rurubu* here contrasts with *o gota*).

The latter contrastive sense of *o rurubu* vis-à-vis *o gota*, of course, is **grerb**. The **vine** term also means "rope."

Case 94a.

Language Waodani (Stage 4)
Classification unclassified
Area Eastern Ecuador
Source M. Catherine Peeke (personal communication)
Life-Form Terms awä **tree** (large woody plant+palm+banana+yucca+
                      bush)/**wood**
               gaguïbæ **grerb** (grass+herb)
               ööbë **vine** (vine)
Discussion Some speakers limit the **tree** term to non-fruitbearing trees. Also the **tree** term has the restricted sense of ligneous tree, and, thus, excludes palms, banana plants, and so on. The source gives "grass and some small herbs" as *gaguïbæ*'s gloss.

Case 95a.

Language Western Subanun (Stage 4)
Classification Mesophilippine, Sulic, Philippine, Northwest Austronesian,
    Austronesian
Area Mindanao, the Philippines
Source William C. Hall (personal communication)
Life-Form Terms kayu **tree** (tree+woody bush)/**wood**
               sigbut **grerb** (grass+herb+grain plant)
               bolagon **vine** (vine)

Case 96a.
_____

Language Wik-Ngathana (Stage 4)
Classification Pama-Maric, Pama-Nyungan, Australian
Area Western Cape York Peninsula, Australia
Source Peter Sutton and Dermot Smyth (personal communication)
Life-Form Terms yuka **tree** (tree)/**wood**

                       yempa **grerb** (grass+herb)

                       nhaya **vine** (vine)

Discussion Succulents, seaweeds, slimes, and mosses are excluded from the above categories. The "vine" term also refers to anything from which string can be derived including trees.

         Three Life-Forms: **tree+grerb+grass.**

97a. Classical Nahuatl (Mexico)

98a. Djinang (Australia)

99a. Gugadja (Australia)

100a. Haida (British Columbia, Canada)

101a. Japanese (Japan)

102a. Mataco (Argentina)

103a. Mitla Zapotec (Mexico)

104a. North Saami (Norway)

105a. Papago (Arizona, U.S.A.)

106a. Southern Paiute (Cedar City dialect) (Utah, U.S.A.)

107a. Tiriyo (Brazil)

108a. Upper Tanana (Alaska, U.S.A.)

109a. Zuni (New Mexico, U.S.A.)

Case 97a.
_____

Language Classical Nahuatl (Stage 4)
Classification Aztecan, Uto-Aztecan, Aztec-Tanoan
Area Mexico
Source Bernardo R. Ortiz de Montellano (1981)
Life-Form Terms quauitl **tree** (tree)

                       xihuitl **grerb** (grass+herb)

                       zacatl **grass** (grass)

Discussion Ortiz de Montellano's paper is based on colonial documents, especially Bernardo de Sahagún's *Florentine Codex: General History of the Things of New Spain* (1575–1577). Inclusive relationships and referential extensions are determined from paragraph headings in the latter work which are presumed to be groupings identified by Classical Nahuatl speakers.

Case 98a.

Language Djinang (Stage 4)
Classification Murngic, Pama-Nyungan, Australian
Area North-Central Arnhem Land, Australia
Source Bruce E. Waters (personal communication)
Life-Form Terms gurrchi or kurrchi **tree** (tree)
                junggi **tree** (tree)/**wood**
                murrur.rt **grerb** (grass+herb)
                yurryarr **grass** (grass)
Discussion Waters writes that *junggi* denotes " 'wood', which includes 'fire-wood' and also refers to 'fire' . . . can also be used as a generic term for 'tree', but *gurrchi* is more correct."

Case 99a.

Language Gugadja (Stage 4)
Classification Wati, Southwest Pama-Nyungan, Pama-Nyungan, Australian
Area Western Australia
Source (1) Anthony R. Peile (personal communication); (2) Anthony R. Peile (n.d.).
Life-Form Terms waḍa **tree** (tree)/**wood**
                waḍa lambanba **grerb** (grass+herb+small bush+fungus)
                yibiṟi **grass** (grass)
Discussion The **grerb** label is created through linguistic modification of the "tree" term and translates literally "small tree."

Case 100a.

Language Haida (Stage 4)
Classification Athapascan-Eyak, Na-Dene
Area British Columbia, Canada
Source Nancy Jean Turner (1974)
Life-Form Terms ihḵ'aayií or ihḵ'aay **tree** (deciduous tree+branching shrub)
                ihḵ'amaál **tree** (coniferous tree)
                tlaas **tree** (coniferous tree)
                ḵaayt or ḵiiyt **tree** (evergreen tree)
                xil **grerb** (herb)
                ḵ'an **grass** (grass)

Discussion The terms *ihk̲'aayií* and *ihk̲'aay* also mean "deciduous branch." A number of nonbranching herbaceous forms are members of the *ihk̲'aay* category. *Ihk̲'amaál* refers more specifically to *Juniperus* and *k̲aayt/k̲iiyt* refers more specifically to *Picea sitchensis*. In addition to "herbaceous plants (other than grasses)" the **grerb** term designates both leaf and medicine. The "grass" term restrictively denotes *Elymus mollis*.

Case 101a.

Language Japanese (Stage 4)
Classification Altaic?
Area Japan
Source Kumiko Yamamoto (1980)
Life-Form Terms ki **tree** (tree)
                kusa **grerb** (grass+herb)
                shiba **grass** (grass)
Discussion Glosses given for the above terms in the source are as follows: *ki* "woody plants having trunks and branches," *kusa* "herbaceous plants which do not have woody characteristics," *shiba* "turf, sod, grass."

Case 102a.

Language Mataco (Stage 4)
Classification Mataco, Macro-Panoan, Ge-Pano-Carib
Area Northern Argentina
Source María Teresa Viñas Urquiza (personal communication).
Life-Form Terms ha?la **tree** (tree)
                jačujah **grerb** (herb)
                hup **grass** (grass)

Case 103a.

Language Mitla Zapotec (Stage 4)
Classification Zapotecan, Oto-Manguean, Mesoamerican
Area Oaxaca, Mexico
Source (1) Ellen Messer (1975); (2) Morris Stubblefield (personal communication); (3) Investigated by the author with Paul K. Chase.
Life-Form Terms yahg **tree** (tree+woody bush)/**wood**
                kʷan **grerb** (herb)
                giš **grass** (grass)
Discussion The above terms and referential extensions are from Messer. Both the **tree** and **grerb** terms can also be used in reference to plants in general.

Messer describes *kʷan* as encompassing plants with green, nonwoody stems having broad leaf morphology. These contrast with plants identified as *giš* which have a blade leaf morphology. The term *giš* can also denote all small vegetation with nearly indistinguishable leaves. It is possible for a plant to be identified by each of the above terms during its life-cycle. For example, Messer writes that "the field weed *yäb* may be called *giš* when very small, *kʷan* when larger and full leaved, and *yahg* when large, dry, and suitable for fuel." Each of the other two sources report a "vine" term, but a different one in each case. Stubblefield gives *bijuc* for "vine" which is a borrowing from Mexican Spanish (*bejuco* "vine"). Chase and I elicited the term *lobaʔa* for "vine." Messer's ethnobotanical study was considerably larger in scope than those of either of the two other sources. Since she does not report a "vine" term, it is assumed here that the category is of low salience and probably unknown to most speakers of the language.

Case 104a.

Language North Saami (Stage 4)
Classification Lappic, Finno-Ugric, Uralic
Area Norway
Source Myrdene Anderson (1978)
Life-Form Terms muorra **tree** (tree)/**wood**
                     rássi **grerb** (herb)
                     suoi'dni **grass** (grass+sedge)
Discussion The "tree" term is applied to all woody species, but it can be used more restrictively in reference to deciduous trees alone contrasting with coniferous trees (*goac'ci muorra*). The source notes that while most members of **grerb** are herbaceous, an important subgroup, *dagɲasat* "heath plants," are woody perennials.

Case 105a.

Language Papago (Stage 4)
Classification Sonoran, Uto-Aztecan, Aztec-Tanoan
Area Arizona, U.S.A.
Source (1) Dean Saxton (personal communication); (2) Madeleine Mathiot (personal communication); (3) Madeleine Mathiot (1964).
Life-Form Terms ú'us **tree** (tree)
                     ṣá'i **grerb** (grass+herb+bush)
                     wáṣai **grass** (grass)
Discussion The above terms and referential extensions are from Saxton. He writes that the "tree" term also encompasses any woody plant that eventually

reaches the size of a tree. The **grerb** term also denotes brush and waste according to Saxton. Mathiot (personal communication) identifies the latter term as referring to "hay, bale of hay, trash" and does not find an extension to "small herbaceous plants." Her 1964 discussion indicates that **grerb** is recognized only implicitly. She (1964: 158) describes for Papago speakers a "subclass" of plants having no "taxonomic tag," encompassing wild perennials. Plants of this unlabeled group are "defined negatively as not belonging with either cacti or trees and bushes." The differences here perhaps are attributable to varying idiolectal and dialectal usage involving extension of a word (*ṣá'i*) primarily meaning "brush, trash, waste," to small herbaceous plants in general (cf. Chapter 6).

Case 106a.

Language Southern Paiute (Cedar City dialect) (Stage 4)
Classification Numic, Uto-Aztecan, Aztec-Tanoan
Area Cedar City, Utah, U.S.A.
Source Catherine Louise Sweeney Fowler (1972)
Life-Form Terms maʔábɨ wɨnídɨ **tree**(tree)
　　　　　　　　maʔábɨ **grerb** (herb(+grass?))
　　　　　　　　pɨ́ɨpɨni **grerb** (herb(+grass?))
　　　　　　　　hukᵂísibɨ **grass** (grass)

Discussion The "tree" term translates literally "standing plant." Fowler writes that the latter label "was recorded only in the context of taxonomic discussions, it may be somewhat artificial." The term *maʔábɨ* has two distinct ranges: (1) all plants except trees (and, possibly, grasses?), and (2) plants in general including trees. Fowler notes that *maʔábɨ* is only rarely used in the more expansive sense of (2). While the primary meaning of *pɨ́ɨpɨni* is clearly "weeds," its **grerb** range is certain since informants apply the term to several plants with uses including even medicinal ones. The "grass" term designates "numerous species of unused grasses." Plant life-form classification in the Cedar City dialect of Southern Paiute is virtually identical to that of the Kaibab dialect also studied by Fowler. For dialectal differences see Southern Paiute (Chemehuevi dialect) (28a) and Southern Paiute (Kawaiisu dialect) (2a).

Case 107a.

Language Tiriyo (Stage 4)
Classification Carib, Macro-Carib, Ge-Pano-Carib
Area Brazil
Source Peter Rivière (personal communication)

Life-Form Terms wewe **tree** (tree)/**wood**
                    itú-pixi **grerb** (herb)
                    oi **grass** (grass)
Discussion The **grerb** term translates literally "small forest" (*itú* = forest, *-pixi* = small in quality). In addition to small nongrass herbaceous plants, the **grerb** term denotes secondary growth.

Case 108a.

Language Upper Tanana (Stage 4)
Classification Northern Athapascan, Athapascan, Athapascan-Eyak, Na-Dene
Area Interior Alaska, U.S.A.
Source Paul Milanowski (personal communication)
Life-Form Terms ts'oo **tree** (tree+woody plant)/**wood**
                    neshee **grerb** (herb(+grass?))
                    tɬ'oh **grass** (grass)
Discussion The **grerb** term is the nominalized form of the verb "it grows." The source is not sure of the inclusion of grasses in **grerb**.

Case 109a.

Language Zuni (Stage 4)
Classification Penutian
Area New Mexico, U.S.A.
Source Willard Walker (1966, 1979)
Life-Form Terms ta'tta:we **tree** (tree)
                    ha'ʔta:we **grerb** (herb+bush(+grass?))
                    pe'ʔta:we **grass** (grass)
Discussion Walker (1966 and 1979) assigns the gloss "weeds" to *ha'ʔta:we*, but describes it as encompassing "all plants or bushes having /ha'we/ or leaves." This category probably extends to all grasses since Walker cites "dropseed grass" as a sample member. He also lists the term *kʷi'mi:we* to which he assigns the gloss "herbs, roots." This term may be an alternate **grerb** label, but it seems more likely that it is restricted to small herbaceous plants and roots used for medicinal and cooking purposes. Walker (1966) writes that only one subcategory of *pe'ʔta:we* (**grass**) is known to him, i.e. *pe':cikowa* "blue gramma," suggesting that the **grass** class is actually an incipient life-form. There is another general plant term, *ła'tta:we*, to which Walker assigns the gloss "bushes." However, his description of this class (1966 and 1979) indicates that membership is based on plant life-state rather

than gross morphology and, thus is actually a special purpose category: "all perennial plants which grow in clumps and have no foliage, hence any bush in winter."

> *Three Life-Forms:* **tree + grerb + bush**.
> 110a. Basari (Senegal, Guinea)
> 111a. Bedik (Senegal, Guinea)
> 112a. Dogon (Mali, Upper Volta)
> 113a. Moore (Ghana)
> 114a. Nya Hon (Laos)
> 115a. Puerto Rican Spanish (Massachusetts, U.S.A.)

Case 110a.

Language Basari (Stage 4)
Classification Northern Branch, West Atlantic, Niger-Congo, Niger-Kordofanian
Area Senegal-Guinea border
Source M.-P. Ferry, M. Gessain, and R. Gessain (1974)
Life-Form Terms a-tʌ́x **tree** (tree)
  ɔ-ndʌs **grerb** (grass + herb)
  a-tyʌ́ty **bush** (bush)

Case 111a.

Language Bedik (Stage 4)
Classification Northern Branch, West Atlantic, Niger-Congo, Niger-Kordofanian
Area Senegal-Guinea border
Source M.-P. Ferry, M. Gessain, and R. Gessain (1974)
Life-Form Terms ga-tɔ̀ **tree** (tree)
  gu-tyàm **grerb** (grass + herb)
  ga-tyéty **bush** (bush)
  ga-tʌs **bush** (bush)

Case 112a.

Language Dogon (Stage 4)
Classification Gur, Niger-Congo, Niger-Kordofanian
Area Mali, Upper Volta
Source Germaine Dieterlen (1952)

Life-Form Terms timmu **tree** (tree)
           dogo timmu **grerb** (grass+herb)
           dogo **grerb** (grass+herb)
           uryo **bush** (bush)

Discussion Dogon seems to have developed a **grerb** term (*dogo timmu*) through linguistic modification of its "tree" term. Apparently, *timmu* can be optionally deleted from *dogo timmu* so that *dogo* can be used on its own as a **grerb** label. The original meaning of the modifier, *dogo*, is not given in the source.

Case 113a.

Language Moore (Stage 4)
Classification Gur, Niger-Congo, Niger-Kordofanian
Area Ghana
Source André Prost (personal communication)
Life-Form Terms tiiga **tree** (tree)
           moogo **grerb** (grass+herb)
           tuugu **bush** (bush)

Case 114a.

Language Nya Hon (Stage 4)
Classification West Bahnaric, Mon-Khmer, Austro-Asiatic
Area South Laos
Source J. E. Vidal and B. Wall (1968)
Life-Form Terms llôông **tree** (tree+erect plant)
           bat **grerb** (grass+herb)
           nwEE **bush** (bush)

Case 115a.

Language Puerto Rican Spanish (Stage 4)
Classification Latin, Italic, Indo-European
Area Massachusetts, U.S.A. (migrants)
Source David F. Mulcahy (1967)
Life-Form Terms palo **tree** (tree)
           planta **grerb** (grass+herb)
           mata **bush** (bush)

Discussion The "tree" category excludes palms. The diminutive suffix *-ita* is often affixed to *planta*. Mulcahy notes that the "criterion which is crucial in describing *plant names* in terms of *plant types* is that of largeness, i.e. *plan-*

tita is the smallest type while *palo* and *palma* [palm tree] are the largest."
Presumably *mata* is somewhere in between.

    Three Life-Forms: **tree+grass+vine**.
116a. Amahuaca (Peru)
117a. Atapec Zapotec (Mexico)
118a. Chewa (Malawi)
119a. Gaviao (Brazil)
120a. Isirawa (Irian Jaya)
121a. Jicaque (Honduras)
122a. Mele-Fila (New Hebrides)
123a. Melpa (Papua New Guinea)
124a. Nimboran (Irian Jaya)
125a. Ninam (Brazil, Venezuela)
126a. Pagan Gaddang (The Philippines)

Case 116a.

Language Amahuaca (Stage 4)
Classification Central Pano, Pano, Pano-Tacana, Ge-Pano-Carib
Area Peru
Source Andre-Márcel d'Ans (1972)
Life-Form Terms hí: **tree** (tree)
                şačí$^{\textrm{ʔ}}$ **grass** (large grass+large sedge)
                wasí$^{\textrm{ʔ}}$ **grass** (small grass+small sedge)
                niši$^{\textrm{ʔ}}$ **vine** (vine)

Case 117a.

Language Atapec Zapotec (Stage 4)
Classification Zapotecan, Oto-Manguean, Mesoamerican
Area Sierra de Juaréz, Oaxaca, Mexico
Source Neal Nellis (personal communication)
Life-Form Terms ya **tree** (tree)/**wood**
                íxxi$^{\textrm{ʔ}}$ **grass** (grass)
                łuɓá **vine** (vine)
Discussion The "grass" term also denotes pasture, high altitude field, and
brush.

Case 118a.

Language Chewa (Stage 4)
Classification Central Eastern Bantu, Bantu Proper, Bantoid, Benue-Congo, Niger-Congo, Niger-Kordofanian
Area Malawi
Source (1) Brian Morris (personal communication); (2) Brian Morris (1980).
Life-Form Terms mtengo **tree** (tree+woody plant)
                   maudzu **grass** (grass+small lily)
                   mtsitsi **vine** (small herbaceous climber)
Discussion **Grass** includes all grasses and grass-like plants. The primary meaning of the **vine** term is "root."

Case 119a.

Language Gaviao (Stage 4)
Classification Monde, Tupi, Equatorial, Andean-Equatorial
Area Brazil
Source Horst Stute (personal communication)
Life-Form Terms ìhv **tree** (tree+tree-like plant)/**wood**
                   pájá sév **grass** (grass)
                   pájá níhn **grass** (grass)
                   dapòh **vine** (vine)
Discussion The "tree" term refers to "all trees and also less woody and smaller tree-like plants (upright standing plants)." The two **grass** labels are probably derived from the Portuguese word for "straw" (*palha*).

Case 120a.

Language Isirawa (also Saberi) (Stage 4)
Classification Upper Tor, North New Guinea?, Indo-Pacific
Area Irian Jaya
Source Carol J. Erickson (personal communication)
Life-Form Terms warara **tree** (tall woody plant)/**wood**
                   saafi **grass** (grass)
                   iriva **vine** (vine)
Discussion The **tree** life-form excludes banana plants and palm type trees. The **grass** term is applied primarily to short grasses. The **vine** category includes both thicker varieties and thinner ones used as string and rope. A fourth term *ufufa*, which covers all small plants that grow where they are not wanted (weeds), also extends to any tall grasses.

Case 121a.

Language Jicaque (Stage 4)
Classification varying opinions, no conclusive argument
Area Honduras
Source Ronald K. Dennis (personal communication)
Life-Form Terms yo **tree** (tree)/**wood**
　　　　　　　　sacate **grass** (grass)
　　　　　　　　'üpü **vine** (vine)
Discussion The "grass" term is borrowed from regional Spanish (*zacate* "grass"). The "vine" label also denotes rope, twine.

Case 122a.

Language Mele-Fila (Stage 4)
Classification Samoic Outlier, Polynesian, Eastern Oceanic, Oceanic, Austronesian
Area Southwest Pacific, New Hebrides
Source Ross Clark (personal communication)
Life-Form Terms raakau **tree** (tree)/**wood**
　　　　　　　　ñaanamu **grass** (grass)
　　　　　　　　vaavaa **vine** (vine)
Discussion The source writes that the "grass" term might be better translated "lawn." Various grasses that are deliberately cultivated as ground cover apparently constitute the focus of *ñaanamu*. The "vine" term also designates rope.

Case 123a.

Language Melpa (Stage 4)
Classification Hagen, Hagen-Wahgi-Jimi-Chimbu, East New Guinea Highlands, Central New Guinea, Indo-Pacific
Area Papua New Guinea
Source Andrew Strathern (personal communication)
Life-Form Terms nde **tree** (tree+bush)/**wood**
　　　　　　　　öi **grass** (grass)
　　　　　　　　kan **vine** (vine)
Discussion The "grass" term often carries the sense of weeds or undergrowth found in fallow or growing in untended gardens. It also means specifically "swordgrass," *Imperata cylindrica*, which is used for house-thatching. "Tail" constitutes a nonbotanical referent of the word. The "vine" term also designates string, rope, and other manmade flexible, elongated objects.

Case 124a.

Language Nimboran (Stage 4)
Classification Nimboran, North Papuan, Central New Guinea or North New Guinea?, Indo-Pacific
Area Grimi River Valley, Irian Jaya
Source Kevin R. May (personal communication)
Life-Form Terms di **tree** (tree+palm)/**wood**
                mesúm **grass** (grass+reed+sugar cane+bamboo)
                tanggang **vine** (vine)

Case 125a.

Language Ninam (Stage 4)
Classification Yanoama, Waican, Macro-Chibchan
Area Brazil and Venezuela border area
Source Carole Swain (personal communication)
Life-Form Terms wiitihik **tree** (tree+woody bush)/**wood**
                kaplixak **grass** (grass)
                thothok **vine** (vine)
Discussion Describing plants in her living compound Swain writes: "There are several kinds of tall, four foot grasses near here. Some qualify as *kaplixak*. Others have their own specific names." This may indicate that *kaplixak* is a label for an incipient, rather than full-fledged **grass** life-form class.

Case 126a.

Language Pagan Gaddang (Stage 4)
Classification Gaddang, Banagic, Cordilleran, Philippine, Northwest Austronesian, Austronesian
Area The Philippines
Source Ben J. Wallace (1970)
Life-Form Terms kayu **tree** (tree+woody bush+bamboo)
                kadat **grass** (grass)
                mapadat **vine** (vine+creeping fern+rattan)

      Three Life-Forms: **tree+grass+bush**.
      127a. Kaguru (Tanzania)
      128a. Nez Perce (Idaho, Washington, Oregon, U.S.A.)

Case 127a.
_____

Language Kaguru (Stage 4)
Classification Central Eastern Bantu, Bantu Proper, Bantoid, Benue-Congo,
  Niger-Congo, Niger-Kordofanian
Area Tanzania
Source T. O. Beidelman (1964)
Life-Form Terms ibike **tree** (tree)
                mabago or mbago **grass** (grass)
                isukusi **bush** (bush)
Discussion Complete glosses assigned to the "grass" and "bush" terms are
as follows: *mabago* or *mbago* "grass, a grassy place, a grassy wilderness, the
bush," and *isukusi* "bush, shrub, stump."

Case 128a.
_____

Language Nez Perce (Stage 4)
Classification Sahaptin-Nez Perce, Penutian
Area Idaho, Washington, Oregon, U.S.A.
Source (1) Haruo Aoki (personal communication); (2) A Missionary of the
  Society of Jesus (1895).
Life-Form Terms tewlíˑkt **tree** (tree)
                číxčix **grass** (grass)
                pátan **bush** (bush)
Discussion The above terms and referential ranges are from Aoki. The 1895
dictionary cited above indicates extension of the **grass** term to nonbladed her-
baceous plants. The latter work assigns the glosses "grass" and "herbage" to
the term. Thus it is possible that *číxčix* labeled **grerb** in the past, perhaps with
a "grass" focus.

STAGE 5 LANGUAGES.

Four Life-Forms: **tree+grerb+grass+vine**.
129a. Akawaio (Guyana)
130a. Amuzgo (Mexico)
131a. Ando (Ivory Coast)
132a. Bunaq (Timor)
133a. Carapana (Colombia)
134a. Colorado (Ecuador)
135a. Daga (Papua New Guinea)
136a. Highland Tequistlatec (Mexico)

137a. Huichol (Mexico)
138a. Kayova (Brazil, Paraguay)
139a. Kekchi (Guatemala)
140a. Makiritare (Venezuela)
141a. Mazatec (Mexico)
142a. Mokilese (Eastern Caroline Islands)
143a. Mopan (Guatemala, Belize)
144a. Muinane (Colombia)
145a. Navaho (Arizona, New Mexico, Utah, Colorado, U.S.A.)
146a. Ndumba (Papua New Guinea)
147a. Sierra Popoluca (Mexico)
148a. Sre (Vietnam)
149a. Tasaday (The Philippines)
150a. Teen (Ivory Coast)
151a. Tepehua (Mexico)
152a. Tewa (New Mexico, U.S.A.)
153a. Texmelucan Zapotec (Mexico)
154a. Tzeltal (Mexico)
155a. Tzotzil (Zinacantan dialect) (Mexico)
156a. Tzutujil (Guatemala)
157a. Yaqui (Mexico and Arizona, U.S.A.)
158a. Yucatec (Mexico)
159a. Zoogocho Zapotec (Mexico)

Case 129a.

Language Akawaio (Stage 5)
Classification Northern Carib, Carib, Macro-Carib, Ge-Pano-Carib
Area Guyana
Source John R. Dorman (personal communication)
Life-Form Terms yöi **tree** (tree)
               d'yek **grerb** (grass+herb+herbaceous vine+soft tree+
                   young wooden tree+small crop plant)
               wānuk **grass** (grass)
               chī'nak **vine** (vine)
Discussion According to Dorman *d'yek* is "any living plant, other than *yöi*."
Thus grasses (*wānuk*) and vines (*chī'nak*) are included in the **grerb** category.
Soft trees included in **grerb** are the banana, pawpaw, and coconut. Dorman
mentions that young wooden trees that will later become *yöi* are known
as *d'yek*.

Case 130a.

Language Amuzgo (Stage 5)
Classification Oto-Manguean, Mesoamerican
Area Oaxaca, Mexico
Source Nicholas A. Hopkins (1980a)
Life-Form Terms tz'on **tree** (tree)
                tzko jndë **grerb** (herb)
                jndë **grass** (grass+maize+cane+reed+garlic+rice)
                tz'ö **vine** (vine)
Discussion The **grerb** term is a combination of the word for leaf, *tzko*, and the word for grass, *jndë*. There is another term, *tzko ndoen*, literally, "wide leaf," which apparently extends to broadleaf herbaceous plants. Whether or not the latter plants are included in *tzko jndë* is not mentioned by the source. The **grass** term also means "brush" (Spanish *monte*).

Case 131a.

Language Ando (Stage 5)
Classification Volta-Comoe, Kwa, Niger-Congo, Niger-Kordofanian
Area Ivory Coast
Source Leotien E. Visser (1975)
Life-Form Terms baka **tree** (tree)/**wood**
                ndri **grerb** (herb+mushroom)
                oua **grass** (savannah grass)
                nyaman **vine** (vine)
Discussion Grasses apparently are not included in **grerb**, although this is not entirely clear. The **grass** term also denotes savannah and dryness.

Case 132a.

Language Bunaq (Stage 5)
Classification Timor, Timor-Alor, "West Papuan," Indo-Pacific
Area Timor
Source Claudine Friedberg (1979)
Life-Form Terms hotel **tree** (tree)
                u **grerb** (herb(+grass?))
                an **grass** (grass)
                mun **vine** (vine)

Case 133a

Language Carapana (Stage 5)
Classification Tucanoan, Macro-Tucanoan, Andean-Equatorial
Area Colombia
Source Ronald G. Metzger (personal communication)
Life-Form Terms yucɨ **tree** (tree)
　　　　　　　moetɨ̃ẽ **grerb** (grass+herb)
　　　　　　　capunirɨ̃jẽ **grerb** (grass+herb)
　　　　　　　carorije **grerb** (grass+herb)
　　　　　　　taa **grass** (grass)
　　　　　　　carupawɛ̄rɨ̄ **vine** (vine)
Discussion The "tree" category excludes palms. All three **grerb** terms refer to small herbaceous plants which are not cultivated. In addition, all three have similar negative literal meanings: *moetɨ̃ẽ* "useless stuff," *capunirɨ̃jẽ* "hurtful stuff," and *carorije* "bad stuff." *Capunirɨ̃jẽ* also encompasses some cultivated poisonous plants.

Case 134a.

Language Colorado (Stage 5)
Classification Cayapa-Colorado, Barbacoan, Macro-Chibchan
Area Ecuador
Source Bruce Moore (personal communication)
Life-Form Terms chide **tree** (tree+bush)/**wood**
　　　　　　　tape **grerb** (herb)
　　　　　　　lapa **grass** (grass)
　　　　　　　sili **vine** (vine)
Discussion Moore describes *tape* as "plants smaller than *chide*, but not grasses."

Case 135a.

Language Daga (Stage 5)
Classification South-East New Guinea, Central New Guinea, Indo-Pacific
Area Papua New Guinea
Source John and Elizabeth Murane (personal communication)
Life-Form Terms oma **tree** (tree)/**wood**
　　　　　　　rarema **grerb** (herb)
　　　　　　　ut **grass** (grass+weed)
　　　　　　　damik **vine** (vine)
Discussion The Muranes write that *oma* "includes any vegetation that is

large, has a wood texture to the trunk (thus bananas are excluded)." Plants identified by *rarema* "basically . . . are any types of vegetation that are smaller than a tree, have no wood texture, are not edible" with the exception of grasses. The term *ut* refers to smaller nonedible vegetation, with grasses constituting the focal type. A field that has no trees is also called *ut*. The "vine" term also designates string.

Case 136a.

Language Highland Tequistlatec (Stage 5)
Classification Tequistlatecan, Hokan
Area Oaxaca, Mexico
Source (1) Investigated by the author with Paul K. Chase; (2) Viola Waterhouse and Muriel Parrott (personal communication).
Life-Form Terms   alhec **tree** (tree+large bush+coconut plant)/**wood**
                       itɬ'e q'uec **grerb** (herb+small cactus)
                       galpajag **grass** (grass)
                       lime **vine** (vine)
Discussion The **tree** term consists of the definite article *al-* "the" plus the stem *-hec* whose sense is roughly reflected by "woody plant, plant in general." Thus the **tree** label is literally "the (woody) plant." The **grerb** term also employs the stem *-hec* and roughly translates "that is plants." However, its literal meaning is clearly subordinate to its designative meaning, **grerb**. The "grass" term may be a borrowing from Mexican Spanish (*paja* "straw"). Waterhouse and Parrott mention another general plant term, *lidamgui*, which extends to "useful plants, edible herbs." This term, of course, labels a special purpose class rather than a life-form category.

Case 137a.

Language Huichol (Stage 5)
Classification Sonoran, Uto-Aztecan, Aztec-Tanoan
Area Jalisco, Mexico
Source (1) Joseph E. Grimes (1980a); (2) P. David Price (1967).
Life-Form Terms   cüyée **tree** (tree)
                               túu.piríiya **grerb** (herb)
                               'uxáa **grass** (grass)
                               naanáa **vine** (vine)
Discussion Price (1967) reports that Huichol totally lacks botanical life-form classes. However, he does refer to two of the above terms but does not describe them as botanical life-form labels: cf. *kʌyé* "tree trunk" and *naná* "flexible (plant part?)." Price's findings may indicate that the above life-form

terms reported by Grimes in a subsequent study are of rather low salience and not known to all speakers of Huichol. Grimes uses "shrubs" as a gloss for *túu.piríiya*, but it is clear from plants listed by him as covered by the latter term that it is a **grerb** label extending to most nongrass herbaceous plants.

Case 138a.

Language Kayova (Stage 5)
Classification Tupi-Guarani, Tupi, Equatorial, Andean-Equatorial
Area Brazil-Paraguay border region
Source Wilson Galhego Garcia (1979)
Life-Form Terms   yvyra **tree** (tree+bush)
                     ka'a **grerb** (herb)
                     kapi'i **grass** (grass)
                     ysypo **vine** (vine)

Case 139a.

Language Kekchi (Stage 5)
Classification Mayan, Mesoamerican
Area Guatemala
Source (1) Ray Freeze (personal communication); (2) Michael R. Wilson (personal communication); (3) Michael Robert Wilson (1972).
Life-Form Terms   če? **tree** (tree+woody bush)/**wood**
                     pim **grerb** (herb)
                     q'e·n **grerb** (herb)
                     k'im **grass** (grass)
                     k'a·m or k'aham **vine** (vine)
Discussion Wilson distinguishes *pim* and *q'e·n* as "weedy herbs" and "leafy herbs" respectively. The use of *pim* in reference to plants implies contempt. The "grass" term also denotes thatch and the "vine" term rope.

Case 140a.

Language Makiritare (Stage 5)
Classification Northern Carib, Carib, Macro-Carib, Ge-Pano-Carib
Area Venezuela
Source Marc de Civrieux (1973)
Life-Form Terms   dih **tree** (tree)
                     mada **grerb** (herb(+grass?))
                     woi **grass** (grass)
                     shlñatte **vine** (vine)

Case 141a.

Language Mazatec (Stage 5)
Classification Popolocan, Oto-Manguean, Mesoamerican
Area Oaxaca, Mexico
Source Eunice V. Pike (personal communication)
Life-Form Terms ya **tree** (tree+bamboo)/**wood**
           ška **grerb** (herb)
           lihi **grass** (grass)
           nʔo **vine** (vine)
Discussion The **grerb** term also denotes leaf and the **vine** term rope.

Case 142a.

Language Mokilese (Stage 5)
Classification Micronesian, Oceanic, Austronesian
Area Mokil Island, Eastern Caroline Islands, Micronesia
Source Barbara Demory (1972)
Life-Form Terms sukaw **tree** (tree+bush)/**wood**
               tuptup **grerb** (grass+herb)
               reh **grass** (grass)
               sukaw kərak **vine** (vine)
Discussion The **tree** life-form encompasses coconut, pandanus, papaya, and banana plants in addition to what are ordinarily trees in English. Demory writes that "overall size and use seem to override stem quality" in the classification of plants as "trees." The term *sukaw* also has the expanded sense of "plants in general." The **grerb** term has "weed" as a distinct narrower meaning. Small plants used for medicine are identified as *sukaw ihn wuhne*, literally, "plant of medicine" rather than as *tuptup*. The "vine" term literally means "crawling plant."

Case 143a.

Language Mopan (Stage 5)
Classification Mayan, Mesoamerican
Area An adjacent region of Guatemala and Belize
Source Rosemary Ulrich (personal communication)
Life-Form Terms čeʔ **tree** (tree)/**wood**
           pokčeʔ **grerb** (herb+bush)
           suʔuk **grass** (grass)
           akʼ **vine** (vine)

Case 144a.

Language Muinane (Stage 5)
Classification Witotoan, Macro-Carib, Ge-Pano-Carib
Area Colombia
Source James W. Walton (personal communication)
Life-Form Terms ɨmohono **tree** (large or small woody plant)
         beeva **grerb** (grass+herb)
         ñaavahu **grass** (nonclustering grass)
         iibaiño **grass** (clustering grass)
         muuhuɨno **vine** (woody vine)

Discussion The **tree** life-form excludes woody vines. The **grerb** category may in fact be an incipient life-form. Walton writes, "lots of the residue [i.e. those herbaceous plants not included in *ñaavahu* and *iibaiño*] seem to be grouped into *beeva*, weeds, grasses, and growth of the small non-woody plants that take over paths, patios, and other cleared areas . . . *beeva*'s literal translation would be 'filth from plant growth.'"

Case 145a.

Language Navaho (Stage 5)
Classification Apachen, Athapascan, Athapascan-Eyak, Na-Dene
Area Arizona, New Mexico, Utah, Colorado, U.S.A.
Source (1) Francis H. Elmore (1944); (2) Oswald Werner, Allan Manning, and Kenneth Y. Begishe (n.d.).
Life-Form Terms tshin **tree** (tree)/**wood**
         tc'il **grerb** (grass+herb(+vine?))
         tł'oh **grass** (grass)
         tc'ilnaaskhaatíih **vine** (vine)

Discussion The above terms and referential extensions are from Elmore. Werner et al. describe the **tree** label as designating "woody plants" and the **grerb** term as denoting "flexible non-woody plants." They do not, however, list a word for "vine." The "vine" term given above translates literally "creeping **grerb**," indicating that vines may be included in the **grerb** life-form.

Case 146a.

Language Ndumba (Tairora) (Stage 5)
Classification Tairora, Gadsup-Anyana-Awa-Tairora, East New Guinea Highlands, Central New Guinea, Indo-Pacific
Area Eastern Highlands of Papua New Guinea
Source Terence E. Hays (1979)

Life-Form Terms sa'tari **tree** (tree+bush+tree fern)/**wood**
　　　　　　　 mauna **grerb** (herb (including fern))
　　　　　　　 muso **grass** (grass+sedge+rush)
　　　　　　　 sana **vine** (vine)

Discussion The **grerb** term in some contexts also seems to mean "useful herbaceous plants" and in others, "plants in general." The **grass** label also applies restrictively to a certain type of grass.

Case 147a.

Language Sierra Popoluca (Stage 5)
Classification Zoquean, Mesoamerican
Area Veracruz, Mexico
Source (1) John Lind (personal communication); (2) Mary L. Foster and George M. Foster (1948).
Life-Form Terms cuy **tree** (tree+bush)/**wood**
　　　　　　　 pɨm **grerb** (grass+herb)
　　　　　　　 múc **grass** (grass)
　　　　　　　 tsay **vine** (vine)

Discussion The above terms and referential ranges, except that of *pɨm*, are from Lind. Lind assigns the gloss "weed" to *pɨm*. Foster and Foster, however, identify the term as referring to grasses. This discrepancy is almost certainly linked to use of the term in reference to small herbaceous plants in general including both weeds and grasses. Lind writes that *múc* designates " 'grass' either short grazing grass or tall grass used for house roofs." While the latter term has a broad range, it may not be a life-form label since the plants it encompasses appear to belong to a special purpose category based on plant use. Lind also gives another general term, *sóc*, which refers to certain kinds of tall grass that can be cut for forage or grazed by livestock.

Case 148a.

Language Sre (Stage 5)
Classification South Bahnaric, Mon-Khmer, Austro-Asiatic
Area Vietnam
Source Jacque Dournes (1973)
Life-Form Terms chi **tree** (tree)/**wood**
　　　　　　　 töm chi **tree** (tree)
　　　　　　　 nyhöt **grerb** (grass+herb)
　　　　　　　 römbu:ng **grass** (grass)
　　　　　　　 chê **vine** (vine)

Discussion Mushrooms are excluded from all of the above categories.

Case 149a.

Language Tasaday (Stage 5)
Classification Sulic, Philippine, Northwest Austronesian, Austronesian
Area Mindanao, the Philippines
Source D. E. Yen (1976)
Life-Form Terms kayu **tree** (tree)
　　　　　　klu'on **grerb** (herb+bush+vine)
　　　　　　dagal **grass** (grass)
　　　　　　bəlagan **vine** (vine)

Discussion With respect to uses of the **tree** and **grerb** terms Yen (pp. 153–154) writes:

> In the large range of shrubby species of the Tasaday forest, *kayu* and *klu'on* were quite inconsistently applied, and the only criterion that suggested itself to this observer in the field was an arbitrary judgement on the size of plants in the informants' eyes. The large, high storey trees like *Vatica* or *Chiseton*, even young sapling specimens, were always recorded as *kayu manəbə* and *kayu mata usa* respectively, and *klu'on* could never be applied. The latter term however, covered not only small trees and shrubs, but climbers like *Freycinetia*, the creeping herb *Commelina*, the upright herbs *Begonia* and *Setaria* grass even though it was later admitted that grasses (including *Setaria*) are classed as *dagal* by the Tasaday.

Case 150a.

Language Teen (also Loron) (Stage 5)
Classification Gur, Niger-Congo, Niger-Kordofanian
Area Ivory Coast
Source Inge Leenhouts (personal communication)
Life-Form Terms dɯjaga **tree** (tree+banana plant)
　　　　　　gusuko **grerb** (herb)
　　　　　　hajaga **grass** (grass)
　　　　　　fanha **vine** (vine)

Discussion The **tree** term also extends to shrubs with tree-like stems. It has another referent, "plants with fruit for sauce," which encompasses such things as tomato, eggplant, okra, and hot pepper plants. The **grerb** term extends to all small herbaceous plants, except grasses, including weeds (labeled *turu*). The **grass** term also refers to "the bush," that is, to all plants which are not "food" (labeled *dɯlɔ*).

Case 151a.

Language Tepehua (Stage 5)
Classification Totonacan, Mesoamerican
Area Where Mexican states of Veracruz, Hidalgo, and Pueblo converge
Source Susan Edgar (personal communication)
Life-Form Terms q'uiu **tree** (tree+woody plant)/**wood**
               ach'itin **grerb** (herb)
               ats'in **grass** (grass+sedge+rush)
               sivic **vine** (vine)

Case 152a.

Language Tewa (Stage 5)
Classification Tanoan, Aztec-Tanoan
Area New Mexico, U.S.A.
Source (1) Randall H. Speirs and Anna F. Speirs (personal communication); (2) Wilfred William Robbins, John Peabody Harrington, and Barbara Freire-Marreco (1916).
Life-Form Terms te: **tree** (tree)
               ɸéʔñǽvi **grerb** (grass+herb)
               tá· **grass** (grass)
               á· **vine** (vine)
               á·ɸǽ· **vine** (vine)

Discussion The above terms are supplied by the Speirs. They note that the **tree** term also refers specifically to the cottonwood tree (*Populus wislizeni*). The account given by Robbins, Harrington, and Freire-Marreco agrees in essential details with the above. However, they describe a somewhat more complex situation with respect to **tree**:

> There is no general word meaning 'tree' unless it be *pᶜe*, 'stiff long object,' 'stick,' 'lumber,' 'plant,' . . . English 'tree' or Spanish *arbol* is sometimes rendered by *te*, Populus wislizeni, ŋwǽŋ, Pinus brachyptera, or some other name of a large 'tree' species. (1916: 8)

Robbins et al. (1916: 8) also mention that there "is no word meaning 'shrub' or 'bush' unless it be this same word *pᶜe*." In addition, they (1916: 9) assign the glosses "rubbish," "litter," "lint," "weed," and "herbaceous plant" to the **grerb** term and write that it ". . . is very common, its application not being restricted to useless plants. It is the nearest equivalent of Spanish *yerba*."

Case 153a.

Language Texmelucan Zapotec (Stage 5)
Classification Popoluco Branch, Zapotecan, Oto-Manguean, Mesoamerican
Area Oaxaca, Mexico
Source Chuck Speck (personal communication)
Life-Form Terms yag **tree** (tree+large bush)/**wood**
                gyiš **grerb** (herb+bush)
                gyizh **grass** (grass)
                lyuky **vine** (vine)

Case 154a.

Language Tzeltal (Stage 5)
Classification Mayan, Mesoamerican
Area Chiapas, Mexico
Source Brent Berlin, Dennis E. Breedlove, and Peter H. Raven (1974)
Life-Form Terms teʔ **tree** (tree)
                wamal **grerb** (herb+bush)
                ʔak **grass** (grass+sedge+narrow-leaved monocotyledon)
                ʔakʹ **vine** (vine)
Discussion Berlin et al. (1974: 30) describe the above life-forms as follows:

teʔ	'plants exhibiting erect to ascending woody stem habit and aborescent stems, generally more than 2 m tall at maturity'
ʔakʹ	'plants exhibiting twining stem habit and lianous stems'
ʔak	'plants exhibiting grass-like leaves and herbaceous stems'
wamal	'plants exhibiting net-veined leaves and herbaceous to infrutescent stems generally less than 2 m tall at maturity'

Case 155a.

Language Tzotzil (Zinacantan dialect) (Stage 5)
Classification Mayan, Mesoamerican
Area Chiapas, Mexico
Source (1) Robert M. Laughlin (personal communication); (2) Robert M. Laughlin (1975).
Life-Form Terms teʔ **tree** (tree)/**wood** (stick)
                ȼiʔlel **grerb** (grass+herb+agave+moss+greens)
                hobel **grass** (grass)
                ʔakʹ **vine** (vine)
Discussion Laughlin (1975) writes that if a species ordinarily classed as **grerb** grows with great vigor, it may be identified as a "tree." Conversely,

stunted trees or those collected in their early stages of growth may be designated **grerb**. This indicates that size is a critical factor in distinguishing **tree** and **grerb**.

Case 156a.

Language Tzutujil (Stage 5)
Classification Mayan, Mesoamerican
Area Guatemala
Source Jim Butler (personal communication)
Life-Form Terms čeʔ **tree** (tree)/**wood**
                ičax **grerb** (herb)
                k'ïm **grass** (grass)
                rëš k'am **vine** (vine)
Discussion The "vine" term translates literally "green rope."

Case 157a.

Language Yaqui (Stage 5)
Classification Sonoran, Uto-Aztecan, Aztec-Tanoan
Area Northern Mexico and Arizona, U.S.A.
Source John M. Dedrick (personal communication)
Life-Form Terms húya-m **tree** (tree)
                ʔóuwo **grerb** (herb+bush)
                básso **grass** (grass)
                wiróa-m **vine** (vine)
Discussion Dedrick mentions that he is in doubt about a bona-fide word for "tree." The above "tree" term is the plural of *húya* which refers in the collective sense to wild vegetation (trees, weeds, cacti, etc.). In the plural, writes Dedrick, it very often refers only to trees. Dedrick also speculates that *húya* may have originally meant "tree." In addition he refers to a "tree" term in a Yaqui grammar and dictionary compiled by Jesuit priests in the late 1590's and early 1600's and later republished under the title *Arte de la Lengua Cahita* (edited by Eustaquio Buelna in Mexico City in 1891). The term mentioned is *buere cutam* (*bʷéere kúta-m*) which translates literally "big woods." Today, Dedrick has only heard the term *kúta-m* used in reference to wood (the material). All of this seems to indicate the very low salience of a "tree" concept for speakers of Yaqui. The **grerb** term refers to "any specific, usually herbaceous plant." The category includes such items as "small plants with stalks or trunks, limbs and leaves, such as corn, wheat, etc., or young trees such as could be transplanted, or shrubs." The **grass** life-form may be incipient since

Dedrick knows of only one named species in the category, *yónso* "Johnson grass." He also notes that the "vine" term may be a borrowing but does not specify a possible lending language.

Case 158a.

Language Yucatec (Stage 5)
Classification Mayan, Mesoamerican
Area Yucatan, Mexico
Source (1) Investigated by the author; (2) Alfredo Barrera Marin, Alfredo Barrera Vazquez, and Rosa Maria Lopez Franco (1976); (3) Ralph L. Roys (1931).
Life-Form Terms čeʔ **tree** (tree + bush + woody plant)/**wood**
                      šiw **grerb** (herb)
                      súʔuk **grass** (grass + sedge)
                      akʲ **vine** (vine)
Discussion The "grass" term is also used to designate thatch and fodder. Roys lists a term for "bush," i.e. *aban*. Barrera Marin et al. give the latter term but with the meaning "weed." My informant did not know the term. The orthography is mine.

Case 159a.

Language Zoogocho Zapotec (Stage 5)
Classification Zapotecan, Oto-Manguean, Mesoamerican
Area Oaxaca, Mexico
Source Inez Butler (personal communication)
Life-Form Terms x̱ag **tree** (tree + cactus)/**wood**
                      x̱iṣeʔ **grerb** (grass + herb)
                      x̱iẑxe **grass** (grass)
                      llba **vine** (vine)
Discussion The "tree" term also refers to plants in general. The **grerb** term also means "wild."

      Four Life-Forms: **tree + grerb + vine + bush**.
      160a. Brunei Malay (Borneo)
      161a. Desana (Colombia)
      162a. Kalam (Papua New Guinea)
      163a. Kumaoni (India)
      164a. Lowland Tequistlatec (Mexico)

165a. Michoacan Nahuatl (Mexico)
166a. Quechua (Peru)
167a. Tifal (Papua New Guinea)

Case 160a.

Language Brunei Malay (Stage 5)
Classification West Indonesian, Hesperonesian, Austronesian
Area Borneo
Source (1) Linda Amy Kimball (personal communication); (2) Linda Amy
   Kimball (1981).
Life-Form Terms puhon **tree** (tree)
                          daundaunan **grerb** (herb)
                          rotan **vine** (vine)
                          belukar **bush** (bush)
Discussion The principal referent of *rotan* is a specific type of vine. Kimball
notes that there may be another term primarily used for vines in general, but
she is not certain. The primary meaning of *belukar* is "secondary growth
area." She (1981) also writes that Brunei Malay does not have a generic term
for "grass." There is, however, a broad, special purpose grass class, *rumput*
"grazing grass."

Case 161a.

Language Desana (Stage 5)
Classification Tucanoan, Macro-Tucanoan, Andean-Equatorial
Area Vaupés territory, Northwest Amazon, Colombia
Source G. Reichel-Dolmatoff (personal communication)
Life-Form Terms yuhkë **tree** (tree)/**wood**
                          taa **grerb** (grass+herb)
                          singá **vine** (vine)
                          poóru **bush** (bush)

Case 162a.

Language Kalam (Stage 5)
Classification Karam, East New Guinea Highlands, Central New Guinea,
   Indo-Pacific
Area Upper Kaironk Valley, Madang District, Papua New Guinea
Source Ralph N. H. Bulmer (1974)
Life-Form Terms mon **tree** (tree)/**wood** (timber)

mj or mjkas **grerb** (herb(+grass?))

mñ **vine** (vine)

bd **bush** (bush)

Discussion The **tree** life-form excludes the Pandanus palms, black-palms, bamboos, hollow-stemmed forms such as Piperaceae, and tree-ferns. Bulmer notes that *mj* (or *mjkas*) refers primarily to leaf and foliage, and, by extension, to leafy plants in general. It is not clear in his account whether grasses are considered kinds of *mj* (or *mjkas*). The "vine" term designates "climbing or creeping plants with strong stems." It also denotes rope, string, and fibre. The "bush" term "can be applied to any free-standing leafy plant from a small *mon* tree or a 20 ft. *Piper* . . . down to quite small 'bushy' garden weeds." A **grass** life-form may be consolidating in the language. The term *ksod*, which refers specifically to the grass species *Themeda australis* (kangaroo grass), has a more general application. In certain contexts it can refer to all short grasses collectively. However, only *Themeda australis* is individually denoted by the term.

Case 163a.

Language Kumaoni (Stage 5)
Classification Pahari, Indic, Indo-Iranian, Indo-European
Area Northwestern India
Source N. C. Shah (personal communication)
Life-Form Terms vota **tree** (tree)

gha **grerb** (grass+herb)

lagil **vine** (vine)

jhar **bush** (bush)

Case 164a.

Language Lowland Tequistlatec (Stage 5)
Classification Tequistlatecan, Hokan
Area Oaxaca, Mexico
Source Viola Waterhouse and Muriel Parrott (personal communication)
Life-Form Terms el'ej **tree** (tree)/**wood**

litʸankʷi **grerb** (grass+herb)

lime **vine** (vine)

a'waj'ej **bush** (bush)

Discussion The "bush" term translates literally "small tree."

Case 165a.

Language Michoacan Nahuatl (Stage 5)
Classification Aztecan, Uto-Aztecan, Aztec-Tanoan
Area Michoacan, Mexico
Source William R. Sischo (personal communication)
Life-Form Terms kʷawil **tree** (tree)/**wood**
                 sakal **grerb** (grass+herb)
                 kʷah'mekal **vine** (vine)
                 kʷahȼindi **bush** (bush)
Discussion The "vine" term translates literally "wood rope" and the "bush" term translates literally "little tree."

Case 166a.

Language Quechua (Stage 5)
Classification Quechumaran, Andean, Andean-Equatorial
Area Peru
Source Gilles Brunel (1976)
Life-Form Terms sac'a **tree** (tree)
                 qora **grerb** (herb(+grass?))
                 lloqaq **vine** (vine)
                 c'afra **bush** (bush)

Case 167a.

Language Tifal (Stage 5)
Classification Ok, Central and South New Guinea, Central New Guinea, Indo-Pacific
Area West Sepik District, Papua New Guinea
Source Al Boush, Jr. (personal communication)
Life-Form Terms as **tree** (tree)/**wood**
                 al **grerb** (grass+herb)
                 sook **vine** (vine)
                 kanaat tuuk **bush** (bush)

        Four Life-Forms: **tree+grass+vine+bush**.
168a. Bororo (Brazil)
169a. Hindi (India)
170a. Kaiwa (Brazil)
171a. Kootenai (Montana, U.S.A.)

172a. Lotuho (Sudan)
173a. Malyalam (India)
174a. Montana Salish (Montana, U.S.A.)

Case 168a.

Language Bororo (Stage 5)
Classification Bororo, Macro-Ge-Bororo, Ge-Pano-Carib
Area Mato Grosso, Brazil
Source (1) Thekla Hartmann (personal communication); (2) Thekla Hartmann (1967, 1972).
Life-Form Terms í **tree** (tree)
            bóe bútu **grass** (grass)
            íwo **grass** (large grass (bamboo+reed plant))
            ikurédu **vine** (vine)
            íka **bush** (bush)
            iwára **bush** (bush)
Discussion The "tree" category excludes palms. In addition, *í* seems to refer more expansively to plants in general, possibly excluding grasses. The label *bóe bútu* translates literally "things that grow." Hartmann notes that in the classification of bushes height or size is not as important as form (bushiness) of a plant. The lack of a **grerb** term may be traced to ecological factors. The "cerrado" flatlands inhabited by the Bororo consist primarily of twisted trees of small or medium height and grasses and bushes as undergrowth.

Case 169a.

Language Hindi (Stage 5)
Classification Central Indic Zone, Indic, Indo-Iranian, Indo-European
Area India
Source N. C. Shah (personal communication)
Life-Form Terms per **tree** (tree)
            ghas **grass** (grass)
            bel **vine** (vine)
            lata **vine** (vine)
            jhari **bush** (bush)

Case 170a.

Language Kaiwa (dialect of Tupi) (Stage 5)
Classification Tupi-Guarani, Tupi, Equatorial, Andean-Equatorial
Area Brazil

Source John Taylor (personal communication)
Life-Form Terms ɨvɨra **tree** (tree) / **wood**
                 kapiˈi **grass** (grass)
                 ɨsapɨ **vine** (vine)
                 ɨvɨraˈi **bush** (bush)
Discussion The "bush" term translates literally "little tree."

Case 171a.

Language Kootenai (Stage 5)
Classification no known genetic affiliation
Area Western Montana, U.S.A.
Source Jeff Hart (1974)
Life-Form Terms nangáki **tree** (standing tree)
                 cəháɬ **grass** (grass)
                 gaʔɬgaʔagawúˀis **vine** (vine)
                 akʷkáʔis **bush** (bush)

Case 172a.

Language Lotuho (Stage 5)
Classification Nilo-Hamitic, Eastern Sudanic, Chari-Nile, Nilo-Saharan
Area Southern Sudan
Source Massimino Allam and P. B. Hollman (personal communication)
Life-Form Terms ayyanii **tree** (tree + palm)
                 amiyaŋir **grass** (grass + grain plant)
                 ayyanii ariak **vine** (vine)
                 eworos **bush** (shrub)
Discussion The **tree** term also designates plants in general. Since native medicines come from leaves, stems, and roots of plants, *ayyanii* also means "medicine." The latter term is used as well in a compound expression which serves as an alternate **tree** label, *ayyanii oŋonyot*, literally, "tree or plant proper." The **vine** term translates literally "creeping plant." This does not encompass creeping grasses which are included in *amiyaŋir*.

Case 173a.

Language Malyalam (Stage 5)
Classification Dravidian
Area Kerala, India
Source N. C. Shah (personal communication)
Life-Form Terms maram **tree** (tree)

vrasham **tree** (tree)
pullu **grass** (grass)
valli-chedi **vine** (vine)
padarpan **vine** (vine)
kutti-chedi **bush** (bush)

Discussion The term *chedi* denotes plants in general.

Case 174a.

Language Montana Salish (Flathead) (Stage 5)
Classification Interior Salish, Salish
Area Montana, U.S.A.
Source Jeff Hart (1974)
Life-Form Terms -ałk **tree** (tree) / **wood**
ʔesšít **tree** (tree)
supúʔlexʷ **grass** (grass)
čiĺyalałkʷ **vine** (vine)
ʔestémp **bush** (bush)

Discussion All but one of the above labels have literal translations: *ʔesšít* "it's standing," *supúʔlexʷ* "hair on earth," *čiĺyalałk* "wrapping, twining around a tree," and *ʔestémp* "it's bunched." There is another term which possibly functions as a **grerb** label: *čəs·upúʔlexʷ* "weeds," literally, "bad hair on the earth."

STAGE 6 LANGUAGES.

Five Life-Forms: **tree+grerb+grass+vine+bush**.
175a. American English (U.S.A.)
176a. Bengali (India)
177a. Central Carrier (Alaska, U.S.A.)
178a. Choctaw (Oklahoma, U.S.A.)
179a. Chol (Mexico)
180a. Chorti (Guatemala, Honduras)
181a. Clallam (Washington State, U.S.A)
182a. Cora (Mexico)
183a. Huastec (Veracruz dialect) (Mexico)
184a. Koya (India)
185a. Lacandon (Mexico)
186a. Malagasy (Madagascar)
187a. Pocomam (Guatemala)
188a. Tzotzil (Chamula dialect) (Mexico)

Case 175a.

Language American English (Stage 6)
Classification Germanic, Indo-European
Area U.S.A.
Source Investigated by the author
Life-Form Terms tree **tree** (tree)
        plant **grerb** (grass+herb+bush+vine)
        grass **grass** (grass)
        vine **vine** (vine)
        bush **bush** (bush)
        shrub **bush** (bush)

Discussion The above terms and ranges are those understood by the author. The **grerb** term also refers more expansively to plants in general. Grasses, vines, bushes, and shrubs are all included in **grerb**. *Bush* also denotes areas with thick, disordered growth. The term *shrub* may be restricted to ornamental bushes in some idiolects.

Case 176a.

Language Bengali (Stage 6)
Classification Eastern Indic Zone, Indic, Indo-Iranian, Indo-European
Area Bengal, India
Source N. C. Shah (personal communication)
Life-Form Terms gacha **tree** (tree)
        aushdhiya ghas **grerb** (herb)
        ghas **grass** (grass)
        lata **vine** (vine)
        jhar **bush** (shrub)
        gulma **bush** (bush)

Case 177a.

Language Central Carrier (Stage 6)
Classification Northern Athapascan, Athapascan, Athapascan-Eyak, Na-Dene
Area Alaska
Source Dick Walker (personal communication)
Life-Form Terms duchun **tree** (tree)
        hanúyeh-i **grerb** (herb)
        tl'o **grass** (grass)
        mai chun **vine** (vine)

dilht'ani **bush** (bush)

Discussion The **grerb** term translates literally "that which grows." The literal meaning of *mai chun* is "fruit pole."

Case 178a.

Language Choctaw (Stage 6)
Classification Muskogean, Macro-Algonquian
Area Oklahoma, formerly Mississippi and adjacent parts of Alabama, U.S.A.
Source Kenneth Jones (1972)
Life-Form Terms ita **tree** (tree)/**wood**
hayyonkpólo **grerb** (herb)
háshshok **grass** (grass)
balálli **vine** (vine)
iti sháwwa **bush** (bush)

Discussion While assigning the gloss "tree" to *ita* Jones writes that the term "may be restricted in meaning and refer only to the wood, i.e. the secondary xylem of the trunk and proximal root and branch areas." The **grerb** term encompasses both nonuseable herbaceous plants (excluding grasses) and medicinal herbaceous plants. In addition, "nonuseable herbaceous plants" constitutes a second, more restrictive range of the term.

Case 179a.

Language Chol (Stage 6)
Classification Mayan, Mesoamerican
Area Chiapas, Mexico
Source (1) Wilbur Aulie (personal communication); (2) John Attinasi (personal communication); (3) Viola Warkentin (personal communication).
Life-Form Terms tʸeʔ **tree** (tree+bush)/**wood**
pimel **grerb** (herb)
ham **grass** (grass)
ak' **vine** (vine)
saj tʸeʔ **bush** (bush)

Discussion Aulie describes *pimel* as "any vegetation which is not a grass and which does not have woody stems." The "bush" term, supplied by Warkentin alone, translates literally "small tree." The orthography for all terms is Warkentin's.

Case 180a.

Language Chorti (Stage 6)
Classification Mayan, Mesoamerican
Area Eastern Guatemala, Western Honduras
Source Charles Wisdom (1949)
Life-Form Terms teʔ **tree** (tree+large bush)
  kʼopot **grerb** (herb+small bush)
  ak **grass** (grass)
  čʼaan **vine** (vine+climbing shrub)
  čʼahn **vine** (vine)
  pʼen **bush** (shrub)

Discussion The original glosses of the above terms are: *teʔ* "plant (as opposed to animal); tree, wild tree; large shrub or bush; cane (especially one with a hard skin)," *kʼopot* "weed; small wild plant; herb; bush; small shrub," *ak* "grass (zacate); grasslike vine or plant; any fodder plant," *čʼaan* "vine (especially an herbaceous vine); climbing shrub; tree with vine-like branches; plant with slender limbs or bark used for tying," *čʼahn* "trailing or climbing vine . . . denotes any strand or twine-like object," *pʼen* "large weed; shrub; shrubbery."

Case 181a.

Language Clallam (Stage 6)
Classification Coast Salish, Salish
Area Washington State, U.S.A.
Source (1) Mark S. Fleisher (personal communication); (2) Mark Stewart
  Fleisher (1976).
Life-Form Terms sqiʔyayŋxʷ **tree** (tree)
  čəniŋł **grerb** (grass+herb)
  sxcaʔyaʔnəqʷ **grass** (grass)
  ʔəsayʔaʔyət **vine** (vine)
  šuʔuʔem **bush** (bush)

Discussion Fleisher (personal communication) writes that *čəniŋł* "probably includes all known plants, i.e. small vegetation." The term apparently is derived from the verb *čən-* "to plant, bury." The **grass** term may be an incipient life-form label since Fleisher's informants did not supply him with named types of grass. The word *sxcaʔyaʔnəqʷ* seems to be derived from the term for "hay," *sxcaʔiʔ*. Fleisher (1976) lists only two labeled members of the **vine** class. The **bush** term is derived from the verb *šaw-* "to grow."

Case 182a.

Language Cora (Stage 6)
Classification Sonoran, Uto-Aztecan, Aztec-Tanoan
Area Jalisco, Sinaloa, Nayarit, Mexico
Source (1) Eugene H. Casad (personal communication); (2) Eugene H. Casad (1980).
Life-Form Terms kɨyé **tree** (woody plant+large cactus?)
  tuʼupí **grerb** (herb+small grass?)
  ɨšá **grass** (large grass)
  náanaʼa **vine** (vine)
  ɨcí **bush** (shrub+small cactus?)

Discussion The **tree** term encompasses woody plants of various sizes and, possibly, large cactuses such as the prickly pear and pitahaya. It also means "trunk." The **grerb** term encompasses nonwoody plants, weeds, thistles and, possibly, small grasses. Some examples of fairly large plants included in **grerb** are the elephant ear plant, the sunflower, sugar cane, and the maguey plant. The **grass** category includes tall, wild grasses of various sorts. The **grass** term may also restrictively designate a specific kind of grass but the source is not absolutely certain of this. The **vine** term also means "root." The source describes the **bush** category as consisting of "wild, medium-sized plant life, including some, at least, with woody stems." Small cactuses may be included as well. The **bush** term also seems to refer to plants and trees that grow in the wild or, in other words, to "brush."

Case 183a.

Language Huastec (Veracruz dialect) (Stage 6)
Classification Mayan, Mesoamerican
Area Northern Veracruz, Mexico
Source Cecil H. Brown (1972)
Life-Form Terms teʔ **tree** (tree)/**wood**
  čʼoho·l **grerb** (herb)
  tom **grass** (grass)
  čʼah **vine** (vine)
  wayelteʔ **bush** (bush)

Discussion The **tree** life-form excludes palms. The "bush" term translates literally "sleeping tree."

Case 184a.

Language Koya (Stage 6)
Classification Dravidian
Area South India
Source Stephen A. Tyler (personal communication)
Life-Form Terms maṛam **tree** (tree)
                 ettu **grerb** (herb)
                 gaḍḍa **grass** (grass)
                 tīga **vine** (vine)
                 poda **bush** (bush)
Discussion The **grerb** term, which labels a class of small herbaceous plants usually having stalks or stems, can be used as well to identify any young, and, hence, small tree.

Case 185a.

Language Lacandon (Stage 6)
Classification Mayan, Mesoamerican
Area Chiapas, Mexico
Source (1) Phillip Baer (personal communication); (2) Ray Freeze (personal communication); (3) William Fisher (personal communication).
Life-Form Terms čeʔ **tree** (tree)/**wood**
                 šiw **grerb** (herb)
                 robir **grerb** (herb)
                 suʔuk **grass** (grass)
                 a·kʼ **vine** (vine)
                 kabar u čeʔer **bush** (bush)
Discussion The "bush" term, supplied only by Phillip Baer, translates literally "low tree." The orthography for all terms is Baer's.

Case 186a.

Language Malagasy (Stage 6)
Classification West Indonesian, Hesperonesian, Austronesian
Area Madagascar
Source Pierre L. Boiteau (personal communication)
Life-Form Terms hazo **tree** (tree)/**wood**
                 ahitra **grerb** (herb)
                 vilona **grass** (grass)
                 ladina **vine** (herbaceous vine)
                 vahy **vine** (ligneous vine)

hazo-kely **bush** (bush)

Discussion The "bush" term translates literally "small tree."

Case 187a.

Language Pocomam (Stage 6)
Classification Mayan, Mesoamerican
Area Guatemala
Source Thom Smith-Stark (personal communication)
Life-Form Terms čieʔ **tree** (tree)/**wood**
  čaːm **grerb** (herb(+grass?))
  kʼim **grass** (grass+grain plant)
  kʼahaːm **vine** (vine)
  ʔakʼun čieʔ **bush** (bush)

Discussion Smith-Stark assigns the gloss "small plant" to *čaːm*. Whether the term encompasses "grass" is not clear. The "bush" term, which is rarely used, translates literally "young tree."

Case 188a.

Language Tzotzil (Chamula dialect) (Stage 6)
Classification Mayan, Mesoamerican
Area Chiapas, Mexico
Source Ken Jacobs (personal communication)
Life-Form Terms teʔ **tree** (tree)/**wood**
  vomol **grerb** (herb)
  yašaltik **grass** (grass)
  akʼ **vine** (vine)
  voȼ voȼ te? **bush** (bush)

Discussion Weeds apparently constitute the focus of the **grerb** category. The "bush" term translates literally "tree in round clumps."

ZOOLOGICAL LIFE-FORM DATA

STAGE 0 LANGUAGES.

No Life-Forms.
1b. Iwaidja (Australia) (has incipient **bird**, **fish**, and **snake**)

Case 1b.

Language Iwaidja (Stage 0) (see case 1a)
Life-Form Terms galagalag **bird** (bird) *I.L.-F.*
  yab **fish** (fish) *I.L.-F.*
  ambij **snake** (snake) *I.L.-F.*
Discussion The above three terms refer only to creatures which lack generic labels or are otherwise unknown. Pym notes that birds, fish, and snakes that are dangerous, edible, or in some way useful tend to have their own generic names. These are not, therefore, identified by the above terms which are labels for incipient life-form classes. Since all Iwaidja animal life-forms are incipient, the language altogether lacks full-fledged zoological life-forms and thus is affiliated with growth Stage 0.

STAGE 1 LANGUAGES.

One Life-Form: **fish**.
2b. Desana (Colombia)
3b. Ngandi (Australia)

Case 2b.

Language Desana (Stage 1) (see case 161a)
Source (1) G. Reichel-Dolmatoff (personal communication); (2) G. Reichel-Dolmatoff (1978).
Life-Form Term vai **fish** (fish)
Discussion The source (personal communication) writes that there is no general term for "bird" in Desana. There are, however, two broad special purpose "bird" categories: (1) *vai-mërá vërá*, referring to game birds, to all edible birds, such as curassow, trumpeter, duck, etc., and (2) *mirimará*, birds that are not eaten, such as song birds, hummingbirds, etc. The label *vai-mërá vërá* translates literally "beasts that fly." The source (personal communication) also reports no general term for "snake" but mentions *anyá* which includes all poisonous snakes and stingrays, and *piróa* "anacondas and boas."

Case 3b.

Language Ngandi (Stage 1) (see case 21a)
Life-Form Term a-jeñ **fish** (fish)
Discussion In addition to not finding words for "snake," "worm," **bird**, **wug**, and **mammal**, Heath notes that he did not record terms for lizard, frog, and turtle/tortoise. He also mentions that absence of a "snake" label may be an elicitation gap, but adds that he is confident that the others are genuine gaps.

> *One Life-Form:* **snake**.
> 4b. Muyuw (New Guinea)

Case 4b.

Language Muyuw (Stage 1) (see case 82a)
Life-Form Term mwatet **snake** (snake)
Discussion There are two other general animal terms mentioned by Lithgow, *man* and *yin*. The word *man* encompasses birds, mammals, insects, and reptiles with legs. Some speakers also include snakes and worms in the category. The term *yin* denotes fish and other water creatures such as turtles and crocodiles. It does not encompass shell-fish. In addition, true fish are definitely not the focus of the category and fish and other sea creatures are not, in fact, called *yin* until they are caught. While it is tempting to regard *man* as a combined **wug-mammal** category, a single feature, terrestrial habitat, apparently is the primary criterion for membership. According to Lithgow, *man* and *yin*

encode the distinction "land creature" versus "sea creature." Thus these appear to be special purpose categories.

STAGE 2 LANGUAGES.

Two Life-Forms: **bird** + **snake**.
5b. Amahuaca (Peru)
6b. Ilongot (The Philippines) (has incipient **fish**)
7b. Jicaque (Honduras)
8b. Karok (California, U.S.A.)
9b. Nimboran (Irian Jaya)
10b. Northern Paiute (Nevada dialect) (Nevada, U.S.A.) (has incipient **fish**)
11b. Papago (Arizona, U.S.A.)
12b. Smith River (California, U.S.A.)
13b. Wik-Ngathana (Australia)

Case 5b.
___

Language Amahuaca (Stage 2) (see case 116a)
Life-Form Terms ʔisa: **bird** (small bird)
ronóʔ **snake** (snake)
Discussion The source is an extensive listing of names for plants and animals in Amahuaca. It does not identify class inclusive relationships in most cases. A third term, *yoʔina*, may possibly have a life-form referential extension. This term is glossed in Spanish *animal, bestia (genérico)* indicating that it is an animal kingdom label for creatures in general. However, it is listed under the section heading *Mamiferos*, "mammals," suggesting that it is possibly restricted in reference to mammals and, thus, possibly should be codified as **mammal**. Here I have taken the actual gloss as decisive evidence for codification.

Case 6b.
___

Language Ilongot (Stage 2) (see case 64a)
Life-Form Terms manuk **bird** (bird)
ʼuleg **snake** (snake)
ʼular **snake** (worm + slug)
rudung **fish** (fish) *I.L.-F.*
Discussion The **bird** term refers more specifically to chicken. The term *rudung* applies primarily to a middle-sized white fish. Rosaldo writes that she

believes *rudung* "can serve generically for 'fish in general' in certain contexts (e.g., when looking at an assortment in a fish tank) but that it would be disallowed in others (e.g., when clearly the referent is *bēyek*, a small sardine river fish)." This indicates that *rudung* labels an incipient **fish** class. Rosaldo also reports two other broad animal classes, *'ayup* "domesticated animal" and *'atap* "wild game animal." While both of these are special purpose categories, *'ayup* can be used expansively for "anything that moves" and, thus, can mean "creature in general."

Case 7b.

Language Jicaque (Stage 2) (see case 121a)
Life-Form Terms tsipyaya **bird** (small bird)
latsj **snake** (snake)
ts'ijiy **snake** (worm + caterpillar)
Discussion Dennis defines *ts'ijiy* as a word for worms in general, but points out that it excludes fly larvae, earthworms, and the roundworm parasite (ascaris). A *tsipyaya* is any small bird, the size of a sparrow, more or less.

Case 8b.

Language Karok (Stage 2) (see case 70a)
Source Jane O. Bright and William Bright (1965)
Life-Form Terms ʔačvi·v **bird** (bird)
ʔápsu·n **snake** (snake)
Discussion The source does not mention worms.

Case 9b.

Language Nimboran (Stage 2) (see case 124a)
Life-Form Terms iú **bird** (bird)
lemo **snake** (snake + lizard)
waipua **snake** (worm)
Discussion The **snake** class includes all snake varieties, plus two varieties of lizards said to resemble snakes and reputedly venomous. The Nimboran term for pig, *ibuo*, is used in reference to all larger imported mammals such as deer, goats, cows, and horses, in addition to pigs. The source mentions that the absence of a **fish** term is surprising since fish are by no means unknown to Nimboran speakers. He speculates that the language may have been brought from further inland where fish would be less plentiful, thus accounting for the **fish** life-form gap.

Case 10b.

Language Northern Paiute (Nevada dialect) (Stage 2) (see case 38a)

Source (1) Arie Poldervaart (personal communication); (2) Catherine Louise Sweeney Fowler (1972).

Life-Form Terms huȝíba **bird** (bird+bat)

  togóg.wa **snake** (snake)

  woʔábi **snake** (worm)

  pakʷí **fish** (fish) *I.L.-F.*

Discussion Fowler assigns the gloss "unnamed fishes" to *pakʷí* indicating that it is an incipient life-form class. Poldervaart also notes that the "fish" term does not designate fish such as the trout and the sucker which have their own separate names. According to Fowler, the principal meaning of *togóg.wa* is "rattlesnake." However, some speakers clearly use this term to designate snakes in general. In addition, some speakers restrict *huȝíba* to "small birds" contrasting with a "large bird" term, *kʷiʔnáʔa*. The latter word refers specifically to eagle.

Case 11b.

Language Papago (Stage 2) (see case 105a)

Source Dean Saxton (personal communication)

Life-Form Terms ˈúˈuwhig **bird** (bird)

  waptopi **snake** (worm+centipede+fish)

Discussion Saxton notes that nonpoisonous snakes in general have a cover term, *wamad*. On the other hand, he has not encountered a term for snakes in general. The lumping of fish with elongated creatures (*waptopi*) is attested in several other languages (Kilangi [133b], Kyaka Enga [69b], and Siane [140b]). This apparently is associated with lack or scarcity of fish in an environment. Saxton believes that the term *waptopi*, meaning "worm," was extended to cover fish when these came into Papago experience.

Case 12b.

Language Smith River (Stage 2) (see case 40a)

Life-Form Terms tšˈeeyáš **bird** (bird)

  tˈaaɣəš **snake** (snake)

Discussion The **bird** term also refers more specifically to duck.

Case 13b.

Language Wik-Ngathana (Stage 2) (see case 96a)
Life-Form Terms thoecha **bird** (bird)
ngenycha **snake** (snake)
Discussion While there is no term for fish in general, the word for scale, *keyngka*, is used in reference to scaled fish. There is also a term for the elasmobranchii (sharks, rays, and sawfish), *kathanga*, which literally means "tying," a reference to the method of cooking these fish. Sutton reports that he has not seen worms in the Western Cape York Peninsula region.

> *Two Life-Forms:* **fish+snake**.
> 14b. Highland Tequistlatec (Mexico)
> 15b. Juchitan Zapotec (Mexico) (has incipient **wug** and **mammal**)
> 16b. Mitla Zapotec (Mexico)
> 17b. Paumari (Brazil)
> 18b. Ritharngu (Australia)
> 19b. Sanuma (Brazil and Venezuela)

Case 14b.

Language Highland Tequistlatec (Stage 2) (see case 136a)
Life-Form Terms ɬadu **fish** (fish)
ɬaynofal **snake** (snake)
ɬabimi **snake** (worm)
Discussion Highland Tequistlatec definitely lacks a **bird** life-form. Birds, if not recognized by a generic name, can be called *ɬaga* which means "small creature in general." Insects and other small creatures—including, for example, small mammals such as mice and rats—are also *ɬaga*. The class *ɬaga* contrasts with *ɬinneja* which encompasses all large creatures. These two terms completely partition the animal kingdom along the dimension size. The term *ɬaga*, then, does not actually label a **wug** category as reported elsewhere by me (1979a), but rather designates a much more general animal class.

Case 15b.

Language Juchitan Zapotec (Stage 2) (see case 69a)
Source Cecil H. Brown and Paul K. Chase (1981)
Life-Form Terms benda **fish** (fish)
beenda **snake** (snake)
bicuti' **snake** (worm)

mani huiini' **wug** (bug+bird+other unknown small creature) *I.L.-F.*

mani' **mammal** (mammal+other unknown large creature)
I.L.-F.

Discussion Two phonological features distinguish terms for "fish" and
"snake": (1) different tones, and (2) vowel length in the first syllables (long
vowels, e.g., -ee-, are "lightly broken"). This case is discussed in detail in
Chapter 6 focusing on incipient life-form classes.

Case 16b.

Language Mitla Zapotec (Stage 2) (see case 103a)

Source (1) investigated by the author with Paul K. Chase; (2) Morris Stubblefield (personal communication).

Life-Form Terms bäjl **fish** (fish)

bä̱l **snake** (snake+worm)

bisiujg **snake** (worm)

Discussion Three words can be used to refer to birds: *manxhiga* literally
"winged creature," *mannirotat* "flying creature," and *maxhaguibaa* "creature of the sky." Each term also denotes creatures which are not birds such as
flying insects. In addition, birds do not seem to form the focus of any of these
three categories. Thus these are special purpose classes.

Case 17b.

Language Paumari (Stage 2) (see case 86a)

Life-Form Terms abaisana **fish** (fish)

makha **snake** (snake)

Discussion Birds are not encoded independently but rather fit into a general
class of creatures (*igitha*) also including bugs, pets and non-dangerous animals. Perhaps the latter category is **wug**, but such a codification is far from
certain. Water snakes are excluded from *makha* and have their own class label, *mabidiri*. There is a tendency to use the **fish** term for small fish which are
caught in large numbers. Larger fish are almost always referred to by their
specific name. Chapman notes that the Paumari tend not to use a generic form
when the specific animal is known. This indicates that the above classes may
be incipient rather than full life-forms.

Case 18b.

___

Language Ritharngu (Stage 2) (see case 24a)
Life-Form Terms guya **fish** (fish)
               ba:pi **snake** (snake)

Case 19b.

___

Language Sanuma (Stage 2)
Classification Yanoama, Waican, Macro-Chibchan
Area Brazil and Venezuela border area
Source (1) Kenneth Iain Taylor (personal communication); (2) Kenneth Iain Taylor (1974).
Life-Form Terms salaga bɨ **fish** (fish)
                olɨgɨgɨ **snake** (snake)
Discussion Taylor (1974) notes that the above two classes are two of very few general categories with labels which are exocentric unitary lexemes. He lists other general zoological categories which are labeled by complex, nonunitary, descriptive lexemes, e.g., *maigi gua wi bɨ* "winged creatures," *hole dimɨ bɨ* "walking (on ground) creatures," and *tuo dimɨ bɨ* "climbing (up trees) creatures." Birds and other winged animals such as bats and flying insects are designated by *maigi gua wi bɨ*. Apparently birds can be distinguished from other members of the latter class through reference to the structure of their wings: thus birds are winged creatures with "solid wings" (*maigi sami*) (Taylor, personal communication). Such a usage is, of course, highly descriptive and for this reason is not judged indicative of a **bird** life-form. (Carol Swain [personal communication] notes the lack of a **bird** term in Ninam. Ninam and Sanuma are very closely related, perhaps only dialects of a single language.) In addition, included among the few exocentric unitary lexemes for general animal categories listed by Taylor (1974) is *kokoi bɨ* which designates birds of prey. The latter, of course, is a special purpose category term. The descriptive label *hole dimɨ bɨ* "walking (on ground) creatures" has a range comparable to that of a **mammal** life-form. It encompasses most terrestrial creatures including ground dwelling mammals, snakes, frogs, alligators, lizards, and turtles (Taylor, personal communication). However, it is clear that the principal criterion for belonging to the latter category is terrestrial habitat. For example, a number of mammals which inhabit trees (coatimundi, squirrel, certain anteaters, etc.) are excluded from the *hole dimɨ bɨ* grouping. These instead are placed in the *tuo dimɨ bɨ* grouping which encompasses "climbing (up trees) creatures."

Two Life-Forms: **bird + fish.**
20b. Sahaptin (Washington, U.S.A.) (has incipient **snake** and **worm**)

Case 20b.

Language Sahaptin (Stage 2) (see case 7a)
Source Eugene Hunn (1980a, b, 1982)
Life-Form Terms kákya **bird** (bird)
            cikᵂácikᵂa **bird** (small bird) *I.L.-F.*
            waykáanaš **fish** (fish)
            núsux̣ **fish** (large fish)
            x̣úlx̣ul **fish** (small fish)
            pyúš **snake** (snake) *I.L.-F.*
            sáysay **snake** (worm + caterpillar + maggot) *I.L.-F.*
Discussion The **bird** term is polysemous, referring more broadly to creatures in general. The "small bird" term is an incipient life-form label used for any smallish bird not otherwise named. The term *waykáanaš* has a complex application. Hunn (1980b: 8) writes:

> The term /*waykáanaš*/ is sometimes used to refer to fish in general, inclusive of the jawless, boneless lampreys . . . but excluding such so-called "fish" as crayfish and shellfish. . . . Yet /*waykáanaš*/ may also mean either "edible fish" or "salmon," . . . particularly in the religious context of the thanksgiving feast; . . . at least the term strongly connotes fish as a sacred food; /*waykáanaš*/ is often described by informants as a "religious word."

Both lampreys and sturgeons are excluded from the ranges of the "large fish" and "small fish" terms. Hunn notes that size is probably not the only feature underlying the *x̣úlx̣ul / núsux̣* distinction. Some fish identified as *x̣úlx̣ul* may in fact grow larger than some identified as *núsux̣*. Included among the "large fish" grouping are various kinds of salmon and the steelhead trout. The following are members of the "small fish" grouping: whitefish, resident trout, Dolly Vardens, smelts, carps, squawfish, chiselmouths, peamouths (?), red-sided shiners, daces, large-scale suckers, bridge-lip suckers, Lost River suckers, and sculpins. Hunn assigns the gloss "salmon" to *núsux̣* and "residual small fish" to *x̣úlx̣ul*. The term for incipient "snake," *pyúš*, is used to designate ten species of snake known in the region. Only one species designated by the term has its own name, i.e. *nč'í pyúš* "gopher snake," literally, "big snake." The term for rattlesnake, *wáx̣ puš*, while clearly derivative from the term for incipient "snake," is not considered to be a kind of *pyúš*. In addition, *pyúš* more specifically designates the garter snake. Hunn (1980a) proposes that this term in the past was a monotypic generic term meaning "garter snake." The term for incipient "worm" refers only to those small elongated creatures not having their own individual names.

STAGE 3 LANGUAGES.

Three Life-Forms: **bird + fish + snake**.

21b. Aguaruna Jivaro (Peru)
22b. Akawaio (Guyana)
23b. Araona (Bolivia)
24b. Asurini (Brazil)
25b. Atapec Zapotec (Mexico)
26b. Bisa (Ghana and Upper Volta)
27b. Bontoc (Guinaang dialect) (The Philippines)
28b. Brunei Malay (Borneo) (has incipient "worm")
29b. Cantonese (Hong Kong Boat People) (Hong Kong)
30b. Carapana (Colombia)
31b. Central Cagayan Agta (The Philippines) (has incipient **wug**)
32b. Chrau (Vietnam)
33b. Chuj (Guatemala)
34b. Colorado (Ecuador)
35b. Djinang (Australia)
36b. Gaviao (Brazil)
37b. Gouin (Upper Volta)
38b. Hopi (Arizona, U.S.A.)
39b. Huastec (Veracruz dialect) (Mexico)
40b. Huichol (Mexico)
41b. Kaingang (Brazil)
42b. Kaiwa (Brazil)
43b. Kenyah (Malaysia)
44b. Keres (New Mexico, U.S.A.)
45b. Lowland Tequistlatec (Mexico)
46b. Machiguenga (Peru)
47b. Mara (Australia)
48b. Mazatec (Mexico)
49b. Mele-Fila (New Hebrides)
50b. Michoacan Nahuatl (Mexico)
51b. Moore (Ghana)
52b. Nez Perce (Idaho, Washington, Oregon, U.S.A.)
53b. Nuaulu (Indonesia)
54b. Nunggubuyu (Australia)

55b. Penang Hokkien (Malaysia)
56b. Semai (Malaysia)
57b. Shoshoni (Utah, Nevada, U.S.A.)
58b. Sisaala (Tumu dialect) (Ghana)
59b. Songhay (Nigeria, Niger, Mali, Upper Volta, Dahomey)
60b. Southern Tiwa (New Mexico, U.S.A.)
61b. Tarahumara (Mexico)
62b. Texmelucan Zapotec (Mexico)
63b. Upper Tanana (Alaska, U.S.A.)
64b. Western Aranda (Australia)
65b. Wik Moŋkan (Australia)
66b. Zoogocho Zapotec (Mexico)

Case 21b.

Language Aguaruna Jivaro (Stage 3) (see case 46a)
Source (1) Michael F. Brown (personal communication); (2) Brent Berlin and Elois Ann Berlin (1977).
Life-Form Terms píshak **bird** (bird)
namák **fish** (fish)
mamayák **fish** (small fish)
dápi **snake** (snake)
námpich **snake** (worm)
Discussion There is another general "bird" term, *chígki*, which is used to refer to large game birds. This category excludes large carrion eaters, birds of prey, and domestic fowl. The **fish** term also means "river." Another term, *kúntin* "game animal," has a referential range resembling that of a **mammal** class. According to Brown, the word is used to designate edible mammals and, for some speakers, edible lizards and amphibians. Brown also notes that some Aguaruna divide *kúntin* into two subgroups: *shíig kúntin* "edible animals" and *kúntin yúchatai* "inedible animals." This usage may indicate that the sense of *kúntin* is expanding from a special purpose "edible mammals" class to "mammals in general."

Case 22b.

Language Akawaio (Stage 3) (see case 129a)
Life-Form Terms torong **bird** (bird)
moruk **fish** (fish)
ögöi **snake** (snake)

Case 23b.

Language Araona (Stage 3) (see case 48a)
Life-Form Terms bakweboni **bird** (bird)
                háikana **fish** (fish)
                bákwakana **snake** (snake)
Discussion Pitman describes *bakweboni* as "air birds . . . this includes most of the birds." There is another term, *wáiboni*, which refers to "ground birds" such as chickens, partridge type birds, and, possibly, turkeys.

Case 24b.

Language Asurini (Stage 3) (see case 11a)
Life-Form Terms wyra **bird** (bird)
                ipira **fish** (fish+sting ray+electric eel)
                masa **snake** (snake)
Discussion A **mammal** life-form may be consolidating under the label *me'ee'ia*. This term, roughly glossed "meat," refers to edible mammals, amphibians, birds, and, apparently, certain reptiles. However, it excludes edible fish, snakes, and insects.

Case 25b.

Language Atapec Zapotec (Stage 3) (see case 117a)
Life-Form Terms bínni **bird** (bird)
                bel.la **fish** (fish)
                bel.la **snake** (snake)
                bel.lato? **snake** (worm)
Discussion The "fish" and "snake" terms are distinguished by different tonal paradigms. The "worm" term translates literally "little snake."

Case 26b.

Language Bisa (Stage 3) (see case 12a)
Life-Form Terms From Prost:
                kyiraw **bird** (small bird)
                zo **fish** (fish)
                mesɛ **snake** (snake)
                From Naden:
                been **bird** (bird+bat)
                zɔ **fish** (fish)
                min **snake** (snake)
                tala-fɔ **snake** (snake)

Discussion With the exception of the **fish** term reports of Prost and Naden (personal communications) are dissimilar. Differences are almost certainly attributable to dialectal variation. Naden notes that *been* does not cover flying domestic animals, not even pigeons. The term *tala-fɔ* translates literally "ground thing." It is also used more generally for "creepy-crawlies," notably termites and snakes.

Case 27b.

Language Bontoc (Guinaang dialect) (Stage 3) (see case 4a)
Source (1) Lawrence A. Reid (personal communication); (2) Lawrence A. Reid (1976).
Life-Form Terms inyólan **bird** (wild bird)
　　　　　　　　ay-áyam **bird** (wild bird)
　　　　　　　　gadiw **fish** (fish)
　　　　　　　　owal **snake** (snake)
　　　　　　　　kelang **snake** (worm)
Discussion Small birds possibly constitute the focus of both **bird** classes. The **fish** term refers specifically to a kind of small fresh water fish species. Reid (personal communication) is not absolutely certain that the term extends to fish in general. However, he does note that it is found in a compound verbal form, *mangadiw*, which means to catch fish, whatever the kind (with the exception of eels).

Case 28b.

Language Brunei Malay (Stage 3) (see case 160a)
Source Linda Kimball (personal communication)
Life-Form Terms burong **bird** (bird + flying insect)
　　　　　　　　lauk **fish** (fish)
　　　　　　　　ular **snake** (snake)
　　　　　　　　chaching **snake** (worm) *I.L.-F.*
Discussion
　　Whether or not birds constitute the focus of *burong* is not clear. Kimball writes that in addition to birds, *burong* "can also mean 'flying bug/insect' . . . if one wants to emphasize that a bird is meant . . . one says *burong bebulu* (feathered bird) . . . but generally one knows from the referent/content what is being meant." The incipient "worm" life-form excludes earthworms since these have specific names.

Case 29b.

Language Cantonese (Hong Kong Boat People) (Stage 3)
Classification Cantonese, Chinese, Sino-Tibetan
Area Hong Kong
Source Eugene N. Anderson (1972)
Life-Form Terms tsök **bird** (bird)
              ü **fish** (fish + sea mammal + cephalopod + abalone)
              se **snake** (snake)

Discussion Other than the fact that Anderson uses *fish* as the primary gloss for *ü*, there is no indication whether or not true fish are the focus of this class. If not, Cantonese should be regarded as a Stage 2 language with **bird** and **snake**.

Case 30b.

Language Carapana (Stage 3) (see case 133a)
Life-Form Terms cawɨrã **bird** (bird + bat + flying insect)
              minia **bird** (small bird)
              wai **fish** (fish)
              ãña **snake** (snake)
              wãsĩã **snake** (worm)

Discussion Whether or not birds constitute the focus of *cawɨrã* is not known. All fish in the Carapana environment are edible except for one type. The non-edible type is called *moena* "useless being" rather than *wai*. The "worm" category excludes nonedible worms. There is an "edible animal" category, *waibɨtoa*, which primarily includes edible mammals, e.g., pacas, wooly monkeys, peccaries, pigs, cows, but also chickens.

Case 31b.

Language Central Cagayan Agta (Stage 3) (see case 55a)
Life-Form Terms manuk **bird** (large bird + large bat)
              mamanuk **bird** (small bird + small bat)
              ikan **fish** (fish)
              ulag **snake** (snake + lizard + centipede + scorpion)
              ulolag **wug** (insect + mite + millipede + worm) *I.L.-F.*

Discussion The word *manuk* specifically designates the domestic chicken. Some large birds denoted by the latter term include giant rufus hornbills, wild and domestic ducks, geese, turkeys, pigeons, eagles, hawks, owls, and cranes. *Manuk* also encompasses the Philippine flying fox (a fruit-bat). Some small birds labeled *mamanuk* include doves and dove-like birds, parrots and parakeets, quails, swifts, kingfishers, crows, ravens, rails, mynahs, and egrets. While true fish constitute the focus of *ikan*, the term is used more broadly to designate eels, squids, octopuses, and turtles. All round bodied fish such as mudfish, catfish, and sharks are excluded from *ikan* and have their own class label, *dalag*. The **snake** term encompasses all legless reptiles plus some poisonous insects. Only one type of lizard is included in the latter grouping. This is a foot long reptile having a body like a snake and barely noticeable legs. The term for incipient **wug**, *ulolag*, translates literally "small snake." The source mentions that this term is used for insects and other small creatures only if the specific name of an organism is not known or not readily recalled.

Case 32b.

Language Chrau (Stage 3)
Classification South Bahnaric, Bahnaric, Mon-Khmer, Austro-Asiatic
Area E.N.E. of Saigon, South Vietnam
Source Dorothy Thomas (1966)
Life-Form Terms sŭm **bird** (bird)
ca **fish** (fish+eel)
vih **snake** (snake)
Discussion Birds of prey, *khlang*, are excluded from the **bird** class *sŭm*. In addition to the above terms, there are three numerical classifiers that tend to map other general classes: (1) *păng*, used in enumerating flat creatures such as turtles, (2) *tong*, used to enumerate long creatures such as lizards, and (3) *vanông*, used in enumerating large mammals. Note that I mistakenly failed to recognize a **snake** life-form for Chrau in an earlier treatment (Brown 1979a).

Case 33b.

Language Chuj (Stage 3) (see case 57a)
Source Nicholas A. Hopkins (1980b)
Life-Form Terms much **bird** (bird)
chay **fish** (fish)
chan **snake** (snake)

Case 34b.

Language Colorado (Stage 3) (see case 134a)
Life-Form Terms pichu **bird** (bird)
watsa **fish** (fish)
pini **snake** (snake)

otoncoro **snake** (smooth long worm)

Discussion The **bird** term also specifically designates a certain type of bird.

Case 35b.

Language Djinang (Stage 3) (see case 98a)
Life-Form Terms wurgi **bird** (bird)
                   guyi **fish** (fish)
                   minarr **snake** (snake)
                   wuyinygurr **snake** (worm)

Discussion A **mammal** life-form may be consolidating under the label *maypal*. This term refers to land mammals, reptiles, and amphibians which are eaten. It also designates crocodiles. It is not normally used in reference to snakes, birds, fish, or bugs.

Case 36b.

Language Gaviao (Stage 3) (see case 119a)
Life-Form Terms íhdún **bird** (small bird)
                   bolív **fish** (fish)
                   baj **snake** (snake)

Discussion A term is found for all edible big birds, i.e. *vajáh*, but there is no word for nonedible large birds such as eagles, vultures, etc. Stute writes, "sometimes the alligator seems to be included [in *bolív*], but not clearly." There is a word, *pòpàga*, for edible big animals such as deer, tapirs, wild pigs, etc., but clearly none for **mammal**, i.e. edible and nonedible mammals.

Case 37b.

Language Gouin (Stage 3) (see case 15a)
Life-Form Terms hùrìmbá **bird** (bird)
                   tètèràambá **fish** (fish)
                   jénáambá **snake** (snake)

Discussion There is a general term, *gbeînî nâ taámbá*, which extends to all creatures which are not birds, snakes, bugs or animals that live in or near the water. This is not considered here to be a **mammal** term since membership in the category is directly based on a single criterion. The term translates literally, "the owners of four legs." Another general term, *bímbámbá*, is a near "unique beginner" or "kingdom" label. It encompasses all creatures (birds, fish, reptiles, worms, bugs, etc.) except fish.

Case 38b.

Language Hopi (Stage 3) (see case 16a)
Source Charles F. Voegelin and Florence M. Voegelin (1957)
Life-Form Terms círo **bird** (bird)
  pá:kiw **fish** (fish)
  lölógaŋ^w **snake** (snake)
Discussion The **bird** term also refers more specifically to snowbird.

Case 39b.

Language Huastec (Veracruz dialect) (Stage 3) (see case 183a)
Source Investigated by the author
Life-Form Terms čʼičin **bird** (bird)
  toʔol **fish** (fish)
  čan **snake** (snake)
  θu·m **snake** (worm)
Discussion Another term, *labaš*, meaning primarily "dangerous snake," is an alternative to *čan* which is fairly frequently used.

Case 40b.

Language Huichol (Stage 3) (see case 137a)
Source Joseph E. Grimes (1980b)
Life-Form Terms vii.quiixi **bird** (bird)
  quee.sûté **fish** (fish)
  cúu.teríixi **snake** (snake)
  cuíisí.teexi or cuíisí.teriixi **snake** (worm+caterpillar)

Case 41b.

Language Kaingang (Stage 3)
Classification Caingang, Ge, Macro-Ge, Ge-Pano-Carib
Area Brazil
Source Herbert Baldus (1946)
Life-Form Terms xanxí or xenxí **bird** (bird)
  pirá **fish** (fish)
  pan **snake** (snake)
Discussion The source does not mention worms.

Case 42b.

Language Kaiwa (dialect of Tupi) (Stage 3) (see case 170a)
Life-Form Terms gwɨra **bird** (bird)
pira **fish** (large fish)
pikɨ **fish** (small fish)
mboi **snake** (snake)

Case 43b.

Language Kenyah (Stage 3) (see case 71a)
Life-Form Terms suwi **bird** (bird)
atok **fish** (fish)
tuꞌdok **snake** (snake)
ulet **snake** (worm)
Discussion The **bird** term designates all birds except the ground dwelling types. The "worm" term refers to all worm-like creatures (caterpillars, grubs, maggots, etc.) excluding earthworms.

Case 44b.

Language Keres (Stage 3)
Classification language isolate
Area New Mexico, U.S.A.
Source Leslie A. White (1947)
Life-Form Terms si·biyó **bird** (bird)
gꞌa·c **fish** (fish)
ckꞌaꞌac^u **fish** (fish)
cro·wi **snake** (snake)
Discussion An informant from Zia Pueblo told White that there is no Keres equivalent for the English word *bird*. An informant from Santa Ana Pueblo, however, gave him the above term for **bird**. The term *gꞌaꞌc* "fish" is used at Santo Domingo and Santa Ana Pueblos and *ckꞌaꞌac^u* is used at Acoma and Laguna. White does not mention worms.

Case 45b.

Language Lowland Tequistlatec (Stage 3) (see case 164a)
Life-Form Terms lakaˀ **bird** (bird)
lat^{y}u **fish** (fish)
layñofał **snake** (snake)
moha **snake** (worm)

Case 46b.

___

Language Machiguenga (Stage 3) (see case 77a)
Life-Form Terms shimeri **bird** (small bird)
                shima **fish** (fish)
                marenkyi **snake** (snake)
Discussion The **fish** term has a second restricted referent, i.e. *Prochilodus magdalenae*, a type of fish known in Peruvian Spanish as *boquichico*.

Case 47b.

___

Language Mara (Stage 3) (see case 20a)
Life-Form Terms ṛayi **bird** (bird)
                waḷañan **fish** (fish)
                ḍawar **snake** (snake)
Discussion The **bird** term is especially applicable to fairly large birds. The word for rainbow fish, *baḷgur*, can be used loosely for any small fish.

Case 48b.

___

Language Mazatec (Stage 3) (see case 141a)
Life-Form Terms nise **bird** (bird)
                hti **fish** (fish)
                ye **snake** (snake)
                čonto **snake** (worm)
Discussion Another term, *čo*, labels a category including all creatures (birds, reptiles, worms, insects, mammals, etc.) with the exception of fish. The "worm" term translates literally "long creature."

Case 49b.

___

Language Mele-Fila (Stage 3) (see case 122a)
Life-Form Terms manu **bird** (bird+bat)
                ika **fish** (fish+whale+porpoise)
                gata **snake** (snake)
Discussion The **bird** life-form possibly also includes butterflies. Snakes are of only one or two species and are neither numerous or conspicuous.

Case 50b.

___

Language Michoacan Nahuatl (Stage 3) (see case 165a)
Life-Form Terms tutol **bird** (bird)

mičin **fish** (fish)

kuwal **snake** (snake)

ʔokʹkʷilin **snake** (worm)

Discussion The **bird** life-form excludes domestic fowl. Some speakers occasionally use Spanish *animal* as if it were a label for a **mammal** life-form encompassing mammals, reptiles (including snakes), and amphibians. The same term is also sometimes restricted in reference to true mammals.

Case 51b.

Language Moore (Stage 3) (see case 113a)

Life-Form Terms liula **bird** (small bird)

zim **fish** (fish)

waafo **snake** (snake)

zurzuri **snake** (worm)

Case 52b.

Language Nez Perce (Stage 3) (see case 128a)

Source Haruo Aoki (personal communication)

Life-Form Terms payó:payo **bird** (bird)

cú:ỷem **fish** (fish)

páyos **snake** (snake)

Case 53b.

Language Nuaulu (Stage 3) (see case 84a)

Source (1) Roy F. Ellen (1973; 1975b); (2) Roy F. Ellen (personal communication); (3) Roy F. Ellen, Andrew F. Stimson, and James Menzies (n.d.).

Life-Form Terms manwe **bird** (bird+bat)

ikai **fish** (fish)

tekene **snake** (snake+worm+centipede+giant millipede)

Discussion The **snake** term is sometimes loosely applied to certain eels. Ellen (personal communication) describes a fourth general term, *ipai*, as being a label for "terrestrial animals, contrasted with those of the sea and air." He (personal communication) writes:

> In this sense the focal reference type is vertebrate quadrupeds. I suspect that on occasions invertebrates might be included by extension, but the contexts in which the term is ordinarily used by no means make this clear.

This discussion suggests that *ipai* may function either as a label for **mammal** or for combined **wug-mammal** although, as Ellen stresses, referential application of the word is not well understood. Ellen also writes that *ipai* is sometimes used in contrast to humans, where it appears to refer to all nonhuman animals. A term for "ritual game animals," *pene*, may in fact label a general purpose category. The latter includes only three creatures: the wild pig, the Moluccan deer, and the cassowary. Since these game animals are the largest wild creatures known, an appropriate codification for *pene* might be **mammal** (large mammal+cassowary). Ellen mentions that at a rather superficial level this term is glossed for outsiders as "meat."

Case 54b.

Language Nunggubuyu (Stage 3) (see case 22a)
Life-Form Terms ŋuṟuḏu- **bird** (bird+bat)
ŋujija- **fish** (fish)
ma:rñ- **snake** (snake+eel)
Discussion The **bird** term is occasionally used to refer to flying insects such as grasshoppers.

Case 55b.

Language Penang Hokkien (Stage 3)
Classification Southern Min, Chinese, Sino-Tibetan
Area West Malaysia
Source E. N. Anderson, Jr. and Marja L. Anderson (1977)
Life-Form Terms ciàu **bird** (bird)
hu or hi **fish** (fish)
chúa **snake** (snake)
thàng **snake** (worm)

Case 56b.

Language Semai (Stage 3)
Classification Sakai, Malacca, Austro-Asiatic
Area Central Malaya
Source (1) Robert K. Dentan (1967, 1968a, 1968b, 1970); (2) Robert K. Dentan (personal communication)
Life-Form Terms cheb **bird** (bird)
ka' **fish** (fish+amphibian+testudinate+aquatic mollusk)
tiji' **snake** (snake)
chachig **snake** (worm)

Discussion The referential extension of *ka'* given above is that known to the unacculturated Semai. In acculturated settlements the word is restricted to true fish. True fish also constitute the focus of the category for unacculturated Semai (Dentan 1970: 21).

Case 57b.

Language Shoshoni (Stage 3) (see case 39a)
Source (1) Ralph V. Chamberlin (1908); (2) Catherine Louise Sweeney Fowler (1972).
Life-Form Terms húču?u **bird** (bird+bat)
                 k^{w}ína?a **bird** (large bird)
                 péŋk^{w}i **fish** (fish)
                 góa or go **snake** (snake)
                 wúabi or wábi **snake** (worm)

Discussion Fowler deals with a dialect of Shoshoni spoken in Owyhee, Nevada and Chamberlin's data are from the Gosiute dialect of Utah. The two **bird** terms and the **fish** term are found in both Fowler's and Chamberlin's descriptions (I use Fowler's orthography). The "snake" and "worm" terms are from Chamberlin alone. These life-form classes probably occur in the Nevada dialect as well. Fowler notes that the term *húču?u* covers all birds for some informants and only small birds for others. She also mentions that bats are thought to be birds or related to birds by most speakers. In Chamberlin's account the "large bird" term apparently refers only to eagles.

Case 58b.

Language Sisaala (Tumu dialect) (Stage 3) (see case 26a)
Life-Form Terms zaara **bird** (bird)
                 biibie **bird** (small bird)
                 cheŋfiliŋ **fish** (fish)
                 dimiŋ **snake** (snake)

Discussion The **snake** term is derived from the verb *dim* "to bite."

Case 59b.

Language Songhay (Stage 3) (see case 27a)
Life-Form Terms kyiraw **bird** (bird)
                 hamisa **fish** (fish)
                 ganda karfu **snake** (snake)
                 noni **snake** (worm)

Case 60b.

Language Southern Tiwa (Stage 3) (see case 42a)
Life-Form Terms šušun **bird** (bird)
           pïmnin **fish** (fish)
           pïřun **snake** (snake)
           pořan **snake** (worm)
Discussion The **bird** life-form apparently excludes domestic fowl.

Case 61b.

Language Tarahumara (Stage 3) (see case 43a)
Source (1) William L. Merrill (personal communication); (2) David Brambila
    (personal communication); (3) Don Burgess (personal communication);
    (4) Kenneth Hilton (personal communication); (5) Andrés Lionnet (1972);
    (6) I. Thord-Gray (1955).
Life-Form Terms chuluwí **bird** (bird)
           rochí **fish** (fish)
           sinó **snake** (snake + lizard species)
Discussion The above terms and extensions are from Merrill who has systematically studied folk zoological classification in Tarahumara. Merrill notes
that a particular lizard, named *ropogópali*, is classed with snakes because it is
said to be poisonous. On the other hand, Burgess reports that *sinó* (or *sinowí*)
is restricted to nonpoisonous snakes. All other sources, however, identify
the word as a label for snakes in general. Merrill also mentions the term
nowí which he reports encompasses caterpillars and other insect larva. Other
sources (Brambila, Hilton, Lionnet, and Thord-Gray) identify this term as a
label for worms in general, possibly excluding earthworms which have their
own cover term. A **wug** category may be in the process of consolidating in the
language. Merrill gives the term *siorí* and writes that it is "apparently a polysemous term that means both 'flying insects' and 'insects,' the latter with
some qualifications." He notes that red ants, black ants, butterflies, moths,
grasshoppers, and several other unidentified insects are associated with the
term, but are not clearly members of a *siorí* class. Hilton also writes that the
term refers to "any fly or insect or bee." The remaining sources do not mention the term or do not report it as a **wug** label. Brambila and Lionnet identify
it simply as the word for "fly (insect)." Thord-Gray writes that *siorí* (*seori*)
designates "fly, flies . . . dipterous insects of which the house fly . . . is the
best known . . . a general term for a fly or winged insect." Merrill also reports that there is no term for **mammal**. Other sources, however, indicate that
mammal too may be in the process of consolidating. Hilton reports the term
namúti meaning both "wild animal" and "thing." This term is limited pri-

marily to mammals since, according to Hilton, it is not used in reference to fish, snakes, and birds. He further states that it is mainly used to denote *unknown* wild animals, thus indicating that it may label an incipient **mammal** life-form class. Lionnet assigns the gloss "animal, thing" to the term. Undoubtedly the rather fluid situation described above for some Tarahumara animal classes reflects extensive idiolectic and dialectic variations.

Case 62b.

Language Texmelucan Zapotec (Stage 3) (see case 153a)
Life-Form Terms čigyiñ **bird** (bird)
　　　　　　　　bel **fish** (fish)
　　　　　　　　bily **snake** (snake+worm)

Case 63b.

Language Upper Tanana (Stage 3) (see case 108a)
Life-Form Terms ts'eht'uudn **bird** (small bird)
　　　　　　　　tuuk **fish** (fish)
　　　　　　　　tɬuh choh **snake** (snake)
　　　　　　　　tɬuh **snake** (worm)
Discussion The **fish** term refers more specifically to white fish. The "snake" label translates literally "large worm." There are no snakes in interior Alaska. There is a fifth term, *noon*, which encompasses all nondomesticated fur-bearing animals. Since designation of creatures by use of the term is apparently based just on their having fur, it is considered a special purpose category label and is not codified as a term for **mammal**.

Case 64b.

Language Western Aranda (Stage 3) (see case 29a)
Life-Form Terms thiypa **bird** (bird)
　　　　　　　　irrpunga **fish** (fish)
　　　　　　　　ampa **snake** (snake)
　　　　　　　　tjapa **snake** (worm+grub+caterpillar)

Case 65b.

Language Wik Moŋkan (Stage 3) (see case 44a)
Life-Form Terms päntj **bird** (bird)
　　　　　　　　ŋa'a **fish** (fish)

tukk **snake** (snake)

Discussion The source does not mention worms.

Case 66b.

Language Zoogocho Zapotec (Stage 3) (see case 159a)
Life-Form Terms be ža ṣil **bird** (bird)
　　　　　　　bx̱inne **bird** (small bird+bat)
　　　　　　　bell (tone 2) **fish** (fish)
　　　　　　　bell (tone 4) **snake** (snake+worm)
Discussion The "bird" term, *be ža ṣil*, translates literally "creature with wings." The latter label encompasses all small birds and other larger birds with the exception of owls. The **snake** life-form excludes caterpillars and centipedes since these have feet.

Three Life-Forms: other than **bird + fish + snake**.
67b. Dalabon (Australia) (**fish + wug + mammal**)
68b. Dugum Dani (West Irian) (**bird + wug + mammal**)
69b. Kyaka Enga (Papua New Guinea) (**bird + snake + mammal**)

Case 67b.

Language Dalabon (Stage 3) (see case 5a)
Source Kenneth Maddock (1972, 1975)
Life-Form Terms djenj **fish** (fish)
　　　　　　　manj **wug** (insect + bird + snake + small marsupial + lizard +
　　　　　　　　　　dingo + emu + crocodile)
　　　　　　　gunj **mammal** (large marsupial)
Discussion Maddock comments on the application of size in distinguishing *gunj* and *manj*:

> When I asked Aborigines whether these small wallabies were *gunj*, I was told that they were 'too small' for this genus. But it would be erroneous to conclude that *gunj* is properly the genus to which large species belong, for if it were, emus, pythons and saltwater crocodiles should be assigned to it instead of to *manj*. Size, then, is not applied systematically to produce genera of species, though it may be used occasionally to rationalize the *manj* membership of creatures felt to be *gunj*-like. That is to say, size is perhaps to be regarded as pertaining to a native model of classification. The explanatory power of this criterion is slight, and I do not remember ever having heard other criteria used (1975: 104).

In any case, the majority of creatures included in *manj* are relatively small and *all* creatures included in *gunj* are large. The referential extensions of *manj* mentioned by Maddock which go against a small size criterion perhaps may be accountable to usages which were originally figurative in nature, for example, a metaphor equating crocodiles with small lizards. The source does not mention worms. Further discussion of this case, bearing on the interpretation that *manj* is **wug** and *gunj*, **mammal**, is undertaken in Chapter 8.

Case 68b.

Language Dugum Dani (Stage 3) (see case 31a)
Life-Form Terms due **bird** (bird+bat)
                       wato **wug** (insect+reptile+amphibian)
                       bpake **mammal** (marsupial+rodent)
Discussion Pigs, dogs, and recently introduced cats are not included in the **mammal** life-form. The absence of **fish** and **snake** life-forms is almost certainly attributable to ecological factors. Heider (1970: 218–219) writes that "fish are totally absent" and that "snakes are rare, but there are two sorts of nonpoisonous ones." The source does not mention worms.

Case 69b.

Language Kyaka Enga (Stage 3)
Classification Enga-Hule-Wiru, East New Guinea Highlands, Central New
    Guinea, Indo-Pacific
Area Papua New Guinea
Source Ralph N. H. Bulmer (personal communication)
Life-Form Terms yaka **bird** (bird+bat+gliding marsupial)
                       kau **snake** (snake+lizard+caterpillar+grub+worm+scorpion+reptile-like insect+fish)
                       wi **mammal** (small mammal (mouse+rat+small marsupial))
                       sa **mammal** (large mammal)
Discussion The absence of a **fish** life-form is almost certainly due to an ecological factor. Bulmer reports that only five fish species are known to Kyaka Enga speakers. The inclusion of fish in **snake** or the "elongated creature" category is also attributable to scarcity of fish. Similar classificatory treatments of fish are reported in this work for Papago (11b), Kilangi (133b), and Siane (126b), all of which are spoken in areas where fish are rare. The "large mammal" class excludes bats, dogs, and other large domestic mammals.

STAGE 4 LANGUAGES.

Four Life-Forms: **bird + fish + snake + wug**.
70b. Catawba (Southeastern U.S.A.)
71b. Clallam (Washington State, U.S.A.)
72b. Cora (Mexico)
73b. Ila (Zambia)
74b. Indonesian (Indonesia)
75b. Kayan (Indonesian Borneo)
76b. Kayapo (Brazil)
77b. Kikamba (Kenya)
78b. Kugu-Nganhchara (Australia)
79b. Malagasy (Madagascar)
80b. Mandarin (China)
81b. Maxakali (Brazil)
82b. Mende (Sierra Leone, Liberia)
83b. Navaho (Arizona, New Mexico, Utah, Colorado, U.S.A.)
84b. Northeastern Thai (Thailand)
85b. Omaha (Nebraska, U.S.A.)
86b. Pashto (Afghanistan)
87b. Sierra Popoluca (Mexico)
88b. Southern Paiute (Cedar City dialect) (Utah, U.S.A.)
89b. Teen (Ivory Coast)
90b. Tok Pisin (Papua New Guinea)
91b. Western Subanun (The Philippines)
92b. Yaqui (Arizona, U.S.A. and Mexico)

Case 70b.

Language Catawba (Stage 4)
Classification Macro-Siouan
Area South Carolina, North Carolina, Tennessee, U.S.A.
Source Frank G. Speck (1946)
Life-Form Terms kutcín **bird** (bird)
               yi· **fish** (fish)
               ya **snake** (snake)
               tcu̧ **wug** (insect)
Discussion The source does not mention worms.

Case 71b.

Language Clallam (Stage 4) (see case 181a)
Life-Form Terms čačəmʔ **bird** (bird)
         sʔiʔɬən **fish** (saltwater fish)
         sxʷaʔxʷč **snake** (snake)
         scəq̓ʷ **snake** (worm)
         sxʷaʔxənʔaʔam **wug** (bug)

Discussion The **fish** term derives from the verb "to eat." There is another general term, *taʔtaʔciŋuxʷ*, which possibly denotes **mammal**. Its referential extensions are unclear, possibly referring just to mammals, or to mammals that are hunted, or to all creatures that are hunted.

Case 72b.

Language Cora (Stage 4) (see case 182a)
Life-Form Terms pína'a **bird** (bird)
         wá'i **fish** (fish)
         kú'uku'u **snake** (snake)
         háhri **snake** (worm)
         tʸi'itɨ **wug** (bug+worm+leech)

Discussion The **fish** term more restrictively refers to catfish, apparently its original meaning. The **wug** term can be more generally glossed "discrete object," in which case it applies to both living and nonliving things. The Spanish word *animal* has been borrowed into Cora and is applied to mammals, lizards, alligators, and turtles. It is not considered here to be a **mammal** label because the term is also occasionally used in reference to birds suggesting that it is in fact a "unique beginner" or "kingdom" label.

Case 73b.

Language Ila (Stage 4)
Classification Central Eastern Bantu, Bantu Proper, Bantoid, Benue-Congo,
     Niger-Congo, Niger-Kordofanian
Area Zambia
Source Rev. Edwin W. Smith and Captain Andrew Murray Dale (1920)
Life-Form Terms bazune **bird** (bird)
         inswi **fish** (fish)
         inzoka **snake** (snake)
         tupuka **wug** (insect)

Discussion The source does not mention worms.

Case 74b.

Language Indonesian (Stage 4)
Classification West Indonesian, Hesperonesian, Austronesian
Area Indonesia
Source Investigated by the author
Life-Form Terms burung **bird** (bird)
  ikan **fish** (fish+whale)
  ulĕr **snake** (snake+worm)
  ular **snake** (snake)
  tjatjing **snake** (worm)
  serangga **wug** (bug)

Case 75b.

Language Kayan (Stage 4)
Classification West Indonesian, Hesperonesian, Austronesian
Area Central Indonesian Borneo
Source Robert H. McDaniel (personal communication)
Life-Form Terms manuk **bird** (bird)
  masik **fish** (fish)
  nyipa **snake** (snake)
  telusung **wug** (insect+spider+maggot)

Case 76b.

Language Kayapo (Stage 4)
Classification Cayapo, Macro-Ge, Ge-Pano-Carib
Area Central Brazil
Source (1) Darrel A. Posey (personal communication); (2) Darrel A. Posey (1981).
Life-Form Terms hak **bird** (bird)
  tep **fish** (fish)
  kangã **snake** (snake)
  pingo **snake** (worm)
  maja **wug** (insect+scorpion+spider+tick+crayfish+pseu-
  doscorpion)
Discussion Posey (1981) notes that the category *maja* has a one-to-one correspondence with the scientific category of Phylum *Arthropoda* and can be described as encompassing "animals with no flesh." This class contrasts directly with *mry* "animals with flesh" which includes birds, fish, snakes,
worms, reptiles, frogs, turtles, and all mammals. The terms *maja* and *mry*

can be interpreted as totally partitioning the animal kingdom into "small creatures" and "large creatures" respectively.

Case 77b.

Language Kikamba (Stage 4)
Classification North Eastern Bantu, Bantu Proper, Bantoid, Benue-Congo, Niger-Congo, Niger-Kordofanian
Area South Central Kenya
Source Janet Ann Shepherd Fjellman (1971)
Life-Form Terms nyūnyi **bird** (bird)
    īkūyū **fish** (fish)
    nzoka **snake** (snake)
    tūsamū **wug** (bug)

Discussion There is a fifth term, *nyamū*, which labels a category resembling a **mammal** life-form. The term refers to any mammal, reptile (including snakes), or fish. This category is in direct contrast with *nyūnyi* **bird** and *tūsamū* **wug**. I have not codified *nyamū* as being a **mammal** life-form term since it designates a much more general grouping of creatures. *Nyamū* and *tūsamū* seem to partition the animal kingdom into "large creatures" and "small creatures" respectively (and thus create a division similar to that reported for Kayapo (76b)). The term *tūsamū* is the diminutive of *nyamū* and roughly translates "little creature." Birds, of course, are excluded from this partitioning and, thus, are not regarded as being "creatures." The source does not mention worms.

Case 78b.

Language Kugu-Nganhchara (Stage 4) (see case 75a)
Life-Form Terms minha thuchi **bird** (small bird)
    minha nga'a **fish** (fish+crustacean)
    thugu **snake** (snake)
    yuku **wug** (insect+insect larva+leech+jellyfish+other)

Discussion The stem *minha* on its own refers primarily to all creatures (excluding humans and the amphibia) which are edible. It is, however, extended to certain nonedible animal species. Whether or not true fish constitute the focus of *minha nga'a* is not known. The latter term is from the Kugu-Muminh dialect of the language. Elsewhere the stem *nga'a* is a prefix in labels for specific fish, shellfish, and crustacea. The "snake" term refers more specifically to a white-bellied black snake considered mildly poisonous.

Case 79b.

Language Malagasy (Stage 4) (see case 186a)
Life-Form Terms vorona **bird** (bird)
            hazan-drano **fish** (fish+crustacean)
            biby-lava **snake** (snake)
            kankana **snake** (worm)
            bibi-kely **wug** (insect)
Discussion The **fish** label is derived from *haza* "hunting" and *rano* "water."
It is not known if true fish constitute the focus of the class. The "snake" term
translates literally "long creature." Similarly, the **wug** term is literally "little
creature." The **wug** label refers principally to insects, but it can also be used
to denote any little creature. Worms are sometimes considered to be the larvae
of snakes or eels.

Case 80b.

Language Mandarin (Stage 4)
Classification Northern Chinese, Chinese, Sino-Tibetan
Area China
Source Investigated by the author
Life-Form Terms nyău **bird** (bird)
            yú **fish** (fish)
            shé **snake** (snake)
            chúng **wug** (insect+worm+nonsnake reptile)
Discussion There is a term used in reference to true mammals, *púrŭdùngwù*.
This is not codified as being a **mammal** term since the class it labels seems to
be a special purpose category. It encompasses specifically creatures which
nurse their young. The term literally means "large animal fed by milk."

Case 81b.

Language Maxakali (Stage 4)
Classification Machacali, Macro-Ge, Ge-Pano-Carib
Area Minas Gerais, Brazil
Source Harold Popovich (personal communication)
Life-Form Terms pɨtɨgi šoëp **bird** (bird)
            mạëm šoëp **fish** (fish)
            kạyạ šoëp **snake** (snake)
            kɨgət šoëp **wug** (insect)
Discussion The term *šoëp* means "group." The source does not mention
worms.

Case 82b.

Language Mende (Stage 4) (see case 80a)
Source Frederick William Hugh Migeod (1913)
Life-Form Terms nwoni **bird** (bird)
                nye **fish** (fish)
                kali **snake** (snake)
                gbǫli **snake** (worm)
                fu-hani **wug** (insect)

Discussion The **wug** label translates literally "living thing." The "worm" category encompasses all worms including earthworms and body-worms. Another term, *hūa*, is glossed "any animal." Since this term occurs in the source in a section listing mammal terms, it is possible that it is actually a **mammal** life-form label.

Case 83b.

Language Navaho (Stage 4) (see case 145a)
Source (1) Berard Haile (1951); (2) Oswald Werner, Allan Manning, and Kenneth Y. Begishe (n.d.); (3) Leland C. Wyman (1964).
Life-Form Terms tsídii **bird** (small bird)
                łóó' **fish** (fish)
                tł'iish **snake** (snake)
                ch'osh **wug** (insect+spider+scorpion+snake+nonsnake
                      reptile)

Discussion The above terms and their referential extensions are from Werner, Manning, and Begishe (n.d.). These authors report that younger Navahos use the "small bird" term to denote birds in general both big and small. There is considerable difference among sources with respect to the range of reference of *ch'osh*. This difference probably reflects usage variation among speakers and the possibility that **wug** is only in the process of consolidating as a full life-form class. Wyman (1964) reports that *ch'osh* encompasses insects and worms. However, only crawling insects, not flying ones, are included in his account. He goes further to write that some people call snakes *ch'osh*, but adds "that is not right." One of his informants stated that "you don't call it *č'oš* [*ch'osh*] if you know the name" of the particular organism thus indicating that the category may be an incipient, rather than full-fledged life-form class. Finally, Haile (1951) in his extensive, if not exhaustive, dictionary of Navaho identifies *ch'osh* as restricted to worms and maggots.

Case 84b.

Language Northeastern Thai (Stage 4)
Classification Kam-Tai
Area Thailand
Source S. J. Tambiah (1969)
Life-Form Terms nog **bird** (bird)
  plaa **fish** (fish)
  nguu **snake** (snake)
  maeng **wug** (insect+centipede+crab)

Discussion The **bird** category does not include domestic fowl, crows, or vultures. In general, *maeng* may be said to consist of insects and a few aquatic invertebrates, the crab being a good example. The source mentions a fifth general term, *sad*, which seems to encompass all creatures except those identified as *nog*, *nguu*, and *maeng*. *Sad*, therefore, resembles a **mammal** label except that it extends to fish. The term is found in the source only in compound forms, e.g., *sad naam* "animals of the water," and is not presented as a unitary lexeme with a **mammal** range. The source does not mention worms.

Case 85b.

Language Omaha (Stage 4)
Classification Siouan, Macro-Siouan
Area Nebraska, U.S.A.
Source Alice C. Flethcher and Francis La Flesche (1906)
Life-Form Terms wazhí^{n}ga **bird** (bird)
  huhu **fish** (fish)
  wéç'a **snake** (snake)
  wagthíshka **wug** (bug+worm)

Case 86b.

Language Pashto (Stage 4)
Classification Iranian, Indo-Iranian, Indo-European
Area Afghanistan
Source Investigated by the author
Life-Form Terms muruwr **bird** (bird)
  mawhi **fish** (fish)
  mawr **snake** (snake+lizard)
  kirm **snake** (worm)
  chinjai **wug** (bug+worm)

Case 87b.

Language Sierra Popoluca (Stage 4) (see case 147a)
Source John Lind (personal communication)
Life-Form Terms jon **bird** (bird)
　　　　　　　　　tɨɨpɨ **fish** (fish)
　　　　　　　　　tsañ **snake** (snake+smooth worm)
　　　　　　　　　xuxutánimat **wug** (insect)
Discussion The **wug** term translates literally "little creature."

Case 88b.

Language Southern Paiute (Cedar City dialect) (Stage 4) (see case 106a)
Life-Form Terms wičíci **bird** (bird)
　　　　　　　　　kʷanánci **bird** (large bird)
　　　　　　　　　pagíʔɨci **fish** (fish)
　　　　　　　　　togóabɨ **snake** (snake)
　　　　　　　　　pabáʔabi **snake** (worm)
　　　　　　　　　paʔábi **wug** (insect+spider)
Discussion Some speakers are reluctant to apply the term *wičíci* to any birds except small ones. The "large bird" term also refers more specifically to eagle. The term *togóabɨ* seems to designate primarily the Great Basin rattlesnake and only secondarily snakes in general. It also denotes the subclass of all poisonous snakes. Worms are said to be related to snakes as "little brothers." The **wug** label also serves as a name for creatures in general. Animal life-form classification in the Cedar City dialect of Southern Paiute is virtually identical to that of the Kaibab dialect also studied by Fowler. For dialectal differences see Southern Paiute (Chemehuevi dialect) (143b).

Case 89b.

Language Teen (also Loron) (Stage 4) (see case 150a)
Life-Form Terms limi **bird** (bird)
　　　　　　　　　busan **fish** (fish)
　　　　　　　　　kpankpoo **snake** (snake)
　　　　　　　　　jɔla **snake** (worm)
　　　　　　　　　bur gɥɛ **wug** (insect)
Discussion The **wug** term translates literally "earth thing." Another life-form class, **mammal**, may be emerging in the language. The term *nama* "meat" is used in reference to mammals and snakes which are either dead or alive. It also denotes fish and birds, but only after these have been killed.

Case 90b.

Language Tok Pisin (Stage 4)
Classification English based Pidgin
Area Papua New Guinea
Source Harry Feldman (personal communication)
Life-Form Terms pisin **bird** (bird+cassowary)
                        pis **fish** (fish)
                        snek **snake** (snake+earthworm+leech)
                        binatang **wug** (bug+grub)

Discussion The above data are from the West Sepik Province dialect of Tok Pisin. *Binatang* apparently is a borrowing from Indonesian where it means "creature."

Case 91b.

Language Western Subanun (Stage 4) (see case 95a)
Life-Form Terms manukmanuk **bird** (bird+bat)
                        soda' **fish** (fish+porpoise+whale+sea cow)
                        mamak **snake** (snake)
                        mamakmamak **wug** (bug+worm+snake+small lizard)

Discussion The unreduplicated term *manuk* designates chicken. Reduplication produces the diminutive; thus, *manukmanuk* is literally "little chicken." Similarly, *mamakmamak* **wug** is literally "little snake." In both cases, according to Hall, literal senses are not conceptually significant. *Manukmanuk*, for example, are thought of as being birds and not as "little chickens." The unusual inclusion of snakes in **wug** is discussed in Chapter 6.

Case 92b.

Language Yaqui (Stage 4) (see case 157a)
Life-Form Terms wiíkit **bird** (bird)
                        kúču **fish** (fish)
                        baákot **snake** (snake)
                        bʷítčia **snake** (worm)
                        yoéria **wug** (insect)

  Four Life-Forms: **bird+fish+snake+mammal**.
  93b. Awtuw (Papua New Guinea)
  94b. Central Carrier (British Columbia, Canada)
  95b. Daribi (Papua New Guinea)

96b. Faiwol (Papua New Guinea)
97b. Hewa (Papua New Guinea)
98b. Ibataan (The Philippines)
99b. Igbira (Nigeria)
100b. Isirawa (Irian Jaya)
101b. Kalam (Papua New Guinea)
102b. Lotuho (Sudan)
103b. Makiritare (Venezuela)
104b. Melpa (Papua New Guinea)
105b. Muinane (Colombia)
106b. Pacaas Novos (Brazil)
107b. Patep (Papua New Guinea)
108b. Tepehua (Mexico)
109b. Tewa (New Mexico, U.S.A.)
110b. Tzeltal (Mexico)
111b. Waodani (Ecuador)
112b. Yolŋu (Australia)
113b. Yurok (California, U.S.A.)

Case 93b.

Language Awtuw (also Autu) (Stage 4) (see case 49a)
Life-Form Terms yi **bird** (bird+cassowary+bat)
ŋale **fish** (fish)
wulæk **snake** (snake)
yiyay **mammal** (mammal+crocodile+turtle)
Discussion Eagles constitute the focus of **bird** and pythons the focus of **snake**. Some speakers include cassowaries in **mammal** as well as in **bird**. The focus of **fish** is a large flat-bodied fish with dorsal and ventral fins. The "ground marsupial" is the focal member of **mammal**. In addition to being a life-form label, *yiyay* seems to carry the meaning "game animal." There is another possible life-form term, *mweymoy*, which may extend to all worms. However, the source reports that only earthworms are known for certain to be referents of the term.

Case 94b.

Language Central Carrier (Stage 4) (see case 177a)
Life-Form Terms dut'ai **bird** (bird)
lho **fish** (fish)
tl'ughus **snake** (snake)
'usgo **snake** (worm)

khunai **mammal** (large mammal)

ts'ant'i **mammal** (small mammal)

Discussion The term *khunai* encompasses all big mammals such as moose, deer, bears, horses, etc., and *ts'ant'i* refers to all smaller mammals such as foxes, wolverines, wolves, etc. While there is no **wug** life-form, there are terms for flying insect and crawling insect. Walker mentions that there are few snakes in the Central Carrier area. The only ones known to speakers of the language are small garter snakes.

Case 95b.

Language Daribi (Stage 4)

Classification Mikaru, East New Guinea Highlands, Central New Guinea, Indo-Pacific

Area Papua New Guinea

Source Roy Wagner (personal communication)

Life-Form Terms ba' **bird** (bird+cassowary)

ai-haza **fish** (fish+eel+crayfish)

sugu **fish** (fish)

hazamani **snake** (snake)

haza **mammal** (mammal)

Discussion Wagner mentions that *haza*, in a certain sense, means "creature in general." The label *ai-haza* translates literally "stream creature." It is not known if true fish are the focus of the term.

Case 96b.

Language Faiwol (Stage 4)

Classification Ok, Central and South New Guinea, Central New Guinea, Indo-Pacific

Area Murray and Luap valleys, Papua New Guinea

Source Fredrick Barth (1975)

Life-Form Terms awon **bird** (bird)

takám **fish** (fish)

dī **snake** (snake)

nuk **mammal** (marsupial+rodent)

Case 97b.

Language Hewa (Stage 4) (see case 59a)

Life-Form Terms noka **bird** (bird+cassowary+fruit bat+butterfly+moth) tui **fish** (fish)

yufɛ **snake** (snake)

pisai **snake** (worm+millipede+centipede+newt+grub+
snail)

wamɛ **mammal** (mammal+lizard)

Discussion Birds constitute the focus of *noka*. Animals specifically mentioned by the source as included in *wamɛ* are the pig, wallaby, rat, phalanger,
tree kangaroo, bandicoot, iguana, and the world's longest monitor lizard. Apparently the **mammal** life-form is mostly limited to those large four-footed
creatures of the forest which are eaten and, thus, actually may be a special
purpose category.

Case 98b.

Language Ibataan (Stage 4) (see case 62a)

Life-Form Terms manomanok **bird** (bird)

among **fish** (fish)

ohed **snake** (worm+caterpillar+maggot)

animal **mammal** (wild mammal+sea turtle+lizard+
snake)

Discussion The "worm" term, *ohed*, does not encompass earthworms. The
mammal term, *animal*, is borrowed from Spanish. Maree writes that creatures classified as *animal* are "left over, do not seem to be grouped or classed
otherwise." Another term borrowed from Spanish, *insekto*, labels a category
including a number of different small creatures: grasshoppers, butterflies,
house flies, horseflies, hair lice, fleas, etc. However, it does not include ants,
wasps, bees, walking sticks, scorpions, cockroaches, and other small creatures typically associated with **wug**. Maree notes that "the class 'insektos'
is not reliable . . . I will guess that the term . . . is a modern way of lumping previously unclassified 'bugs.'" He also assigns the glosses "pest" and
"left over animals" to the term. *Insekto*, then, seems to label an emerging
wug life-form.

Case 99b.

Language Igbira (Stage 4) (see case 17a)

Life-Form Terms inómí **bird** (bird)

ìvòvò **fish** (fish)

ẹwụ **snake** (snake)

ìkùkùrúmí **snake** (worm+maggot)

uye **mammal** (mammal+nonsnake reptile)

Discussion Scholz writes that *uye* encompasses most or all of the four-legged animals, i.e. all mammals and most reptiles. He identifies some of the creatures included in the latter category: goats, leopards, lions, monitor lizards, hippopotami, manatees, hares, and tortoises. He also mentions that *uye* has "meat" as a secondary sense.

Case 100b.

Language Isirawa (also Saberi) (Stage 4) (see case 120a)
Life-Form Terms apre **bird** (bird+cassowary)
       avisi **fish** (fish+shrimp)
       poii **snake** (snake+snake-like insects)
       sokaara **mammal** (small mammal)
Discussion The Isirawa language is also known as Saberi. The **fish** class does not include crabs or shellfish. Some people, however, extend it to turtles while others include turtles in a "crab" category. It is not known if true fish constitute the focus of *avisi*. Millipedes and centipedes are examples of snake-like insects included in the **snake** life-form. The latter is also extended to biting insects such as scorpions. The "small mammal" term refers specifically to a certain kind of rat. In its more general use it encompasses rats, mice, and possums. At least 13 kinds of animals are included in "small mammal."

Case 101b.

Language Kalam (Stage 4) (see case 162a)
Source (1) Ralph N. H. Bulmer (1974); (2) Ralph N. H. Bulmer and J. I. Menzies (1972–1973); (3) Ralph N. H. Bulmer, J. I. Menzies, and F. Parker (1975); (4) Ralph N. H. Bulmer and M. J. Tyler (1968).
Life-Form Terms yakt **bird** (bird+bat)
       kobsal **fish** (fish)
       yñ **snake** (snake+lizard)
       soyn **snake** (small snake)
       ñom **snake** (snake)
       as **mammal** (small mammal+frog)
       kmn **mammal** (large mammal)
Discussion The **bird** life-form excludes cassowaries, the **fish** life-form excludes eels, and the "small mammal" category excludes the common household rat. A **wug** life-form may be consolidating in the language. The term *joŋ*, which refers specifically to certain insects of the order Orthoptera (locusts, grasshoppers, and crickets), has a more general application. Bulmer writes:

. . . if one says that a particular individual insect is a *joŋ*, this means unambiguously that it is a grasshopper, locust or cricket. However if one is told that a certain bird eats *joŋ*, this does not mean that it eats only grasshoppers etc.—in fact it may be known hardly ever to eat grasshoppers. It means that the bird is an insectivore, *joŋ* here referring to a collectivity including all insects and insect-like arachnids (1974: 15).

Since insects other than grasshoppers, etc. cannot be identified individually by the term, it is not quite a full-fledged life-form label.

Case 102b.

Language Lotuho (Stage 4) (see case 172a)
Life-Form Terms aheny **bird** (bird)
aham **fish** (fish)
amunok **snake** (snake)
acyaŋi **mammal** (mammal+nonsnake reptile)

Case 103b.

Language Makiritare (Stage 4) (see case 140a)
Life-Form Terms tonoro **bird** (bird)
kan'Fwe **fish** (fish+?)
Oko'YA **snake** (snake)
O'kedu **snake** (snake)
orokuato **mammal** (mammal+?)
Discussion The source notes that *kan'Fwe* encompasses other aquatic creatures in addition to true fish without specifying what these are and without mentioning whether or not true fish constitute the category's focus. The source also describes the membership of *orokuato* as being "predominantly mammals" thus implying that some nonmammals belong to the category.

Case 104b.

Language Melpa (Stage 4) (see case 123a)
Life-Form Terms köi **bird** (bird+bat)
oma **fish** (fish+eel)
kimbukla **snake** (snake+worm+grub+caterpillar+lizard)
kui **mammal** (marsupial+rat+cat)

Case 105b.

Language Muinane (Stage 4) (see case 144a)
Life-Form Terms joomɨ **bird** (bird+bat)
        taava **fish** (fish+eel+stingray+porpoise)
        jiinimo **snake** (snake)
        asimɨ **mammal** (mammal+alligator+lizard+frog+turtle)
Discussion The term for **mammal** also means "meat." Earthworms and the roundworm parasite which are called *tuhujɨmɨ* are thought to be related to other small elongated creatures such as centipedes, snails, and the like; but since the category is restricted to only two types, it is not codified as **snake** (worm).

Case 106b.

Language Pacaas Novos (Stage 4) (see case 45a)
Life-Form Terms me **bird** (bird)
        hwam **fish** (fish+shrimp+crab)
        em' **snake** (snake)
        mete' **snake** (worm)
        carawa **mammal** (mammal+large nonsnake reptile+
          turtle)
Discussion The words *me*, *hwam*, and *carawa* in fact refer only to members of the categories **bird**, **fish**, and **mammal** respectively which are eaten. When these terms are modified by *caji* meaning "different, strange, wrong, bad, evil," e.g., *caji me*, they refer to organisms belonging to **bird**, **fish**, and **mammal** classes respectively which are not eaten. The source does not mention whether or not true fish are the focus of *hwam*. Some Pacaas Novos clans use the "snake" term in reference to worms. The word *carawa* also means "meat," "thing," or "something."

Case 107b.

Language Patep (Stage 4) (see case 85a)
Life-Form Terms menac **bird** (bird+cassowary)
        beac **fish** (fish)
        myel **snake** (snake+worm+lizard+centipede)
        lɨlii **mammal** (mammal+frog+turtle+shrimp+crab+
          fish)
Discussion The **bird** class includes all varieties of birds both domestic and wild. The **mammal** class, *lɨlii*, is unusual since it encompasses fish as well as other water creatures and mammals. The inclusion of fish in **mammal** may be

traced to the fact that the Patep are mountain people and are only acquainted with a few varieties of fish which occur in nearby streams. This is similar to other cases reported here (see Kilangi [133b], Papago [11b], Kyaka Enga [69b], and Siane [140b]) in which scarcity of fish in environments is correlated with their unusual suprageneric categorization. However, in the latter cases fish are included in **snake** rather than in **mammal**. The term *lilii* also designates animal flesh (of mammals and water creatures) which is eaten.

Case 108b.

Language Tepehua (Stage 4) (see case 151a)
Life-Form Terms ts'ok'nin **bird** (bird)
pamata **fish** (fish)
lu **snake** (snake)
tsapu **snake** (worm+coral snake+eel species)
maktilin **mammal** (mammal+lizard+snake+frog+toad)

Case 109b.

Language Tewa (Stage 4) (see case 152a)
Source (1) Randall H. Speirs and Anna F. Speirs (personal communication); (2) Junius Henderson and John Peabody Harrington (1914).
Life-Form Terms círé **bird** (bird+bat)
pa: **fish** (fish)
pǽ·ñu· **snake** (snake)
pubǽ́ **snake** (worm)
tsí:wi:ʔê **mammal** (mammal+reptile)
Discussion The above orthography is that supplied by the Speirs. Henderson and Harrington report that the "worm" term may be loosely applied to all worm-like animals, perhaps even to insects and spiders but the latter application is not usually made. The **mammal** term, reported by the Speirs, is not mentioned by Henderson and Harrington (1914).

Case 110b.

Language Tzeltal (Stage 4) (see case 154a)
Source Eugene S. Hunn (1977)
Life-Form Terms mut **bird** (bird)
čay **fish** (fish+aquatic crustacean)
čan **snake** (snake)
čanbalam **mammal** (mammal)
Discussion The **bird** term more specifically refers to chicken. True fish con-

stitute the focus of *čay*. A fifth term, *lukum*, is used to designate earthworms and intestinal worms, but is not codified here as "worm" since it does not extend to many other small elongated creatures usually associated with the category. The **mammal** term is also used to designate creatures in general. Hunn, however, does not claim that the word has two distinct referential applications. Rather, it seems that the most typical or representative *čanbalam* "creature" is found in the mammal grouping. The term functions as a **mammal** label when the referential cutoff point for any Tzeltal speaker using it is something short of animals in general.

Case 111b.

Language Waodani (Stage 4) (see case 94a)
Life-Form Terms ayabö **bird** (bird)
  yæyæ **fish** (fish + crustacean + caiman + eel + stingray)
  tætæ **snake** (snake)
  ööïgä **mammal** (mammal)
Discussion Some speakers include all birds and fowl in the **bird** class, while some exclude parrots, some exclude the larger fowl, some exclude hummingbirds, and most exclude hawks. These excluded groupings constitute their own categories denoted by generalized application of generic labels for focal members. True fish constitute the focus of *yæyæ*. The source reports that a few people recognize *tætæ* "snake" as a subclass of **mammal**. The **mammal** label has a second, more specific use as a term for "fleshy animal, prey." Most speakers use the term in its general sense vacillating with regard to its more specific application. A few, however, use the term consistently in the specific sense and some use it only with its general meaning. Some creatures included in **mammal** listed by the source are monkeys, peccaries, deer, tapir, rodents, dogs, cats, marsupials, edentates, manatee, hoofed mammals, and bats. The source notes that, with the exception of the **mammal** label, the above terms are used by some speakers only in reference to unknown and unnamed creatures. Thus for some speakers these label incipient life-form classes.

Case 112b.

Language Yolŋu (Stage 4) (see case 30a)
Source (1) Stephen Davis (personal communication); (2) Stephen L. Davis (1980).
Life-Form Terms warrakan **bird** (bird)
  warrakan **bird** (large bird)
  djikay **bird** (small bird)

guya **fish** (fish)

bäpi **snake** (snake)

warrakan **mammal** (land mammal+reptile+fresh water turtle+bird)

Discussion The term *warrakan* is three ways polysemous, designating (1) large birds, (2) birds in general, and (3) a grouping of land mammals, reptiles, and birds. These three referential ranges are apparently acquired by speakers in a set order. Davis writes in a personal communication:

> "Warrakan," for example, is used by children up to 10 years of age to refer to large birds, in contrast to "djikay" which refers to small birds. For 11 to 18 years "warrakan" is used to refer to both large and small birds. From 19 to the early 30's "warrakan" refers not only to all birds but mainly to large edible birds classified by their habitat from sea to bush. Older persons use "warrakan" to refer to both large land animals, reptiles, bats, echidnas, birds.

The unusual inclusion of birds in a **mammal** class is discussed in Chapter 6. The **fish** term is restricted to bony fish. Cartilaginous fish (sharks and stingrays) have their own term, *maranydjalk*. Sea turtles are not included in the **mammal** category as are fresh water turtles, rather they are lumped with dugongs, dolphins, and whales in a grouping labeled *miyapanu*.

Case 113b.

Language Yurok (Stage 4)

Classification Macro-Algonquian

Area Northwestern California, U.S.A.

Source Jane O. Bright and William Bright (1965)

Life-Form Terms c'uc'iš **bird** (small bird)

nunepuy **fish** (fish)

leyes **snake** (snake)

ho·re⁷mos **mammal** (mammal)

Discussion The Brights assign the gloss "bird, especially small bird" to *c'uc'iš*. They do not mention worms.

Four Life-Forms: **bird**+**fish**+**snake**+combined **wug-mammal**.

114b. Koiwai (West Irian)

115b. Mokilese (Eastern Caroline Islands)

116b. Tzotzil (Zinacantan) (Mexico)

Case 114b.

Language Koiwai (Stage 4) (see case 74a)
Life-Form Terms manu **bird** (bird+butterfly)
           don **fish** (fish+whale+porpoise+lobster+crab+croco-
               dile+octopus)
           aroi **snake** (snake+lizard+caterpillar+leech+centipede+
               worm+starfish)
           binatang combined **wug-mammal** (bug+mammal)
Discussion True fish constitute the focus of *don*. The combined **wug-mammal**
term is a loan from Bahasa Indonesian. Starfish apparently are included in
snake because these creatures, like most elongated animals, "squirm."

Case 115b.

Language Mokilese (Stage 4) (see case 142a)
Life-Form Terms maan səng **bird** (bird)
           mwumw **fish** (fish)
           mawj **snake** (worm+caterpillar)
           maan combined **wug-mammal** (rat+dog+cat+pig+fruit
               bat+lizard+monitor+worm+bug+bird)
Discussion The **bird** term translates literally (and roughly) "flying creature."
The term *maan*, which labels a combined **wug-mammal** class including
birds, has two other distinct referential ranges: one more expansive (creatures
in general) and one less expansive (combined **wug-mammal** excluding birds).
The unusual inclusion of birds in combined **wug-mammal** is discussed in
Chapter 6. Snakes apparently do not inhabit Mokil Atoll.

Case 116b.

Language Tzotzil (Zinacantan dialect) (Stage 4) (see case 155a)
Source (1) Nicholas H. Acheson (1966); (2) Robert M. Laughlin (1975).
Life-Form Terms mut **bird** (bird)
           choy **fish** (fish+shrimp)
           kiletel chon **snake** (snake)
           xuvitetik **snake** (worm+caterpillar)
           chon combined **wug-mammal** (mammal+nonsnake rep-
               tile+snake+worm+insect+frog+turtle)
Discussion The above terms and referential extensions, with the exception of
one item, are from Acheson. The **fish** label is from Laughlin, a dictionary
treatment which is very thorough with respect to names for plants and animals
and their classification. Acheson's failure to mention fish is perhaps attribut-

able to the fact that there are very few of these creatures known to Highland Chiapas peoples. It is not known whether or not true fish are the focus of *choy*. Acheson notes that some speakers include bats in the **bird** life-form. The term *chon* has two distinct referents according to Acheson: (1) creatures in general, and (2) all creatures which are not birds or fish (combined **wug-mammal**). The **snake** label, *kiletel chon*, translates literally (and roughly) "dragging creature." It refers specifically to snakes and more generally to all reptiles. The unusual inclusion of snakes in combined **wug-mammal** is discussed in Chapter 6.

      Four Life-Forms: **bird+snake+wug+mammal**.
      117b. Gimi (Papua New Guinea)
      118b. Maring (Tsembaga dialect) (Papua New Guinea)
      119b. Ndumba (Tairora) (Papua New Guinea)

Case 117b.
―――

Language Gimi (Stage 4) (see case 14a)
Life-Form Terms nimi **bird** (bird)
               kuri **snake** (snake+lizard+worm)
               kaba **wug** (insect+spider)
               umi **mammal** (large mammal [e.g., marsupial])
               atumi **mammal** (small mammal [e.g., rat])
Discussion Glick assigns the glosses "large furred animals" and "small furred animals" to *umi* and *atumi* respectively. The **snake** term is glossed "elongated animals." The absence of a **fish** life-form is almost certainly due to an ecological condition. According to Glick, the Gimi, who live in a steeply mountainous region, are familiar with only two varieties, the eel and tinned fish.

Case 118b.
―――

Language Maring (Tsembaga dialect) (Stage 4)
Classification Jimi, Hagen-Wahgi-Jimi-Chimbu, East New Guinea High-
    lands, Central New Guinea, Indo-Pacific
Area Bismarck Mountains, Papua New Guinea
Source Ray A. Rappaport (1967)
Life-Form Terms kabaŋ **bird** (bird+cassowary)
                 noma **snake** (snake)
                 baŋ **wug** (insect)
                 ma **mammal** (large mammal)

koi **mammal** (small mammal)

Discussion The "large mammal" category includes wild mammals over 4 or 5 inches high when standing on all fours, essentially large marsupials and giant rats. This class excludes pigs and bats. The "small mammal" category encompasses rats and small marsupials, i.e. all mammals under 4 or 5 inches high when standing on all fours. The absence of a **fish** life-form is almost certainly due to ecological factors. Only two native taxa of fish are known: *kobe* "eel" and *tuoi* "catfish" both of which are eaten. The source does not mention worms.

Case 119b.

Language Ndumba (Tairora) (Stage 4) (see case 146a)

Source (1) Terence E. Hays (personal communication); (2) Terence E. Hays (1983).

Life-Form Terms kuri **bird** (bird+cassowary+bat)

kaapa'raara **snake** (snake+eel+lizard+gecko+skink+ worm+leech+centipede)

to'vendi **wug** (insect+spider+snail+frog+toad+snake+ lizard+gecko+skink+worm+leech+centipede)

fai **mammal** (large mammal [marsupial+monotreme])

faahi **mammal** (small mammal [mouse+rat])

Discussion Nearly all *kaapa'raara* (**snake**) are included in *to'vendi* (**wug**). Lack of a **fish** life-form is almost certainly traced to ecological factors. Hays (personal communication) notes that eels are the only native fish known to Ndumba (Tairora) speakers. Domestic mammals (dogs, cats, pigs, and other livestock) are excluded from the ranges of both **mammal** terms.

STAGE 5 LANGUAGES.

Five Life-Forms: **bird+fish+snake+wug+mammal**.

120b. American English (U.S.A.)
121b. Anindilyakwa (Australia)
122b. Azande (Sudan)
123b. Chorti (Guatemala, Honduras)
124b. Classical Nahuatl (Mexico)
125b. Czech (Czechoslovakia)
126b. Delaware (Oklahoma, U.S.A.)
127b. Eskimo (Northwest Territory, Canada)
128b. Fipa (Central Eastern Africa)
129b. Fore (Papua New Guinea)

130b. Gbaya Kara (Central African Republic)
131b. Hill Pandaram (India)
132b. Japanese (Japan)
133b. Kilangi (Tanzania)
134b. Komo (Zaire)
135b. Mataco (Argentina)
136b. Minnesota Ojibwa (Minnesota, U.S.A.)
137b. Montagnais (Cree) (Quebec, Canada)
138b. Northern Ojibwa (Ontario, Canada)
139b. North Saami (Norway)
140b. Siane (Papua New Guinea)
141b. Tifal (Papua New Guinea)

Case 120b.

Language American English (Stage 5) (see case 175a)
Life-Form Terms bird **bird** (bird)
                fish **fish** (fish)
                snake **snake** (snake)
                worm **snake** (worm)
                bug **wug** (insect+spider+tick+mite+centipede+milli-
                    pede+micro-organism)
                insect **wug** (insect+spider+tick+mite+centipede+
                    millipede)
                animal **mammal** (mammal+nonsnake reptile+amphibian)
                mammal **mammal** (mammal)

Discussion The above terms and ranges are those understood by the author. The term *animal* (**mammal**) also has the expanded sense "creature in general." The term *mammal* is primarily a scientific label. However, it apparently has filtered into folk usage, the result of widespread schooling.

Case 121b.

Language Anindilyakwa (Stage 5) (see case 10a)
Source (1) Julie Waddy (personal communication); (2) Dulcie Levitt (personal communication); (3) Julie Waddy (1979, 1980, 1982); (4) John W. Harris (1979).
Life-Form Terms wurrajija **bird** (bird+flying mammal)
                akwalya **fish** (fish)
                yingarna **snake** (snake+legless lizard)
                wurrajija **wug** (bug+bird+flying mammal)

yinungwungwangba **mammal** (nonflying mammal+liz-
ard+frog+crocodile+fresh water
turtle)

Discussion The term *wurrajija* serves as a label for two different life-form classes, **bird** and **wug**, the latter class encompassing members of the former. Since true birds constitute the focal referents of the term (Waddy, personal communication and 1982), it may be the case that the more inclusive **wug** application developed through expansion of reference from a **bird** range (see related discussion, Chapter 6). Waddy (personal communication) speculates that *wurrajija* meaning "bird" was first extended to other flying creatures such as bats and winged insects and, subsequently, to nonflying insects and similar creatures such as spiders and ticks. She (personal communication) writes, ". . . it's probably worth commenting that ants are seen as *wurrajija* because they know that winged forms of at least one of the ants common here are found at certain times of the year . . . since ants crawl on the ground and up trees and so on, it's a relatively simple step to add ticks, scorpions and spiders." The **fish** term, *akwalya*, has two additional and more expansive ranges: (1) all animals in the sea including fish, crabs, turtles, sea birds, etc., and (2) all animal life. Levitt writes that the **fish** term was originally used only for fish and that it now is often used for "meat in general." She also notes that worms are not very common but those that do occur are classed with snakes. The **mammal** term also has a more expansive sense: animals on the land including mammals, bugs, reptiles, land birds, etc. (Waddy, personal communication). Such a sense emerges when land animals are being thought of as a group distinct from sea animals (cf. meaning [1] of *akwalya* given above).

Case 122b.

_____

Language Azande (Stage 5)
Classification Eastern (of Adamawa-Eastern), Adamawa-Eastern, Niger-
    Congo, Niger-Kordofanian
Area Sudan
Source E. E. Evans-Pritchard (1963)
Life-Form Terms azile **bird** (bird)
                atio **fish** (fish)
                awo **snake** (snake)
                agbiro **wug** (insect+small nonsnake reptile+toad+
                    tortoise)
                anya **mammal** (mammal+large nonsnake reptile)
Discussion The iguana is an example of a large nonsnake reptile included in the **mammal** life-form. The source does not mention worms.

Case 123b.

Language Chorti (Stage 5) (see case 180a)
Life-Form Terms mut **bird** (bird)
čiʔik **bird** (bird)
čai **fish** (fish)
čan **snake** (snake+long worm)
lukum **snake** (long large worm+small snake)
upʼiʔ **snake** (small worm)
yarqʼir **wug** (insect)
ar **mammal** (mammal)
Discussion The **bird** term, *mut*, does not encompass domestic fowl. The word *čiʔik* is not often used. There are apparently three sizes of elongated creatures, *čan* (large), *lukum* (medium), and *upʼiʔ* (small). The "insect" term refers specifically to the honey bee. The **mammal** label is also used for "creatures in general."

Case 124b.

Language Classical Nahuatl (Stage 5) (see case 97a)
Life-Form Terms tototl **bird** (bird)
michin **fish** (fish)
coatl **snake** (snake)
tlalapan nemi **wug** (insect+worm+snake)
manenemi **mammal** (mammal)
Discussion Ortiz de Montellano's paper is based on colonial documents, especially Bernardo de Sahagún's *Florentine Codex: General History of the Things of New Spain* (1575–1577). Inclusive relationships and referential extensions are determined from paragraph headings in the latter work which are presumed to be groupings identified by Classical Nahuatl speakers. There is another general term, *yoyoliton*, which refers to small insects, including scorpions, bedbugs, lice, fleas, fireflies, flies, mosquitoes, and others. This term does not encompass worms, ants, locusts, and butterflies. The **wug** label translates literally "lives on land."

Case 125b.

Language Czech (Stage 5)
Classification West Slavic, Slavic, Balto-Slavic, Indo-European
Area Czechoslovakia
Source Mark Flotow (personal communication)

Life-Form Terms ptar **bird** (bird)
  ryba **fish** (fish+jellyfish+seahorse+other)
  had **snake** (snake)
  červ **snake** (worm)
  hmyz **wug** (bug+worm)
  zvíře **mammal** (mammal+snake+frog+snail+toad+
  crab+lobster+octopus)

Discussion True fish constitute the focus of *ryba*. The **mammal** term has the more expansive sense "creature in general."

Case 126b.

Language Delaware (Stage 5) (see case 13a)
Life-Form Terms -ehʊle **bird** (bird+bat)
  nʌmḗs **fish** (fish+shellfish+sea mammal)
  xkuk **snake** (snake)
  muxwɛs **wug** (bug)
  ayɛsəs **mammal** (land mammal)

Discussion Whether or not true fish constitute the focus of *nʌmḗs* is not mentioned. Also there is no mention of worms by the source. The "land mammal" term can also be used in reference to creatures in general.

Case 127b.

Language Eskimo (Stage 5) (see case 32a)
Life-Form Terms tiŋmiat **bird** (large bird)
  qupanuat **bird** (small bird)
  iqalluit **fish** (fish)
  guglugiaq **snake** (worm)
  qupilruit **wug** (insect+spider+worm)
  niryutit **mammal** (large mammal)
  uumayuit **mammal** (small mammal+large mammal)

Discussion The category *tiŋmiat* "large bird" includes geese, swans, loons, ducks, gulls, terns, owls, falcons, hawks, ravens, and cranes. The "small bird" class, *qupanuat*, encompasses larks, buntings, robins, jays, sparrows, grouse, and the like. Stilt-legged birds do not fit into either of the latter two classes and do not form a third labeled "bird" category. Dogs, polar bears, and sea mammals are excluded from both **mammal** classes. Lack of a "snake" term is almost certainly attributable to the rarity, if not complete absence, of snakes in the region.

Case 128b.

Language Fipa (Stage 5)
Classification Fipa-Mambwe, Central Eastern Bantu, Bantu Proper, Bantoid, Benue-Congo, Niger-Congo, Niger-Kordofanian
Area Central Eastern Africa
Source Roy Willis (1974)
Life-Form Terms ifyuuni **bird** (bird)
　　　　　　　inswi **fish** (fish)
　　　　　　　amasoka **snake** (snake)
　　　　　　　ifyoongoli **wug** (insect)
　　　　　　　inyama **mammal** (mammal+nonsnake reptile)
Discussion The source does not mention worms.

Case 129b.

Language Fore (Stage 5)
Classification Fore, Gende-Siane-Gahuku-Kamano-Fore, East New Guinea Highlands, Central New Guinea, Indo-Pacific
Area Eastern Highlands, Papua New Guinea
Source J. M. Diamond (1966)
Life-Form Terms kábara **bird** (bird)
　　　　　　　úba **fish** (fish)
　　　　　　　kwiyágine **snake** (snake+lizard)
　　　　　　　kabágina **wug** (insect+spider+worm)
　　　　　　　úmu **mammal** (small marsupial+rodent)
　　　　　　　íga **mammal** (large marsupial+echidna+giant rat)
Discussion The **bird** life-form does not include the cassowary. Neither **mammal** class includes bats.

Case 130b.

Language Gbaya Kara (Stage 5)
Classification Eastern (of Adamawa-Eastern), Adamawa-Eastern, Niger-Congo, Niger-Kordofanian
Area Central African Republic
Source Paulett Roulon (1977)
Life-Form Terms nɔ́é **bird** (bird+bat)
　　　　　　　zòrò **fish** (fish+crab+shrimp)
　　　　　　　gɔ́k **snake** (snake)
　　　　　　　kókódó·mɔ̀ **wug** (insect+spider+centipede+larva)

sàdì **mammal** (mammal+nonsnake reptile+turtle+
toad+frog)

Discussion Birds constitute the focus of the **bird** life-form and true fish apparently are the focus of **fish**. The term *sàdì* has two distinct applications: (1) as a label for **mammal** (as above), and (2) as a label for a category encompassing all creatures, all of which are vertebrates, which are not included in **wug**, all of which are invertebrates. At one level of abstraction, then, *sàdì* and *kókódó·mɔ̀* completely partition the universe of animals into "large creatures" and "small creatures" respectively. The **mammal** term also means "meat." The source does not mention worms, such as earthworms, but these are almost certainly included in **wug** along with other small elongated animals such as insect larvae and centipedes.

Case 131b.

Language Hill Pandaram (Stage 5) (see case 60a)
Life-Form Terms pakshi **bird** (bird+bat)
min **fish** (fish)
pambu **snake** (snake)
puchi **wug** (insect+crustacean+small nonsnake reptile+
amphibian)
mrgam **mammal** (mammal+large nonsnake reptile)

Discussion Morris notes that *pakshi* is also used to refer to some winged insects. He does not mention whether or not birds constitute the focus of the category. In addition, worms are not discussed. The large nonsnake reptiles included in **mammal** are the land tortoise, the monitor lizard, and two species of crocodiles.

Case 132b.

Language Japanese (Stage 5) (see case 101a)
Life-Form Terms tori **bird** (bird)
uo **fish** (fish)
sakana **fish** (fish)
hebi **snake** (snake)
mushi **wug** (bug+worm+snail)
dō-butsu **mammal** (mammal+turtle?)
ho-nyū-rui **mammal** (mammal+turtle?)

Discussion Sakana (**fish**) also means "side dish." The source notes that speakers of Classic Japanese included snakes in the **wug** class *mushi* and sometimes referred to these creatures as *naga-mushi* "long wug." This earlier usage is reflected by the contemporary Japanese term for adder, *mamushi*, which is a compound label consisting of the **wug** term and another constituent. The **mammal** term *dō-butsu* translates literally "moving thing." This label originally designated creatures in general and has subsequently taken on **mammal** as a second, more restricted referent. The other **mammal** label, *honyū-rui*, is a scientific term which has entered folk usage. It translates literally "group raising children with milk." The latter two labels have replaced the traditional term for **mammal**, *kedamono*.

Case 133b.

Language **Kilangi** (Stage 5) (see case 19a)
Life-Form Terms ndee **bird** (bird+bat)
          samaki **fish** (fish)
          njoka **snake** (snake)
          kinyúlulu **snake** (worm+worm-like lizard)
          makoki **wug** (insect+spider+tick+mite+worm+snake+
               nonsnake reptile+frog+toad+centipede+slug+
               snail+leech)
          vanyama **mammal** (mammal)

Discussion Kesby suspects that the chameleon merges with *njoka* "snake," mentioning that Kilangi speakers are not explicit about this point. The wormlike lizards included in *kinyúlulu* belong to the family Amphisbaenidae. Some speakers occasionally treat small mammals, such as the slender mongoose, as belonging to the **wug** category. Kesby (1979) notes that two of the above terms, *vanyama* (**mammal**) and *samaki* (**fish**), are relatively recent borrowings from Swahili. While there is no evidence that Kilangi had a **mammal** term before borrowing one from Swahili, it clearly had an earlier **fish** label. When Kesby's middle-aged informants were boys, the word *soompa* designated **fish**. This term itself was borrowed from the neighboring Sandawe sometime between 1880 and 1890. At that time there were no fish in Kilangi territory. Kesby (1979) writes that middle-aged men state that formerly fish were forbidden as food because they were considered to be snakes (*njoko*). This earlier understanding, according to Kesby (1979), conforms exactly with that of the Gogo and other groups of the Eastern Rift Highland Zone. The classificatory lumping of fish and elongated animals (snakes and worms) is also reported in this work for Papago (11b), Kyaka Enga (69b), and Siane (140b). In all cases this characteristic is correlated with scarcity or absence of fish in environments.

Case 134b.

___

Language Komo (Stage 5)
Classification North Eastern Bantu, Bantu Proper, Bantoid, Benue-Congo, Niger-Congo, Niger-Kordofanian
Area Zaire
Source W. de Mahieu (1980)
Life-Form Terms mbaú aoɣala **bird** (bird)
                    sú **fish** (fish + aquatic crustacean)
                    ǹdjóka **snake** (snake)
                    mpaphá **wug** (insect)
                    nyama **mammal** (large mammal + crocodile)
                    mbaú **mammal** (small mammal + bird)
Discussion The **bird** term translates literally "flying small mammal." The source does not mention whether or not true fish constitute the focus of *sú*. Some of the large mammals included in *nyama* are gorillas, chimpanzees, antelopes, elephants, buffaloes, large monkeys, large cats, ant-eaters, and otters. Some of the small mammals included in *mbaú* are various rodents (mice, rats, squirrels, etc.). The unusual inclusion of birds in "small mammal" is discussed in Chapter 6.

Case 135b.

___

Language Mataco (Stage 5) (see case 102a)
Life-Form Terms ahʷenče **bird** (bird)
                    wahat **fish** (fish)
                    amɬäh ta wuh **snake** (snake)
                    iwo **snake** (worm)
                    wo **wug** (insect + spider + worm)
                    icawet **mammal** (mammal + lizard + frog + crab + snake +
                             bat + duck + white snail)
Discussion The **bird** life-form excludes ducks and, possibly, other domestic fowl and the ostrich. Domestic fowl and the ostrich possibly are placed in the **mammal** category along with ducks. The "snake" term is derived from *amɬäh* which on its own means "viper."

Case 136b.

___

Language Minnesota Ojibwa (Stage 5) (see case 37a)
Source Mary Rose Bartholomew Black (1967)
Life-Form Terms binešị·yag **bird** (bird)
                    gi.gọ.yag **fish** (fish)

ginebig **snake** (snake)
manido.šag **wug** (insect + snake + toad)
manido.weyišag **mammal** (small mammal)
awesị.yag **mammal** (large mammal)

Discussion There is some variability with respect to membership of **wug**, "small mammal," and "large mammal." For example, snakes can be placed in either **wug** or "small mammal," although the usual assignment seems to be **wug**. Other creatures which shift between two of these three classes are mice, crabs, frogs, toads, woodchucks, squirrels, foxes, gophers, and the dog. The latter mammals, with the possible exception of mice, presumably shift between "small mammal" and "large mammal" classes. One creature, the turtle, can enter into any one of the three categories apparently depending on actual size. The source does not mention worms.

Case 137b.

Language Montagnais (Cree) (Stage 5)
Classification Algonquian, Macro-Algonquian
Area Quebec, Canada
Source (1) Serge Bouchard (1973); (2) Serge Bouchard and José Mailhot (1973).
Life-Form Terms pine.hi.h **bird** (bird)
neme.h **fish** (fish)
ačine.pukw **snake** (snake)
ka.tapa.skunče.t **snake** (worm)
ha.čime.w **wug** (insect + spider)
awe.hi.h **mammal** (mammal)

Discussion The above terms are all from the Mingan dialect of Montagnais. Bouchard and Mailhot (1973) also outline classificatory features of the Schefferville dialect. The latter differs from Mingan Montagnais in that it distinguishes "large bird" (*pine.šu*) and "small bird" (*pine.ši.š*) and does not have a single term encompassing birds of all sizes. There are some notable exclusions from the **wug** category: bees, parasite insects such as lice, and, possibly, ants.

Case 138b.

Language Northern Ojibwa (Stage 5)
Classification Algonquian, Macro-Algonquian
Area Weagamow Lake, Ontario, Canada
Source Mary B. Black (1976)

Life-Form Terms bineši.ns **bird** (small bird)
(term?) **fish** (fish)
ginebig **snake** (snake)
manijo.š **wug** (insect+spider)
aweši.ns **mammal** (large mammal)

Discussion Black reports much variability among informants with respect to knowledge of terms and their referential extensions. The above terms and ranges are those apparently understood by the majority of informants interviewed by Black. A minority of informants, mostly younger ones, use the term *bineši.ns* in reference to all birds large and small. A minority of informants restrict the term *manijo.š* to crawling bugs alone and a very few even state that it refers only to spider. A number of informants also associate turtles, frogs, snakes, crayfish, clams, and snails with *manijo.š* with the remark that these are *gega.d manijo.š*, "nearly" *manijo.š*. A large majority agree that *aweši.ns* denotes large mammals such as moose, caribou, deer, and, possibly, bear and wolf. A minority do not recognize the latter term or category. Black discusses another word, *awiya.ši.š*, without giving a breakdown with respect to numbers of informants using it in various ways. This term demonstrates at least three distinct extensions: (1) to all creatures (mammals, birds, fish, snakes, insects, etc.) except people, (2) to all mammals large and small, and (3) to all smaller mammals, and for some, to all smaller mammals plus large birds such as ducks, loons, and geese. Black attributes much of the reported variability to a system in flux. The above rendition of this system apparently represents a change from an older one which reconstructs roughly as follows:

bineši.ns **bird** (small bird)
(term?) **fish** (fish)
ginebig **snake** (snake)
manijo.š **wug** (insect+spider [and possibly +snake+
frog+turtle+crayfish+clam+snail])
aweši.ns **mammal** (large mammal)
awiya.ši.š **mammal** (small mammal+large bird)

Black does not give a term for **fish**, but her discussion clearly indicates that there is one. In addition, she does not mention worms.

Case 139b.

Language North Saami (Stage 5) (see case 104a)
Life-Form Terms lod'di **bird** (bird+bat)
cizaš **bird** (small bird)
guolli **fish** (fish)
gearmaš **snake** (snake)

mátto **snake** (worm + larva)

divri **wug** (insect + worm + larva + snake + spider + slug +
crab + shrimp + crill + snail + sea shell)

spire **mammal** (mammal + nonsnake reptile + amphibian)

Discussion The **bird** term, *lod'di*, is also used to refer to flying invertebrates, but the two senses are clearly distinct. Although there is a word for snakes, these creatures have never been experienced in the arctic according to Anderson. The **wug** term has a second sense which is restricted to "elongate crawling invertebrates." This encompasses all creatures of its expanded sense with the exception of beetles, globular invertebrates, and shelled invertebrates such as snails, sea shells, etc. The **mammal** term has a second expanded range in which birds are lumped with mammals and other land vertebrates. This usage, however, is rare.

Case 140b.

Language Siane (Stage 5)

Classification Siane, Gende-Siane-Gahuku-Kamano-Fore, East New Guinea Highlands, Central New Guinea, Indo-Pacific

Area Eastern Highlands, Papua New Guinea

Source Peter D. Dwyer (1978)

Life-Form Terms nema **bird** (bird + bat)

laiva **fish** (fish)

hoiafa **snake** (snake + earthworm + centipede + millipede +
leech + mollusk + land planarian + scincid lizard +
agamid lizard + crocodile + fish)

hanu **wug** (insect + spider + frog)

hunembe **mammal** (small mammal [marsupial mouse +
pygmy possum + small rodent])

hefa **mammal** (large mammal + dwarf cassowary + eel)

Discussion The **bird** life-form includes all birds except cassowaries and all bats except one species. The term *hefa* encompasses all large mammals including the introduced varieties, cat, sheep, goat, cow, and horse. Only two types of fish other than eels are known to Siane speakers. Fish, in addition to having their own cover label, *laiva*, are included within the **snake** category, *hoiafa*, by older men in all contexts. Younger men in formal contexts usually assign an independent or primary status to *laiva*, but in informal situations treat fish as included in *hoiafa*. The lumping of fish with elongated animals is also attested for Papago (11b), Kyaka Enga (69b), and Kilangi (133b). This classificatory feature is correlated with lack or scarcity of fish in environments.

Case 141b.

Language Tifal (Stage 5) (see case 167a)
Life-Form Terms awoon **bird** (bird)
aniing **fish** (fish)
inab **snake** (snake)
beem **snake** (worm)
keeng **wug** (bug)
taloob kiilim **mammal** (mammal + large reptile)
Discussion The **mammal** term translates literally "large creature." Most of the time the Tifal "pig" term is used in reference to the larger imported mammals such as cows and horses. In the past pigs were the largest creatures known.

> *Five Life-Forms:* **bird** + **fish** + **snake** + **wug** + combined **wug-mammal**.
> 142b. Daga (Papua New Guinea)
> 143b. Southern Paiute (Chemehuevi dialect) (Nevada, U.S.A.)

Case 142b.

Language Daga (Stage 5) (see case 135a)
Life-Form Terms nenip **bird** (bird)
meo **fish** (fish)
mokare **snake** (snake + worm)
motamot **wug** (insect + tick + mite)
man combined **wug-mammal** (bug + mammal + snake + worm + cassowary + eel)
Discussion The combined **wug-mammal** term also means "meat." The **wug** class does not include spiders.

Case 143b.

Language Southern Paiute (Chemehuevi dialect) (Stage 5) (see case 28a)
Life-Form Terms wičici **bird** (bird)
pagí'ɨcu **fish** (fish)
kwiyáču **snake** (snake)
pa'ávivim **wug** (insect + spider)
pa'abi combined **wug-mammal** (insect + spider + snake + mammal + lizard + frog)
Discussion The **wug** term, *pa'ávivim*, apparently is the plural of *pa'abi*

(combined **wug-mammal**). The source does not mention worms. For dialectal differences see Southern Paiute (Cedar City dialect) (88b).

> *Six Life-Forms:* **bird + fish + snake + wug + mammal** + combined **wug-mammal**.
> 144b. Tahitian (South Pacific)

Case 144b.

Language Tahitian (Stage 5)

Classification Eastern Polynesian, Polynesian, Eastern Oceanic, Oceanic, Austronesian

Area Tahiti, South Pacific

Source (1) Yves Lemaitre (1973, 1977); (2) Edmund Andrews and Irene D. Andrews (1944); (3) Tepano Jaussen (1969).

Life-Form Terms manu **bird** (bird + certain flying insect)
ʔapaʔapa **bird** (bird)
iʔa **fish** (fish + porpoise + dolphin + whale + tortoise + octopus)
paru **fish** (fish or small fish)
ʔōfī **snake** (snake)
iro **snake** (worm)
manumanu **wug** (nonflying insect + certain flying insect)
ʔānīmara **mammal** (mammal + chicken + lizard + centipede + large-bodied spider)
manu combined **wug-mammal** (mammal + insect + bird + chicken + lizard + centipede + large-bodied spider)

Discussion Four of the above terms are not given in the primary source (Lemaitre 1977). One of the two **bird** terms, *ʔapaʔapa*, is from the dictionary sources Andrews and Andrews (1944) and Jaussen (1969). Jaussen notes that the latter term is less commonly used for **bird** than *manu*. One of the two **fish** terms, *paru*, is also from the latter two dictionary sources in which it is assigned the glosses "small fish" and "fish" respectively. The "snake" term, *ʔōfī*, is from Lemaitre (1973, also a dictionary) and is found as well in Andrews and Andrews (1944) and Jaussen (1969). The "worm" term, *iro*, is from Andrews and Andrews (1944) and Jaussen (1969). It is possible that this term is not a full-fledged life-form label and actually refers only to "maggot." The term *manu* has three distinct designative ranges: (1) birds, (2) birds and certain flying insects, and (3) birds, insects, mammals, and certain other creatures. Lemaitre (1977) notes that for more highly acculturated speakers *manu* designates only "bird." However, it is not clear from his account whether or not true birds constitute a focus of *manu* for those speakers associating the term with ranges (2) and (3). Nor is the possibility that true fish constitute the focus of *i?a* mentioned, although this is suggested by glosses for the term given in Andrews and Andrews (1944) and in Jaussen (1969). The "snake" term is a corruption of the Greek word for "serpent" (*ophis*) (Ross Clark, personal communication). As Lemaitre (1973: 176) notes, in order to translate the Bible into Tahitian, missionaries created a large number of animal names from Hebrew, Greek, and Latin. Since snakes do not inhabit Tahiti, there was no native term for these creatures (Brown 1981b). The **wug** term, *manumanu*, is formed by reduplicating *manu* (combined **wug-mammal**), a common method of giving the idea of smallness and great numbers (Lemaitre 1977: 174). Lemaitre (1977: 180) notes that informants characterize *manumanu* (**wug**) as creatures of "small size" and *manu* (**bird**) as creatures "that fly." Thus flying insects tend to fall into one or the other of these two categories depending on size and flying ability. Lemaitre writes: "Flies and mosquitoes are small enough to be *manumanu* and/or do not fly well enough to be *manu*. Butterflies fly well enough to be *manu* and/or are not small enough to be *manumanu* (1977: 181)." Creatures regularly designated by *manumanu* include grasshoppers, lice, fleas, ants, flies, mosquitoes, and woodlice. *Manu* (**bird**) consistently encompasses phasmids, moths, butterflies, dragonflies, bees, wasps, and all birds (with one exception). Other creatures, such as crickets and cockroaches, are sometimes placed in *manumanu* (**wug**) and sometimes in *manu* (**bird**). In addition, there is some ambiguity with respect to the life-form classification of chickens. Since chickens do not fly very much, some speakers apparently do not recognize them as kinds of *manu* (**bird**). Instead, they lump these domesticated fowl with mammals and other large creatures in the **mammal** class. In addition to dogs, cats, pigs, and chickens, some speakers include rats, lizards, and even centipedes and large-bodied spiders in **mammal**. The **mammal** term, *?ānīmara*, is a borrowing from French. The unusual inclusion of birds in the combined **wug-mammal** class is discussed in Chapter 6.

NOTES

1. In preliminary studies (Brown 1977, 1979a) cross-language data were compiled from two major sources: (1) dictionaries and (2) nondictionary sources. Nondictionary data were collected through personal communications with individuals who gathered information firsthand in the field, through reference to published and unpublished monographs and articles treating folk biological classification, and by me directly from informants. Of the 105 languages surveyed for plant classification (Brown 1977) dictionaries were primary sources for 76 cases and nondictionary sources were drawn on for the remaining 29. Among the 112 languages sampled for animal classification (Brown 1979a) 78 cases were based on dictionary sources and 34 on nondictionary sources.

    Since nondictionary sources deal primarily with plant and animal classification, they are obviously more reliable with respect to thoroughness and accuracy of biological reference than dictionary sources. The fact that most data assembled in the original studies were gathered from dictionaries meant that the initial investigations were necessarily pilot studies. Ideally most data in terms of which uniformities in folk biological classification are determined should be compiled from nondictionary sources. A major contribution of the present work is presentation of nondictionary data bearing on folk plant and animal classification in very large numbers of languages (188 and 144 cases respectively).

CHAPTER 1: INTRODUCTION

1. I borrow the expression "life-form" from Brent Berlin's work (1972, 1973, 1976; with Breedlove and Raven 1973, 1974). Berlin enumerates several strict criteria that biological classes must meet in order to qualify as life-form categories. These are outlined presently in this chapter. However, as explained in Chapter 2, my usage of "life-form" departs somewhat from Berlin's. I apply it to all general plant and animal classes which reflect certain pan-environmental, large biological discontinuities in nature. Such classes usually, but not always, conform to Berlin's life-form criteria. In addition, Chapter 2 discusses in detail precisely what is meant by "pan-environmental, large biological discontinuity."
2. Generic categories occurring at Level 1, which are not included in any major life-form class, are "unaffiliated generics" (Berlin et al. 1974: 30). Unaffiliated plant generics invariably are cultivated and/or morphologically peculiar in some way.
3. Berlin et al. (1974: 34) specify certain conditions in which secondary lexemes are in evidence even though all items of a class are not labeled by equivalent composite terms.

4. Of course, the composite forms *oak tree*, *walnut tree*, and *maple tree* also occur. *Oak*, *walnut*, and *maple* respectively are in effect abbreviated versions of the latter composite lexemes. Secondary lexemes cannot be similarly abbreviated: e.g., *white oak* to *white, *pin oak* to *pin. Some productive primary lexemes also cannot be abbreviated, e.g. *tulip tree* to *tulip (Berlin 1976: 397).

CHAPTER 2: LIFE-FORM CLASSES AND DISCONTINUITIES IN NATURE

1. **Grerb** is a mnemonic derived from *grass* and *herb*. In American English *plant* is used to refer to small herbaceous plants as opposed to trees. Since *plant* is also used as a unique beginner term to refer to botanical organisms in general (including trees), **grerb** is used in this work to avoid ambiguity of reference. Unless otherwise indicated, throughout this book *plant* is used only in its more expansive sense.
2. **Wug** is a mnemonic derived from *worm* and *bug*.
3. *Animal* is more commonly used than *mammal* as a **mammal** class label by speakers of American English. Since *animal* is also used as a unique beginner term to refer to creatures in general, it is not employed as a category gloss to avoid ambiguity of reference. Unless otherwise indicated, throughout this book *animal* is used only in its more expansive sense.
4. Tables 5–7 suggest that "frog/toad" is commonly encoded by languages and regularly found to be among the more polytypic animal classes of languages. Given this, it is possible that this discontinuity participates in some manner in regular encoding patterns to be described in Chapter 3. This possibility has yet to be systematically investigated.
5. Labels for categories having referential foci are often polysemous terms, the fully extended class constituting one referent, and the more restricted focus another. Such polysemy sometimes develops through expansion of reference whereby a term which originally designated only the focal referent extends to a broader category encompassing that referent. When terms for general purpose classes are expanded in this manner, the resulting broader class is sometimes a special purpose category, for example, the expansion of a term for **fish** to all aquatic creatures. The reverse development also occurs, that is, expansion of a special purpose category term, e.g. "weed," to a broader general purpose class, e.g. small herbaceous plants in general (**grerb**). Examples of such developments are extensively cited in Chapter 6.

CHAPTER 3: ANALYSIS OF CROSS-LANGUAGE DATA

1. The encoding sequence of Figure 2 is revised from that presented in Brown (1977). In the original formulation **grerb**, the only life-form proposed as ever emerging second after **tree**, was viewed as having two possible referential ranges: (1) encompassing grasses and nongrass herbaceous plants, and (2) encompassing grasses alone. If **grerb** were encoded with range 1, the subsequent encoding of **grass** by a language would result in the restriction of **grerb** to nongrass herbaceous plants. If **grerb** were encoded with range 2, a term for nongrass herbaceous plants added subsequently would be considered **grerb** and the original **grerb** term (restricted to grasses) would then be reinterpreted as being a **grass** label. In the revised encoding sequence (Figure 2) these complexities are eliminated by simply recognizing the possible encoding of **grass** immediately after **tree** and the possible addition of **grerb** after **grass**.
2. The encoding sequence of Figure 3 is revised from that presented in Brown (1979a). In the latter work, Stage 0 was not recognized. In addition, the earlier version of the sequence pro-

posed that **wug** regularly precedes **mammal**. Data assembled in the present work do not support such a proposal. The original determination of the priority of **wug** vis-à-vis **mammal** was influenced in part by the fact that the vast majority of language cases surveyed were extracted from dictionaries (see Brown 1981a for a discussion of this point).

3. The zoological life-form encoding sequence predicts the occurrence of 11 different combinations of animal life-form classes. Hence, one of the predicted combinations, **bird** on its own, does not occur in the sample of 144 language cases.

4. Terence E. Hays working with Ndumba (Tairora) speakers of New Guinea and Eugene S. Hunn working with Tzeltal speakers of Mexico independently identified "residual" biological classes during the early 1970's. For discussions of the role of residualness in folk biological classification, see Hays (1974) and Hunn (1976, 1977).

CHAPTER 4: LANGUAGE RELATEDNESS AND GROWTH STAGES

1. In addition to the New Guinea and North American cases, the "small mammal"/"large mammal" contrast is encoded by only one other language surveyed, Komo, spoken in Zaire.

CHAPTER 5: LEXICAL RECONSTRUCTION AND LIFE-FORM GROWTH

1. Language sources used in Brown and Witkowski's (1982) study were mostly dictionaries and vocabulary lists and thus were uneven in nature, some more reliable with respect to thoroughness and accuracy of biological reference than others. Some Mayan languages, then, may actually have more life-form terms than those reported by Brown and Witkowski, as these authors have noted in their article.

2. The Polynesian plant and animal life-form studies (Brown 1981b, 1982a), like the Mayan animal study (Brown and Witkowski 1982), are based primarily on dictionary and vocabulary lists and are thus subject to the limitations of such sources (see Note 1).

3. As it happens, Nukuoro was the only exception to the encoding sequence found among the 105 languages surveyed in the original botanical life-form study (Brown 1977). Since the source for Nukuoro (Carroll and Soulik 1973) is a dictionary rather than a detailed treatment of folk botanical classification, it is possible that Nukuoro may eventually prove not to be problematic. For example, the language has a reflex of the Proto-Polynesian word for **tree**, but the meaning assigned to it in the dictionary source is "wood." A detailed study may show that **tree** exists as a secondary, less salient referent of the term.

4. If Proto-Numic did have terms for **bird**, **fish**, and **snake**, examination of labels for these categories in contemporary languages suggests that considerable lexical replacement has occurred since Proto-Numic times.

5. The measure of societal scale which I have used is from Marsh (1967). In addition to Marsh's index, several other measures of societal scale employing a wide range of variables have been devised (e.g., Freeman 1957 and Naroll 1956). Significantly, all of these correlate strongly with one another (Schaefer 1969) indicating that a wide range of different variables can serve as reliable measures of societal scale. Marsh's (1967: 338–347) work indexes societal scale primarily in terms of size and integration of political units and degree of social stratification.

    The correlation between societal scale and size of botanical life-form vocabularies given in Brown (1977: 331) is relatively strong: gamma = .59 ($p < .05$, $N = 54$). A correlation based on botanical life-form data reported in this work (Appendix A) is considerably larger: gamma = .83 ($p < .02$, $N = 50$). The correlation between societal scale and zoological life-form vocabularies given in Brown (1979a: 805) is also relatively strong: gamma = .66 ($p < .02, N = 49$). A correlation based on animal life-form data reported in this work (Appendix B) is in the same range: gamma = .59 ($p < .30, N = 33$). However, the latter association is not statistically significant. This is due mainly to the small number of cases utilized ($N = 33$). (Of the 144 languages surveyed for animal classification, only 33 were found on the list of 500 languages [societies] compiled by Marsh [1967] which I consulted for societal scale scores.) The present data (Appendix B) seem to show that while languages associated with small-scale societies sometimes have large animal life-form vocabularies, languages associated with large urban societies never have small animal life-form lexicons.

While the correlation coefficients for the associations between societal scale and size of biological life-form lexicons are moderately high, they are not, of course, perfect. Thus among the world's languages there are exceptions to the generalization that languages having many zoological and botanical life-forms are associated with large-scale societies and those having few with small-scale societies. This indicates that societal scale is not the only factor that affects size of biological life-form lexicons. However, the correlations show that a significant percentage of languages having many zoological or botanical life-form terms are associated with large-scale societies and that a significant percentage of those having few with small-scale societies. Thus, societal scale constitutes a common factor underlying biological life-form growth. There is, then, a strong worldwide tendency for languages to add plant and animal life-form terms as societal scale expands.

6. Frequency of occurrence of terms for these concepts are extracted from word frequency books, respectively Thorndike and Lorge (1944), Landau (1959), and Buchanan (1941). In the case of American English, only one frequency count of the several found in Thorndike and Lorge (1944) is used, i.e., the "Lorge-Thorndike Semantic Count." In Tables 12, 14, and 15 Arabic and Spanish concepts are denoted by English glosses. Associated frequency scores are those of actual plant and animal terms. Actual terms and their frequency scores are given in Tables 11 and 13 for American English.

Terms for certain biological concepts were excluded from consideration in Tables 11–15. Words for special-purpose classes such as "flower," "herb," "weed," "pet," and so on were not included (see Chapter 2 for a discussion of special-purpose as opposed to general-purpose biological categories). In addition, terms for products of plants such as English *apple*, *grape*, *potato*, *tobacco*, etc. were not included if these did not also designate plants that produce them. For example, *lemon* is excluded because it does not denote lemon tree, but only its fruit. There are of course polysemous terms such as *onion* which denote both the plant and its product. Such terms are included in Tables 11 and 12. Since term polysemy or lack of it could not be determined for Arabic, Arabic exclusions were modeled on those for American English. For example, if an Arabic term had the gloss "lemon" in Landau's (1959) word frequency book, it was excluded. Thus it is probable that some Arabic plant concepts were unjustifiably deleted.

7. In American English the term *animal* is used to designate both "creature in general" and **mammal**. Consequently, two distinct usages contribute to the high salience of this term (frequency count = 849, see Table 13). Such a dual application may also pertain to the equivalent Spanish word *animal*. It is, of course, impossible to determine what proportion of frequency counts for such polysemous items trace to one usage as opposed to the other.

8. Size of plant life-form lexicon correlates with botanical species diversity somewhat less strongly than with societal scale: gamma = .34 ($p < .001, N = 105$) versus gamma = .59 ($p < .05, N = 54$) (Brown 1977: 331). Number of zoological life-forms was not similarly found to be significantly correlated, either positively or negatively, with species diversity.

9. Gamma = .45, $p < .02, N = 54$ (Brown 1977: 331).

CHAPTER 6: NOMENCLATURAL DEVELOPMENT

1. This discussion of **tree** innovation is based on Witkowski, Brown, and Chase (1981).
2. Gamma = .81 ($p < .001$, $N = 66$) (Witkowski, Brown, and Chase 1981).
3. The term *plante* was actually known to speakers of Old English (Anglo-Saxon), but with the meaning "young tree, sapling" (Weekley 1967). Reflections of this early usage are seen in modern compound forms such as *ash-plant*.
4. Motu and Arosi are both geographically and genetically removed from one another: Motu (New Guinea) is a Papua Austronesian language within Oceanic and Arosi (San Cristobal, southern Solomons) is an Eastern Oceanic language.
5. See Pawley and Green (1971: 32) for Proto-Polynesian results and Kaufman (1964: 96–100) for Proto-Mayan reconstructions.
6. This discussion of incipient life-forms is based on Brown and Chase (1981).

CHAPTER 7: LIFE-FORMS AND LINGUISTIC MARKING

1. Parts of this chapter are based on Brown (1982b and n.d.).
2. The following word frequency books were used as sources for data presented in Tables 16 and 17: Arabic (Landau 1959), Brazilian Portuguese (Brown, Carr, and Shane 1945), Chinese (Liu 1973), French (Vander Beke 1929), German (Morgan 1923), Italian (Juilland and Travera 1973), Japanese (Miyaji 1966), Peninsular Spanish (Buchanan 1941), Rumanian (Juilland, Edwards, and Juilland 1965), Russian (Josselson 1953) and American English (Thorndike and Lorge 1944). Thorndike and Lorge (1944) present several different counts for American English. Frequencies for American English plant life-forms given in Table 16 are from the "Lorge-Thorndike Semantic Count." Frequencies for American English animal life-forms given in Table 17 are aggregated figures from two counts, i.e. from the "Lorge Magazine Count" and the "Lorge-Thorndike Semantic Count."

    The approximate number of running words (tokens) pertaining to each word frequency study is as follows: American English (4,500,000), Arabic (272,178), Brazilian Portuguese (1,200,000), Chinese (250,000), French (1,147,748), German (10,910,777), Italian (500,000), Japanese (250,000), Peninsular Spanish (1,200,000), Rumanian (500,000), Russian (1,000,000). The considerable differences in ranges of frequency counts for different languages reflect the fact that counts for these languages are based on tokens that vary considerably in size.

    Several word frequency books consulted break counts down according to genre of written materials surveyed, e.g., drama, essays, newspapers, technical/scientific literature. These include sources for Chinese, Italian, Japanese, Rumanian, and Spanish. In each of these cases, frequency figures from technical/scientific literature are excluded from counts presented in Tables 16 and 17 since these do not reflect "folk" usage.

    In compiling frequency data of Tables 16 and 17, life-form terms for languages other than American English and Japanese were looked up in standard English–other-language dictionaries, and these were then searched for in alphabetical listings of terms in individual word-frequency books. Since dictionary sources do not deal primarily with biological naming and classification, it is possible that some life-form terms were missed. Thus life-form inventories described for some languages of Tables 16 and 17 may be incomplete.

    In Tables 16 and 17, some frequency scores are only close estimates. In the case of German, no absolute frequencies are given in the source (Morgan 1923) for individual lexical items, only narrow frequency ranges for groupings of words close in frequency of use. Most word-frequency books omit terms having frequencies below a certain cutoff point, for example, 5 occurrences. In some cases, two or more nonlisted terms (of a single language) may designate the same life-form class. Thus it is impossible to give exact aggregated scores for these life-forms. Instead, an estimated figure, usually based on the cutoff point, is given.

3. Since the Russian **tree** term also denotes wood, the usage frequency relating to its life-form application is almost certainly something less than 166 occurrences given in Table 16 and therefore possibly less than the frequency score pertaining to Russian **grerb** (146 occurrences).

4. The frequency count for American English **mammal** given in Table 17 is the frequency of occurrence of the word *mammal*.

5. The exception is French, frequency data for which have been extracted from Vander Beke (1929). However, other French word frequency investigations indicate that the language is not exceptional. A study by Juilland, Brodin, and Davidovitch (1970) lists French "snake" as occurring 13 times in approximately 500 thousand tokens compared to 3 times for "worm" (with technical/scientific genre counts excluded). In addition, an anonymous study (1971) tabulates 1961 occurrences of French "snake" in 71 million tokens compared to only 621 for "worm." Clearly, Vander Beke's (1929) counts for "snake" and "worm" are anomalous, perhaps somehow an artifact of sampling procedure.

6. Orthography used for transcribing life-form terms (Appendices A and B) regrettably is not uniform across language cases. In all cases, orthography supplied by sources is utilized. In this counting of orthographic segments, all symbols occupying spaces in the horizontal presentation of a word are tallied. This includes symbols indicating vocalic length and symbols indicating glottalization and aspiration of consonants. For example, Kekchi (139a) *q'e·n* **grerb** is judged as having five orthographic segments. When a language has two or more terms for a single life-form class, e.g., Southern Paiute (Cedar City) (88b) with **bird** (bird) and **bird** (large bird), segments of all terms are counted and figure into calculations for that life-form.

7. It might also be argued that **fish** and **snake** categories of younger American children are incipient life-form classes since names of included members are not known. This would clearly be the case if several fish and snakes with known names were excluded from **fish** and **snake**. Since children did not know the individual names of any fish and snake exemplars with one exception, a definitive argument concerning this issue cannot be made here. Of course, the exception suggests that **fish** may be a complete life-form class for these children: the shark, identified by several as *jaws*, is in all cases included in **fish**.

8. Terms for incipient "snake" and "worm" classes are not included in these counts. It should be noted that many sources for language cases fail to refer to worms either as encoded as a unique zoological class or otherwise classified. Consequently, more than 59 languages of the sample probably have "worm" terms. Of course, failure to mention worms is some index of their lack of salience.

9. Four exceptions to this implicational relationship are Papago (11b), Ibataan (98b), Mokilese (115b), and Eskimo (127b). These four languages have "worm" terms but lack "snake" labels. Two of these exceptions can be explained by ecological factors. Snakes are absent in environments of speakers of Mokilese (Micronesia) and Eskimo. While Papago lacks a "snake" term, i.e., a label encompassing all true snakes, it nevertheless has a word for nonpoisonous snakes in general.

CHAPTER 8: EXPLANATORY FRAMEWORK

1. I do not presume to view the framework put forth in this chapter as the final and definitive explanation of cross-language regularities described in preceding chapters. I do, naturally,

believe it to be a highly plausible account and predict that much of it will survive further scholarly consideration by myself and/or others. Be that as it may, the proposed explanation should be judged independently from the uniformities described. In other words, whether the explanation is found acceptable in total or in part, the cross-language data assembled and the patterns to which they attest can stand on their own merit and challenge all to interpret them.

2. This tendency is also reflected in zoological classification where "snake" (large elongated creature) is universally unmarked vis-à-vis its contrasting class "worm" (small elongated creature) which is marked (cf. Chapter 7).

3. I am grateful to Stanley R. Witkowski for suggesting this distinction to me.

4. I am not suggesting that botanical classes defined principally in terms of functional or utilitarian features, e.g., "vegetable," are in some sense primary or fundamental units in systems of folk plant classification. Rather, I would argue that utilitarian considerations—such as an enhanced need for general plant terms in languages of urban societies—are often related to priorities concerning which discontinuities in the plant world will be lexically encoded and which ones will not be at any given time.

5. In some cases **grass** may enter into a marking sequence based on size. This is presumably the case when the initial binary opposition involves a **tree/grass** rather than **tree/grerb** contrast. Size, of course, is one of several dimensions along which **grass** contrasts with **tree** (others include ligneousness, leaf morphology, and the presence or absence of a central support). **Bush**, then, may emerge as a category which is intermediate in size relative to **tree** and **grass**. However, since small size is only one distinctive feature of grasses, and probably not the most important one, the pertinence of size to a **tree/grass** contrast may not be as obvious as the dimension's pertinence to a **tree/grerb** distinction. As a consequence, chances that **bush** will be distinguished as a category intermediate in size between **tree** and **grass** are something less than if **tree** and **grerb** were involved. This is perhaps reflected by the fact that only two Stage 4 languages, Kaguru (127a) and Nez Perce (128a), have a **tree+grass+bush** combination.

6. For discussions of residualness in folk biological classification, see Hunn (1976, 1977) and Hays (1974).

CHAPTER 9: CONCLUSION

1. The status of **wug** and **mammal** as true discontinuities in nature is problematic. This is discussed in Chapter 8.

2. The discussion of color encoding in this section is based on Witkowski and Brown (1977).

3. Witkowski and Brown (1981) argue that a need for referring to colors in a general manner arises with emergence of color manipulating technologies. This argument is based on the observation that as societies grow in scale there is a tendency for the number of basic color terms to increase. This probably relates to increasing control over color in the form of dyeing, painting, and other activities which usually accompany the overall technological advances associated with societal growth.

4. My colleague, Stanley R. Witkowski, is responsible for the idea that total referential coverage of the color space through use of general terms is more useful than partial coverage. In Chapter 8 his notion of domain coverage and utilitarianism is extended by me to plants and animals. I am grateful to him for sharing this idea with me.

REFERENCES CITED

Acheson, Nicholas H.
1966   Etnozoologia Zinacanteca. *In* Los Zinacantecos: Un Pueblo Tzotzil de los Altos de Chiapas, Evon Z. Vogt, ed., pp. 433–454. Mexico: Instituto Nacional Indigenista.

Anderson, Eugene N.
1972   The Ethnoicthyology of the Hong Kong Boat People. *In* Essays on South China's Boat People, by Eugene N. Anderson. Taipei: The Orient Cultural Service.

Anderson, Eugene N. and Marja L. Anderson
1977   Fishing in Troubled Waters: Research on the Chinese Fishing Industry in West Malaysia. Taipei: The Chinese Association for Folklore.

Anderson, Myrdene
1978   Saami Ethnoecology: Resource Management in Norwegian Lapland. Ph.D. thesis, Yale University.

Andrews, Edmund and Irene D. Andrews
1944   A Comparative Dictionary of the Tahitian Language. Chicago: The Chicago Academy of Sciences

Anonymous
1971   Dictionnaire des Fréquences: Vocabulaire Littéraire des XIXe et XXe Siècles—II—Table des Fréquences Décroissantes. Nancy, France: Centre de Recherche pour un Trésor de la Langue Française.

d'Ans, Andre-Márcel
1972   Repertorios Etno-botánico y Etno-zoológico Amahuaca. Revista Museo Nacional, Lima 38: 352–384.

Baldus, Herbert
1946   Vocabulário Zoológico Kaingang. Arquivos Meseu Paranaense 6: 149–160.

Barrera Marin, Alfredo, Alfredo Barrera Vazquez, and Rosa Maria Lopez Franco
1976   Nomenclatura Ethnobotanica Maya: Una Interpretación Taxonómica. Mexico, D.F.: Instituto Nacional de Antropología e Historia.

Barth, Fredrick
1975   Ritual and Knowledge among the Baktaman of New Guinea. New Haven: Yale University Press.

Beidelman, T. O.
  1964   Some Kaguru Plants: Terms, Names and Uses. Man 64: 79–82.
Berlin, Brent
  1972   Speculations on the Growth of Ethnobotanical Nomenclature. Language in Society 1: 51–86.
  1973   Folk Systematics in Relation to Biological Classification and Nomenclature. Annual Review of Ecology and Systematics 4: 259–271.
  1976   The Concept of Rank in Ethnobiological Classification: Some Evidence from Aguaruna Folk Botany. American Ethnologist 3: 381–399.
Berlin, Brent and Elois Ann Berlin
  1977   Ethnobiology, Subsistence, and Nutrition in a Tropical Forest Society: The Aguaruna Jívaro, Studies in Aguaruna Jívaro Ethnobiology, Report No. 1, Language Behavior Research Laboratory, University of California, Berkeley.
Berlin, Brent, James Shilts Boster, and John P. O'Neill
  1981   The Perceptual Bases of Ethnobiological Classification: Evidence from Aguaruna Jívaro Ornithology. Journal of Ethnobiology 1 (1): 95–108.
Berlin, Brent, Dennis E. Breedlove, and Peter H. Raven
  1966   Folk Taxonomies and Biological Classification. Science 154: 273–275.
  1973   General Principles of Classification and Nomenclature in Folk Biology. American Anthropologist 75: 214–242.
  1974   Principles of Tzeltal Plant Classification: An Introduction to the Botanical Ethnography of a Mayan-speaking People of Highland Chiapas. New York: Academic Press.
Berlin, Brent and Paul Kay
  1969   Basic Color Terms: Their Universality and Evolution. Berkeley: University of California Press.
Black, Mary B.
  1967   An Ethnoscience Investigation of Ojibwa Ontology and World View. Ph.D. thesis, Stanford University.
  1969   Eliciting Folk Taxonomy in Ojibwa. In Cognitive Anthropology, Stephen A. Tyler, ed., pp. 165–189. New York: Holt, Rinehart and Winston, Inc.
  1976   Semantic Variability in a Northern Ojibwa Community. Papers in Linguistics 9 (3–4): 129–157.
Bornstein, Marc H.
  1973   The Psychophysiological Component of Cultural Difference in Color Naming and Illusion Susceptibility. Behavior Science Notes 8: 41–101.
  1975   The Influence of Visual Perception on Culture. American Anthropologist 77: 774–798.
Bornstein, Marc H., William Kessen, and Sally Weiskopf
  1976   The Categories of Hue In Infancy. Science 191: 201–202.
Bouchard, Serge
  1973   Classification Montagnaise de la Faune: Etude en Anthropologie Cognitive sur la Structure du Lexique "Animal Indien" Chez les Montagnais de Mingan. M.A. thesis, Laval University.
Bouchard, Serge and José Mailhot
  1973   Structure du Lexique: Les Animaux Indiens. Recherches Amèrindiennes au Quèbec 3 (1–2): 39–67.

Breedlove, Dennis E. and Nicholas A. Hopkins
    1970   Study of Chuj (Mayan) Plants, with Notes on their Uses. I. The Wasmann Journal of Biology 28: 275–298.

Bright, Jane O. and William Bright
    1965   Semantic Structures in Northwestern California and the Sapir-Whorf Hypothesis. American Anthropologist 67: 249–258.

Brown, Cecil H.
    1972   Huastec Plant Taxonomy. Katunob 8 (2): 74–78.
    1977   Folk Botanical Life-Forms: Their Universality and Growth. American Anthropologist 79: 317–342.
    1979a Folk Zoological Life-Forms: Their Universality and Growth. American Anthropologist 81: 791–817.
    1979b Growth and Development of Folk Botanical Life-Forms in the Mayan Language Family. American Ethnologist 6: 366–385.
    1981a More on Folk Zoological Life-Forms. American Anthropologist 83: 398–401.
    1981b Growth and Development of Folk Zoological Life-Forms in Polynesian Languages. Journal of the Polynesian Society 90: 83–110.
    1982a Growth and Development of Folk Botanical Life-Forms in Polynesian Languages. Journal of the Polynesian Society (in press).
    1982b Folk Zoological Life-Forms and Linguistic Marking. Journal of Ethnobiology 2 (1): 95–112.
    n.d.   Folk Botanical Life-Forms and Linguistic Marking. Unpublished manuscript, Northern Illinois University.

Brown, Cecil H. and Paul K. Chase
    1981   Animal Classification in Juchitan Zapotec. Journal of Anthropological Research 37: 61–70.

Brown, Cecil H. and Stanley R. Witkowski
    1979   Aspects of the Phonological History of Mayan-Zoquean. International Journal of American Linguistics 45: 34–47.
    1980   Language Universals. In Toward Explaining Human Culture, David Levinson and Martin Malone, principal authors, pp. 359–384. New Haven: HRAF Press.
    1982   Growth and Development of Folk Zoological Life-Forms in the Mayan Language Family. American Ethnologist 9: 97–112.
    n.d.   Size Terminology, Societal Complexity, and Linguistic Marking. Unpublished Manuscript.

Brown, Charles B., Wesley M. Carr, Milton L. Shane
    1945   A Graded Word Book of Brazilian Portuguese. New York: F. S. Crofts & Co.

Brunel, Gilles
    1976   The Evolution of Quechua Life Forms. Paper given at the 75th Annual Meeting of the American Anthropological Association, Washington, D. C.

Bruner, J. S., J. J. Goodnow, and G. A. Austin
    1956   A Study of Thinking. New York: Wiley.

Buchanan, Milton A.
    1941   A Graded Spanish Word Book. Toronto: The University of Toronto Press.

Buck, Carl Darling
1949   A Dictionary of Selected Synonyms in the Principal Indo-European Languages. Chicago: University of Chicago Press.
Bulmer, Ralph N. H.
1970   Which Came First, the Chicken or the Egg-head? *In* Échanges et Communications, Mélanges offerts à Claude Lévi-Strauss à l'Occasion de son 60ème Anniversaire, J. Pouillon and P. Maranda, eds, pp. 1069–1091. The Hague: Mouton.
1974   Folk Biology in the New Guinea Highlands. Social Science Information 13 (4/5): 9–28.
Bulmer, Ralph N. H. and J. I. Menzies
1972   Karam Classification of Marsupials and Rodents. Journal of the Polynesian Society 81: 472–499.
1973   Karam Classification of Marsupials and Rodents—Pt. 2. Journal of the Polynesian Society 82: 86–107.
Bulmer, Ralph N. H., J. I. Menzies, and F. Parker
1975   Kalam Classification of Reptiles and Fishes. Journal of the Polynesian Society 84: 267–308.
Bulmer, Ralph N. H. and M. J. Tyler
1968   Karam Classification of Frogs. Journal of the Polynesian Society 77: 333–385.
Burris, Harold W., Jr.
1979   Geometric Figure Terms: Their Universality and Growth. The Journal of Anthropology 1 (2): 18–41.
Carroll, Vern, and Tobias Soulik
1973   Nukuoro Lexicon. Honolulu: The University Press of Hawaii.
Casad, Eugene H.
1980   Life-Form Classification in Cora. Unpublished manuscript.
Casson, Ronald, ed.
1981   Language, Culture, and Cognition: Anthropological Perspectives. New York: Macmillan.
Chamberlin, Ralph V.
1908   Animal Names and Anatomical Terms of the Goshute Indians. Proceedings of the Academy of Natural Sciences of Philadelphia, Vol. LX, pp. 74–103.
1964   The Ethno-botany of the Gosiute Indians of Utah. Memoirs of the American Anthropological Association, Vol. II, Part 5, pp. 329–405 (reprinted by the Kraus Reprint Corporation, 1964).
Chase, Paul K.
1980a   Acquisition of Folk Zoological Life-Forms by American and Zapotec Children. M.A. thesis, Northern Illinois University.
1980b   Acquisition of Folk Zoological Life-Forms by American Children. The Journal of Anthropology 2 (2): 104–121.
Chomsky, Noam
1975   Reflections on Language. New York: Pantheon.
de Civrieux, Marc

1973 Classification Zoologica y Botanica entre los Makiritare y los Kariña. Antropológica 36: 3–82.

Clark, Herbert H.
1973 Space, Time, Semantics, and the Child. *In* Cognitive Development and the Acquisition of Language, Timothy E. Moore, ed., pp. 27–63.

Conklin, Harold C.
1954 The Relation of Hanunóo Culture to the Plant World. Ph.D. thesis, Yale University.

Cruse, D. A.
1977 A Note on the Learning of Colour Names. Journal of Child Language 4: 305–311.

Davis, Stephen L.
1980 Aboriginal Science: Language, Learning and World View. Paper given at the 1980 Teacher/Linguist Conference for the Northern Territory Department of Education.
1981 Principles of Yolŋu Classification: Some Possible Universals in Cognition and Lexical Encoding. Unpublished manuscript.

Deighton, F. C.
1957 Vernacular Botanical Vocabulary for Sierra Leone. London: The Crown Agents for Oversea Governments and Administrations.

Demory, Barbara
1972 A Preliminary Survey of the Ethnobiology of a Micronesian Atoll: Mokil or "A Rat is a Hairy Lizard." Unpublished manuscript.

Dentan, Robert K.
1967 The Mammalian Taxonomy of the Sen'oi Semai. Malayan Nature Journal 20: 100–106.
1968a The Semai: A Nonviolent People of Malay. New York: Holt, Rinehart and Winston.
1968b Notes on Semai Ethnoentomology. Malayan Nature Journal 21: 17–28.
1970 Labels and Rituals in Semai Classification. Ethnology 9 (1): 16–25.

Diamond, J. M.
1966 Zoological Classification System of a Primitive People. Science 151: 1102–1104.

Dieterlen, Germaine.
1952 Classification des Végétaux Chez les Dogon. Journal de la Société de Africanistes 22 (1–2): 115–158.

Dougherty, Janet W. D.
1978 Salience and Relativity in Classification. American Ethnologist 5: 66–80.
1979 Learning Names for Plants and Plants for Names. Anthropological Linguistics 21: 298–315.

Dournes, Jacques.
1968 Bois-Bambou: Aspect Végétal de l'Univers Jörai. Paris: Editions du Centre National de la Recherche Scientifique.
1973 Chi-Chê: La Botanique des Srê. Paris: Laboratoire d'Ethnobotanique.

Durbin, Marshall
    1972   Basic Colors—Off Color? Semiotica 6: 257–277.
Dywer, Peter D.
    1978   The *Muruk* is not a Bird, It is an Animal: Higher Categories of a New
            Guinea Zoological Taxonomy. Unpublished manuscript.
Ellen, Roy F.
    1973   Nuaulu Settlement and Ecology: An Approach to the Environmental Rela-
            tions of an Eastern Indonesian Community. Ph.D. thesis, University of
            London.
    1975a   Non-domesticated Resources in Nuaulu Ecological Relations. Social Sci-
            ence Information 14 (5): 127–150.
    1975b   Variable Constructs in Nuaulu Zoological Classification. Social Science In-
            formation 14 (3/4): 201–228.
Ellen, Roy F., Andrew F. Stimson, and James Menzies
    n.d.   On Some Aspects of Nuaulu Classification of Snakes and Other Reptiles.
            Journal d'Agriculture et de Botanique Appliquée (in press).
Elmore, Francis H.
    1944   Ethnobotany of the Navajo. Albuquerque: The University of New Mexico
            Press.
Evans-Pritchard, E. E.
    1963   Notes on Some Animals in Zandeland. Man 63: 139–142.
Ferry, M.-P., M. Gessain, and R. Gessain
    1974   Ethno-Botanique Tenda. (Documents du Centre de Recherches Anthropo-
            logiques du Musée de l'Homme.) Paris: Laboratoire d'Anthropologie Biolo-
            gique, Démographique et Génétique.
Fjellman, Janet Ann Shepherd
    1971   The Myth of Primitive Mentality: A Study of Semantic Acquisition and
            Modes of Categorization in Akamba Children of South Central Kenya.
            Ph.D. thesis, Stanford University.
Fleisher, Mark Stewart
    1976   Clallam: A Study in Coast Salish Ethnolinguistics. Ph.D. thesis, Washington
            State University.
Flethcher, Alice C. and Francis La Flesche
    1906   The Omaha Tribe. Bureau of American Ethnology Annual Report No. 27.
Foster, Mary L. and George M. Foster
    1948   Sierra Popoluca Speech. Institute of Social Anthropology, Publication No. 8.
            Washington, D.C.: Smithsonian Institution.
Fowler, Catherine Louise Sweeney
    1972   Comparative Numic Ethnobiology. Ph.D. thesis, University of Pittsburgh.
Fox, C. E.
    1970   Arosi-English Dictionary. Canberra: The Australian National University.
Fox, Robert B.
    1952   The Pinatubo Negritos: Their Useful Plants and Material Culture. Philippine
            Journal of Science 81 (3–4): 173–414.
Frake, Charles O.

1964   A Structural Description of Subanun "Religious Behavior." *In* Explorations in Cultural Anthropology: Essays in Honor of George Peter Murdock, Ward H. Goodenough, ed., pp. 111–129. New York: McGraw-Hill.

Freeman, L. C.

1957   An Empirical Test of Folk-Urbanism. Ann Arbor: University Microfilms.

French, David

1957   An Exploration of Wasco Ethnoscience. *In* American Philosophical Society Year Book 1957, pp. 224–226. Philadelphia: The American Philosophical Society.

Friedberg, Claudine

1979   Socially Significant Plant Species and Their Taxonomic Position Among the Bunaq of Central Timor. *In* Classifications in their Social Context, Roy F. Ellen and David Reason, eds., pp. 81–101. London: Academic Press.

Fuentes, Jordi

1960   Dictionary and Grammar of the Easter Island Language. Santiago, Chile: Editorial Andre Bello.

Galhego Garcia, Wilson

1979   O Dominio das Plantas Medicinais entre os Kayová de Amambai: Problemática das Relações entre Nomenclatura e Classificação. Unpublished manuscript, Universidade de São Paulo.

Garnier, Pierre.

n.d.   Noms de Plantes en: Langue Mandingue: Bamana (Bambara), Dioula, Maninka (Malinké). Langue Baoulé. Essai de Classification Logique des Noms Populaires de Plantes. Docteur d'Université these, Université d'Aix-Marseille.

Glick, Leonard B.

1964   Categories and Relations in Gimi Natural Science. American Anthropologist 66 (no. 4, pt. 2): 273–280.

Goodenough, Ward

1957   Cultural Anthropology and Linguistics. *In* Report of the 7th Annual Round Table Meeting on Linguistics and Language Study, Monograph Series on Languages and Linguistics No. 9, Paul L. Garvin, ed., pp. 167–173. Washington, D.C.: Georgetown University.

Greenberg, Joseph H.

1966   Language Universals with Special Reference to Feature Hierarchies. The Hague: Mouton.

1969   Language Universals: A Research Frontier. Science 166: 473–478.

1975   Research on Language Universals. Annual Review of Anthropology 4: 75–94.

Grimes, Joseph E.

1980a   Huichol Life Form Classification II: Plants. Anthropological Linguistics 22: 264–274.

1980b   Huichol Life Form Classification I: Animals. Anthropological Linguistics 22: 187–200.

Groves, Barbara

1978 English Linguistic Development of the Life-Form *Plant*. Unpublished manuscript.

Haile, Berard
1951 A Stem Vocabulary of the Navaho Language. St. Michaels, Arizona: St. Michaels Press.

Harrington, John P.
1932 Tobacco among the Karuk Indians of California. Bureau of American Ethnology, Bulletin 94. Washington, D.C.: Smithsonian Institution.

Harris, John W.
1979 Ethnoscience and its Relevance for Education in Traditional Aboriginal Communities. M.A. thesis, University of Queensland.

Hart, Jeff
1974 Plant Taxonomy of the Salish and Kootenai Indians of Western Montana. M.A. thesis, University of Montana.

Hartmann, Thekla
1967 A Nomenclature Botânica dos Borôro. São Paulo, Brasil: Instituto de Estudo Brasileiros.
1972 Zur Botanischen Nomenklatur der Bororo Indianer. Zeitschrift für Ethnologie 96 (2): 234–249.

Hays, David G., Enid Margolis, Raoul Naroll, and Dale Revere Perkins
1972 Color Term Salience. American Anthropologist 74: 1107–1121.

Hays, Terence E.
1974 Mauna: Explorations in Ndumba Ethnobotany. Ph.D. thesis, University of Washington.
1976 An Empirical Method for the Identification of Covert Categories in Ethnobiology. American Ethnologist 3: 489–507.
1979 Plant Classification and Nomenclature in Ndumba, Papua New Guinea Highlands. Ethnology 18: 253–270.
1982 Utilitarian/Adaptationist Explanations of Folk Biological Classification: Some Cautionary Notes. Journal of Ethnobiology 2 (1): 89–94.
1983 Ndumba Folk Biology and General Principles of Ethnobiological Classification and Nomenclature. American Anthropologist (in press).

Headland, Thomas N.
1981 Taxonomic Disagreement in a Culturally Salient Domain: Botany Versus Utility in a Philippine Negrito Taxonomic System. M.A. thesis, University of Hawaii.

Heath, Jeffrey
1978 Linguistic Approaches to Nunggubuyu Ethnozoology and Ethnobotany. *In* Australian Aboriginal Concepts, L. R. Hiatt, ed., pp. 40–55. Canberra: Australian Institute of Aboriginal Studies.

Heider, Karl G.
1970 The Dugum Dani: A Papuan Culture in the Highlands of West New Guinea. Chicago: Aldine Publishing Company.

Henderson, Junius and John Peabody Harrington

1914   Ethnozoology of the Tewa Indians. Bureau of American Ethnology, Bulletin 56. Washington, D.C.: Smithsonian Institution.

Hopkins, Nicholas A.

1980a   Amuzgo Ethnobotanical Structure and Terminology. Paper presented at the American Anthropological Association meeting, Washington, D.C., December 1980.

1980b   Chuj Animal Names and their Classification. Journal of Mayan Linguistics 2 (1): 13–39.

Hunn, Eugene S.

1976   Toward a Perceptual Model of Folk Biological Classification. American Ethnologist 3: 508–524.

1977   Tzeltal Folk Zoology: The Classification of Discontinuities in Nature. New York: Academic Press.

1980a   Final Project Report, Technical Description of Project Results, Sahaptin Ethnobiology. Unpublished manuscript.

1980b   Sahaptin Fish Classification. Northwest Anthropological Research Notes 14 (1): 1–19.

1982   The Utilitarian Factor in Folk Biological Classification. American Anthropologist 84: 830–847.

Jakobson, Roman

1941   Kindersprache, Aphasie, und allgemeine Lautgesetze. Uppsala, Sweden: Almqvist and Wiksell.

Jauseen, Tepano

1969   Grammaire et Dictionnaire de la Langue Tahitienne. Cinquième édition revue par Mgr. Mazé et le R.P.H. Coppenrath. Paris: Musée de l'Homme.

Johnson, E. G.

1977   The Development of Color Knowledge in Preschool Children. Child Development 48: 308–311.

Jones, Kenneth

1972   An Introduction to Choctaw Ethnobotany. M.A. thesis, University of Kansas.

Jordan, Julia Anne

1965   Ethnobotany of the Kiowa-Apache. M.A. thesis, University of Oklahoma.

Josselson, Harry H.

1953   The Russian Word Count and Frequency Analysis of Grammatical Categories of Standard Literary Russian. Detroit: Wayne University Press.

Juilland, Alphonse, Dorothy Brodin, and Catherine Davidovitch

1970   Frequency Dictionary of French Words. The Hague: Mouton.

Juilland, Alphonse, P. M. H. Edwards, and Ileana Juilland

1965   Frequency Dictionary of Rumanian Words. The Hague: Mouton.

Juilland, Alphonse and Vincenzo Travera

1973   Frequency Dictionary of Italian Words. The Hague: Mouton.

Kaufman, Terrence

1964   Materiales Lingüísticos para el Estudio de las Relaciones Internas y Externas de la Familia de Idiomas Mayanos. *In* Desarrollo Cultural de los Mayas, E. Vogt, ed., pp. 81–136. México: Seminario de Cultural Maya.

Kay, Paul and Chad K. McDaniel
  1978   The Linguistic Significance of the Meanings of Basic Color Terms. Language 54: 610–646.
Kesby, John D.
  1979   The Rangi Classification of Animals and Plants. *In* Classifications in Their Social Context, Roy F. Ellen and David Reason, eds., pp. 33–56. New York: Academic Press.
Kimball, Linda Amy
  1981   On "Wood" and "Tree" in Brunei Malay. Unpublished manuscript.
Landau, Jacob M.
  1959   A Word Count of Modern Arabic Prose. New York: American Council of Learned Societies.
Lanyon-Orgill, P. A.
  1969   The Language of Eddystone Island (Western Soloman Islands). Balmains, Scotland: The Crichton Press.
Laughlin, Robert M.
  1975   The Great Tzotzil Dictionary of San Lorenzo Zinacantán. Smithsonian Contributions to Anthropology, No. 19. Washington, D.C.: Smithsonian Institution.
Lemaitre, Yves
  1973   Lexique du Tahitien Contemporain. Paris: Office de la Recherche Scientifique et Technique Outre-Mer.
  1977   Tahitian Ethnozoological Classification and Fuzzy Logic. *In* Language and Thought: Anthropological Issues, William C. McCormack and Stephen A. Wurm, eds., pp. 171–183. The Hague: Mouton.
Lindfors, Judith Wells
  1980   Children's Language and Learning. Englewood Cliffs, New Jersey: Prentice-Hall, Inc.
Lionnet, Andrés
  1972   Los Elementos de la Lengua Tarahumara. México: Universidad Nacional Autónoma de México.
Lister-Turner, R.
  1931   A Dictionary of the Motu Language of Papua. Sydney, New South Wales: A. H. Peittifer, Government Printer.
Liu, Eric Shen
  1973   Frequency Dictionary of Chinese Words. The Hague: Mouton.
Luomala, Katharine
  1953   Ethnobotany of the Gilbert Islands. Bernice P. Bishop Museum Bulletin 213. Honolulu: Bernice P. Bishop Museum.
Maddock, Kenneth
  1972   The Australian Aborigines: A Portrait of their Society. London: Allen Lane The Penguin Press.
  1975   The Emu Anomaly. *In* Australian Aboriginal Mythology, L. R. Hiatt, ed., pp. 102–122. Canberra: Australian Institute of Aboriginal Studies.
Mahar, James Michael

1953   Ethnobotany of the Oregon Paiutes of the Warm Springs Indian Reservation. B.A. thesis, Reed College.

de Mahieu, W.
1980   Structures et Symboles. London: International African Institute of London.

Malinowski, Bronislaw
1965   Coral Gardens and their Magic, Vol. II, The Language of Magic and Gardening. Bloomington: Indiana University Press.

Marsh, Robert M.
1967   Comparative Sociology: A Codification of Cross-societal Analysis. New York: Harcourt, Brace and World.

Martin, Marie A.
1971   Introduction a l'Ethnobotanique du Cambodge. Paris: Éditions du Centre National de la Recherche Scientifique.

Mathiot, Madeleine
1964   Noun Classes and Folk Taxonomy in Papago. *In* Language in Culture and Society: A Reader in Linguistic Anthropology, Dell Hymes, ed., pp. 154–163. New York: Harper and Row.

Matras, Jacqueline and Marie A. Martin
1972   Contribution a l'Ethnobotanique des Brou (Cambodge—Province de Ratanakiri). Journal d'Agriculture Tropicale et de Botanique Appliquée 19: 93–139.

Mayers, Marvin K.
1958   Pocomchi Texts. Norman, Oklahoma: Summer Institute of Linguistics.

Messer, Ellen
1975   Zapotec Plant Knowledge: Classification, Uses, and Communication about Plants in Mitla, Oaxaca, Mexico. Ph.D. thesis, The University of Michigan.

Migeod, Frederick William Hugh
1913   Mende Natural History Vocabulary. London: Kegan Paul, Trench, Trübner and Co. Ltd.

Miller, Jay
1975   Delaware Alternative Classifications. Anthropological Linguistics 17: 434–444.

Missionary of the Society of Jesus, A
1895   A Dictionary of the Numípu or Nez Perce Language. Montana: St. Ignatius Mission Print.

Miyaji, Hiroshi
1966   A Frequency Dictionary of Japanese Words. Ph.D. thesis, Stanford University.

Morgan, B. Q.
1923   German Frequency Word Book Based on Kaeding's Häufigkeitswörterbuch der deutschen Sprache. New York: The Macmillan Company.

Morris, Brian
1976   Whither the Savage Mind? Notes on the Natural Taxonomies of a Hunting and Gathering People. Man 11: 542–557.
1980   Folk Classification. Paper presented to the National Fauna Preservation Society of Malawi.

Mulcahy, David F.
  1967   A Preliminary Ethnoscientific Analysis of Puerto Rican Folk Medicine. M.A. thesis, University of Massachusetts.
Naroll, Raoul S.
  1956   A Preliminary Index of Social Development. American Anthropologist 58: 687–715.
Ortiz de Montellano, Bernardo R.
  1981   El Conocimiento de la Naturaleza Taxonomia Azteca. *In* La Historia General de la Medicina en Mexico, A. Lopez Austin, ed. Mexico: Academia Nacional de Medicina.
Paillet, Jean Pierre R.
  1973   Eskimo Language Animal and Plant Taxonomies in Baker Lake. Unpublished manuscript.
Palmer, Gary
  1975   Shuswap Indian Ethnobotany. Syesis 8: 29–81.
Pawley, Andrew and Kaye Green
  1971   Lexical Evidence for the Proto-Polynesian Homeland. Te Reo 14: 1–35.
Peile, Anthony R.
  n.d.   Preliminary Notes on the Ethno-botany of the Gugadja Aborigines at Balgo, Western Australia. Western Australian Herbarium Research Notes (in press).
Peña, Andrés
  1980   Plantas Medicinales de San Marcos Tlacoyalco y Otras Plantas y Árboles que la Gente Conoce. México, D.F.: Instituto Lingüístico de Verano.
Pennoyer, III, Fredrick Douglas
  1975   Taubuid Plants and Ritual Complexes. Ph.D. thesis, Washington State University.
Peterson, Roger Tory
  1980   A Field Guide to the Birds East of the Rockies. (4th Edition) Boston: Houghton Mifflin Company.
Posey, Darrel A.
  1981   Wasps, Warriors and Fearless Men: Ethnoentomology of the Kayapó Indians of Central Brazil. Journal of Ethnobiology 1: 165–174.
Price, P. David
  1967   Two Types of Taxonomy: A Huichol Ethnobotanical Example. Anthropological Linguistics 9 (7): 1–28.
Randall, Robert A.
  1976   How Tall is a Taxonomic Tree? Some Evidence for Dwarfism. American Ethnologist 3: 543–553.
Rappaport, Roy A.
  1967   Pigs for the Ancestors: Ritual in the Ecology of a New Guinea People. New Haven: Yale University Press.
Reichel-Dolmatoff, G.
  1978   Desana Animal Categories, Food Restriction, and the Concept of Color Energies. Journal of Latin American Lore 4 (2): 243–291.
Reid, Lawrence A.

1976   Bontok-English Dictionary. Pacific Linguistics Series C—No. 36. Canberra: The Australian National University.

Reid, Lawrence and Domingo Madulid
1972   Some Comments on Bontoc Ethnobotany. Philippine Journal of Linguistics 3 (2): 1–24.

Robbins, Wilfred William, John Peabody Harrington, and Barbara Freire-Marreco
1916   Ethnobotany of the Tewa Indians. Bureau of American Ethnology, Bulletin 55, Washington, D.C.: Smithsonian Institution.

Roulon, Paulett
1977   Classification Gbaya des Animaux. *In* Langage et Cultures Africaines: Essais d'Ethnolinguistique, Geneviève Calame-Griaule, ed., pp. 52–83. Paris: François Maspero.

Roys, Ralph L.
1931   The Ethno-Botany of the Maya. Middle American Research Series, No. 2. New Orleans: Tulane University.

Rudder, John
1979   Ethnobiology among the Yolŋu (Northern Territory). Paper presented at the 49th ANZAAS Conference, Auckland, New Zealand.

Schaefer, James M.
1969   A Comparison of Three Measures of Social Complexity. American Anthropologist 71: 706–708.

Smith, Rev. Edwin W. and Captain Andrew Murray Dale
1920   The Ila-Speaking Peoples of Northern Rhodesia. Volume II. London: Macmillan and Co., Ltd.

Speck, Frank G.
1946   Ethnoherpetology of the Catawba and Cherokee Indians. Journal of the Washington Academy of Sciences 36 (10): 355–360.

Stevenson, Matilda Coxe
1915   Ethnobotany of the Zuni Indians. Bureau of American Ethnology Annual Report No. 30, pp. 31–102. Washington: Government Printing Office.

Stross, Brian
1973   Acquisition of Botanical Terminology by Tzeltal Children. *In* Meaning in Mayan Languages, Munro S. Edmonson, ed., pp. 107–141. The Hague: Mouton.

Tambiah, S. J.
1969   Animals Are Good to Think and Good to Prohibit. Ethnology 8: 423–459.

Taylor, Kenneth Iain
1974   Sanumá Fauna: Prohibitions and Classifications. Monografía No. 18. Caracas: Fundación La Salle de Ciencias Naturales, Instituto Caribe de Antropología y Sociología.

Taylor, Paul Michael
1979   Preliminary Report on the Ethnobiology of the Tobelorese of Halmahera (North Moluccas, Indonesia). Paper presented at the Halmahera Research Workshop, Ternate, July 10–20, 1979.

Thomas, Dorothy

1966   Chrau Zoology: An Ethnolinguistic Study. *In* Papers on Four Vietnamese Languages, David D. Thomas, ed., pp. 1–14. Auckland: Linguistic Society of New Zealand.

Thomas, Jacqueline
1977   A Propos de la Structure du Vocabulaire Botanique en Ngbaka-ma'bo. *In* Langage et Cultures Africaines: Essais d'Ethnolinguistique, Geneviève Calame-Griaule, ed., pp. 37–51. Paris: François Maspero.

Thomson, D. F.
1946   Names and Naming in the Wik Moŋkan Tribe. The Journal of the Royal Anthropological Institute of Great Britain and Ireland 76 (2): 157–168.

Thord-Gray, I.
1955   Tarahumara-English, English-Tarahumara Dictionary. Coral Gables, Florida: University of Miami Press.

Thorndike, Edward L. and Irving Lorge
1944   The Teacher's Word Book of 30,000 Words. New York: Bureau of Publications, Teachers College, Columbia University.

Trager, George L.
1939   'Cottonwood' = 'Tree': A Southwestern Linguistic Trait. International Journal of American Linguistics 9: 117–118.

Turner, Nancy
1974   Plant Taxonomic Systems and Ethnobotany of Three Contemporary Indian Groups of the Pacific Northwest (Haida, Bella Coola, and Lillooet). Syesis 7: 1–107.

Turner, Nancy and Marcus A. M. Bell
1971   Ethnobotany of the Coast Salish Indians of Vancouver Island. Economic Botany 25: 63–104.
1973   The Ethnobotany of the Southern Kwakiutl Indians of British Columbia. Economic Botany 27: 257–310.

Tyler, Stephen·A., ed.
1969   Cognitive Anthropology. New York: Holt, Rinehart and Winston.

Vander Beke, George E.
1929   French Word Book. New York: The Macmillan Company.

Vanoverbergh, Morice
1927   Plant Names in Iloko. Journal of the American Oriental Society 47: 133–173.

Vergiat, A.-M.
1969   Plantes Magique et Médicinales des Féticheurs de l'Oubangui (Région de Bangui). Journal d'Agriculture Tropicale et de Botanique Appliquée 16: 84–110.

Vidal, Jules
1963   Systématique, Nomenclature et Phytonymie Botanique Populaire au Laos. Journal d'Agriculture Tropicale et de Botanique Appliquée 10 (10–11): 433–448.

Vidal, J. E. and J. Lemoine
1970   Contribution a l'Ethnobotanique des Hmong du Laos. Journal d'Agriculture Tropicale et de Botanique Appliquée 17: 1–59.

Vidal, J. E. and B. Wall
  1968   Contribution a l'Ethnobotanique des Nya Hön (Sud Laos). Journal d'Agri-
          culture Tropicale et de Botanique Appliquée 15 (7–8): 243–264.
Visser, Leotien E.
  1975   Plantes Médicinales de la Côte d'Ivoire (Mededelingen Landbouwhoge-
          school, Vol. 75, no. 15). Wageningen, Nederland: V. Veenman and Zo-
          nen B.V.
Voegelin, Charles F. and Florence M. Voegelin
  1957   Hopi Domains: A Lexical Approach to the Problem of Selection. Indiana
          University Publications in Anthropology and Linguistics, Memoir 14 of the
          International Journal of American Linguistics. Supplement to International
          Journal of American Linguistics Vol. 23, no. 2.
  1977   Classification and Index of the World's Languages. New York: Elsevier.
Waddy, Julie
  1979   The Aborigines and the Birds. Unpublished manuscript.
  1980   Biological Classification from an Anindilyakwa Speaker's Point of View. Pa-
          per presented at the ANZAAS Conference, May 1980.
  1982   Biological Classification from a Groote Eylandt Aborigine's Point of View.
          Journal of Ethnobiology 2 (1): 63–77.
Walker, Willard
  1966   Inflectional Class and Taxonomic Structure in Zuni. International Journal of
          American Linguistics 32: 217–226.
  1979   Zuni Semantic Categories. *In* Handbook of North American Indians, Vol-
          ume 9, Southwest, William C. Sturtevant, general ed., Alfonso Ortiz, vol-
          ume ed., pp. 509–513. Washington, D.C.: Smithsonian Institution.
Wallace, Ben J.
  1970   Hill' and Valley Farmers: Socio-Economic Change Among a Philippine
          Péople. Cambridge, Massachusetts: Schenkman Publishing Company, Inc.
von Wattenwyl, A. and H. Zollinger
  1979   Color Term Salience and Neurophysiology of Color Vision. American An-
          thropologist 81: 279–288.
Weekley, Ernest
  1967   An Etymological Dictionary of Modern English. New York: Dover Publica-
          tions, Inc.
Werner, Oswald, Allan Manning, and Kenneth Y. Begishe
  n.d.   A Taxonomic View of the Traditional Navajo Universe. Unpublished
          manuscript.
White, Leslie A.
  1947   Notes on the Ethnozoology of the Keresan Pueblo Indians. Papers of the
          Michigan Academy of Science, Arts, and Letters, Volume XXXI (1945),
          pp. 223–243. Ann Arbor: The University of Michigan Press.
Whiting, Alfred F.
  1939   Ethnobotany of the Hopi. Museum of Northern Arizona Bulletin No. 15.
          Flagstaff: Northern Arizona Society of Science and Art.

Willis, Roy

    1974   Man and Beast. London: Hart-Davis, MacGibbon.

Wilson, Michael Robert

    1972   A Highland Mayan People and Their Habitat: The Natural History, Demography and Economy of the K'ekchi'. Ph.D. thesis, University of Oregon.

Wisdom, Charles

    1949   Materials on the Chorti Language. Microfilm Collection of Manuscripts in Middle American Cultural Anthropology. Number 28. Chicago: University of Chicago Library.

Witkowski, Stanley R. and Cecil H. Brown

    1977   An Explanation of Color Nomenclature Universals. American Anthropologist 79: 50–57.

    1978a Lexical Universals. Annual Review of Anthropology 7: 427–451.

    1978b Mesoamerican: A Proposed Language Phylum. American Anthropologist 80: 942–944.

    1981   Lexical Encoding Sequences and Language Change: Color Terminology Systems. American Anthropologist 83: 13–27.

Witkowski, Stanley R., Cecil H. Brown, and Paul K. Chase

    1981   Where do Tree Terms Come From? Man (N.S.) 16: 1–14.

Wyman, Leland C.

    1964   Navaho Indian Ethnoentomology, University of New Mexico Publications in Anthropology, Number 12. Albuquerque, New Mexico: The University of New Mexico.

Yamamoto, Kumiko

    1980   Japanese Folk Biology. M.A. thesis, Northern Illinois University.

Yen, D. E.

    1976   The Ethnobotany of the Tasaday: II. Plant Names of the Tasaday, Manobo Blit and Kemato Tboli. In Further Studies on the Tasaday, D. E. Yen and John Nance, eds., pp. 135–158. Makati, Rizal, Philippines: Panamin Foundation.

Zipf, G. K.

    1935   The Psycho-Biology of Language. Boston: Houghton Mifflin.

    1949   Human Behavior and the Principle of Least Effort. Cambridge, Mass.: Addison Wesley Publishing.

INDEX

Page numbers given in italic type following language names indicate where detailed data on language cases are presented in appendices. Blind entries to cases in Appendix B refer readers to sources for the same case number in Appendix A.

Atapec Zapotec, 106, *176*, 216, *218*
Attinasi, J., 201
attribute: abstracted, 11; clustering, 12;
  "white-breasted nuthatchness," 11
Aulie, W., 201
Austin, G. A., 9, 16
Australia: languages of, 37, 74, 133, 135,
  137, 141, 143, 148, 160, 168, 169, 207,
  208, 212, 214, 222, 225, 227, 230, 231,
  236, 249, 254, 255
Austronesian language family, 37, 45, 61, 66
Awtuw, 29, 72, 77, 149, *151*, *242*
Ayres, G., 157
Azande, 109, 110, 253, *255*
Aztec-Tanoan languages, 37

Baer, P., 204
Baldus, H., 223
Bambara, 149, *152*
Banda, 149, *152*
Baoule, 149, *152*
Barth, F., 243
Basari, *174*
Bedik, *174*
Begishe, K. Y., 187, 238
Beidelman, T. O., 180
Belize: languages of, 43, 186
Bell, M. A. M., 145, 147
Bella Coola, 28, 77, *134*
Bengali, 199, *200*
Benue-Congo languages, 74
Berkeley, California, 92
Berlin, Brent, 3, 5–14, 16, 18, 19, 50,
  58–60, 76, 121, 123, 150, 191, 217, 230,
  269n3; formal criteria of, 20; framework of
  ethnobiological ranks of, 5, 6, 11, 20;
  general principles of, 4; proposals of, 6
Berlin, Elois, 150, 217
Bible, 47
binary contrast (*see* binary opposition)
binary opposition, 74, 99–102, 104, 106,
  124, 126, 127; based on size, 99, 100,
  108, 271; classification through, 99, 100;
  encoding one-half of, 41; initial, 275n5;
  initial for color, 124–126; as prevalent in
  encoding biological life-forms, 21; related
  to conjunctivity, 100; **tree/grass**, 275n5;
  tree/grerb, 101, 275n5
biological categories: composite labels for, 6;
  "empty," 21; general purpose, 117, 272n6;

generic, 269n2; lack of specific wiring for,
  129; monotypic, 12; polytypic, 117;
  "residual," 271n4; salience of, 7, 50;
  special purpose, 272n6
biological class name: construction of, 3
biological classes (*see* biological categories)
biological phenomena: strategies in
  organizing, 3
biology, folk, 4, and passim
bird: definition of, 15; encoded through
  binary opposition, 100; encoding priority
  of, 107; environmental factors in
  expanding, 75; included in **wug-mammal**,
  73; referential expansion of, 73, 74; passim
Bisa, 136, *138*, 216, *218*
Black, M. R., 92, 145, 261, 262
Boiteau, P. L., 204, 237
Bolivia: languages of, 151, 218
Bontoc, 28, *134*, 216, *219*
Borneo: languages of, 194, 219, 238
Bornstein, M. H., 123
Bororo, 188, *197*
borrowing: of "large/small mammal"
  distinction, 40; of life-forms, 59
Borthakur, S. K., 162
Boster, J. S., 11
botanical species: diversity of, 56; passim
Bouchard, S., 262
Boush, A., Jr., 196, 265
Brambila, D., 147, 229
Brazil: languages of, 137, 149, 164, 172,
  177, 179, 185, *197*, 213, 214, 218, 222,
  223, 235, 237, 247
Brazilian Portuguese, 85, 87, 273n2
break: generic (*see* discontinuities)
Breedlove, D. E., 3, 4, 6, 7, 16, 18, 76, 154,
  191, 230, 269n3
Bright, J. O., 147, 210, 211, 250
Bright, W., 147, 210, 211, 250
British English, 110
Brodin, D., 274n5
Brou, 149, *153*
Brown, C. B., 273
Brown, C. H., 4, 7, 14–16, 18–21, 36, 40,
  43–45, 50–52, 54, 55, 58–60, 65, 71,
  73, 78, 86, 87, 91, 94, 100, 120, 121,
  122, 124, 126, 129, 203, 212, 269, 270n1,
  271n1, 271n2, 271n5, 272n5, 272n8,
  273n2, 275n3
Brown, L. K., 164

Brown, M. F., 217
Brunei Malay, 77, 193, *194*, 216, *219*
Brunel, G., 196
Bruner, J. S., 9
Buchanan, M. A., 55, 272n6, 273n2
Buck, C. D., 61
Bulmer, R. L., 6, 10, 17, 18, 194, 232, 245
Bunaq, 180, *182*
Burgess, D., 148, 229
Burris, H., 58
bush: definition, 13; descriptive labels for, 68; innovation of, 68; as least distinctive discontinuity, 107; passim
Butler, I., 193, 231
Butler, J., 192
Bye, R. A., Jr., 147

Cakchiquel, 63, 73, 76
California: languages of, 147, 159, 210, 211, 250
Cambodia: languages of, 139, 153
Canada: languages of, 134, 136, 144, 145, 147, 169, 257, 262
canonical position: of humans, 103
Cantonese, 90, 216, *220*
Carapana, 63, 72, 130, 180, *183*, 216, *220*
Carr, W. M., 273n2
Carroll, V., 271n3
Casad, E. H., 203, 234
Casiguran Dumagat, 149, *153*
Casson, R. W., 3
cassowaries: as residual animals, 110
Catawba, *233*
Central African Republic: languages of, 152, 161, 163, 258
Central America: languages of, 48
Central Cagayan Agta, 77, 149, *153*, 216, *220*
Central Carrier, 41, 199, *200*, 241, *242*
Central East Africa: languages of, 258
Chamberlain, R. V., 146, 228
Chamorro, 61
Chapman, S., 164, 213
Chase, P. K., 21, 60, 77, 78, 80, 93–96, 158, 170, 171, 184, 213, 273n2
Chewa, *177*
China: languages of, 85, 87, 88, 237
Chinese, 273n2 (*see* Mandarin)
Choctaw, 29, 199, *201*
Chol, 73, 77, 199, 201

Cholan Mayan languages, 71
Cholti, 71
Chomsky, N., 120
Chontal, 77, 149, *154*
Chorti, 71, 199, *202*, 253, *256*
Chowning, A., 66
Chrau, 17, 18, 20, 216, *221*
Chuj, 149, *154*, 216, *221*
Chung, C. S., 159, 224
Clallam, 29, 33, 37, 77, 199, *202*, 233, *234*
Clark, R., 103, 178, 225, 246
classes: general/special purpose (*see* biological categories)
Classical Nahuatl, 112, *168*, 253, *256*
classification: general principles of, passim; of languages, 34–36, 38–40, 130; of plants by children/adults, 92, 93; suprageneric, 8
classificatory systems: of large/small scale human groups, 7
clustering: by attribute, 9; by morphological features, 10, 17
cognates: in Benue-Congo languages, 74; in Polynesian languages, 62, 71
cognition: human, 2, 119
cognitive anthropology, 1–3
cognitive maps, 3
cognitive psychologists, 120
cognitive structures: underlying cultures, 3
Colombia: languages of, 183, 187, 194, 208, 220, 247
color: categorization of, 3, 122; domain of, 120
color categories: basic, 58, 121; "composite," 122; focal members of, 122; marking hierarchy of, 123; neurophysiologically wired, 123
color classes (*see* color categories)
color encoding, 121, 122, 275n2
color space: coverage of, 275n4
color terms: basic, 3, 4, 121, 275n2; combinations of, 122; orthographic length of, 123
color vocabularies: native, 121
Colorado, 180, *183*, 216, *221*
Colorado: languages of, 187, 238
combined **wug-mammal**, 90, 92, 97, 118, 130; created from **bird** and **snake**, 75; definition of, 17, 18; in encoding sequence, 26; implicational relationships of, 27; as a

Lacandon, 199, *204*
La Flesche, F., 239
Landau, J. M., 52, 54, 272n6, 273n2
language acquisition: by children, 84, 92–96, 115
language change: regularity of, 24
languages: classification of, 34–36, 38–40, 130; deviant from encoding sequence, 25, 27, 29, 30–32; diffusion of, 36, 40; genetically related, 33, 37, 40, 41; geographically contiguous, 33, 37
language regularities, 7, 8; passim
Lanyon-Orgill, P. A., 66
Lao, 150, *161*
Laos: languages of, 156, 161, 175
Latin, 47, 64
Lauber, E., 139, 222
Lauck, L., 164, 247
Laughlin, R. M., 191, 251
Leenhouts, I., 189, 240
Lemaitre, Y., 76, 266
Lemoine, J., 156
Lemordant, M. D., 151
length of words: average orthographic, 89–90; phonological, 84; as related to frequency of use, 84
lexemes: composite, 269n3, 270n4; productive primary, 270n4; secondary, 269n3, 270n4; (*see* secondary lexemes)
lexical domains, 2, 3
lexical encoding sequences (*see* encoding sequences)
lexical overextensions: by children, 94
lexical reconstructions (*see* reconstructions)
lexicon: size of life-form, 272n8
Liberia: languages of, 162
life-form: children's inventories of, 94; dual classification of, 94, 112; encoding sequences of, passim; initial triad of, 46, 71, 87, 92, 109; salience of, 50; unexpected singleton, 45; uniform acquisition of, 59
life-form categories: actually occurring combinations of, 25, 26; embryonic, 77 (*see* incipient life-forms); fully-developed, 80, 81; patterning of, 24; possible combinations of, 24, 25, 26; predicted combinations of, 26; passim
life-form classes (*see* life-form categories)
life-form classification: natural constraints on, 24

life-form encoding sequences (*see* encoding sequences)
"life-form" rank, 4, 18, 19
life-form studies: Mayan, 271n2, 271n3; Polynesian, 271n2, 271n3
ligneousness, 100–102, 124, 275n5
Lillooet, 28, 77, 143, *145*
Lind, J., 188, 240
Lindfors, J. W., 94
Lionnet, A., 148, 229
Lister-Turner, R., 66
Lithgow, D., 162, 208
Liu, E. S., 273n2
Lorge, I., 51, 52, 272n6, 273n2
Lotuho, 106, 197, *198*, 242, *246*
Lowland Tequistlatec, 193, *195*, 216, *224*
Luomala, K., 144

Machiguenga, 150, *161*, 216, *225*
"macro-black," 121, 122, 124–126
macro-colors: non-attested, 124
"macro-red," 121–123, 125, 126
"macro-white," 121, 123–125
Madagascar: languages of, 204, 237
Maddock, K., 135, 231
Madulid, D., 134
Mahar, J. M., 135
Mailhot, J., 262
Makiritare, 181, *185*, 242, *246*
Malagasy, 111, 199, *204*, 233, *237*
Malawi: languages of, 177
Malaysia: languages of, 159, 224, 227
Mali: languages of, 142, 152, 174, 228
Malinowski, B., 159
Malyalam, 197, *198*
mammal: definition of, 16; encoded through binary contrast, 40, 74; inclusion of fish in, 32; innovation of, 72; from "meat" terms, 72; rarity of in Polynesia, 46; relative indistinctness of, 108; residual nature of, 111; as a true discontinuity, 275n1; passim
Mandarin, 90, 233, *237*
Mangaian, 46, 47, 72
Mangarevan, 46
"mani'," 78–80
"mani huiini'," 78–80
Manja, 150, *161*
Manning, A., 187, 238
Manobo Blit, 150, *161*

neural circuitry: of humans, 122, 127
neurophysiological mechanisms: of humans,
123; wiring of, 124, 125
Nevada: languages of, 142, 146, 211, 228,
265
New Guinea: languages of, 12, 17, 31, 32,
40, 110, 187, 271n4, 273n4 (*see* Papua
New Guinea)
New Hebrides: languages of, 178, 225
New Mexico: languages of, 147, 173, 187,
190, 224, 229, 238, 248
New Zealand: languages of, 46
Nez Perce, 33, 37, 179, *180*, 216, *226*,
275n5
Ngandi, 29, 137, *140*, 207, *208*
Ngbaka Ma'bo, 29, 100, 150, *163*
Nicholson, V. C., 137, 218
Niger: languages of, 142, 228
Niger-Congo, 37
Nigeria: languages of, 139, 142, 228, 244
Nimboran, 30, 176, *179*, 209, *210*
Ninam, 71, 176, *179*
Niuean, 63, 72
nomenclature: general principles of, passim
North America: areal features of, 41
North American Indians, 2
North Carolina: languages of, 233
Northeastern Thai, 90, 233, *239*
Northern Ojibwa, 32, 41, 110, 112, 254, *262*
Northern Paiute, 57, 77, 105
Northern Paiute (Nevada dialect), 30, 33, 37,
48, 49, 143, *146*, 209, *211*
Northern Paiute (Oregon dialect), 28, 33, 48,
134, *135*
North Saami, 32, 110, 112, 168, *171*, 254,
263
Norway: languages of, 171, 263
Nuaulu, 72, 150, *163*, 216, *226*
Nukuoro, 45, 62, 71, 72, 271n3
Numic languages, 37, 48, 57
Nunggubuyu, 137, *141*, 216, *227*
Nya Hon, 174, *175*

Oaxaca: Mexico, 78, 94, 129
Oceania: languages of, 43, 66, 75, 273n4
Oklahoma: languages of, 145, 201, 257
Old English (Anglo Saxon), 62, 273n3
Omaha, 233, *239*
O'Neill, J. P., 11

Oregon: languages of, 180, 226
orthographic length: of color terms, 123 (*see*
length of words)
orthographic segments: counts of, 274n6; of
words, 89
orthography: used in appendices, 130
Ortiz de Montellano, B. R., 168, 256
Oxford English Dictionary, 64

Pacaas Novos, 26, 28, 72, 77, 106, *149*, 242,
247
Pagan Gaddang, 176, *179*
Paillet, J. P. R., 144, 257
Palmer, G., 136
Pama-Ngungan, 37
Papago, 30, 31, 33, 37, 63, 168, *171*, 209,
211, 274n9
Papua New Guinea: languages of, 138, 155,
162, 163, 178, 183, 194, 196, 208, 232,
241–247, 252, 253, 258, 264, 265
Paraguay: languages of, 185
parent languages: break-up of in Polynesia,
43; of Mayan languages, 43; of Numic
languages, 48; possessing few life-form
terms, 36 (*see individual entries under*
Proto-)
Parker, F., 245
Parrott, M., 184, 195, 212, 224
"part of" path: and expansion of reference,
60; and innovation of **vine**, 67
Pascuense, 75 (*see* Easter Island)
Pashto, 112, 233, *239*
Patep, 32, 72, 110, 150, 242, *247*, *277*
Paumari, 30, 77, 150, *164*, 212, *213*
Pawley, A., 46, 273n5
Peeke, M. C., 167, 249
Peile, A. R., 169
Penang Hokkien, *227*
Peninsular Spanish, 54, 55, 85, 156, 273n2
Pennoyer, F. D., 166
Perkins, D. R., 123
Peru: languages of, 150, 161, 196, 209, 217, 225
Pfitzner, J. C., 143, 230
Philippines: languages of, 37, 134, 153, 154,
156, 157, 161, 165, 167, 179, 189, 209,
219, 220, 241, 244
Pike, E. V., 186, 225
Pileni, 66 (*see* Polynesian Outliers)
Pitman, M., 151, 218

plant: in English, 4, 64, 65, 270n1; **grerb** as derived referent of, 65; as a large biological discontinuity, 13; polysemy of, 64, 65; as a unique beginner, 270n1

plant category: special purpose, 68, 69; utilitarian, 69

plants: native classification of, 2, 21, passim

Pocomam, 63, 76, 199, *205*

Pocomchi, 73, 76, 150, *164*

Poldervaart, A., 211

Polynesia: languages of, 43, 45–47, 57, 62–64, 66–68, 70, 72, 77, 96, 103

Polynesian Outliers, 45

polysemy: through expansion of reference, 270n5; of life-form terms, 60, 85, 272n6; of plant, 65; of **tree**, 60, 61, 131; of **vine**, 65, 67

polytypic categories: as criteria of life-form rank, 18, 21; general purpose, 24 (*see* biological categories)

Popoluca, 137, *141*

Popovich, H., 237

Posey, D. A., 235

prairies, 105

Price, P. D., 184

primary colors: conjunctive, 124

primary lexemes: labeling life-forms, 18; productive, 5, 6, 20 (*see* lexemes)

Prost, A., 138, 142, 175, 218, 226, 229

Proto-Mayan, 57, 63, 71; reconstruction of life-form inventories in, 43, 44, 273n5; "tongue" in, 76; "worm" in, 96

Proto-Numic, 48–50, 57, 271n4

Proto-Polynesian, 45–48, 57; "maggot" in, 71; prominence of birds in, 75; reconstructions of life-form inventories in, 62, 96, 273n5

Proto-Quichean, 63

psycholinguistic literature, 94

Puerto Rican Spanish, 174, *175*

Pym, N., 133, 207

Quechua, 194, *196*

questioning: techniques of in ethnoscience, 92, 94

Quiche, 63, 73

rain forests: tropical, 56

Randall, R. A., 165

Rappaport, R. A., 252

Rarotongan, 46, 47

Raven, P. H., 3, 4, 6, 16, 18, 76, 191, 230, 269n1

reconstructions: and life-form growth, 43–58, 118; of Mayan life-form vocabularies, 43, 44; of Polynesian life-form vocabularies, 45; of Proto-languages, 119, 273n5

reduplication, 74–76

reeds: grouped with vines, 28

reference: expansion of, 59–60, 62, 63, 66, 67, 69, 71–75, 270n5; restriction of, 59, 64, 76

referent: focal, 270n5

referential histories: reconstructed, 71

reflexes: in post-Proto-Oceanic times, 66, 121; of Proto-Mayan, 67, 71, 73; of Proto-Numic, 49; of Proto-Polynesian, 46, 62, 66, 71, 72, 271n3; unitary, 66

regularities: of color encoding, 120; cross-language, passim; lexical, 4; perceptual, 122

Reichel-Dolmatoff, G., 194, 208

Reid, L. A., 134, 219

related words (*see* cognates)

relationships: implicational, 84, 85, 96, 97; inclusive, 95

Renard-Casevitz, F.-M., 161, 225

Rennellese, 72

"residual" category: of life-form classes, 108–112, 118; of plants not in **tree** and **grerb**, 28

residualness: lack of, 112; role of in folk classification, 271n4, 275n6

"rich cognition" model: of human language faculty, 120, 127

Ritharngu, 30, 137, *141*, 212, *214*

Rivière, P., 172

Robbins, W. W., 2, 190

Rogers, M. B., 145 (*see* Black, M. R.)

Roglai, 150, *164*

Romance languages, 86

Rosaldo, M. Z., 156, 209

Roulon, P., 258

Roys, R. L., 193

Rudder, J., 143

Rumanian, 85, 88, 273n2

Russian, 88, 273n2, 274n3

Sahaptin, 28, 33, 37, 77, 134, *135*, *215*
salience: linguistic, 11, 115; perceptual, 11, 55, 97
salience rankings: of plant and animal concepts, 50–55
Samal, 150, *165*
Sambal, 150, *165*
Sanuma, 30, 212, *214*
savannahs, 65
Saxton, D., 171, 211
Schaefer, J. M., 271n5
Scholz, H.-J., 139, 244
secondary lexemes, 6, 20; as criteria of generics, 20; (*see* lexemes)
Semai, 217, *227*
Senegal: languages of, 152, 174
Shah, N. C., 195, 197, 198, 200
Shane, W. M., 273n2
Sherbro, 137, *141*
Shoshoni, 28, 37, 48, 49, 143, *146*, 217, *228*
Shuswap, 28, 134, *136*
Siane, 12, 31, 32, 40, 110, 254, *264*
Sierra Leone: languages of, 141, 160, 162, 166
Sierra Popoluca, 29, 111, 181, *188*, 233, *240*
Sisaala (Tumu dialect), 137, *142*, 217, *228*
Sischo, W. R., 196, 225
size: dimension of, 58, 275n5; terms for, 58 (*see* dimension)
Smith; Rev. E. W., 234
Smith River, 30, 33, 37, 143, *147*, 209, *211*
Smith-Stark, T., 205
Smyth, D., 168, 212
"snake": lack of salience of, 88; marking and encoding of, 96, 97; relative marking values of, 91; as unmarked, 275n2
snake: definition of, 15; encoded through binary opposition, 100; encoding priority of, 107; as highly heterogeneous, 31; inclusion of fish in, 32; scarcity of in northern latitudes, 32; unusual treatment of, 32; passim
social stratification: degree of, 271n5
societal scale: associated with technological advances, 275n3; changes in, 70, 80, 81; correlation with species diversity, 56; correlation with wood/**tree** polysemy, 61, 62; correlation with zoological life-form vocabularies, 271n5, 272n5; index of,

272n5; and life-form growth, 50–58; measure of, 272n5
societies: large, nation-state, 7, 50, 56, 61, 85, 87, 88, 90–92, 272n5, 275n4; small-scale, 7, 61, 70, 90, 91, 119, 272n5, 275n4
Solomons: San Cristobal, 273n4
Songay, 137, *142*, 217, *228*
Soulik, T., 271n3
South Carolina: languages of, 233
Southern Kwakiutl, 143, *147*
Southern Paiute (Cedar City dialect), 29, 33, 37, 48, 49, 168, *172*, 233, *240*, 274n6
Southern Paiute (Chemehuevi dialect), 31, 33, 37, 48, 49, 89, 112, 137, *142*, *265*
Southern Paiute (Kawaiisu dialect), 27, 28, 36, 48, 49, *133*
Southern Tiwa, 36, 37, 105, 143, *147*, 217, *229*
Spanish (*see* Peninsular Spanish; Puerto Rican Spanish)
special purpose classes, 10 (*see* biological categories)
species diversity: botanical, 56; lack of, 12
specific categories, 4, 7, 11; encoding discontinuities, 11; marking relationships of, 7
specific classes (*see* specific categories)
"specific" rank, 4
specifics: labeled, 12
Speck, C., 191
Speck, F. G., 233
Speirs, A. F., 190, 248
Speirs, R. H., 190, 248
Sre, 181, *188*
stage affiliation, 130; of animal life-forms, 29–31; of plant life-forms, 27-29
Stark, S., 141
Stevenson, M. C., 2
Stimson, A. F., 226
Strathern, A., 178
Stross, B., 93
Stubblefield, M., 170
Stute, H., 177, 222
Sudan: languages of, 198, 246, 255
Sutton, P., 168, 212
Swahili, 74
Swain, C., 179
syntax: universals of, 120